The Sovereign Citizen

DEMOCRACY, CITIZENSHIP,
AND CONSTITUTIONALISM

Rogers M. Smith and Mary L. Dudziak, Series Editors

A list of books in the series
is available from the publisher.

The
Sovereign Citizen

Denaturalization and the Origins
of the American Republic

Patrick Weil

PENN

UNIVERSITY OF PENNSYLVANIA PRESS

PHILADELPHIA

Published by
University of Pennsylvania Press
Philadelphia, Pennsylvania 19104-4112
www.upenn.edu/pennpress

Printed in the United States of America on acid-free paper
10 9 8 7 6 5 4 3 2 1

Library of Congress Cataloging-in-Publication Data
Weil, Patrick.
The sovereign citizen : denaturalization and the origins of
the American Republic / Patrick Weil. — 1st ed.
    p. cm. — (Democracy, citizenship, and constitutionalism)
    Includes bibliographical references and index.
    ISBN 978-0-8122-2212-8 (pbk. : alk. paper)
    1. Expatriation—United States—History—20th century.
2. Citizenship, Loss of—United States—History—20th century.
3. Citizenship—United States—History—20th century. I. Title.
    KF4715.W45 2013
    342.7308'3—dc23   2012022653

CONTENTS

═══════════

Introduction

Present-day Americans feel secure in their citizenship. They are free to speak up for any cause and to oppose their government, to marry a person of any nationality, and to live wherever they decide, in the United States or abroad. Many Americans consider their citizenship the most "cherished" status in the world.[1] This is why most foreign-born U.S. residents look forward to the day they can apply for citizenship, once the required five-year waiting period has passed. For many, the day they pledge allegiance to the United States will be one of the most memorable of their lives.

.Yet there was a time, not long ago, when the American government expatriated—or forcibly stripped the citizenship of—certain American citizens. Beginning in 1907, American women marrying foreign husbands, as well as previously naturalized Americans who later moved abroad, could lose their citizenship. Although the former provision would later be repealed,[2] the Nationality Act passed in 1940 expanded the automatic loss of citizenship to include several new categories of American-born citizens, including those who engaged in foreign military service, voted in foreign elections, or were convicted of treason or of desertion from the armed forces of the United States.

While American-born citizens could lose their citizenship in limited circumstances, naturalized foreign-born Americans were at special risk because they could be deprived of their citizenship, or denaturalized, for a wide variety of reasons. It might come as no surprise that the citizenship of the naturalized could be revoked if their naturalization application was tainted by fraud or other illegal acts. But foreign-born Americans could also be denaturalized: if they spoke out or took action against the U.S. government during wartime or were otherwise involved in "radical" organizations; if they belonged to ethnic or political groups that were perceived as "un-American"; or if they resided abroad, in any country around the world, regardless of how many years they had been American citizens. Although denaturalization had similar consequences for the individual as another phenomenon called denationalization, the two are distinct: denationalization denotes a loss of citizenship, whereas, in theory, a denaturalized person has never been a citizen.[3]

During the course of the twentieth century, more than twenty-two thousand Americans were denaturalized. Even decades after becoming Americans, the foreign-born risked losing their citizenship in denaturalization proceedings initiated by the executive branch and tried in the courts. This book tells the unique story of these Americans for the very first time.

Denaturalization and denationalization are most often associated with twentieth-century authoritarian regimes. The Soviet Union revoked the citizenship of 1.5 million individuals. The Nazi regime denaturalized forty thousand people and revoked the citizenship of another forty thousand native-born citizens. In France, between 1940 and 1944, the Vichy regime denaturalized fifteen thousand people and stripped the citizenship of five hundred native-born French nationals.

But denaturalization existed in democracies as well. The United States first established the practice through the Naturalization Act of 1906. Only three years later, in 1909, Emma Goldman became the first American denaturalized for political reasons. Following the United States, the United Kingdom introduced denaturalization in 1914, and further reinforced its procedures in 1918. France temporarily installed a denaturalization policy in 1915, for the duration of World War I, and made the practice permanent through legislation passed in 1927.[4] Many other countries followed suit.

In 1933, twenty-four years after having been deprived of her citizenship, Goldman would write of the trend:

> To have a country implies, first of all, the possession of a certain guarantee of security, the assurance of having some spot you can call your own and that no one can alienate from you. That is the essential significance of the idea of country, of citizenship. Divested of that, it becomes sheer mockery.
>
> Up to the World War citizenship actually did stand for such a guarantee. . . . But the War has entirely changed the situation. Together with countless lives, it also destroyed the fundamental right to be, to exist in a given place with any degree of security. . . . Citizenship has become bankrupt: it has lost its essential meaning, its one-time guarantee. Deprivation of citizenship, exile and deportation are practiced by every government; they have been established and accepted methods. . . . Yet, for all their "legality," denaturalization and expatriation are of the most primitive and cruel inhumanity.[5]

The majority of denaturalizations in France and the United Kingdom can be connected to the two world wars and their consequences—the proceedings were performed to protect national security and in response to perceived acts of treason and disloyalty. Yet in the United States, only 1 percent (approximately two hundred) of the twenty-two thousand denaturalizations conducted during the twentieth century were connected to wars. These few "political" acts of denaturalization have been the subject of valuable studies,[6] but the vast majority of the denaturalizations in the United States reflect an exceptional and much more complex history.[7]

This study of denaturalization examines, but also searches beyond, the personal ordeals and destinies of the denaturalized by casting light on neglected dimensions of America's understandings of *citizenship*. The institution of denaturalization, from its first appearance in America in 1906, made a quiet yet major contribution to the transformation of contemporary American citizenship in at least two ways. The first of these was in the federalization of the naturalization process. Today a foreign resident who wants to become an American citizen looks for the nearest federal office—and not to the local and state courts. This was not always the case. The second of denaturalization's contributions is the role it played in a series of twentieth-century Supreme Court decisions that would redefine the country's understanding of sovereignty and citizenship.

In 1790, Congress established, for the first time, a uniform rule of naturalization.[8] Despite legislative tinkering with the naturalization process in 1798, 1802, and 1906,[9] it remained the case from the Founding until 1930 that the majority of new Americans were naturalized in state courts. The state judiciary, however, did not always respect citizenship requirements set by federal law.

In the first part of the nineteenth century, the federal government fought for its sovereignty on several fronts, against states of the Union that challenged the supremacy of federal citizenship—culminating in the bloody and hard-fought Civil War—and against foreign countries that contested the power of the United States to naturalize their former citizens. But by 1868 these early battles were over. One day before Congress ratified the Fourteenth Amendment, which unified American citizenship and proclaimed the precedence of federal citizenship over state citizenship, it also passed the Expatriation Act of 1868. This Act proclaimed the right of American citizens to expatriate, or acquire a foreign nationality, and the equal right of all naturalized citizens to travel abroad under the protection of the United States. The latter was made possible only by the Bancroft Treaties—signed with Prussia in 1868, the United Kingdom in 1870, and later with almost three dozen other countries— according to which countries of origin would recognize the American nationality of their own expatriated citizens.[10] It was only then, when American citizenship became "paramount and dominant instead of being subordinate and derivative," that the old issue of fraud in the naturalization processes was tackled at the federal level.[11]

At the beginning of the twentieth century, the U.S. government was determined to crack down on fraud to ensure the dignity of the naturalization procedure in courts and to protect the sacrosanct status of American citizenship.[12] In 1903, President Theodore Roosevelt proclaimed, "We poison the sources of our national character and strength at the fountain, if the privilege is claimed and exercised without right, and by means of fraud and corruption." "The body politic," Roosevelt explained, "cannot be sound and healthy if many of its constituent members claim their standing through the prostitution of the high right and calling of citizenship."[13] The Naturalization Act of 1906 responded to these concerns by introducing denaturalization as a new instrument for deterring any fraud and illegality that might occur during the naturalization process.[14]

Denaturalization, however, would also serve another purpose. Buoyed by a growing public discourse in favor of purifying America's citizenry, denaturalization became a tool for the expulsion of those deemed to possess "un-American" characteristics. The U.S. government targeted those new citizens who were later discovered to be of "un-American" opinion, race, or residence and stripped them of their citizenship. Foreign-born Americans were not the only ones at risk. When denaturalization became a central part of the government's national security policy during World War II, the 1940 Nationality Act also expanded the number of American-born citizens subject to automatic loss of citizenship. American citizenship had become conditional.

This was precisely when the Supreme Court inserted itself into the denaturalization debate. Although intensely divided, the Court progressively reduced the scope of the federal government's authority to revoke American citizenship. It did so, in part, by upholding free speech and procedural guarantees for foreign-born Americans. But the most significant limits on the scope of the federal government's denaturalization authority came later, in the middle of the 1960s, when the Supreme Court began to grapple with and question the constitutionality of denationalizing native-born Americans.

The result of these rulings was nothing short of a revolution in the definition of American citizenship—one brought about by a reversal of the traditional concept of sovereignty. There is no better way to understand how this new definition of citizenship emerged than to follow the battles that broke out on the Supreme Court, first over denaturalization, and then over denationalization. During the first half of the twentieth century, citizenship was still defined as a constellation of rights contingent on the satisfaction of certain obligations, a regime in which the law could say: "if you act this way, you will lose your citizenship." Yet as this book reveals in great detail, through a series of fascinating and sometimes rancorous clashes between the justices of the Supreme Court, a new definition of citizenship was slowly forged. The citizen was no longer required to submit to a sovereign power able to change and nullify his or her status. American citizens, naturalized and native-born, were redefined as possessing sovereignty themselves. Citizenship had moved from an era when it was provisional, qualified, and unsecure to one in which it was nearly unconditionally guaranteed.

The concept of citizenship has always enjoyed multiple and varying definitions, but three of its dimensions are invoked most frequently. First, citizenship is sometimes described as possessing an affective dimension: "the feeling that one belongs, is connected through one's sense of emotional attachment, identification and loyalty."[15] In nation-states, this feeling is sustained by membership in an "imagined community," constructed from official cultural frames of social belonging within a nation-state.[16] The second dimension of citizenship is political and civic. In a democracy, adult citizens elect their representatives, while foreign residents and citizen minors participate in civil and political society in other ways. As political theorist Judith Shklar notes, this dimension of "American nationality has its own history of exclusions and inclusions, in which xenophobia, racism, religious bigotry, and fear of alien conspiracies have played their part." Rogers Smith has masterfully explained that in this history of citizenship exclusion occurs from *within* the bounds of formal nationality, as the tales of women and the descendants of American slaves show.[17]

Although the affective and civic notions of citizenship will appear occasionally, it is the third, legal, dimension of citizenship that is the focus of this book. The legal dimension of citizenship reflects the formal linkage of each individual to the nation-state. It is manifested in the passports and national identification documents that confer the official status of national citizen on roughly 99 percent of all human beings. Legal citizenship exists independently of an individual's sense of belonging or degree of participation in national and patriotic institutions.[18]

This book's investigation of denaturalization may not tell the entire history of American citizenship since 1906, but it does illuminate a significant yet overlooked aspect of it. By focusing on the practice of denaturalization and applying a micro-historical approach to the laws surrounding and institution of naturalization, I was able to discover phenomena that had not previously been observed and to uncover details and broader trends that have not previously been written about. Reducing the scale of observation and engaging in an intensive study of archival materials[19] allows this book to reveal what were unknown dimensions of American political development and to unearth "how, and with what effect, American citizenship has changed over time."[20] In doing so, this study of denaturalization sheds light on three broader social historical phenomena, which are developed, respectively, in the three sections of this book.[21]

As I describe in Part I, beginning in 1906 denaturalization provisions were established as the primary mechanism through which the government could exert control over citizenship status after it had been conferred by a court. Originally, this federal intervention in the citizen-making process served two principal purposes: deterring the fraud and illegality that could occur in naturalization and, at the same time, preserving a system for conferring American citizenship on foreigners by (mainly state) courts. But the competition for authority over the naturalization process—held simultaneously by state and federal courts as well as by various executive agencies (including the Departments of Justice and Labor), to say nothing of the specialized committees of Congress that also influenced naturalization procedures—created opportunities for changes.[22]

Denaturalization became an instrument through which the Division of Naturalization (later the Immigration and Naturalization Service), created in 1906, consolidated its power. The threat of *denaturalization* proceedings accelerated the transfer of the management of *naturalization* applications from the judiciary to the Division of Naturalization. This uneven trend, which proceeded through multiple stages, accompanied the transformation over time of naturalization from an institution largely controlled at the state-level into one entirely managed by an extensive federal bureaucracy.[23] The federalization of American citizenship was fully realized when responsibility over naturalization was transferred from the Department of Labor to the Department of Justice. Interestingly, the original target of these denaturalization proceedings was emphatically not the individuals being denaturalized: the denaturalized were often encouraged to reapply for citizenship. Rather, the government's real interest was in the *institution* of naturalization, which it wanted to purge of fraud and illegality, and misbehaving courts, which the government wanted to force in line.

At precisely the same moment that the federal government was consolidating its authority, the use of denaturalization as a tool for ridding the American citizenry of "undesirables" surged to the forefront. This brand of denaturalization was not entirely novel: it originated in 1907 as part of a restrictive and racist immigration policy illustrating the rise of a "conditional citizenship."[24] New Americans could lose their citizenship if they violated certain standards not applied to the native-born: if a naturalized citizen was Asian, spoke out against war, was a Socialist, a Communist, or a fascist, or lived abroad, she risked the loss of her American citizenship. As I describe in Part II, these grounds rapidly became the primary justifications for denaturalization. They were rooted in both the explicit wording of statutes (for example, in the case of residence abroad), as well as in extensive interpretations of the law by the executive branch and the courts as a means for assessing loyalty to the United States. These interpretations left open the possibility of an ongoing evaluation of a new citizen's allegiance to the United States.

Yet three of the principal grounds for denaturalization—residence abroad, race, and political belief—would ignite a series of conflicts within the executive branch (among the Justice, State, and Labor Departments) and the courts, which until 1940 had limited the scope of expatriation. But when World War II broke out, denaturalization, together with Congress's denationalization of numerous American-born citizens, moved from the margins of the U.S. government's policy to the front and center. Under the personal supervision of Francis Biddle, President Franklin Roosevelt's Attorney General, denaturalization became an integral part of a proactive program by the Justice Department to bolster national security against threats from America's "enemies."

However, as I detail in Part III, even as the United States was caught in the upheaval of World War II, the Supreme Court intervened and began to reduce the scope of the federal government's denaturalization authority. Before the outbreak of war, the Supreme Court had backed the authority of the executive to pursue the denaturalization of new Americans for failing to adhere to a myriad of legal minutiae, from the form of naturalization applications, to the duration of U.S. residence, to the age of their arrival in the United States.

After 1943, however, the Supreme Court reversed course and began protecting denaturalized individuals. The first of these trailblazing new decisions was issued in 1943, in favor of William Schneiderman, the Secretary of the Communist Party in California. It was followed in 1944 by an even more surprising ruling to save Hugo Baumgartner, a former German citizen accused of harboring Nazi sympathies, from losing his American citizenship.

The *Schneiderman* and *Baumgartner* decisions put an end to America's World War II denaturalization program. Yet denaturalization remained available on a number of grounds. The scope of the government's denaturalization power would not be further reduced until the Supreme Court later intervened in cases involving the stripping of citizenship from native-born Americans. On the eve of the war, only American-born citizens acquiring another nationality risked losing their citizenship. But in 1940, a new law extended the denationalization power to include those Americans who had evaded the draft, joined a foreign army, or participated in foreign elections.

The Supreme Court reacted over a sixteen-year period from 1955 until 1971 by splitting on several occasions over the question of the constitutionality of forced denationalization provisions. About half of the Court, depending on the particulars of a given case, continued to uphold the authority of Congress to deprive naturalized and native Americans alike of their citizenship. As the basis for its decisions, the Court asserted judicial restraint and the exclusive authority of the elected branches over foreign affairs. The other half of the Court, however, invoked a number of constitutional rights in support of striking down and restricting laws permitting denaturalization and expatriation.

Denaturalization had provoked a fierce debate on the Supreme Court between these two factions. And, eventually, the practice of denaturalization was sharply restricted. Nevertheless, a nearly unanimous Court permitted—and still permits, in narrow circumstances—a naturalized citizen to lose her American citizenship.[25]

But for the native-born, the situation was different. Some justices were aghast at the possibility of forced denationalization of American-born citizens. "I am convinced that such a suggestion would have been shocking to the Founding Fathers and the American people and it should still be shocking," wrote Chief Justice Earl Warren at the beginning of 1958 on a stenography pad found in his personal archives.[26] At that moment Warren was in the middle of a fight with his brethren on the Court over that very issue in the *Perez v. Brownell* case and lacked a majority supporting his views. But thanks to Justice Hugo Black and with the help of his clerk, Jon Newman, Warren was in the process of developing a reasoned criticism of expatriation that was rooted in the language of the Constitution. Several members of the Court, principally Justices Felix Frankfurter and Tom Clark, invoked the war powers, the exclusive authority of the elected branches to manage foreign affairs, and the sovereignty of the state with respect to its citizens to limit judicial intervention. Warren replied to them that, on the basis of the founding principles of the American Republic crystallized in the Fourteenth Amendment, American sovereignty was derived not only from the state but belonged to citizens themselves. At the time, Warren's view was in the minority, and his approach was detailed only in a dissenting opinion. Eventually, however, Justice Warren and his allies on the Court were able to marshal several other constitutional provisions in support of their view that the denationalization of Americans was unconstitutional, including the Eighth Amendment (which prohibits cruel and unusual punishment) and the Fifth Amendment (which protects due process). The road was a bumpy one, however, and Warren's rough coalition would lose some cases before winning several others.

It was only in 1967, in *Afroyim v. Rusk*, that Justice Black was finally able to outline an interpretation of the Fourteenth Amendment that secured for all—native-born and naturalized—the full set of privileges entailed in American citizenship. American citizenship was no longer a contingent benefit conferred by a sovereign state in exchange for its citizens' respect for the laws. As Justice Warren put it in his *Perez* dissent, "their citizenship is not subject to the general powers of their government." Citizens themselves were now a fount of sovereignty.

Contrary to the definition of citizenship as "the right to have rights," the concept of citizenship as the source of sovereignty could cover and protect all citizens, including those with dual citizenship and the foreign-born. By the time *Perez* was reversed in 1967 in the *Afroyim* decision, the concept of citizen sovereignty had become the jurisprudence of the land. And what is more, it had achieved, without much notice, a revolution in the definition of American citizenship.

The evolution of denaturalization in twentieth-century America carries us from the edges to the very heart of the American story by revealing the transformation of Americans' understanding of citizenship. Changes in America's management of naturalization and denaturalization reflect larger structural phenomena such as the rise of the state and the growing recognition of basic civil and human rights, but these changes were not the inevitable product of broader forces.

Before naturalization could become the federal institution that it is now, a foundation first had to be laid. Richard Campbell, the first Chief of the Division of Naturalization, served from 1906 to 1922. A policy entrepreneur, Campbell initially took his post with relatively few resources at his disposal, his denaturalization authority among them, but succeeded in using the minor clout of the position to his full advantage. His successes were less the result of intra-governmental competition than they were born of cooperation and the forging of bureaucratic alliances. The federalization process did not occur without resistance, but in contrast to other policy areas where units of government typically compete to exercise and extend the authority at their disposal, in the case of naturalization, many of the political stakeholders were eager to transfer power to the rising Division—and, later, Bureau—of Naturalization.[27]

Although the executive branch and the wider public backed a vigorous and aggressive denaturalization policy, several dissenting figures played a major role in preventing hundreds of thousands of foreign-born Americans from losing their citizenship. These advocates were not prophets of a future where Americans were fully secure in their citizenship, but they were able to find in the law of the land—or, at least, in their interpretations of the law—a basis for a position that favored the preservation of citizenship.[28] From the end of the 1930s until the 1960s, courageous lawyers defended their clients from the trial courts all the way up to the Supreme Court. It took years before mounting judicial losses finally yielded to substantial legal gains. But without these efforts, the federal judiciary might have continued to denaturalize hundreds of American citizens for such causes as "mental reservation" at the moment of the pledge of allegiance or for "lack of attachment" to the Constitution.[29] Among these advocates were Harry Weinberger from New York, who represented the famed anarchist Emma Goldman; Ernie Goodman from Detroit, who defended numerous Communists during the Cold War; and their colleague from New York, Carol King, who worked on behalf of radicals like Harry Bridges and William Schneiderman. For instance, had King not possessed the audacity to ask Wendell Willkie, a former Republican presidential candidate who received nearly 45 percent of the vote in the 1940 election, to represent the communist Schneiderman in front of the Supreme Court (and had Willkie himself not summoned the courage to take on the case), the fate of many leftist activists targeted for denaturalization in the 1950s might have been quite different.

Still, perhaps the most forgotten, yet important, historical player in reducing the scope of denaturalization was George Wickersham, U.S. Attorney General under President Taft. Wickersham was skeptical of denaturalization, and immediately upon his arrival at the Justice Department in 1909, he issued an instruction called Circular 107 ordering the Department not to initiate denaturalization proceedings against new Americans who had by accident or circumstance failed to follow the letter of the law when they were naturalized. Instead, Justice Department lawyers were only to pursue denaturalization proceedings in instances where a substantial result could be achieved "in the way of the betterment of the citizenship of the country." In this manner, Circular 107 played a major role in reducing the impact of denaturalization prior to World War II. Similarly, Wickersham fought against the State Department to prevent it from adopting a policy that would deprive naturalized citizens living abroad of their citizenship. Instead, he prevailed on the State Department to impose the much less severe consequence of loss of U.S. consulate protection. His interpretation again preserved the citizenship of thousands of naturalized Americans. Wickersham was also an early defender of a liberal approach to free speech. In 1912, outraged that a socialist union leader had been denaturalized through proceedings initiated by an assistant U.S. attorney, he ordered the attorney to work to reestablish the man's American citizenship.[30]

Finally, there is a serendipitous dimension to the Supreme Court's revolutionary jurisprudence. If certain provisions permitting the forced expatriation of many categories of Americans had not been inserted in the 1940 Nationality Act at the request of the State Department and the Department of War, perhaps the Supreme Court would not have been forced to enter the fray, redefining American citizenship in the process. President Franklin D. Roosevelt, for one, opposed many if not all of these provisions.[31] Had he prevailed, American law would have permitted only the expatriation of Americans who acquired a foreign nationality—a type of expatriation that did not divide the Court as strongly.

But this is not how events unfolded. Instead, the United States greatly expanded the grounds for which Americans could be stripped of their citizenship and relied on denaturalization more often than any other democracy. This frequency was due, in part, to America's federal system of government. In addition, owing to the United States' heavy reliance on immigration in comparison to much older European nations, America became the home of large numbers of the foreign-born, whose differences in appearance, ethnicity, and ideas allowed denaturalization to become an instrument of racism, bigotry, and fear.

Yet today, severely limited by Supreme Court jurisprudence,[32] denaturalization remains on the books less as a reflection of America's past prejudices than as a symbol of its commitment to human rights. Nowadays, denaturalization is used primarily as a tool for targeting individuals who commit crimes against humanity, including former Nazis and others responsible for acts of genocide. This is the story of how, during the twentieth century, denaturalization evolved in tandem with fundamental assumptions about American citizenship.

PART I

The Federalization of Naturalization

The only means given to the Government, therefore, to avoid the application of the law in different ways and thus destroying that uniformity of operation required by law—the Federal Constitution—is by cancellation proceedings. . . . It stops other courts of original jurisdiction from applying a contrary view of law and authoritatively advises the public, the administrative officers and the courts as to what the law is, for the information and guidance, thus making the rule of naturalization uniform in operation, as intended.

—*Annual Report of the Commissioner of Naturalization* (1921)

CHAPTER 1

Denaturalization, the Main
Instrument of Federal Power

Naturalization fraud was not a new phenomenon in nineteenth-century America, but it reached its peak in New York City in the November 3, 1868, election that placed Ulysses S. Grant in the presidency. In October 1868 alone, fifty-four thousand foreigners were naturalized in New York City by only two judges.[1] Grant ultimately lost the state by ten thousand votes to his opponent Democrat Horatio Seymour, a New York governor. A senatorial inquiry later showed that, in addition to New York, the Democrats won three other states—New Jersey, Georgia, and Louisiana—through fraud.[2]

In response, the Republican leadership in Congress proposed to cede exclusive jurisdiction for naturalization to the federal courts. But just as had happened after the contested 1844 election,[3] a congressional inquiry did not lead to any major change in the law. Instead, western Republicans joined Democrats in opposing the granting of exclusive authority over naturalization proceedings to the federal courts.[4] At the time, naturalization was a tool for political machines to increase the number of loyal voters on the eve of local, state, and federal elections. For the naturalized themselves, naturalization provided access to jobs restricted to those possessing American citizenship. Furthermore, naturalization was a means for the clerks of local courts to generate revenue.[5] Finally, naturalization fraud was not a priority for reformers, who wanted to cure and purify citizenship in all its dimensions and who had placed the elimination of patronage jobs in civil service and reform of the ballot higher on their agenda.[6]

On April 1, 1890, the House of Representatives ordered a subcommittee of the Committee on the Judiciary to investigate the naturalization practices of American courts. In a March 1893 report, its chairman, Congressman William

Oates of Alabama, described them as completely dysfunctional: "What a ridiculous farce! The making of citizens out of aliens, which should be a grave judicial proceeding in the exercise of a constitutional function, is left by the courts to its mere ministerial officers who can exercise no judicial power, but run the machine merely for the fees they can make out of it."[7]

A 1902 scandal in St. Louis, in which several politicians were indicted for violating naturalization laws, finally turned the wheels of naturalization reform.[8] But it was not until March 1903, in reaction to the assassination of President William McKinley,[9] that Congress passed a bill prohibiting the naturalization of those opposed to organized government and who advocated the killing of government officials. The bill also included a provision that required courts to record the affidavits of applicants for citizenship and their witnesses and to check "the truth of every material fact requisite for naturalization."[10] At that time, many judges eventually discovered the requirements of the law; they undertook efforts to implement them, but they did so with uneven results: "some of the certificates [contained] less than 200 words and others 4000, some [created] new forms, others [used] the old ones."[11]

At around the same time that Congress launched legislative reform efforts, in April 1903, Joel Marx, special assistant to the U.S. attorney for the Southern District of New York, began an investigation into immigration fraud which had become endemic to New York, the epicenter of naturalization.[12] In a single two-year period, from April 1903 to May 1905, "through the efforts" of the U.S. attorney's office, there were 791 arrests for naturalization fraud in New York, with 685 convictions. Of these, 418 arrests were based on either false testimony or an ineligible age of arrival in the United States while 89 others were for lacking the five years of residence required prior to naturalization.[13]

Based on the first results of Marx's efforts—as presented to a federal grand jury in New York[14]—President Theodore Roosevelt called on December 7, 1903, "for the immediate attention of the Congress." Railing against current naturalization practices, he exclaimed: "Forgeries and perjuries of shameless and flagrant character have been perpetrated, not only in the dense centers of population, but throughout the country; and it established beyond doubt that very many so-called citizens of the United States have no title whatever to that right, and are asserting and enjoying the benefits of the same through the grossest frauds."[15]

One year later, President Roosevelt called for "a comprehensive revision of the naturalization laws" and for an inquiry into the subjects of citizenship, expatriation, and protection of Americans abroad, with a view towards mending the problems with appropriate legislation. Toward that end, Roosevelt suggested that naturalization authority be vested exclusively in certain courts that would require written naturalization applications and deliver regular reports to the Secretary of State. Under this plan, Congress would clarify the evidentiary standards that courts should apply. On March 1, 1905, Roosevelt appointed a commission to further investigate this proposal.[16]

By the time Roosevelt began lobbying for naturalization legislation, many of the previous obstacles to reform had dissipated. Perhaps most important, the interest of party machines in minting new voters before elections had declined. The inauguration of the secret ballot in the majority of the states by 1892 had made the control of voters at the ballot box difficult and even inefficient.[17] The political parties thus no longer resisted naturalization reform.

Roosevelt's new Presidential Commission on naturalization reform comprised three members: the chairman, Milton D. Purdy, from the Department of Justice; Gaillard Hunt, from the Department of State; and Richard K. Campbell, from the Department of Commerce and Labor. They were the foremost experts on naturalization in their respective departments. The Purdy Commission delivered its report on November 8, 1905. It would become the basis for the 1906 Naturalization Act, which, for the first time, created a mechanism for statutory denaturalization.[18]

Before the 1906 Act, in order to be naturalized, an alien was required to have resided in the United States for five years and within the state where the naturalizing court was located for one year.[19] He had to have "behaved as a man of good character, attached to the principles of the Constitution of the United States, and well disposed to the good order and happiness of the same."[20] Furthermore, the applicant was required to make a *declaration of intention* to become a citizen, before a court with naturalization power, at least two years prior to his actual application.[21] Yet if the alien had come to the United States under eighteen years of age, he was exempted from the preliminary declaration of intention.[22] In the Commission's opinion, the exemption of the two-year waiting period, normally imposed after the declaration was registered, was the primary source of fraud. It encouraged youthful-looking immigrants who had attained the age of majority to commit perjury by swearing that they had arrived prior to their eighteenth birthday.

The Commission also identified several other deficiencies and inequities. For one, the court procedure was discreet and *ex parte*, taking place between the applicant and the court, with no "interested party on the other side to oppose the applicant's claim, pose tough questions or dig up coun-ter-evidence."[23] Additionally, naturalization fees were entirely regulated by state law and varied widely. In California, for instance, there was no charge of any kind. But in Alabama, Florida, Georgia, Mississippi, Pennsylvania, South Carolina, and Texas, the fee was five dollars, and in Nevada, it was ten dollars.

Finally, the Commission cited competition among the courts as another source of fraudulent and improper naturalizations. Under the United States' original federal naturalization law, passed on March 26, 1790, naturalization could be conferred by any common law court of record.[24] In 1802, additional requirements were added: in order to naturalize new citizens, courts should have a clerk and a seal.[25] This meant that more than five thousand courts were legally authorized to compete for the approximately hundred thousand original naturalization applications processed each year across the United States.[26] For the courts, naturalization was a business, and court clerks reaped the dividends: "One court bids for business against another, and the court which is strict in en-forcing the law loses the fees which a more lax court gets."[27] When state courts in New Jersey, New York, and Rhode Island began to require that "public notice . . . be given in advance of a hearing for naturalization, all the naturalization busi-ness went to the Federal Court, where the procedure was not strict so far."[28]

According to the Commission the bottom line was clear: uniformity in both fees and procedure were a necessity. In its view, the Constitution left no doubt as to the Congress's right to provide for effective federal control of the naturalization machinery and to create a "uniform rule of Naturalization."[29]

The Commission recommended that only federal courts in cities of over a hundred thousand inhabitants be given the power to naturalize alien resi-dents.[30] In addition, it proposed a uniform naturalization fee of at least seven dollars throughout the United States and a cap on the revenue that admin-istration of the naturalization process could generate for clerks. Half of the collected fees, up to $3,000, would be subject to the court's disposition; every-thing collected beyond that amount would go to the federal government.[31] The Purdy Commission also suggested mandating permanent residence in the United States and requiring knowledge of English as preconditions for naturalization. And, in order to discourage fraud, naturalization would be for-bidden in the thirty days preceding a presidential or congressional election.[32]

Additionally, the commission proposed that the preliminary declaration of intention which meant "little or nothing," be eliminated. As a substitute, all aliens would be required to file a petition at least ninety days before a hearing by the court. Meanwhile their petitions would be transmitted immediately to a new Bureau of Naturalization, which would be created within the Department of Commerce and Labor[33] to supervise the execution of the naturalization laws.[34]

Ultimately, many of the Purdy Commission's recommendations became part of the Naturalization Act of June 29, 1906. For example, the Act mandated that aspiring citizens be able to speak English. It also required applicants to have lived *continuously* in the United States during the five years directly prior to naturalization and to continue to reside in the United States afterward.

However, the Naturalization Act did not include the Commission's proposal to eliminate the declaration of intention, nor did it provide that federal courts in large cities possess exclusive jurisdiction over naturalization. Indeed, many cities of more than a hundred thousand inhabitants did not possess a federal court. New Jersey, for example, had a federal court in Trenton but lacked one in Newark or Hudson City.[35] As a result, Congress preserved the authority of state courts to naturalize new citizens—with the condition that, in addition to having a seal and a clerk, the courts should exert universal competence.

Nevertheless, the new law did reinforce a certain degree of federal control over naturalization. Now, proceedings were required to be held in open court, and a representative of the United States would have the right to appear. Under the new procedures, the federal government could cross-examine the petitioner and his or her witnesses, as well as subpoena its own witnesses, produce relevant evidence, and "be heard in opposition to the granting of any petition in naturalization proceedings."[36] A new Bureau of Immigration and Naturalization within the Department of Commerce and Labor was given the task of enforcing naturalization laws.

In addition, Section 15 of the Act conferred upon U.S. attorneys the authority to institute denaturalization proceedings "in any court having jurisdiction to naturalize aliens . . . for the purpose of setting aside and canceling the certificate of citizenship on the ground of fraud or on the ground that such certificate of citizenship was illegally procured."[37] Another provision in the same section also permitted denaturalization on grounds previously raised by Theodore Roosevelt in response to the common practice of newly naturalized returning to their native countries as soon as they secured U.S. citizenship.

The Naturalization Act went into effect on September 27, 1906. The newly established Division of Naturalization, responsible for overseeing the implementation of the law, settled into the Munsey Building on Pennsylvania Avenue in Washington, D.C. Twenty-five hundred square feet of office space was rented to house seventeen people, including fourteen clerks.[38] Within several months, the chief of the new division, Richard Campbell, expressed his satisfaction: "That something has been accomplished in the direction of reducing the notorious and long-continued abuses in conferring citizenship by naturalization is palpable." He noted that the new regime's success was reflected in a number of new trends: "First the greatly reduced number of naturalizations, and, second, the high grade of the petitioners, as stated by the U.S. attorneys, and partly shown by the small portion of denials. . . . The number of cancellations, secured or pending, of certificates improperly issued is another evidence of the practical value of the new law as a reform measure."[39]

Indeed, in the years following its passage, the effect of the 1906 Act was immediate and quantifiable. Before 1906, the number of naturalizations was estimated at 100,000 per year. In 1907, however, the number of certificates issued plummeted to 7,953. Just one year later, in 1908, the number of naturalizations had tripled, to 25,963, and in 1909, it rose to 38,372.[40] But it would be several years before the pace of naturalization again reached pre-1906 levels.

The courts and assistant U.S. attorneys did not share Campbell's contentment with the effects of the broad reforms and felt overwhelmed by their new tasks. Part of the problem was that the Naturalization Act cut in half the number of courts offering naturalization proceedings. Under the old system, nearly 5,160 different state and federal courts were qualified to conduct naturalization procedures.[41] Under the new criteria fixed by the 1906 Act, even though there were upward of 3,000 courts vested with the authority to conduct naturalizations,[42] the number of courts actually offering naturalizations settled at around 2,200 and 90 percent of these were state courts. And while the courts remained in charge of receiving and registering applications for naturalization and of delivering the oath of citizenship, they now also had to fulfill new legal requirements, which increased their workload. Court clerks were obligated to shoulder these additional burdens despite a decline in resources. Some came to the conclusion that the financial benefit of offering naturalization service was not worth the additional work required and decided to abandon the naturalization process altogether.[43]

In addition, the new naturalization process was cumbersome, with numerous actors tasked with participating across four distinct stages. First, a naturalization application had to be filed with a competent court, most often in a clerk's office. Second, in the three months following the application, the court or the federal government could investigate the facts alleged by the applicant and the applicant's two witnesses. Third, the naturalization hearing would then take place in open court, and the government could intervene if it felt it necessary. Fourth, at any time after the successful completion of the naturalization process, a U.S. attorney could institute proceedings for the cancellation of the naturalization on the grounds of fraud or illegality.

The new scheme did not clearly delineate the authority and responsibilities of the various interested parties and opened the ground for conflicts

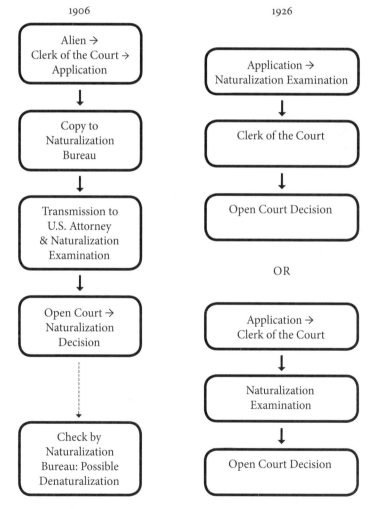

Figure 1. U.S. Naturalization Process, 1906–1926

between the courts—federal and state—and between the Division of Naturalization and the Department of Justice. For example, the new law permitted the executive to intervene at stages 2, 3 and 4 of the naturalization process. But if the law was clear in assigning to the U.S. attorneys the tasks of instituting cancellation procedures, no mention was made of which department was in charge of intervening in open court at the naturalization proceeding itself, and, prior to it, in the examination of the application.

At first, in 1906 and 1907, the Department of Justice was able to represent the executive branch's interests in the naturalization process because, as noted earlier, the number of naturalization proceedings was very low in the first year after the passage of the Naturalization Act. Moreover, in order to support its new responsibilities, the Department of Justice received an appropriation of $100,000.[44] With this new funding source, a number of assistant U.S. attorneys were appointed to work at headquarters in large cities around the country.[45] Additionally, in order to relieve these assistant attorneys of the eventual enormous volume of naturalization-related issues, Alford W. Cooley, assistant attorney general, recruited a "considerable number of examiners"—forty to fifty—who were dispatched to the same principal cities as the new attorneys.[46] These examiners were authorized to initiate the preliminary naturalization examination, check applications, correct minor errors, turn away individuals who were clearly unable to meet the requirements of the new law, and transmit contested cases to assistant U.S. attorneys.[47]

Campbell, the primary architect of the Department of Commerce and Labor's naturalization machinery, viewed with disfavor the development of a new administration within the Department of Justice, under the supervision of Cooley. But in 1907 Campbell's small new division did not possess sufficient resources to fulfill his goal of managing a uniform and centralized naturalization process without additional help. Soon after the Naturalization Act's passage, Congress had rebuffed Campbell's request to form a new team of examiners, choosing to allocate to the Department of Justice responsibility for naturalization attorneys and examiners.[48]

With the drafting of a uniform application form, responsibility for overseeing *denaturalization* proceedings was the only real power given to Campbell's Division of Naturalization. It was not much. But creative use of denaturalization authority would gradually but radically reinforce the new Division's central role in transforming American citizenship.

As described above, under Section 15 of the new law, U.S. attorneys were obligated to institute proceedings for the cancellation of naturalization

certificates upon affidavit showing that a certificate had at any time been illegally or fraudulently procured. Once informed of an instance of illegality or
fraud, they could not refuse to act.

In the years just following the passage of 1906 Act, evidence supporting
denaturalization typically originated from a few common sources. Interestingly, the majority of denaturalization cases arose when witnesses for new
citizens were required to produce their own certificates of naturalization.
While ascertaining the competence of these witnesses, examiners and judges
would often uncover fraud or illegality in a witness's naturalization proceeding. Confronted with contradictory information and documents relating to
a witness's declaration of intention or date of arrival in the United States, it
might become clear that a witness's citizenship had been illegally procured.[49]

The Civil Service Commission was another source of denaturalization
proceedings due to legal requirements restricting classified civil service positions to American citizens. The Commission required that foreign-born applicants for these positions submit their naturalization certificates, which it
would then check.[50] Counterfeit certificates were promptly reported. Similarly, denaturalization cases would even arise when the certificates of naturalized persons applying for licenses to serve as officers of steam vessels, a
position reserved for citizens of the United States, were investigated. Of the
415 applicants in 1908 for such positions, 59 became the subjects of cancellation proceedings.[51] A number of denaturalization cases were also passed
along from the State Department,[52] which sometimes discovered illegality or
fraud when naturalized citizens submitted passport requests.

One year after it was established by the 1906 Act, the new naturalization
system was in crisis. U.S. attorneys were overwhelmed by their responsibility
for intervening in open court—the third stage of the naturalization process.
But the investment of time and resources in naturalization cases paled in
comparison to what was required in *denaturalization* cases.[53] This put a significant strain on the system, because the number of denaturalization cases
increased dramatically during the earlier years of the new regime: from 86 in
1907 to 457 in 1908 (see Appendix 3).

Officially, the increase in denaturalization cases was not caused by "the
result of a search by government officials for violations of law." The Division
of Naturalization would declare in its 1907 Annual Report, "They were all developed as an incident of administrative work either in this or in some other
department or branch of the Government."[54] In truth, however, the Division
of Naturalization played a proactive role in encouraging the different agencies

U. S. DEPARTMENT OF LABOR
NATURALIZATION SERVICE

No. ....

ORIGINAL.

UNITED STATES OF AMERICA

PETITION FOR NATURALIZATION

To the Honorable the .... *Court of* .... *at* ....

The petition of .... *hereby filed, respectfully showeth:*

First. My place of residence is ....

(Give number, street, city or town, and State.)

Second. My occupation is ....

Third. I was born on the .... *day of* .... *anno Domini 1*........ *at* ....

Fourth. I emigrated to the United States from .... *on or about the* .... *day of* .... *anno Domini 1*........, *and arrived in the United States, at the port of* .... *on the* .... *day of* .... *anno Domini 1*........, *on the vessel* ....

(If the alien arrived otherwise than by vessel, the character of conveyance or name of transportation company should be given.)

Fifth. I declared my intention to become a citizen of the United States on the .... *day of* ...., *anno Domini 1*........ *at* .... *in the* .... *Court of* ....

Sixth. I am .... *married. My wife's name is* ....; *she was born on the* .... *day of* ...., *anno Domini 1*........ *at* ...., *and now resides at* ....

(Give number, street, city or town, and State.)

I have .... *children, and the name, date and place of birth, and place of residence of each of said children is as follows:*

....
....
....
....
....
....

Seventh. I am not a disbeliever in or opposed to organized government or a member of or affiliated with any organization or body of persons teaching disbelief in or opposed to organized government. I am not a polygamist nor a believer in the practice of polygamy. I am attached to the principles of the Constitution of the United States, and it is my intention to become a citizen of the United States and to renounce absolutely and forever all allegiance and fidelity to any foreign prince, potentate, state, or sovereignty, and particularly to .... *of whom at this time I am a subject, and it is my intention to reside permanently in the United States.*

Eighth. I am able to speak the English language.

Ninth. I have resided continuously in the United States of America for the term of five years at least immediately preceding the date of this petition, to wit, since the .... *day of* ...., *anno Domini 1*........, *and in the State of* .... *continuously next preceding the date of this petition, since the* .... *day of* ...., *anno Domini 1*........, *being a residence within this State of at least one year next preceding the date of this petition.*

Tenth. I have not heretofore made petition for citizenship to any court. (I made petition for citizenship to the .... *Court of* .... *at* ...., *on the* .... *day of* ...., *anno Domini 1*........, *and the said petition was denied by the said Court for the following reasons and causes, to wit:* .... *and the cause of such denial has since been cured or removed.)*

Attached hereto and made a part of this petition are my declaration of intention to become a citizen of the United States and the certificate from the Department of Labor, together with my affidavit and the affidavits of the two verifying witnesses thereto, required by law. Wherefore your petitioner prays that he may be admitted a citizen of the United States of America.

....

(Complete and true signature of petitioner.)

Declaration of Intention No. .... *and Certificate of Arrival No.* .... *from Department of Labor filed this* .... *day of* ...., *191*....

NOTE TO CLERK OF COURT.—If petitioner arrived in the United States on or before JUNE 29, 1906, strike out the words reading "and Certificate of Arrival No. .... from Department of Labor."

AFFIDAVITS OF PETITIONER AND WITNESSES

.... } *ss:*

The aforesaid petitioner being duly sworn, deposes and says that he is the petitioner in the above-entitled proceedings; that he has read the foregoing petition and knows the contents thereof; that the said petition is signed with his full, true name; that the same is true of his own knowledge, except as to matters therein stated to be alleged upon information and belief, and that as to those matters he believes it to be true.

....

(Complete and true signature of petitioner.)

...., *occupation* .... *residing at* ....

and ...., *occupation* .... *residing at* ....

each being severally, duly, and respectively sworn, deposes and says that he is a citizen of the United States of America; that he has personally known .... *the petitioner above mentioned, to have resided in the United States continuously immediately preceding the date of filing his petition, since the* .... *day of* ...., *anno Domini 1*........, *and in the State in which the above-entitled petition is made continuously since the* .... *day of* ...., *anno Domini 1*........; *and that he has personal knowledge that the said petitioner is a person of good moral character, attached to the principles of the Constitution of the United States, and that the petitioner is in every way qualified, in his opinion, to be admitted a citizen of the United States.*

....

(Signature of witness.)

....

(Signature of witness.)

Subscribed and sworn to before me by the above-named petitioner and witnesses in the office of the Clerk of said Court this .... *day of* ...., *anno Domini 191*......   [SEAL.]

...., *Clerk.*

By ...., *Deputy Clerk.*

[OVER.]

Figure 2. Petition for Naturalization, Form 2204, in use from 1913 to June 30, 1929.

IN THE MATTER OF THE PETITION OF

....

TO BE ADMITTED A CITIZEN OF THE UNITED STATES OF AMERICA.

Filed ...., 19......

OATH OF ALLEGIANCE

I hereby declare, on oath, that I absolutely and entirely renounce and abjure all allegiance and fidelity to any foreign prince, potentate, state, or sovereignty, and particularly to .... the .... of .... of whom I have heretofore been a subject; that I will support and defend the Constitution and laws of the United States of America against all enemies, foreign and domestic; and that I will bear true faith and allegiance to the same.

Subscribed and sworn to before me, in open Court, this .... day of ...., A. D. 19......

...., Clerk.

NOTE.—In renunciation of title of nobility, add the following to the oath of allegiance before it is executed: "I further renounce the title of (give title), an order of nobility, which I have heretofore held."

ORDER OF COURT ADMITTING PETITIONER

Upon consideration of the petition of ...., and affidavits in support thereof, and further testimony taken in open Court, it is ordered that the said petitioner, who has taken the oath required by law, be, and hereby is, admitted to become a citizen of the United States of America, this .... day of ...., A. D. 19......

(It is further ordered, upon consideration of the petition of the said ...., that his name be, and hereby is, changed to ...., under authority of the provisions of section 6 of the act approved June 29, 1906 (34 Stat. L., pt. 1, p. 596), as amended by the act approved March 4, 1913, entitled "An act to create a Department of Labor.")

By the Court:

...., J ....

ORDER OF COURT DENYING PETITION

Upon consideration of the petition of .... and the motion of .... for the United States in open Court this .... day of ...., 19......, it appearing that.. ....

THE SAID PETITION IS HEREBY DENIED.

...., J ....

MEMORANDUM OF CONTINUANCES

REASONS FOR CONTINUANCE

Continued from..., 19......   ....
to..., 19......   ....
Continued from..., 19......   ....
to..., 19......   ....

NAMES OF SUBSTITUTED WITNESSES

...., occupation ...., residing at ....

...., occupation ...., residing at ....

Certificate of Naturalization, No. ...., *issued on the* .... *day of* ...., *A. D. 19......*

14—532   [INSERT ON FOLLOWING LINES MARRIAGES AND BIRTHS OCCURRING AFTER PETITIONING AND BEFORE NATURALIZATION.]

....

....

to convey information regarding naturalization fraud to U.S. attorneys' offices. The division was eager to have assistant U.S. attorneys mobilized across the country working on denaturalization proceedings, and it asked them to gather and report information about any naturalization cancellations that occurred within their districts.[55]

The Department of Justice was crushed under the weight of these obligations. The required tasks were so arduous and numerous for the U.S. attorneys that "in many naturalization petition hearings, it was impossible for the Government to appear, so the applicants received their citizenship without objection." Despite a surge in the number of applicants for citizenship, Congress appropriated only $150,000 to the Department of Justice for the supervision of naturalization, compared to an estimated need of $325,000 for the 1909 fiscal year. From the perspective of the Department of Justice, this was unfortunate: it thought applicants were best served by having their cases thoroughly investigated prior to their admission to citizenship. Doing so would avoid the need for unpleasant proceedings later to revoke citizenship.[56]

The Division of Naturalization took advantage of the situation. As early as 1908,[57] it pointed to the Department of Justice's struggles as proof that it should be permitted to recruit field examiners to work on the naturalization proceedings. Eventually, Campbell was successful in convincing Congress to sign off on this plan.

The good news for Campbell and the Division of Naturalization was that Theodore Roosevelt's Attorney General, Charles Bonaparte, had no desire to retain control over the naturalization examiners.[58] In fact, Bonaparte stated in the 1907 *Annual Report of the Department of Justice* that, in his view, "the naturalization examiners should be transferred to the Department of Commerce and Labor," even though, within the Department of Justice, "he was in a small minority on that subject."[59]

So, at the beginning of 1909, Bonaparte, who was on excellent terms with the Commerce and Labor Secretary, Oscar Straus, accepted the latter's suggestion that he meet with Campbell to discuss how the two of them could "shape [their] request for appropriation harmoniously."[60] Despite the potential for interagency conflict, when Campbell and Bonaparte met, they rapidly came to an agreement. Instead of waiting for a prospective citizen to go to court, where precious resources might be needed in order to contest the denaturalization application, it was better, as Bonaparte would testify to Congress a few weeks later, "to advise him how that informality could be removed." He continued, "In other words it seems to me that the tail is wagging the dog. The court work is a mere incident of a thorough investigation of the facts connected to the case."[61] In the alternative, Bonaparte suggested that responsibility for checking all applications during the ninety-day period between registration with the clerk of court and the swearing of allegiance to the United States be transferred to the Department of Commerce and Labor.

At first, the joint proposal divided the congressional committee, but eventually Congress followed the joint suggestion of Bonaparte and Campbell. As requested, the employment of the naturalization examiners and clerks[62] would be transferred from the Department of Justice to the Division of Naturalization in the Department of Commerce and Labor for the 1910 fiscal year, with $125,000 appropriated to cover necessary expenses.[63] During the year following this change, the Attorney General expressed his satisfaction over its result: "that, with the exception of some portions of the Southern States which it has not had the means to cover, the naturalization work seems to be most effectively administered."[64] The U.S. attorneys' offices were, from that point on, only required to participate in contested cases, appeals, and cancellation proceedings, "all of which have been reduced to a minimum."[65] With this adjustment, the Departments of Justice and Labor were able to forge a strong cooperative relationship on naturalization policy, even if they lacked the means to actively represent the government in every court proceeding.

But, while they might increasingly see eye-to-eye on naturalization policy, the views of the two departments diverged with respect to their approaches to denaturalization. The Division of Naturalization advocated an amendment to the existing statute to automatically validate naturalization certificates issued at least ten to fifteen years prior to individuals who had been continuous residents of "the United States and who, appear to have possessed (at the time they were naturalized) the prescribed personal qualifications at the time of their naturalization."[66] Attorney General Bonaparte disagreed with this lax approach. Instead of legalizing illegal naturalizations that occurred under the previous naturalization law, he urged Congress to amend the 1906 Act so that it would place clearly within the scope of its denaturalization provision "certificates issued under the old naturalization law as well as those issued under the present law."[67]

But this first conflict over denaturalization ended swiftly with the arrival of the new Taft Administration. On September 20, 1909, after receiving approval from Campbell at the Division of Naturalization,[68] George W. Wickersham, Taft's new Attorney General,[69] sent out an important circular to all U.S. attorneys:

In the opinion of the Department, as a general rule, good cause is not shown for the institution of proceedings to cancel certificates of naturalization alleged to have been fraudulently or illegally procured *unless some substantial results are to be achieved thereby in the way of the betterment of the citizenship of the country.* The legislation referred to, being retroactive, is construed to be *remedial rather than penal* in its nature; for the protection of the body politics rather than for the punishment of the individual concerned. Ordinarily, *nothing less than the betterment of the citizenship of the country should be regarded as sufficient to justify the disturbance of personal and property rights which cancellation proceedings may occasion.* This does not mean that such proceedings should not be instituted in any case where willful and deliberate fraud appears, as the perpetration of such fraud would indicate lack of the moral qualifications necessary for citizenship. If, however, many years have elapsed since the judgment of naturalization was apparently so procured, and the party has since conducted himself as a good citizen and possesses the necessary qualifications for citizenship, cancellation proceedings should not, as a rule, be instituted.

Cancellation proceedings should not be instituted merely for correction of errors and irregularities in the naturalization of a person which would properly have been the subject of consideration at the hearing or of correction on appeal.

Mere consent to the cancellation of a certificate of naturalization by the holder thereof, for some defect or irregularity, should not be regarded as in itself sufficient to justify such procedures.[70] (Emphasis added)

With this circular, denaturalization was redefined in order to avoid targeting *every* American fraudulently or illegally naturalized—these first years of implementation had demonstrated that those fitting into this category were far too numerous. Denaturalization would now be pursued only if "some substantial results" could be "achieved thereby in the way of the betterment of the citizenship of the country."

The result of this new policy was significant: the Circular established a new logic for denaturalization as a tool for the protection of the body politic, rather than for punishment applied, without further judgment, to every individual who violated mere technical requirements. Yet, despite a fleeting appearance of unity, the nomination of Wickersham foreshadowed tension between the Justice, Labor, and State Departments over the enactment and interpretation of denaturalization rules for years to come.

CHAPTER 2

The Installment of the Bureau
of Naturalization, 1909–1926

The chief examiner of the Naturalization Service, Morris Bevington, described the pre-1906 naturalization process in St. Louis as follows: "Before elections, the ward leaders would drum up all the alien residents of their particular districts, and herd them together before some one of the courts, and have naturalization papers issued to them, usually 'minor papers.' They were entirely innocent of any wrongdoing and more often secured naturalization against their own will, and most reluctantly. They were simply coerced by American citizens, who wanted their votes and who had a stronger will power than they themselves possessed."[1]

As the 1909 circular made clear it was this kind of person that the Naturalization Bureau and the new attorney general, George Wickersham, no longer wanted to pursue. The consequence of Wickersham's instruction was that, only when cases transmitted by the State Department, the Civil Service Commission, or the Steamboat Inspection Service showed fraud or a will to deceive the court, would proceedings be initiated to revoke citizenship. Otherwise, "when the holders of illegally obtained papers were themselves the victims of deception, and not guilty of any design to break the law," no action would be taken by the Division of Naturalization. In addition, the Division would continue to use cancellation proceedings as a means for protecting the proper functioning of the naturalization process: for instance, when the courts that naturalized immigrants lacked proper jurisdiction, when the naturalization applications were found to have been completed on incorrect forms, or when a court clerk was indicted for corruption.[2]

The impact of Wickersham's 1909 instruction was clear and immediate. The number of citizens who were denaturalized dropped from a high of 921 in 1909 to 397 in 1910. From there, the numbers continued to fall: to 225 in 1911 and to 212 in 1912. The trend in St. Paul, Minnesota, was typical. Between July and November 1908, thirty certificates of naturalization were cancelled on various grounds including: false declarations concerning the place of residence or age of naturalized citizens, naturalization petitions signed on the day of the hearing, and witnesses who themselves lacked American citizenship. But within two years the number of denaturalization cases plunged. In 1910 the only denaturalization case in St. Paul concerned Johann Penner, a naturalized American citizen who had since moved back to his native Canada. After a short-lived surge in 1914 (to 414 denaturalization cases), the numbers remained low throughout the rest of the decade with 319 cases in 1915, 184 cases in 1916, 152 cases in 1917, 154 cases in 1918, and 115 cases in 1919.

For Richard Campbell, now the Commissioner of Naturalization within the Department of Labor, this decline was too dramatic. It illustrated a new conflict between his new Bureau and the Department of Justice. On March 4, 1913, Congress had passed a law that split the Department of Labor and Commerce into two separate departments: the Department of Labor and the Department of Commerce. The act also divided up the functions of the former Bureau of Immigration and Naturalization and placed the newly created Bureau of Naturalization under the Department of Labor. Campbell was designated as Commissioner of the Bureau of Naturalization and reported directly to the Labor Secretary. Campbell understood that the 1909 Circular would limit the circumstances in which individuals who gained American citizenship *prior* to the passage of the 1906 Naturalization Act could be denaturalized. But he believed that the government should not be similarly constrained when dealing with individuals naturalized *after* 1906.[3] The Department of Justice, however, sought to limit the reach of the United States' denaturalization authority and took a stand against denaturalizing Americans who gained their citizenship after 1906 unless such proceedings were necessary for the betterment of the citizenry.

In reaction, the Naturalization Bureau initiated a new policy. Instead of using Section 15 of the 1906 Act, which required a U.S. attorney to institute denaturalization proceedings, with long and costly delays, Campbell decided to direct his naturalization examiners to informally approach judges to have them revoke their naturalization decisions on the grounds of illegally procured evidence.[4] Many judges cooperated. In 1913, half the cancellation cases were handled without the involvement of U.S. attorneys, and in 1914, that proportion rose to two-thirds of cases. Yet some judges refused to cooperate and requested that the Bureau of Naturalization go through normal adversarial proceedings.

When in 1915 the Department of Justice submitted a revised version of the 1909 Circular that explicitly applied its restrictions on denaturalization to individuals granted citizenship after 1906,[5] Richard Campbell protested:

> There are more than two thousand courts engaged in admitting aliens to citizenship. There is a great diversity of opinion in regard to what the law means in its various details. . . . There are many reasons, too numerous to state within the compass of this memorandum, which lead to varying and contradictory decisions of courts of coordinate jurisdiction all over the United States on many points of the law. In actual practice, therefore, the law is not uniform in its operation throughout the United States. . . . Since the Department of Justice has held that there is no review by the ordinary processes resorted to in contested cases, there remains as a means of correcting errors of law, or at least of unifying the constructions of the law by the various courts, the proceeding to cancel.[6]

But on June 1, 1916, the same denaturalization circular that Wickersham had sent in 1909 was resent, unchanged, by his new replacement Attorney General T. W. Gregory, to all U.S. attorneys, keeping alive the clashing interpretations between the Bureau of Naturalization and the Justice Department.

Commissioner Campbell reacted aggressively. In addition to continuing the Bureau of Naturalization's policy of asking courts directly for cancellation, thereby bypassing the U.S. attorneys, in 1914 Campbell requested that Congress give the Bureau independent legal authority to bring denaturalization proceedings.[7] Three years later Campbell pleaded, in a 1917 report, that "the practical result of the situation was an absence of uniformity in the rules of naturalization, the discouragement of the examiners in their efforts to secure the correction of palpable errors in the granting of certificates, and the loss of much time that was spent in the fruitless endeavor to bring cases of such error within the administrative ruling referred to."[8] He also emphasized the contradictory standards for naturalization that had emerged: "We have the Supreme Court [in *Johannessen v. United States*,][9] saying in effect to alien candidates for citizenship 'at your risk, you must comply with all the requirements of the law; otherwise your certificate is worthless,' while the administrative ruling says 'unless you are personally unfit to be an American citizen, your certificate shall not be questioned, although you may not have complied in all respects with the law.' "[10] For Campbell, in the end, "the obvious remedy for this condition is to place the control of this provision of the law in this bureau."[11]

Congress heard Campbell's pleas—in part because, since 1914, his Bureau of Naturalization had become increasingly popular as a facet of the Americanization campaign developing across the country through the efforts of various civil society organizations.[12] Raymond Crist, the Deputy Commissioner of the Naturalization Bureau, endorsed with enthusiasm the idea of Clarence N. Goodwin, a naturalization judge from Chicago, to provide applicants for citizenship with civic education and training. Woodrow Wilson agreed to preside over the first national large-scale Americanization event on May 10, 1915, in Philadelphia, attended by more than fifteen thousand people. Building on the momentum of this event, the Bureau contracted with state and local governments, schools, and organizations to provide them with civic education resources. By linking itself with a national citizenship education program, the Bureau was able to gain greater public legitimacy while also promoting its goals of standardizing and enforcing the uniform Federal naturalization application process. Congress backed the Bureau and increased its appropriation so that it could better fulfill its new patriotic tasks. And on May 9, 1918, Congress passed a bill giving the Commissioner of the Bureau of Naturalization his long-sought-after concurrent authority with U.S. attorneys to institute proceedings to cancel certificates of citizenship.[13]

The Bureau of Naturalization had triumphed. Twelve years after the passage of the 1906 Act, "by successive steps full authority commensurate with its responsibility has been conferred upon one administrative officer, under the supervision of one department, to supervise and administer the 'uniform' rule of naturalization authorized by our organic law, the Federal Constitution."[14] Back in 1905, the Purdy Commission had proposed to preserve the competence of the courts for naturalization, not because it was the best method for minting new citizens ("experience has shown that they are a very defective machinery for the purpose"),[15] but because no preferable alternatives were available. Campbell's ambition had been to build that missing institution, and he was succeeding.

In addition, since 1906, the courts had endorsed the denaturalization provisions of the 1906 Naturalization Act almost entirely without reservation. The courts cast aside challenges to the Act's constitutionality that alleged that it operated as retroactive or ex post facto legislation and deprived defendants of their right to a trial by jury.[16] In *United States v. Mansour* in 1908,[17] for instance, a federal judge found that denaturalization cases were considered to lie in "equity" rather than to constitute civil or criminal legal proceedings. Therefore, they were not covered by the Constitution's Sixth and Seventh Amendment guarantees of the availability of jury trials.[18]

Just four years later, the Supreme Court held, in *Johannessen v. United States*,[19] that Congress could authorize the government to bring a separate suit attacking the validity of a naturalized American's citizenship. Because naturalization proceedings were, before 1906, "ex parte"—involving only a judge and an individual seeking citizenship—no legal principles prevented the government from bringing an adversarial suit later in order to revoke the original judgment granting citizenship. The *Johannessen* Court also rejected the argument that the 1906 Naturalization Act was an unconstitutional ex post facto law, finding that the statute "makes nothing fraudulent or unlawful that was honest and lawful when it was done." A certificate of citizenship, the Court found, should be considered an instrument conferring certain political privileges that could be revoked, like grants of public land, in situations where it was unlawfully or fraudulently obtained.

The Court confirmed the *Johannessen* ruling in the 1917 case *United States v. Ness* for naturalizations obtained after 1906.[20] In *Ness* the Court decided that the presence of a U.S. attorney as a party to a naturalization proceeding (under Section 11 of the Naturalization Act) did not prevent the United States from initiating a separate denaturalization proceeding (under Section 15), when an individual's citizenship was "illegally procured."[21] Justice Louis Brandeis, who delivered the opinion of the Court, asserted that "section 11 and section 15 were designated to afford cumulative protection against fraudulent or illegal naturalization."[22]

In 1926, in *Tutun v. United States*, the Supreme Court finally decided that a naturalization proceeding in a federal court was a case within the meaning of the Constitution, the Judicial Code, and the act establishing the Court of Appeals.[23] The Court ruled that the cancellation proceedings authorized by section 15 of the 1906 act were not a denial of the usual method of pursuing appeals in courts. In the matter of contesting naturalization, the United States was given another "cumulative remedy":[24] it could both appeal a naturalization decision and start a suit to attack the same decision for having been "illegally procured." For the Naturalization Bureau, the separate denaturalization procedure still had some clear advantages: the right to appeal decided in *Tutun* by the Supreme Court did not concern naturalization by state courts,[25] and there was no time limit for denaturalization proceedings.[26]

In addition, the Supreme Court had interpreted "illegally procured" based on the doctrine of jurisdictional fact.[27] To be legally naturalized, an alien had to:

1. fulfill certain procedural requirements such as filing a certificate of arrival, a declaration of intention, or a petition for naturalization; or obtain the decree of naturalization in open court,
2. be "racially" eligible, either black or white;
3. be able to speak English;
4. have established permanent residence in the United States for five years and have waited two years between the day of the declaration of intention and of the application for naturalization;
5. be of "good moral character";
6. be attached to the "principles of the Constitution" and to organized government in general;
7. take an oath of allegiance to the United States.[28]

Any decree of naturalization that had not been obtained in full compliance with the letter of the law could be revoked. Under the pressure of an increasingly burdensome number of tasks, courts seemed increasingly agreeable to transfer their power to treat the first stage of the naturalization application. In 1909, naturalization examiners began using a creative interpretation of the 1906 Act as authority to conduct interviews with applicants for citizenship *before* they appeared in court.[29] When a large number of petitions for naturalization began being filed each year, one federal district court decided to formally require that citizenship candidates and witnesses meet with a naturalization examiner in advance of appearing before the clerk of court.[30] In other jurisdictions, however, pre-court interviews were used without this formal recognition.[31]

By 1914, the Division of Naturalization could claim that 50,000 of the 123,000 applicants for citizenship sat through a preexamination interview conducted by a naturalization examiner. It was easier for citizenship applicants to appear before examiners because the Bureau's district headquarters were located in many of the United States' largest cities and in close proximity to the courts (sometimes even in the same building). This system saved the clerks time and permitted the examiners to review the greatest number of cases, "all at a far less expense and embarrassment to the applicants for citizenship."[32] The eleven chief examiners running the country's eleven naturalization districts performed the work, assisted by forty-eight assistant examiners and fourteen clerks.[33]

In addition, the outbreak of World War I and America's eventual military involvement drove the creation of a special new procedure permitting aliens who volunteered for the armed forces to be naturalized rapidly without meeting many requirements of the 1906 Act—including the normally required delay of ninety days. Under the wartime measure passed on May 9, 1918, before filing a naturalization petition, aliens who enlisted in the armed forces of the United States could pass a preliminary examination and appear with two witnesses before a representative of the Bureau of Naturalization. In order to operate the new system, which made official the centrality of the Bureau's role in the naturalization process, new examiners were recruited and trained by more experienced naturalization officers. By the end of June 1918, 63,993 foreigners serving in the military were naturalized.[34] One year later, on June 30, 1919, the total number had reached 128,335[35] and rose still further to 244,300 by the end of 1920.[36] At the same time, the Bureau's force of examiners increased, and its appropriations doubled from $305,000 in 1918 to $675,000 in 1919.[37] The Bureau of Naturalization was able to take satisfaction in demonstrating that the administrative naturalization process could work: "This particular provision has made it possible for the machinery of the law to operate with the minimum of friction."[38]

But the Naturalization Bureau's satisfaction was short-lived. After 1918, the number of declaration of intentions and naturalizations rose to double their previous levels. At the same time, in the years following the war, the Bureau of Naturalization was forced to process these under a significantly reduce budget.[39] Eventually, the Bureau staff began to examine the documents of many candidates for naturalization by correspondence.[40] In such instances, an alien would file a petition for naturalization before a clerk of a court who would contact the Bureau so that it could send the applicant a questionnaire through the mail. Each applicant's witnesses also received by mail a written questionnaire that asked them about their knowledge of the applicant. Largely on the basis of these written statements, "made ex parte of course, the court [would] admit[] that man to citizenship," after he appeared in person.[41]

In 1922, of the 170,000 aliens applying for citizenship, 29,000 mailed in applications. In areas where it lacked offices, mainly in the western part of the country, the Bureau found that, "We do not have the force to go and investigate those cases as they should be investigated, and as a consequence we must adopt this expedient." The Bureau of Naturalization found this new mail-based process "totally and entirely unsatisfactory,"[42] carrying with it considerable risks: "Now, with all the isms rampant as they are, it seems to me that at a time like this we should stop that sort of practice." At the beginning of 1923, the Bureau launched a program to extend its preliminary investigation process to every court with naturalization authority around the country. In order to implement the expanded program, Bureau officials tried to convince "the more than 2,000 clerks of courts . . . engaged in naturalization transactions" to require each applicant to establish contact with the naturalization examiner "*before* he files his naturalization petition."[43] But in large cities, where the Bureau of Naturalization had existing agreements with the courts to investigate applicants, examiners were overwhelmed with a flood of applications. In 1925, only 20 percent of all the naturalization papers were fully completed in the presence of a naturalization examiner.[44]

In response, the Bureau pursued a successful strategy of increasing its authority—and budget—by tapping into the currents of political paranoia and anticommunism. It urged Congress to allocate more resources, and insisted that, without that increase, it could not prevent a growing tide of "reds" from becoming American citizens: "There are reports showing that socialist organizations are urging their members to become naturalized. We cannot withstand that action without funds. If they have funds, as they seem to have, from abroad and other sources, to carry on their propaganda work, in 90 days you will have them coming into citizenship."[45]

To prevent the naturalization of Communists, the Bureau cooperated with civil society organizations, which it used to feed it with information: "the Americanization societies . . . and the American Legion are pointing out to our men daily cases — I should not say daily, perhaps, but cases which require more careful investigation, all of which necessarily takes time."[46] Raymond Crist, who in 1923 was selected as the new Commissioner of the Bureau of Naturalization, also strove to develop strong ties with industry, "so that we can arrange to get reports from employers about their employees who are coming into citizenship." But he pleaded that relying on outside groups was plainly insufficient and that the Bureau required additional funds to recruit new examiners to investigate so "that we can not only know what the candidates for citizenship are doing in the day time, but we can know the associates they keep, the societies they attend, and the character of thought which they express."[47] Congress' eventual decision to increase the Bureau's budget allocation allowed it to reduce the number of naturalization investigations handled through correspondence from twenty-nine thousand in 1922 to fifteen thousand within only two years.[48]

But there was another problem, present since 1906 but growing more serious over time. Section 13 of the 1906 Naturalization Act prescribed the duties of naturalization court clerks: making, filing, and docketing naturalization papers and collecting fees. Yet state court clerks, often elected for a limited term, typically entered office lacking experience in performing the complex and demanding tasks required by their naturalization responsibilities.[49] Furthermore, the fees they could collect under the 1906 Act from any single applicant were not high—five dollars for a full naturalization procedure.[50] The clerks were authorized to retain only half of these fees, not to exceed $3,000 per year.[51] The other half, and all additional fees collected beyond the maximum, had to be sent to the Bureau of Naturalization for deposit in the U.S. Treasury.[52] Even if the entirety of naturalization fees could be used to supplement clerk salaries (rather than, as is more likely, used to satisfy expenses incident to the naturalization process),[53] clerks were receiving little additional compensation in exchange for taking on substantial responsibilities. James Farrell, the Chief Naturalization Examiner in the naturalization district of Boston, summed up the situation in 1922:

> In those outside courts, the matter is unwelcome, at least, in many of them, and especially where they have but little of it, because every case that comes before a clerk is a burden on him. He is unfamiliar with the law, and in every case he has to make an inquiry, de novo; he has to look up the requirements and he groans and in some places he says to the petitioner—this actually so—"I will give you $4 if you would go somewhere else and file this." It is a burden in that way because you are only giving that man half the fees and because of the time it takes, especially in those country courts; he is not recompensed or compensated for the efforts he makes. It is in the big centers that there is money for the clerk and there you try to shut him off with $3,000.[54]

Naturally, this system encouraged clerks, once they reached the statutory limit of $6,000 in total fees collected, to virtually refuse to entertain additional naturalization business.[55] Additional appropriations had permitted the Bureau, since 1909, to pay some assistants to facilitate the work of the clerks in the cities where collection typically exceeded $6,000.[56] In 1919, however, "Congress changed the method of compensation of the United States court clerks from emoluments to the salary basis" and prohibited "the allotment of any money" from the Naturalization Bureau budget for the compensation of assistants to clerks of the U.S. courts.[57]

In 1924 the naturalization work of the Bronx, Kings, and New York City county courts collapsed. Given the critical location of the failure, an alternative means for processing naturalization applications had to be created as quickly as possible. The New York state court clerks' funding was halted and applicants were redirected to naturalization examiners recruited by the Bureau of Naturalization. Within a few days, the work performed previously by thirty-seven county clerks and their assistants[58] was now completed by eight clerks working directly under the supervision of the district director of naturalization in New York City. Once their applications were treated, future naturalized citizens were sent to the two U.S. district courts in New York City, which handled 8,885 declarations and petitions per month in 1924, compared to 1,758 the previous year.[59]

The crisis, despite its challenges, produced an example that the Bureau of Naturalization wanted to expand nationally. But the Democrats did not like the reform implemented in New York and did not want to eliminate state courts from the naturalization business. The Democratic members of the Committee on Appropriations persuaded the House, over the protests of the Commissioner of Naturalization to allocate $370,000 for payments to state court clerks. However, a Republican representative from New York, Ogden Mills, succeeded in having the Senate strike the appropriation language from the bill, and final appropriations were left to the discretion of the secretary of the Department of Labor. Following that decision, on February 28, 1925, Mills wrote a draft letter to President Calvin Coolidge and enjoined him to pass it along to the secretary of labor. Coolidge did so just a few days later on March 2, 1925. "It seems to me," the letter read, "that, in view of the fact that the Bureau of Naturalization is able to do the work more cheaply and more efficiently than the County Clerks, that . . . the policy should be continued and you should not return to that policy abandoned by your Department a year ago."[60]

In 1925 four different sets of naturalization procedures were being used in parallel. In larger cities, the Bureau of Naturalization concluded agreements directly with the courts to have applicants meet with a naturalization examiner immediately before (1) or after (2) registering with the clerk of court.

Outside of the cities, state courts staff were subsidized by the federal government to perform the task of filing and checking applications in place of the naturalization examiners (3). Finally, applicants and witnesses were investigated through the postal system (4).

The naturalization examiners needed to be well trained to deal with the complexities of the system: they were required to possess a law degree or to pass, under the supervision of the Civil Service Commission, an examination on the relevant laws.[61] They also needed a background in typewriting and stenography, as they had clerical as well as legal responsibilities.[62] Despite their expertise, the examiners were often overwhelmed by their various tasks. They worked "overtime constantly," often on weekends and during vacations.[63]

For the Bureau of Naturalization, the lack of standardized naturalization practices and the impossibility of appealing judicial decisions conferring citizenship made *de*naturalization the last chance for creating and maintaining the "uniformity of rule" that Campbell had originally envisioned. A single procedure is "of the utmost practical importance in maintaining the uniformity of the rule of naturalization required by the Constitution," Campbell noted, "It stops other courts of original jurisdiction from applying a contrary view of law and authoritatively advises the public, the administrative officers and the courts as to what the law is, for their information and guidance, thus making the rule of naturalization uniform in operation, as intended."[64]

Yet if, in the early years following the 1918 Act, many more denaturalization cases were directly managed by the Bureau of Naturalization than funneled through the U.S. attorneys, by the middle of the next decade, the situation was reversed. In 1919 the U.S. attorneys received 13 cases, while 135 were handled by the commissioner of naturalization; and in 1921 U.S. attorneys managed 11, and the commissioner of naturalization 65. But in 1923, 640 cases were referred to the U.S. attorneys while only 96 were handled by the Bureau of Naturalization.[65]

Campbell had fought hard to secure authority to institute denaturalization proceedings, but five years after having obtained it in 1918, he was forced to abandon it. There were several reasons for Campbell's reversal. First, U.S. attorneys and naturalization examiners weren't accustomed to working within the new framework. For example, it took more than three years for the Bureau of Naturalization to obtain a decision in the case of Georges Dumas, a native of Canada, naturalized in 1900, who had returned to live permanently in Canada in 1901. In April 1919, a petition to cancel his certificate was filed in the name of the commissioner of naturalization by a naturalization examiner.

The case had been originally referred by the Minneapolis U.S. attorney's office, but the judge refused to receive the petition for denaturalization on the grounds that, apart from the U.S attorney, only the commissioner of naturalization or his deputy possessed concurrent authority in the matter of cancellation. After multiple exchanges of letters, Campbell refiled the petition himself and obtained a court decision on November 13, 1922.[66] These troubles were not isolated to the *Dumas* case. As a result, on February 28, 1923, the solicitor of the Department of Labor reminded naturalization examiners that cases for denaturalization should be submitted first to the Commissioner for him to decide to institute proceedings for cancellation, or to refer the case to the appropriate U.S. attorney.[67]

Second, the absence of any separation of powers between the handling of naturalization and denaturalization cases encouraged fraud. In San Francisco, for instance, a scandal exploded involving the complicity of a naturalization examiner in the issuing of fraudulent naturalization certificates.[68] Ultimately, cases that resulted in twenty-seven denaturalizations and five criminal prosecutions were handled by the Department of Justice. The district director of naturalization who had manifested a "lack of interest" in ordering an investigation, was eventually replaced, but not before he attempted to implicate the commissioner of naturalization in the charges of corruption.[69]

As a result, between 1922 and 1926, a compromise was negotiated regarding the management of naturalization and denaturalization procedures between the Justice, Labor, and State Departments, the Supreme Court, and finally Congress. The Bureau of Naturalization agreed to accept the Department of Justice's resumption of its leadership in denaturalization proceedings: denaturalization cases would be handled exclusively by U.S. attorneys. The decision to institute cancellation proceedings would be approved centrally by the Department of Justice before being dispatched to the appropriate U.S. attorney's office.[70] The Department of Justice, in turn, backed the Bureau of Naturalization in its effort to attract into its sphere of competence naturalization responsibilities that had formerly been performed by the courts.

At the request of several judges, and with the strong backing of Supreme Court Chief Justice and former president William Howard Taft, Congress decided to intervene.[71] At a series of hearings entitled "Relief of Judges in Naturalization Cases," Taft pleaded for changes to be made to the naturalization process in order to relieve the federal judiciary of overly burdensome tasks and to preserve the judges from an atmosphere that threatened to soil their dignity. He quoted the complaints of Judge Augustus Hand, a renowned federal trial court judge from the Southern District of New York: "The whole courthouse is swamped with 1,800 persons a week who hang around for the purpose of being naturalized. That is not a good environment for the court. It makes the going to court very burdensome to the litigants who have to be there." Taft advocated in favor of a new naturalization process "by which these applicants can be disposed of somewhere away from the court, and the intervention of the judges to be limited to a mere office examination of the work of some subordinate . . . who is more familiar . . . with the details of the facts, and relieve our court atmosphere of this great burden."[72]

In response, on June 8, 1926, Congress passed amendments to the naturalization laws authorizing federal courts to designate one or more officers of the Bureau of Naturalization to conduct preliminary hearings on petitions for naturalization and to make findings and recommendations to the courts.[73] If the examiner found the testimony of the witnesses satisfactory, he was given authority to exempt them from attending a final judicial hearing. Under this procedure, the petitioner was only required to appear before the court to take the oath of allegiance, "thus relieving the court of a large amount of work."[74]

The 1926 Act was of great satisfaction to the interested parties. It benefited the Bureau of Naturalization, which was now permitted to hire additional examiners and to involve itself more directly with naturalization cases handled by federal courts.[75] At the same time, the federal district courts were freed from a tedious and demanding task, even while they preserved their right under the law to exercise final authority in naturalization cases.[76]

In considering the original bill, Congress also debated extending the new procedures to the various state courts. Democratic Congressman Adolph Sabath, for instance, advocated strongly for placing the state courts on an equal footing with the federal courts—this would have helped to preserve the economic windfall and the influence conferred by the naturalization business on many state courts. But, in the end, only the federal courts were permitted to partake in the benefits of the new system.[77]

The passage of 1926 amendments to the Naturalization Act was a key moment in the history of the naturalization authority in the United States. Its impact was immediately measurable. Within six years, 90 percent of the federal judiciary availed itself of the new procedures permitted under the 1926 Act.[78] In those areas where state courts were still permitted to confer citizenship, the less demanding procedures available to those applying for citizenship in federal courts—requiring only appearance of witnesses and one examination for applicants, in most cases—provoked a decided shift in favor of increasing the proportion of federal court naturalizations.[79] At the same time, the allowances to clerks at state courts, already reduced more than 50 percent in 1924, faced further reductions every year between 1927 and 1930. Thereafter, many of the states' courts surrendered naturalization jurisdiction altogether. In 1926, state courts still conducted the majority of civilian naturalizations, 79,515 of 146,239 or 54 percent. Five years later, they conducted only 34 percent (48,256 of 140,271).[80] Slowly but surely, the naturalization process was becoming federalized.

CHAPTER 3

The Victory of the Federalization
of Naturalization, 1926–1940

Nonetheless, in the period between the 1926 amendments to the Naturalization Act and the outbreak of World War II, denaturalization was at its peak. The number of revocations of citizenship averaged about a thousand a year between 1935 and 1941, reflecting three historical phenomena.

First, the Bureau of Naturalization continued to be vigilant in ensuring that state courts respected the requirements of federal naturalization laws. Thomas Ellis Isaac, for instance, was naturalized on March 18, 1926, at the Court of Common Pleas for Clarendon County, South Carolina. But the Court of Common Pleas had not been authorized to conduct naturalizations since 1911. As a result, Isaac's certificate was annulled in 1927 for having been illegally procured.[1] The Bureau eventually discovered that the Clarendon court had illegally naturalized six other people as well and decided to pursue the denaturalization of all of them.[2]

Just as often, however, after the Bureau targeted the courts themselves, it endeavored to protect the interests of the denaturalized. Edla Lund, a Swedish widow and music teacher born in Stockholm in 1867, arrived in the United States at the age of twenty. She had been naturalized on December 5, 1932, not using the appropriate forms. Her naturalization was cancelled on April 9, 1934, but, characteristically, the district director of naturalization was asked to assist Lund in regaining American citizenship. Others were advised to reapply for naturalization after their certificates were cancelled.[3]

Second, a general toughening in immigration law combined with some liberal provisions aimed at naturalizing World War I foreign combatants and seamen, encouraged fraud. Before 1921, an immigrant entering and residing in the United States illegally, who was also interested in becoming a naturalized citizen could follow an easy procedure. He could cross into Mexico or Canada and have his subsequent reentry into the United States officially recorded.[4] This would serve as a record of legal entry into the country and would begin the official countdown toward citizenship.

After the Immigration Restriction Act was passed on May 19, 1921, however, immigrants to the United States had to be admitted within a national quota, with the exception of immigrants from nations in the Western Hemisphere. This meant that many immigrants could no longer "reset" the record of their arrival through a quick jaunt south of the border. Moreover, many immigrants who had arrived before 1921 could not prove their entry date—some arrived before records of arrival were kept at all ports of entry, while in other cases entry records were lost or destroyed.[5] With legal methods for circumventing America's entry requirements no longer available, some individuals seeking American citizenship used the assistance of dishonest immigration bureaucrats to modify boat records from years past.

The new system reinforced the Bureau of Naturalization's control of the naturalization process. On August 1, 1924, the Bureau requested that the clerks of naturalization courts throughout the United States forward the declarations of intention of applicants for citizenship who had arrived in the United States after June 2, 1921. The Bureau also asked clerks to defer filing these applications with the courts until proof had been furnished that the applicants' entry into the United States was by a permanent admission: "Large numbers of aliens who had entered the country illegally or who were unlawfully remaining in the United States after having entered the country for temporary periods of residence only were attempting to make declarations of intention."[6] Under the plan adopted by the Bureau, applications from aliens arriving after June 30, 1924, were compared with the immigration visas in the Bureau's custody in order to defeat "attempts to become citizens by those who entered the United States in defiance of the provisions of the quota and visa restrictions of the immigration law."[7]

Illegal naturalization also involved individuals who feigned inclusion in two categories of foreigners whose naturalization had been statutorily facilitated since World War I. On May 9, 1918, Congress had passed an act providing for the immediate naturalization of alien soldiers in the U.S. military, permitting them to become citizens without the typically required certificate of arrival. The same act provided that any alien who had been a member of the armed forces for three or more years could file a petition for naturalization without proof that they had met the five-year residency requirement, and that any applicant who had served during World War I was exempt from the requirement to file a declaration of intention.[8] Between May 9, 1918, and June 1, 1919, a total of 128,000 foreign soldiers were naturalized under these provisions.[9]

In the San Francisco naturalization district, fraudulent naturalizations of "draft evaders, slackers posing as honorably discharged soldiers and sailors," and "men claiming merchant service through forged seamen's discharges" were cancelled in 1924.[10] Over the course of 1929, proceedings for the violation of naturalization laws on similar grounds were also initiated in Pittsburgh, New York City, and Boston.[11] In the middle of 1930, it was discovered that a New York City-based group was providing fraudulent naturalization documents, taking advantage of the exemptions conferred on veterans, to immigrants who had arrived after the end of World War I. Individuals typically paid between $500 and $800 for their fraudulent naturalizations. Confessions were obtained from four individuals who secured their naturalization by falsely alleging World War I service. Up to twelve other individuals were involved in the fraud.[12]

Third, the number of denaturalizations rose rapidly in the late 1930s and early 1940s to levels unseen in American history. Naturalizations also unexpectedly rose during this period, reaching a peak in 1940.[13] This rise came despite the fact that immigration declined from 6.3 million individuals in the years between 1910 and 1919 to 4.3 million in the 1920s, dropping below 700,000 over the course of the 1930s.[14] The 1936 *Annual Report of the Department of Labor* observed that "normally it might be expected that a decline in immigration would be followed by a corresponding decline in naturalization, but this has not been true in the past 4 years. Immigrants admitted between 1933 and 1936, inclusive, numbered 123,823 and during the same period 475,767 declarations of intention were filed. It is evident that the majority of aliens who are now seeking naturalization are not recent immigrants but have been in the country for some time."[15] The era of "hostile legislation" was among the reasons invoked for this rush of hitherto indifferent aliens.

But, in actuality, the increase after 1934 in the number of aliens going through the naturalization process was primarily the product of the dramatic rise of unemployment caused by the Great Depression. The resulting response by President Roosevelt creating social programs reserved exclusively for citizens generated a strong incentive for aliens to seek naturalization. Aliens were commonly barred from employment on public works, private employers preferred hiring citizens, and only citizens could qualify for old-age pensions and other benefits under social security laws. These considerations impelled the alien to seek naturalization and the citizens to prove her citizenship. Both trends provoked a denaturalization surge.[16]

Two primary social benefits seem to have been particularly important to immigrants: old-age assistance and public employment programs such as the Works Progress Administration (WPA). In a 1932 article, "Is Citizenship a Fair Requirement in Old Age Assistance Acts?" sociologist Dallas Hirst points out: "All but one of the eighteen states which have passed old age assistance acts requires that the recipients of such aid be citizens. . . . In other words, one old person out of every five is ineligible for state old age assistance because he or she has failed to become a citizen."[17]

The federal Social Security Act, passed in 1935, established certain basic federal contours for state old-age assistance programs, among them the proviso that state plans could not include "any citizenship requirement which excludes any citizen of the United States."[18] But the phrasing left it up to each state to decide what, if any, coverage to provide to noncitizens. In April 1936, thirty-eight of the forty-eight states, plus the District of Columbia, had state old-age assistance laws in place. Of these thirty-nine jurisdictions, twenty-eight required U.S. citizenship as a prerequisite to receiving old-age aid.[19]

Consequently, the new Immigration and Naturalization Service (INS), reuniting in 1933 the Bureau of Immigration and the Bureau of Naturalization into a single agency, began uncovering numerous cases of immigrants who were naturalized illegally before 1906 and requested old age benefits. Under the Justice Department's original 1909 Circular interpreting and applying the Naturalization Act, the citizenship—and social security benefits—of these individuals would be protected.[20]

However, for the large number of immigrants fraudulently naturalized after 1906, the INS tightened the noose. On November 17, 1938, it instituted denaturalization proceedings against five immigrants, all of whom were naturalized in 1936 or 1937 by a court that had not possessed jurisdiction since February 3, 1912.[21]

During this time of economic crisis, various regulations restricted legal employment to American citizens. A 1933 study by social scientist Harold Fields found that, starting in 1928, "the majority of jobs in basic industries and also membership in the majority of the largest unions were reserved to American citizens." In fact, Fields listed "eighteen professions, eleven types of public employment, forty-three kinds of occupational licenses, and ten miscellaneous categories of activity which required either first papers or full citizenship according to the statutes of various states and the District of Columbia."[22] Historian Mary Anne Thatcher writes that, by 1941, "eight or nine of every ten jobs in the United States were denied to aliens by statute or local ordinance, by the regulations of licensing boards, or by the prejudices of private employers."[23] Employment was becoming ever more tied to citizenship.

When the Works Progress Administration (WPA) was created, administrator Harry Hopkins was hard-pressed to answer congressional requests to provide data on how many aliens were receiving public services. He responded only that, "Many of the initial office forms designed for the WPA provided no place for giving information on race, religion, citizenship, or politics."[24] Despite the resolve of Hopkins and Roosevelt, Congress passed in 1936 the first restrictions on employment by the WPA, prohibiting the agency from "knowingly" hiring aliens who were in the United States illegally, though also directing that "prompt" employment was not to be infringed upon by any new controls.[25]

By 1939, the WPA had banned noncitizen employment entirely.[26] Applicants for jobs and recipients of agency services were often asked to fill out informational forms about their citizenship. These forms would eventually reveal a certain number of illegal or fraudulent naturalizations that had not been cancelled due to the protections afforded by the 1909 Circular. Many of the fraudulent naturalizations uncovered were performed for the parents of Depression-era aid recipients. The citizenship they received when they were minors could be one day at risk.[27] In order to avoid a situation that could lead to a sudden loss of social benefits and jobs or to deportation, these citizens were often advised to seek their own denaturalization, so that they could reapply and regularize their citizenship status.

These requirements encouraged foreign immigrants to naturalize. And this pressure for naturalization also, inevitably, increased naturalization fraud. An investigation that began in December 1933 uncovered evidence of systematic fraud in naturalization cases in the New York district, perpetrated since 1924 "by racketeers acting in collusion with employees of this Service having access to official records." Fifty-six investigators were assigned to examine 4 million arrival records and 150,000 naturalization petitions, files, and court records in New York and Brooklyn over a nine-year period. Evidence of fraud, such as altered boat manifests and missing files, was detected. Bribes of between $100 and $1,200 had been extracted from immigrants. The payments collected even at this early point in the scheme totaled over a million dollars.[28]

In April 1935, Samuel H. Kaufman, Special Assistant to the Attorney

General, was assigned to the federal district courts surrounding the port of New York to help organize the prosecution of the large number of local denaturalization cases, including those of "aliens who have entered the country unlawfully, persons who have aided in such entry, and perpetrators of naturalization fraud."[29] In 1937, four years after the fraud investigation had begun in New York, 174 indictments were handed down in fraudulent naturalization cases. Among those indicted were ten former employees and two then-current employees of the Immigration and Naturalization Service. In all, 3,336 aliens were arrested for deportation proceedings, 140 certificates of naturalization were cancelled, and an additional 279 naturalizations were pending cancellation.[30]

While denaturalization was higher than ever, the transfer of power between state courts and the federal administration concerning naturalization accelerated in several stages.

First, the Nationality Act of 1940 extended to the state courts the system of INS examiners that was already operating in conjunction with the federal courts.[31] State courts that did not elect to adopt the new system were permitted to continue to grant citizenship under the original procedure, requiring the full examination of the petitioner and witnesses at the final hearing. But, as time went on, nonadopting courts were fewer and fewer in number. Court reliance on the conclusions of examiners made judicial naturalization a mere formality (since judges invariably and unquestioningly followed the recommendations of the Immigration and Naturalization Service). As a result, the 1940 Act, in effect, bypassed the courts and conferred the power of designation of examiners directly on the Commissioner of Immigration and Naturalization.

Second, on May 22, 1940, at the suggestion of Undersecretary of State and close confidant Sumner Welles, Franklin Roosevelt announced the transfer of the Immigration and Naturalization Service to the Department of Justice.[32] Since January 1940, Roosevelt had been under pressure from Congress to remove Secretary of Labor Frances Perkins from her post. She had been accused of not enforcing immigration laws when she lobbied to welcome Jewish refugees from Europe and obtained the right to remain for German Jewish visitors already in the United States at the outbreak of World War II.[33] And when Perkins dismissed charges against the alleged Communist union leader Harry Bridges, her decision provoked a political firestorm.[34]

Welles, to whom the president often turned "for fresh ideas and quick action,"[35] had convinced him that the transfer of the INS to the Department of Justice was justified because there were various aspects of naturalization and of immigration problems in which the collaboration of the courts was essential, and because, in many cases, investigations were necessary and had to be carried out by the FBI.[36] The transfer would also permit Roosevelt to keep Perkins in his cabinet, while placating her opponents.[37]

On May 21, Roosevelt summoned Attorney General Robert Jackson for a lunch at the White House. "Shortly after lunch arrived," reported Jackson, "he handed me an Executive Order which proposes immediate transfer of the Bureau of Immigration and Naturalization from the Department of Labor to the Department of Justice." Jackson recalled that Roosevelt "turned to his soup and left the move to me." He read the order and told the President that "he had no desire to undertake this task; that it was one which no man could long perform acceptably in a period of public excitement; that there was somewhat the same tendency in America to make goats of all aliens that in Germany had made goats of all Jews." Jackson explained, "I told him that I favored a much stronger border control and a stricter supervision of aliens in the country than we had had in the past, but that I was utterly opposed to a new policy of persecuting or prosecuting aliens just because of alienage." With all of this Roosevelt agreed, and, his complaints satisfied, Jackson accepted the responsibility of transferring the INS to the Department of Justice.[38]

This departmental transfer was the last major step toward the federalization of naturalization authority. As a consequence, "the Government need for denaturalization as a remedy for naturalization abuses" decreased "with the increasing supervision of the Department of Justice over naturalization process."[39]

The power exercised by the Naturalization Service was also reinforced by the war. Beginning around 1940, naturalization applications poured in: aliens submitted to registration by the Alien Registration Act wanted to express their loyalty and secure their status as citizens[40] while an increasing number of companies—particularly in war industries—were reluctant to hire noncitizens. Because, at the time, it employed only 147 naturalization examiners, the INS faced an increasingly long backlog of petitions; in 1941, an applicant was typically required to wait between fourteen and eighteen months before she could become naturalized. Realizing the severity of the problem, Congress increased the Immigration and Naturalization Service's funding, allowing it to raise the total number of examiners to approximately 400 by 1944.[41] The INS assigned these additional examiners "to districts where the demand for naturalization was unusually heavy and arrearages unusually formidable," including areas such as New York, Newark, Buffalo, Boston and Cleveland.[42] With the additional cooperation of the courts, the number of civilian naturalizations rose from 185,000 in 1939 to 393,000 in 1944.

Congress also authorized for the first time in U.S. history, a designated representative of the INS Commissioner to "combine the powers of naturalization examiner and of a naturalization judge" and confer, on foreign soil, American citizenship to noncitizens serving with armed forces abroad.[43] Finally in August 1943, in order to "produce uniformity and improvement"[44] in the naturalization process, the Immigration and Naturalization Service instituted a centralized review of examiners' recommendations.[45] Under this new system, petitions recommended either for denial or for approval with facts presented to the court, or regarding which the field officer was in doubt as to the proper recommendations, were submitted to the central office for review.[46]

Additional statutory authority for the INS review process was introduced by the Internal Security Act, passed on September 23, 1950.[47] Already, the large-scale administrative review of the naturalization examiners' work had fulfilled an important purpose: "in achieving uniformity in recommendations and decisions."[48] The 1950 Act relabeled the initial hearing conducted by a naturalization examiner as a "preliminary examination," and made preliminary examination records admissible as evidence at subsequent final judicial hearings. Naturalization examiners were granted the authority to subpoena a naturalization application and to compel by subpoena the production of relevant evidence.

In the mid-1950s, the INS initiated a program to reduce the number of courts exercising naturalization jurisdiction and to encourage the filing of naturalization petitions in larger courts. In 1955, a total of 950 courts exercised naturalization jurisdiction. This number dropped to 752 in 1958, to 622 in 1964, and to 450 in 1977.

Thirteen years later, naturalization—a responsibility of the judiciary since America's founding—became a wholly administrative procedure after the passage of the Immigration Act of 1990.[49] In removing naturalization authority from the judiciary, Congress castigated some courts for tolerating delays of up to two years in processing applications.[50] Courts, exclusively those in the federal system, retained only the authority to formally administer the citizenship oath.[51] Because of these changes, the age when thousands of courts performed the work of minting America's citizens was confined to the memory of a small cadre of experts and scholars.

The denaturalization provision of the 1906 Act was originally and primarily conceived as a means of redressing naturalization fraud and illegality committed prior to or during the naturalization process itself—before the moment an alien obtained American citizenship. But, in practice, the Wickersham 1909 Circular limited the cancellation of certificates of citizenship that had been fraudulently or illegally procured to those instances where revoking naturalization would substantially better the country's citizenry.

Yet even at the height of naturalization corruption in the 1930s, cases where individuals obtained citizenship through fraud or illegal behavior committed before or during the naturalization process constituted a minority of the cancellations of naturalization certificates.[52] The bulk of denaturalizations after 1909 resulted not from an intent to clean up the naturalization process or to make naturalization procedures more administrative in nature. Rather, these naturalizations occurred out of a desire to expel from the body politic "un-American" citizens: most of them not for fraud or illegality committed *before* they were naturalized, but because of who they were or what they had done *after* they obtained American citizenship.

The goal of "bettering the citizenry," along with the vesting of denaturalization authority in federal hands, paved the way for interpreting the 1906 denaturalization provision in a new direction. Denaturalization became a means for cleansing the American body politic of those naturalized citizens who behaved in ways considered un-American, due to their attachment to a "foreign" morality or to their race, land of origin, or political ideas—sometimes before their naturalization, but, most often, developed afterward.

"Former" Americans of this sort were never encouraged to reapply after they were stripped of their citizenship. To the contrary, expelled from American citizenry, they would become foreigners again or, worse, stateless. They were often deported from the United States or, if already abroad, forbidden to reenter.

PART II

=====

A Conditional Citizenship

John Raker (Democrat, California). If a man appears
  before a court with his witnesses and soft pedals himself
  through, and he is an anarchist at the time, and within
  five years after he has received his papers he commences
  to practice anarchy, there is no provision whereby you
  can take his naturalizations papers from him.
Mr. Crist. There are judicial decisions by which that has
  been done, in construing the present law.
[Raker:] Do they go so far?
[Crist:] Yes, sir. There have been several cases, and the
  Wurstenbarth case is an outstanding case.
[Raker:] If all the proceedings are in good shape, but
  within two, three four or five years he begins to practice
  sabotage, becomes an anarchist or I.W.W., and it can
  be established that at the time he was naturalized
  he held those views, can you cancel his certificate of
  naturalization?
[Crist:] I think so.
Albert Johnson (Republican, Washington) Chairman. We
  intend to provide a means for reopening such a case.
>   —House of Representatives, Hearings Before the
>   Committee on Immigration and Naturalization,
>   October 19, 1921

CHAPTER 4

The First Political Denaturalization:
Emma Goldman

In the evolution of its purpose and interpretation, the 1906 denaturalization clause took American citizenship in a new direction. Immigration from Europe was at its peak in 1907 with 1,285,349 entries.[1] The dramatic reaction to this surge—restrictionist and racist—was reinforced later in the context of World War I and the rise of revolutionary ideologies. One of the primary objectives of the immigration and naturalization policies was to detect and prevent "un-American" immigration and to exclude and deport those who had succeeded in settling in the country. "Un-Americanism" was defined politically and encompassed opinions, acts, practices, or simply ethnicity.

In the context of the creation of the Dillingham Commission by the Immigration Act of February 20, 1907,[2] whose report led to the adoption of the literacy test in 1917, and to the quota laws of 1921 and 1924,[3] loyalty became an important concern of the government.

This trend resulted in the creation of a *conditional citizenship* for some categories of citizens. The Expatriation Act of March 2, 1907, promoted the goal of "reducing the number of Americans who, in the eyes of the federal government, have compromised their status as citizens by maintaining or establishing foreign liaisons of a certain type."[4] The quasi-simultaneity of the 1906 Naturalization Act, designed to create a standard on naturalization and to combat fraud and illegality, and the 1907 Expatriation Act, which created this conditional citizenship, is deceptive: one concerns mainly procedural fraud, the other xenophobia and fear of foreign and radical ideologies. While the 1906 act was the culmination of a legislative debate on fraud that had started in the 1840s, the 1907 act began a period of fear and paranoia that would greatly expand by 1940.

This conditional citizenship applied in 1907 to different categories of native-born Americans: women marrying foreigners and Americans acquiring another nationality. Even though the provision concerning American women was by then obsolete,[5] in 1940 the scope of conditionality would expand to include American-born citizens evading the draft, joining a foreign army, or participating in foreign elections. But naturalized citizens remained the main target of crusaders against un-Americanism. If they were residing abroad, they were the object of both the 1906 and 1907 laws. The latter expanded the scope of the former to include naturalized citizens living two years in their country of origin or five years in any foreign country at any time after their naturalization.

New Americans living in the United States could also lose their citizenship if they violated certain standards. Let's put aside the "criminals." Today all democracies provide for the possibility of voiding a citizenship recently granted if a naturalized person is found to have lied about a criminal record prior to accession to citizenship. That provision was more expansive in the interwar period than it is today. It included in the scope of bad moral character, for example, cases involving extramarital relations, defense or advocacy of free love, the practice of plural marriage or polygamy,[6] the possession and sale of intoxicating liquor in violation of the National Prohibition Act of 1922,[7] or working as a pimp.[8] These restrictions reflected the values and social norms of the time. Yet additional restrictions—based on race and politics—rose after 1906. A naturalized person who was Asian, spoke out against the war, or was a socialist, a communist, or a fascist risked the loss of his American citizenship.

Citizenship could be lost by acts or speech now considered basic rights. But this conditionality of the status of naturalized citizen would provoke conflicts within the executive branch—between the Justice and the State departments—and with and between the courts. Conditionality of citizenship was rooted in both the explicit language of the statute (for the naturalized citizen moving and living abroad) as well as in more expansive interpretations of the law's intent. For instance words pronounced or acts committed after naturalization could serve as a *post facto* indication of a mental reservation, a lack of attachment to the U.S. Constitution at the moment of or before the naturalization. Sometimes an illegality committed before naturalization—like an error or a lie on the date of arrival in the United States—could serve as a pretext for a denaturalization for political reasons. This is how it started for Emma Goldman, the subject of the first political denaturalization in the United States in 1909.

*   *   *

Goldman was born in 1869 in Lithuania, where she was introduced to anarchist principles at the factory where she worked. She emigrated to the United States at the age of seventeen and married fellow Russian-born factory worker Jacob Kersner, through whom she acquired American citizenship. The two separated not long thereafter, and subsequently divorced.

Goldman eventually became the "most prominent anarchist of the era" and was known by most Americans of the time as "Red Emma" and the "High Priestess of Anarchism."[9] Her involvement as a revolutionary grew in the aftermath of the Haymarket Riot in 1886, where a bomb had been thrown at police during a protest in favor of a shorter workday. The subsequent execution of several anarchists in connection with the attack galvanized many American anarchists, including Goldman. Six years later, Goldman is believed to have participated in the attempted assassination of factory owner and future philanthropist Henry Clay Frick. Goldman's long-time companion and fellow anarchist Alexander Berkman was the would-be assassin. Though not personally involved, Goldman served as an inspiration to, and briefly met, Leon Csolgosz, the insurrectionary Polish anarchist and the assassin of President William McKinley.

Based on these revolutionary activities, the U.S. government wanted to deport Goldman.[10] The government's original strategy was simply to bar her reentry to the United States when she left the country in the fall of 1907 for speaking engagements at the International Anarchist Congress in Europe.[11] On September 24, 1907, Frank Sargent, the commissioner general of immigration, sent a "strictly confidential" telegram to the New York, Philadelphia, and Baltimore immigration offices declaring that "Emma Goldman, the notorious anarchist, is now out of the United States, but intends to return very shortly to resume her propaganda in this country. . . . It is desired that either or both of these persons [the other was Max Baginski] who may arrive at your port should be detained and rigidly examined; any claims of American citizenship to be fully verified before being accepted as correct."[12]

Goldman was returning with fellow anarchist Max Baginski,[13] and immigration officials initially attempted to treat and quickly deport her as an alien. But Goldman traveled from Liverpool to Montreal and "experienced no trouble whatever getting into Canada."[14] On the train from Montreal to New York, the porter took her ticket, "together with a generous tip, and he didn't show up again" for the rest of the journey. Two weeks later, at her first public appearance, the newspapers, the public, and the government were informed of her arrival back in the States.[15] Oscar S. Straus, secretary of commerce and labor, pronounced Goldman to be in violation of a 1907 act of Congress, known as the Anarchist Law, and issued an order "to take into custody the said alien, and convey her before a Board of Special Inquiry, at Ellis Island, to enable her to show cause why she should not be deported in conformity with the law."[16]

On November 17, a memo of the Bureau of Immigration sent to Straus listed Goldman's criminal record as well as the many anarchist speeches she had delivered in recent years, including the most recent one, on November 11 in New York City. But it also warned Straus of the possibility of deporting her, especially since it was still unclear whether or not Goldman was a citizen: "The general opinion of the officers who have been following her up is that she will welcome arrest; that it will not only advertise her and add to her prestige, but will be the means of bringing her in considerable sums in the way of contributions."[17] On November 19, 1907, Straus withdrew the warrant for Goldman's arrest, pending an investigation on her citizenship status.[18]

On March 10, 1908, Sargent requested that Richard K. Campbell, the chief of the Division of Naturalization, open an inquiry into Goldman's assertion that she was truly an American citizen via her naturalized father, as she had originally declared.[19] On March 13, Assistant U.S. Attorney Palmer S. Chambers telegraphed Campbell: "Investigation progressing satisfactorily, very probably E.G. is not a citizen. Will write you when sure."[20] On March 18, 1908, Chambers submitted an eight-page report to Campbell,[21] based on the investigation he had performed that day in Rochester, New York, with naturalization examiner Abraham L. Zamosh: "Goldman was born in Popolan, County of Shavel State of Kovno, Russia, on June 16th, 1870, Russian date (American date June 29, 1870). . . . In December 1885 she left there with her half sister Helena Zodokoff for the United States." Goldman arrived in Rochester, New York, on January 1, 1886. The report notes that Emma Goldman's father Abraham Goldman was naturalized on October 13, 1894, when Emma Goldman was over twenty-four years of age, and she could not, therefore, claim naturalization through him. "Emma Goldman was married to Jacob Kersner in the spring of 1887. . . . In the latter part of 1888 or early in 1889, Emma Goldman and her purported husband were divorced according to the Jewish law by Rabbi Abe Chajin Levinson. [A few months after this], Goldman fell in love with Abraham [sic] Berkman, the man who shot Henry Clay Frick during the Homestead riot."

The report then moves to Jacob Kersner.

The son of Abraham Kersner, born in Niemiroff, State of Kaminits Podolsk, Russia in approximately April, 1868, he arrived in June 1883 or 1884. From there, he went to Rochester, back to New York City, and finally back to Rochester to live with his parents. The following entry appears on the naturalization records of Monroe County: Jacob A. Kersner, born at Belgrade Serbia, Germany, April 1st, 1868, landed in the United States June 18, 1879, date of naturalization October 18, 1884. Witnesses Simon Goldstein and Samuel Cohen. Charge to the Democratic County Committee." The father believes that the above record is that of the naturalization of his son Jacob.

This report's findings demonstrate that Kersner was naturalized before the age of eighteen and the investigation is therefore pursued in two directions: proof of the identity of Kersner and of his marriage with Emma Goldman.

On May 27, 1908, inspector John Gruenberg, from the Bureau of Immigration of New York City, reported to Sargent that he now had enough evidence to denaturalize Kersner: "I have obtained their [Kersner's parents and brother] affidavits, whereby it is shown beyond a doubt that Jacob A. Kersner, under whom Emma Goldman claims citizenship, is the identical person who migrated to the United States from Russia, in the year 1882, at the age of about 16 years, and that he was not of age, nor had he been 5 years continuously in the United States on the 18th day of October, 1884, and therefore his naturalization was obtained fraudulently."[22] Inspector Gruenberg concluded his memo with a call for action: "I most respectfully suggest that, should proceedings be instituted eventually resulting in the annulment of the order of Naturalization, that it would have a very salutary moral effect, in so far as it would deprive Emma Goldman of that feeling of security which she now manifests, believing herself to be a citizen of the United States."[23]

Two days later, on May 29, Straus updated the status of the case. He was ready to act but remained prudent: "For many reasons it is not desirable to institute such a suit unless there are reasonable grounds for concluding that such a suit would be successful. The failure of the suit would tend to martyrise Emma Goldman in the estimation of her ill guided followers. You will observe that the whereabouts of Jacob Kersner or Jacob A. Kersner is not known. He seems to be a fugitive from justice."[24]

On June 11, 1908, Campbell officially responded to Straus that enough evidence had been gathered to initiate an action for the cancellation of Kersner's naturalization certificate. Straus approved the order by his personal signature and a handwritten notation: "Approved. Have action taken accordingly. Signed: OSS."[25] On September 24, 1908, the Department of Justice filed a bill of complaint against Kersner.[26]

The hearing, postponed two or three times on account of other business was finally set for some time in the week of January 25, 1909 at the U.S. district court at Buffalo.[27] Then, suddenly, Chambers had second thoughts and sent a letter to Charles J. Bonaparte, the attorney general. Chambers agreed, with all the assistant U.S. attorneys involved in the case, that "the denaturalization of the husband *ipso facto* denaturalizes the wife." But as "in this particular case the wife's interests are the only ones in which the government is particularly interested," he wondered if Goldman should not be "made a party to the suit." "Should we obtain judgment against Kersner and discover later that Emma Goldman . . . is not affected thereby, the whole object to be obtained by the suit would be lost."[28]

But on February 2, 1909, William R. Harr, an assistant attorney general, recommended that the government not join her in a suit to cancel her husband's certificate: "the wife acquired, not by any act of her own, but simply by grant from the Government. This grant was based however, upon a condition that she married a citizen. In the eye of the law, it may be said, that if her husband's certificate of naturalization was obtained by fraud, he was never a citizen and therefore his wife acquired no rights of citizenship."[29] Bonaparte thought it advisable to request the opinion of the secretary of commerce and labor on the matter[30] and on February 11, Straus answered that he seriously doubted the wisdom of making Emma Goldman a party in the case. Straus explained, "It would too obviously indicate that the ultimate design of the proceedings is not to vindicate the naturalization law, but to reach an individual, and deprive her of an asylum she now enjoys as a wife of an American citizen."[31]

On February 16, Chambers was ordered by the attorney general to proceed without involving Goldman in the case.[32] And on April 8, 1909, the U.S. District Court of the Western District of New York invalidated Kersner's citizenship.[33] The defendant did not appear at the hearing. However, Kersner's father testified to his date of birth as 1865 or 1866 and to their date of arrival in the United States as 1882. Simon Goldstein, his former employer and his witness at the time of his naturalization, confirmed that Kersner and Goldman were husband and wife and were living together as a real couple.[34]

Goldman's eventual deportation would not occur until a decade later. In a memorandum dated March 21, 1908, to Straus, Charles Earl, solicitor of the Department of Commerce and Labor, wrote that he had examined the legal prospects of deporting Goldman, and had concluded that if the government took away Kersner's citizenship, Goldman's long residence in the United States would protect her.[35]

"Before a person can be legally deported under the immigration act," he explained, "it must first appear that such a person is 'an alien' within the meaning of that act. . . . It yet remains exceedingly doubtful whether she is 'an alien' within the meaning of the immigration act and as such liable to deportation. Goldman has permanently domiciled in the U.S. for over 32 years since she was 15." In the most recent federal court decision on the issue, *Rodgers v. United States ex rel. Buchsbaum*, the court held that "we are clearly of the opinion that an alien who has acquired a domicile in the United States cannot thereafter while still retaining such domicile legally be treated as an immigrant on his return to this country after a temporary absence for a specific purpose not involving a change of domicile."[36] But in 1914, the Supreme Court would reverse this holding in *Lapina v. Williams.*[37]

After deciding not to pursue Goldman, the Department of Justice nevertheless hoped she would leave the country unaware that, in its view, she had lost her citizenship. Then the government could bar her from reentering the United States.[38] Goldman in fact had heard about the denaturalization of her former husband. The secret service of the Anarchist Bureau of the Chicago Police Department had, at the beginning of 1909, intercepted a letter from Goldman to a fellow anarchist. In it Goldman wrote: "At first I took this case of the U.S. Authorities of taking my papers away as a joke but now it turns out serious; altogether too serious. The U.S. Authorities are planning to take us by surprise. We, a few of us, had a meeting and decided to be prepared. Now what I ask of you is very important and you should attend to it at once. Go to his brother and find out how long since Jac. K. left Rochester, how long since he last heard from him and if he is alive. If he is dead that alters my case. I am worried to death over it and hope that you will do your share [to] relieve me from it."[39]

Later, after both she and her former husband were denaturalized, Goldman published a first version of "A Woman Without a Country" (see Appendix 1). In this short pamphlet written in a sarcastic tone, she narrates the government's obsessive chase and concludes: "You have Emma Goldman's citizenship. But she has the world, and her heritage is the kinship of brave spirits—not a bad bargain."[40]

In subsequent years Goldman became involved in the opposition to

World War I: "She could not understand how professed liberals could in one breath denounce Prussian militarism and in the next propose conscription."[41] In protest against the Selective Service Act of 1917, which required all males aged twenty-one to thirty to register for the draft, she and Berkman organized the No Conscription League of New York, which proclaimed: "We oppose conscription because we are internationalists, antimilitarists, and opposed to all wars waged by capitalistic governments."

On June 15, 1917, Goldman and Berkman were arrested and charged with conspiracy to "induce persons not to register" under the newly enacted Espionage Act, and were held on $25,000 bail each.[42] Defending herself and Berkman during their trial, Goldman invoked the First Amendment, asking how the government could claim to fight for democracy abroad while suppressing free speech at home.

The jury found them guilty and the judge imposed the maximum sentence of two years' imprisonment, a $10,000 fine each, and the possibility of deportation after their release from prison. Goldman served two years in the Missouri State Penitentiary.[43] Just before the expiration of her sentence, on September 5, 1919, the Department of Labor ordered Goldman's arrest in order to deport her on the basis of the 1918 Anarchist Exclusion Act.[44] Harry Weinberger, her lawyer, tried to argue before the commissioner general of immigration that the denaturalization of her former husband did not affect the citizenship of Emma Goldman. "The citizenship of her husband made her a citizen," he declared, "the same as if she had applied on her own account."[45] The final decision was submitted to Louis F. Post, assistant secretary of labor.[46] He concluded that "the revocation of her husband's citizenship, upon which hers depended, operated automatically to subject her to the disabilities of an alien." "If I erred," he wrote later in his memoirs, "my decision was jurisdictional and would have been reviewed by the courts in habeas corpus proceedings. But Miss Goldman didn't take her case to the courts."[47]

On December 8, 1919, Goldman and Berkman appeared in federal court before Judge Julius M. Mayer, who declared that as aliens, they had no constitutional rights. In court, Goldman argued: "The apparent cancellation of my citizenship by starting an action against Jacob A. Kersner without giving me an opportunity to defend or show the falsity of the government's position, shows how any woman married to a naturalized citizen and feeling secure in her citizenship, may suddenly find herself an alien, and because of some opinion she may hold which may be unpopular, find herself an arrested alien and deported from the country she may come from more than 30 years ago, as is my case today."[48]

Goldman and Berkman remained in detention at Ellis Island. On December 10, 1919, U.S. Supreme Court Justice Louis Brandeis declined to overrule the lower court's decision in their case. On December 13, her lawyer obtained the guarantee that Goldman and Berkman would be deported to the country of their choice, Soviet Russia, instead of to Germany, the first option of the Bureau of Immigration. And at dawn on December 21, 1919, Goldman, Berkman, and 247 aliens set sail on the SS *Buford*, bound for Russia. Fifty-one were considered anarchists and 184 were members of the Union of Russian Workers who had been arrested during the first Palmer Raids, conducted in eighteen U.S. cities in November 1919.[49] Already working for the Justice Department, a young J. Edgar Hoover had supervised the deportation proceedings and was present when the boat deporting Goldman set sail.[50]

Later, on December 9, 1921, Goldman would write from Riga to Harry Weinberger. She was just out of Russia and in despair over her experience in the Soviet Union:

> My dear, dear Councelor:
> It is a long time between letters. Is it not? I will make no idle apologies. Living in Dante's Inferno is not conducive to communication with the outside world. It is not only the censorship which prevented my writing. It was much more my own disturbed and harassed spirit which could find no peace or comfort long enough to write serenely.
> . . . The only difference between Russia and other countries is that in Russia the very elements who have helped to unfurl the Revolution have also helped to carry the Revolution to her grave—and that pain eats more into one's vitals than the existence of reaction in other lands. One can survive the betrayal of an enemy but one you believe in and loved—one can never survive.[51]

She implored Weinberger:

> I want you to write me with perfect frankness about my chance of returning to America. It is no use deceiving myself and others by saying I will feel at home and be able to take root anywhere out of America. If I had unlimited means and could reconcile myself to a life of leisure, Europe would be preferable. Even though the world is one black

dungeon, one could travel comfortably and without annoyance, if one had means and would change one's name. It might even be profitable to cruise the world and write one's impression. But I have no means and I cannot continue being dependent much longer. Nor can I continue inactive much longer. I must really know how I stand in regard to the States, so it's up to you to tell me.

First, any sense in pressing the "Kersner" claim? Secondly, any good in going through with the marriage farce. I mean any good for a deported woman to attach herself to an American Gentleman? I mean will the fact of marriage to an American annul my deportation? I don't say I have already found the unfortunate one who will sacrifice himself for a "good cause." Still I meant to be prepared—meant to get my nadan[52] ready. Please write me at your earliest opportunity.

It was a case of unfortunate timing that just months later American feminists, who had campaigned for the elimination of the clause in the 1907 law that prescribed deprivation of nationality for an American woman marrying a foreigner, saw their efforts rewarded with the passage of the Cable Act of September 22, 1922.[53]

The Cable Act thereafter disconnected marriage and nationality. American women were allowed to retain their nationality after marrying foreigners.[54] But, likewise, foreign women would no longer automatically become American by marrying an American man.[55] Henceforth, if Emma Goldman remarried to an American man, she would be required to go through naturalization proceedings, which allowed for greater federal government control.

CHAPTER 5

Radicals and Asians

In 1912, a few years after Emma Goldman's denaturalization, Leonard Oleson was denaturalized on new legal grounds—"lack of attachment" to the U.S. Constitution. On September 21, 1910, the chief naturalization examiner in Seattle requested that the U.S. attorney institute a denaturalization proceeding.[1] During his hearing, Oleson denied that he was an anarchist or opposed to organized government. He declared himself a socialist, "willing for people to retain their money, but insisting that all the land, buildings and industrial institutions should become the common property of all the people." Oleson declared that this object could be attained "by the power of the ballot" and "when that object shall be attained the political government of the country will be entirely abrogated, because, there will be no use for it." U.S. District Judge Cornelius H. Hanford declared that Oleson had no reverence for the Constitution, nor any intention to support and defend it against its enemies and was not "well disposed toward the peace and tranquility of the people."[2] Hanford cancelled Oleson's certificate of naturalization on May 10, 1912.

In the following days, letters of protest were sent to President William Howard Taft, and the Attorney General asked the U.S. attorney involved in the case for more information.[3] After receiving his report, Wickersham sent a short and firm reply: "Department thinks Judge Hanford has committed grave error in cancelling Oleson's certificate of naturalization upon grounds stated in his opinion. You are instructed to cooperate with respondent in effort to have case responded and judgment set aside."[4]

Wickersham was again proving himself a defender of civil liberties. A few weeks earlier, he had refused to prosecute the Industrial Workers of the World (IWW or Wobblies) under federal law for "seditious conspiracy" in a Southern California free speech case.[5] Despite strong pressure from the superintendent of the San Diego Police Department, Senator John Works of

California, and President Taft himself "to show the strong hand of the United States"[6] against the IWW, Wickersham followed the advice of his assistant attorney general, William Harr: he instructed the reluctant local U.S. attorney not to prosecute the IWW.[7] Harr had argued that despite the fact that the Wobblies were "self-confessed liars and lawbreakers," there was nothing indicating a specific attack on the U.S. government.[8]

A few weeks later, in regard to the Oleson case, Wickersham explained his position:

> As I read Judge Hanford's opinion, it proceeds upon the idea that Oleson is disqualified because he is a socialist and advocates radical changes in the institutions of this country—specifically communal instead of individual ownership of land, buildings and industrial institutions, such changes to be brought about by the use of the ballot. This view rests upon the theory that the Constitution of the United States is immutable, whereas it provides in itself for amendment by the people through the use of the ballot. If Oleson is disqualified because he advocates communal ownership of certain property, to be brought about by the use of the ballot, so also are they disqualified who advocate the direct election of United States Senators and Government ownership of railroad, which is to be accomplished in the same way. It needs no citation of authority to demonstrate the right of every citizen to seek within the Constitution, to accomplish such changes in the structural Government as he thinks wise. The fact that the doctrines avowed by Oleson may be repugnant to the majority of the people is no reason for denying to him the equal protection of the laws.[9]

Wickersham also thought that the suit to cancel Oleson's certificate of naturalization was based upon an erroneous interpretation of the law. The Naturalization Act required from the applicant that "he has behaved as a man . . . attached to the principles of the Constitution of the United States." In other words, it requires *behavior* and not belief.[10] Judge Hanford's opinion indicates that he regarded the question as one of "belief" rather than "behavior," which was for Wickersham clearly erroneous.[11] Congress had disqualified on account of belief only those who "disbelieve[d] in or [were] opposed to organized government." Oleson denied that he was an anarchist or opposed to organized government; he also denied that he was in favor of overthrowing the government by force or violence. "There is nothing in the facts as found by Judge Hanford," Wickersham wrote, "to indicate that during the period mentioned Oleson had behaved in a manner indicating that he was not attached to the principles of the Constitution of the United States."[12]

After his opinion was made public, letters of protest arrived in droves at the Department of Justice. Wickersham replied that he relied in his actions "entirely upon Judge Hanford's own opinion which says that Oleson stated that he proposed to accomplish the objects of his views through the power of the ballot."[13] Immediately after Judge Hanford's decision, socialists all across the country also protested, and on June 7, 1912, at the request of the Socialist congressman from Wisconsin, Victor Berger, a unanimous House of Representatives directed an inquiry into Hanford's conduct—the first step in impeachment proceedings. He had been charged with "a long series of corrupt and unlawful decisions"[14] dating back twenty-two years and including the Oleson case, and also with "being in a drunken condition while presiding the court."[15]

On June 19, Judge Hanford refused to vacate and set aside his previous judgment in the Oleson case. Eight days later a three-member investigating committee sent to Seattle to conduct the inquiry opened its hearings on the Oleson case. The first witness called was Oleson himself. He testified that Hanford had asked him if he was "devotedly attached to the Constitution of the United States," and that he had replied that although he had no "superstitious reverence for the document," he was "willing to abide by the laws of the country." He testified also that he was a member of the Socialist Labor Party and of the Detroit wing of the IWW, drawing a sharp line between the two wings—his being socialistic, the other one being anarchistic—of the latter organization.[16]

On July 22, by agreement with the congressional committee, Hanford resigned and the impeachment procedure was stopped.[17] Hanford was about to face documentary evidence showing that the Northern Pacific Railroad had sold him land "on very favorable terms shortly after Hanford had rendered a decision that saved the company more than $60,000 in taxes."[18] Hanford's judgment was reversed and a new hearing ordered by the Court of Appeals on the Oleson case on February 13, 1913.[19] The case was reassigned for trial on March 9, 1914, but was dismissed by the newly appointed U.S. attorney Clay Allen. Oleson's citizenship had been reestablished and was no longer at risk. This position was imposed on Allen against his will by the Labor Department opinion that the evidence was insufficient to properly establish a case for the cancellation of naturalization.[20]

As a consequence of this case, Wickersham and Secretary of Commerce and Labor Charles Nagel decided that all requests for cancellation proceedings on political, racial, and religious grounds should be presented by the Department of Commerce and Labor to the Department of Justice in Washington, D.C., and not to the U.S. attorneys. Instructions were given to naturalization examiners to report such cases to the Department of Commerce and Labor.[21]

Recalling the Oleson case in 1921, John Speed Smith, chief naturalization examiner for the Ninth District, Seattle, gave the following statement: "When the case came up for a hearing on the cancellation proceeding, our judge went off into the question of socialism. . . . That got all the Socialists arrayed against us. . . . At that time, in our country out there, there were a lot of people that thought that a man had a right to be a member of the IWW. While we were fighting them a lot of good citizens . . . thought that a man under the Constitution could be an IWW and a Socialist. I could not ask a man in court whether he had any Socialistic tendencies and one judge barred me from asking a petitioner if he was an IWW . . . he considered it immaterial. . . . The whole sentiment of the people has changed, and I think the war has a lot to do with it."[22] In April 1917 when the United States entered World War I, the climate became more ominous, and the reaction of the Wilson administration's attorney general, Thomas Gregory, changed completely.

During World War I, some German Americans were denaturalized because they expressed sympathy for their country of origin. They were condemned as having lacked "complete renunciation of all foreign allegiance at the time citizenship" was granted.[23]

Pressure had increased on the U.S. government to curtail the free speech rights of Americans of German origin both because of the general fear of disloyalty and a recent change in the German nationality law. By virtue of the law of July 22, 1913, known as the Delbrück Law, Germans living abroad would lose their nationality if naturalized in their new country, unless they obtained explicit prior authorization from the German government. Authorization would be granted only to candidates who agreed to carry out their military service.[24]

However, once war broke out, the adoption of that provision—the explicit right for Germans naturalized abroad to keep their German nationality—provoked very strong reactions in all Western countries; it contributed to the development of legislation on denaturalization for disloyalty in France (in 1915) and in the United Kingdom (in 1918) that was aimed in particular at naturalized persons of "enemy" origin.

In the United States, as early as July 1914, Richard Flournoy, assistant to the solicitor at the State Department, considered that "the introduction of a quite novel provision, according to which Germans residing in foreign countries may keep their German nationality, under certain conditions, after obtaining naturalization as citizens of such countries" seemed "to carry the principle of dual nationality further than it [had] ever been carried before."[25] And when war broke out, the reactions grew stronger still. In June 1915, in an article titled, "When Is an American Not an American?" former president Theodore Roosevelt called the German law into question.[26]

On August 25, 1916, Attorney General Gregory was requested by George A. Dew, editor and publisher of *The Messenger* in Toledo, Washington, to act against naturalized Germans' "disloyal and traitorous in sentiment."[27] He replied that "utterances, such as you describe, are clearly evidence that when they were made, the person guilty thereof was bearing allegiance to Germany, his motherland. The open question would be whether he had returned to German allegiance, since his naturalization, or whether the expression was of mental reservation which he had always entertained. If the former, it would not constitute a ground for cancelling his naturalization certificate. If the latter, it would." And Gregory concluded that the court would determinate the answer and decide whether or not to cancel the certificate of naturalization.[28]

Many Americans had entered into what Christopher Cappozola calls "vigilant citizenship," which heightened demands for volunteer neighborhood policing and closer cooperation with the state during wartime.[29] German Americans had become the enemy for many, along with anything that carried a trace of German origins.[30] Gregory commented later that

> during the early period of our participation in the war much complaint was current[ly] growing out of disloyal utterances on the part of naturalized Americans of German and Austrian origin. Many of these utterances, while entirely disloyal, did not fall within the scope of the criminal statutes. The department reached the conclusion, however, that in certain individual cases these utterances were of a character that demonstrated that the naturalized citizen had never in good faith renounced his allegiance to the country of his origin. A number of civil actions were therefore instituted. . . . The successful outcome of these early litigations and the accompanying wide publicity had a

marked effect upon naturalized citizens of disloyal tendency throughout the country and greatly lessened the volume of these utterances.[31]

Denunciations flourished, but they did not necessarily provoke denaturalization. One illustrative case was that of August Weiler, born in Germany
in 1846 and naturalized in Illinois in 1888. Thirty years later, on May 21, 1918,
Weiler was arrested in St. Louis, following notification of the authorities by
Harry Rosecarr, a customer at Yawitz Tailoring Company, Weiler's place of
employment. Rosecarr had gone to the tailor shop to solicit contributions
to the Red Cross. Weiler responded to this request by saying, "I am born in
Germany and you cannot tear the German out of my heart. . . . My cradle was
there and it is my country. . . . The Kaiser has done nothing to me and I can't
see why the U.S. went into that war, we ought to stay out of it."[32]

After his arrest, the seventy-one-year-old Weiler was locked up by local
police pending his transfer to national authorities. Two days later, on May 23,
the Office of the Chief Examiner of the Naturalization Service in St. Louis
recommended to Campbell that he endorse a denaturalization procedure
against Weiler.[33]

A subsequent August 8, 1918, letter to the commissioner revealed that
Weiler had also been indicted for "violation of the Espionage Act." However,
the local U.S. attorney was "very much in doubt as to the value of the evidence
against said Weiler. He recommended the cancellation suit only in the event
of conviction in the criminal case." On September 7, the commissioner endorsed this strategy and denaturalization proceedings were never initiated.[34]

Another case concerned Victor Schneider, who was born in Austria in 1871,
arrived in the United States in 1893, and filed his declaration of intention in
1899, a few days before his naturalization. According to the information gathered by the local Bureau of Investigation, at the beginning of 1918, it appeared
to the chief examiner in Chicago that Schneider was pro-German and was still
in allegiance to the emperor of Austria as he "has declined to work on war materials." On March 11, 1918, the chief examiner referred the matter to the U.S. attorney in order to institute denaturalization proceedings. During the following
months the U.S. attorney certified to the Naturalization Service that he wanted
to use Schneider as a test case and that he had only delayed it on account of
other work. He promised the case was a priority, but that was not exactly the
truth. Still, three years later, on February 2, 1921, he again promised the naturalization office that the case would be tried at the earliest date. Finally, on January
13, 1922, he wrote the chief naturalization examiner in Chicago that the disloyal

statements had been made in December 1917, too much time had passed, there was a risk of not finding the witnesses, and finally that it would be impossible for the government to succeed in court, and the case was therefore dropped.[35]

But when suits occurred, courts accepted the order to denaturalize U.S. citizens based on evidence of present disloyalty as a retroactive indication of disloyalty *at the time of naturalization.* This assumption necessitated inquiries, and the courts' decisions were consistent during the period from 1916 to 1923, with the exception of one case, *Woerndle.*

The District Court of Washington set the tone on May 10, 1918, by denaturalizing Carl August Darmer.[36] On October 17, 1917, Darmer, a German-born citizen naturalized in 1888, had refused to buy a Liberty Bond. He told the sellers that "if he bought any Liberty Bonds it would be the same as kicking his own mother." He added "he would rather throw all his property into the bay than buy one $50 Liberty Bond." The court reasoned that since "attachments generally are weakened by length of time and absence from the cherished object, the contention that it is more likely that it was stronger then than now cannot be said, in the absence of explanation, to be altogether unreasonable."

Three days after the Darmer decision, on May 13, 1918, in the District Court of New Jersey, the *Wursterbarth* case[37] echoed the sentiment that loyalty and allegiance to the United States should increase with the defendant's stay there, and that the subject's alien allegiance should correspondingly decrease. A native of Germany, naturalized in 1882, Frederick W. Wursterbarth refused repeatedly to give money to or become a member of the American Red Cross, or to subscribe to the Young Men's Christian Association fund. At these occasions, he made statements that he would do nothing to defeat his country of origin, and that he did not wish the United States to win the war. The question for Judge Thomas G. Haight, Sr. was "whether it may be legitimately inferred as a fact, from his present state of mind, that he was of the same mind at the time he took the oath of allegiance and renunciation." And the judge provided an answer that would become a point of reference for the attorney general:

> As the years succeeding his naturalization passed, coupled with the fact that he continued to dwell within our midst, associate with our citizens, receive the benefits . . . it is natural to presume that his affection and feeling of loyalty and allegiance to this country would increase, and that any ties which bound him to the country from which he came would correspondingly decrease. If therefore, under such

circumstances, after 35 years, he now recognizes an allegiance to the sovereignty of his origin, superior to his allegiance to this country, it seems to me that it is not only permissible to infer from that fact, but that the conclusion is irresistible, that at the time he took the oath of renunciation, he did so with a mental reservation as to the country of his birth, and retained toward that country an allegiance which the laws of this country required him to renounce before he could become one of its citizens. Indeed, for the reasons just stated, his allegiance to the former must at that time has been stronger than it is at present.[38]

Immediately, Gregory sent a circular, with the court decision, to all U.S. attorneys, emphasizing "the doctrine enunciated by the court in the *Wursterbarth* case": "This decision is of great and immediate importance because of the far reaching effect which it should have in discouraging disloyalty in the part of naturalized citizens." Gregory added, "It is the desire of the Department that similar proceedings be commenced at once wherever the facts appear to warrant such action."[39]

A year and a half later, on December 23, 1919, the Fifth Circuit Court of Appeals confirmed the *Wursterbarth* doctrine. Herman Kramer, a German naturalized in 1912, was denounced by A. H. Rebentish, a Secret Service agent, for telling him that he would do all he could against the United States. A keeper of a saloon near an aviation field in San Antonio, he told Rebentish that any information he could get from soldiers at the aviation field, he would send to Germany. The court asserted that "American citizenship is a priceless possession, and one who seeks it by naturalization must do so in entire good faith, without any mental reservation whatever, and with the complete intention of yielding his absolute loyalty and allegiance to the country of his adoption. If he does not, he is guilty of fraud in obtaining his certificate of citizenship."[40]

The Ninth Circuit Court, on May 3, 1920, refused the appeal from F. H. Schurmann to have his certificate of naturalization, which had been issued to him in Los Angeles on December 17, 1904, restored.[41] Schurmann published a book in August 1916, *The War as Seen in German Eyes*, to convince Americans not to go to war against Germany, his country of origin. When the United States entered the war, Schurmann wanted to continue to sell his book but, cautiously, asked his U.S. attorney and the attorney general about its legality. He was denaturalized for having responded to an American who asked him whether it was possible that he would not defend the shores of the United States: "Well Allen I will tell you. I have sworn allegiance to your flag or country, but I am going to tell you this much: That I didn't swear away my birthright. And this is the crisis where every German, whether he is a socialist or not, this is the time that it is up to him to defend the fatherland."[42]

On April 2, 1921, a federal court in Washington State stripped Paul Herberger of his citizenship, which was acquired in 1912, on the grounds that he had not been loyal to his country.[43] He wrote numerous letters to his sister in Germany, excerpts of which served as evidence of "a legal fraud." He wrote in one, for example, "I cannot write you anything of the war and the feeling here, because, if I did, the censor would keep the letter as a souvenir. This much I can tell you, that this famous liberty stuff here does not amount to much. Over there in Germany we had much more liberty than we have here; militarism is absolute trump here."[44] In another letter, he wrote, "If you did not have to reckon with America's friendship, the submarines would have long since brought England to her knees through hunger. It is hoped that someday Germany may repay America like with like."[45] The court reasoned that "it is not necessary that a man be shown to be guilty of treason in order to conclude from his actions and speech that he is not loyal and has not been loyal."[46] And the court concluded with a sort of sociological and psychological tone:

> Loyalty or allegiance, is necessarily, of slow growth; therefore somewhat involuntary, not fully subject to the will. Those who lightly, for temporary advantages, undertake to change their allegiance, are liable to overlook the deep seated nature of this feeling; but the fact that not until afterwards, in times of stress, is it made manifest that the desires, suffered to lie dormant, are stronger for their native than for their adopted country, although this fact may not be fully realized at the time of their realization, renders it none the less a legal fraud for the applicant to fail to disclose his true, although latent, feeling in such matter.[47]

These above cases could be contrasted with *Woerndle*, a Ninth Circuit case decided in 1923, in which the court held that letters showing sympathy with Germany were neither "clear" nor "convincing" enough to prove that the defendant had fraudulently taken the oath of allegiance when he applied for naturalization, especially because "from and after the date when the United States entered the war there is no evidence of any disloyal utterance or any disloyal act on the part of the appellee. On the contrary, the testimony was that, outwardly at least, he conducted himself as a loyal American citizen, that he purchases Liberty Bonds to the maintenance of the Red Cross and to the war activities of the YMCA."[48] The court concluded that "citizenship, once bestowed upon proceedings in the federal courts, should not be lightly taken away. The evidence . . . should be more clear and convincing than it is in the present case."[49]

At the same time, courts were starting to denaturalize anarchists, not on the ground of mental reservation projected retroactively back to the moment of their pledge of allegiance, but for a lack of attachment to the principles of the Constitution. In 1918, the District Court of Oregon decided in *Swelgin* that persons who advocate anarchism cannot really avow allegiance to this government "for they do not intend to submit themselves to its Constitution, laws, rules and regulations, nor to defend it in time of insurrection, or against an aggression from abroad, or when it is at war with other nations."[50] Carl Swelgin had been, since 1911, a member and even an organizer of the IWW. The court described extensively the official program and statutes of the organization, that it advocated "resistance to the existing governmental authority of the United States, and the complete control and ownership of all property in the United States through the abolition of all other classes of society."[51] The court concluded that the defendant was a disbeliever in and opposed to organized government, beliefs about which he fraudulently misled the court.

The target of a similar case, Samuel Applefeld was a native of Ostrog, Russia. He arrived in America in June 1910, on a ship called the *Rhein*. Based on documents in his file,[52] he was naturalized sometime shortly after March 11, 1918, and was denaturalized not long thereafter.

In the government report on his case, he is described as "Race: Hebrew" and "Alleged Anarchist." At the core of his file is a report submitted by FBI agent William Doyas, in response to a request from others at the FBI, dated in early 1918. The agent explained that prior to interviewing Applefeld, he spoke with Applefeld's neighbor, "a colored man who appeared quite intelligent." The neighbor, Thomas Muse, said that he had never heard Applefeld say anything pro-German or anti-American. While visiting Muse, Doyas did notice that Applefeld "is being patronized by a great number of colored people; he also employs colored help."[53]

Doyas then interviewed Applefeld "under a pretext" and gathered his basic biographical information. Doyas reported that Applefeld "spoke quite freely and stated that his sympathies are with the Socialists, and voluntarily stated that about three years ago he heard Emma Goldman speak." He detailed his subscriptions to magazines edited by Emma Goldman and Alexander Berkman, until these magazines were "suppressed," plus "magazines of every description printed in English and Hebrew languages." During the interview, Agent Doyas said, Applefeld "failed to utter a word in favor of the United States but appeared to be pleased to say that he approved the steps taken by the Bolsheviks in Russia." The report concluded, "No doubt Applefeld will deny believing in the teachings of anarchy when applying for final naturalization papers" and it warned the Bureau of Naturalization to take the appropriate steps against his naturalization.

And yet Applefeld was eventually issued a certificate of naturalization. Richard Campbell probably directed one of his naturalization examiners to approach the relevant judge to revoke naturalization decision on the grounds of illegally procured evidence. A few weeks later he could inform the chief clerk of the Department of State, "By direction of the Secretary of Commerce and Labor, I have to advise you that the order of admission to citizenship of the following-named person, made on the date given below, was set aside and held for naught and the certificate of citizenship issued there under cancelled."[54]

The federal court in New York also followed this reasoning when on September 10, 1919, it denaturalized Michael Stuppiello, an American citizen since March 6, 1915. Stuppiello had confessed after his arrest in May 1918 to being an anarchist.[55] The court said that a disbeliever in organized government "is barred . . . from the privilege of naturalization" regardless of whether he is a philosophical anarchist or an activist. This line of reasoning was upheld in *Glaser v. United States* by the Seventh Circuit Court of Appeals in 1923.[56] But the Ninth Circuit Court in *Rowan v. United States* reversed the district court decision to denaturalize James Rowan, a naturalized U.S. citizen originally from Great Britain.[57] Assistant Secretary of Labor Louis Post had initiated the proceedings. He argued that Rowan's conviction under the Espionage Act for conspiracy and his sentence to twenty years of imprisonment "raises a serious question as to the bona fide of the oath he took at the time of naturalization" in 1907.[58]

Speaking through Judge William H. Hunt, the Ninth Circuit Court rejected this analysis and held, on March 28, 1927, that Rowan's violation of the Espionage Act of 1917 "is not logically probative of his state of mind in 1907." Based on a recent Supreme Court decision, Solicitor General William D. Mitchell thought there was no chance to get the Supreme Court to grant certiorari and the government stopped there.[59] It was the last case in its deportation campaign against members of the IWW.

                              *   *   *

The same year, in 1927, the Supreme Court denied certiorari in an appeal from a decision of a circuit court to maintain a naturalized South Asian American in his American citizenship. After that decision, the Bureau of Naturalization ended the campaign to denaturalize Asian Americans, which had been rooted in one of the earliest and oldest exclusions.

In 1790, Congress, on the basis of its constitutional power to establish uniform rules of naturalization, stipulated that only free white persons could be naturalized.[60] In 1870 a post–Civil War act of July 14, extended the privilege of naturalization to "aliens of African nativity and persons of African descent."[61] The leader of the Radical Republicans in the Senate, Charles Sumner from Massachusetts, a fervent abolitionist, wanted the elimination of the mention of race in the provision, but was defeated. Congress added "African descent" to the category "free white persons" so as to exclude Asians. Yet some local courts naturalized Asians anyway. Starting in 1906, however, the Naturalization Bureau began to pursue a mission of denaturalizing Asians, whenever it came into contact with them, when, for example, they requested an American passport or any other official document.

The legal status of the Chinese was clear: an 1882 act of Congress prohibited the admission of Chinese individuals to American citizenship.[62] It is less clear, however, what drew the attention of immigration authorities to Moy Sing Bo, naturalized in Iowa on October 24, 1892, more than twenty years after his naturalization, but he was subsequently denaturalized by the same court that naturalized him on December 2, 1913, simply because he was Chinese.[63]

Similary, Pablo Loynaz, naturalized in 1878 in Louisiana, was subsequently determined to be of Chinese ancestry, and then was denaturalized on January 5, 1911.[64] Chung Bark Hing, a native of China, arrived in the United States in September 1881. He became a member of an American church in Los Angeles, and then moved to Iowa, where he made his declaration of intention in 1897. He was admitted as a citizen by the Circuit Court of Lafayette County, Wisconsin, on October 31, 1900, in Darlington, where he owned and ran a laundry. Hing returned regularly to China, where he had a wife and children. He still resided in Darlington when, for some reason, he requested information from the Bureau of Naturalization about his right to return to the United States if he went back to China in the middle of 1918. Immediately, steps were taken to have Hing's certificate of naturalization cancelled, which a judge of the Circuit Court of Lafayette County did on January 13, 1919.[65]

Less clear was the status of the Japanese. In July 1906, Charles Bonaparte, the attorney general, specifically held the Japanese to be ineligible for citizenship.[66] Clerks of the courts were instructed in 1911 not to register applications of Japanese citizens for naturalization. Some courts did, however, grant them citizenship. Ulysses Kaneko was naturalized by the Superior Court of San Bernardino County, California, in 1896. Misuji Miyakawa was naturalized by the Monroe Circuit Court of Indiana on October 9, 1905. Taneumatseu Matsuki was naturalized on January 7, 1907, by the U.S. District Court of Northern Florida.[67]

A few years later, examiner A. M. Simmons reported in August 1911 that the Civil District Court in New Orleans had naturalized a Japanese individual on September 4, 1906. After examining the court's registers, Simmons determined that thirty-eight Chinese and Japanese natives had been naturalized in 1878. The government pursued denaturalization for as many of these individuals as it could, but many had died or returned to their home countries. The others were in fact denaturalized.[68]

In 1916, the clerk of a court in Tacoma discovered in one of the court's registers that a Japanese individual named Henry Matsumato had been naturalized in 1896. The FBI initiated action in the case, but the U.S. attorney resisted:

> It is possibly known in the department, the extreme sensitiveness of the Japanese people to every question touching upon their admission into the U.S. or their acceptance as citizens here. It occurs to me that since this certificate has so long been in existence, that any action in respect to it might be considered in one or two aspects. If the holder is reputable Japanese, in good standing in the community, that no action should be had. If on the contrary, he is a citizen, generally undesirable, that action might be taken to cancel his certificate. In this connection, I might suggest that I discussed the matter with Naturalization examiner John Speed Smith, and he has promised to make some investigations regarding the man.[69]

A few years later, Charles Benedict came to the attention of American authorities when he applied for an American passport, enclosing a copy of his 1902 naturalization in Galveston County, Texas. In response to his request, H. L. Hershey, the secretary to the governor-general of the Philippines,[70] citing Benedict's mention of his Chinese origins in his passport application, invoked the 1882 act of Congress that prohibited the admission of Chinese individuals to American citizenship. Hershey forwarded the case to Washington for action. The State Department corrected the information the governor-general received by mentioning the fact that Benedict was Japanese and not a Chinese-born American. Post was being prudent, concerned about protecting Benedict's status as a citizen until it could be proven to have been acquired illegally.

In a March 11, 1918 letter to the secretary of state, Post noted that the investigation had failed to disclose that Benedict belonged to an excluded class insofar as the naturalization law was concerned: "It has not been possible to establish that he is not a white person. The fact that he was born in China or Japan does not, of itself, bring him within any of the excluded naturalization classes."[71] He continued, "if Benedict was Chinese, this must be proven. If he was Japanese, the question of Japanese admissibility to American citizenship remained to be decided by the Supreme Court." Post concluded, "until such time that the facts turn definitely against Benedict, he should continue to enjoy all the benefits of citizenship, and should face no criminal action." On March 23, 1918, the State Department furnished a copy of Benedict's passport with his photo. Joseph C. Hutcheson, Jr., the U.S. district judge for the Southern District of Texas decided on June 17, 1919, that the "photograph on the attached passport application was not deemed sufficient."[72] The court requested depositions from the clerk of the court before whom the passport application was sworn to as to bring evidence that the applicant "belongs either to the Chinese or Japanese race."[73] Depositions to this effect were most likely presented, because on June 16, 1920, Judge Hutcheson cancelled Benedict's certificate of naturalization.[74]

In 1922 the Supreme Court confirmed that courts were not authorized to naturalize Japanese.[75] Takao Ozawa, born in Japan in 1875, immigrated to the United States in 1894. Ozawa studied at the University of California at Berkeley, and settled in Hawaii, from where in 1914 he applied for naturalization.[76] He pleaded that he was a true American: he sent his children to American schools and churches and spoke with them only in English, and he was not a registered member of any Japanese organizations. The District Court of Hawaii held that, having been born in Japan and being of the Japanese race, he was not eligible for naturalization.[77] Ozawa appealed to the Court of Appeals for the Ninth Circuit, which sent certified questions to the Supreme Court before deciding on his case.

Wickersham, now a former attorney general, represented Ozawa in the Supreme Court and argued that the 1906 act had trumped the exclusionary provisions of the 1875 act and also that the Japanese possessed white skin, and thus were white.[78] But the Supreme Court concluded that "manifestly the test afforded by the mere color of the skin of each individual is impracticable, as that differs greatly among persons of the same race, even among Anglo-Saxons, ranging by imperceptible gradations from the fair blond to the swarthy brunette, the latter being darker than many of the lighter hued persons of the brown or yellow races. Hence to adopt the color test alone would result in a confused overlapping of races and a gradual merging of one into the other, without any practical line of separation." The Court added: "The determination that the words 'white person' are synonymous with the words 'a person of the Caucasian race' simplifies the problem, although it does not entirely dispose of it."[79]

Three years later, the Supreme Court confirmed the cancellation of a certificate of naturalization granted in 1921 to Hidemitsu Toyota while he was serving in the U.S. Army. The act of May 9, 1918 (section 7), permitted the expedited naturalization of "any alien" who had honorably served in the army or navy of the United States. But with the exception of the privilege extended to Filipinos, the act said nothing which could be construed as changing the racial prerequisites then applicable. With World War I at its peak and its outcome still uncertain, some Asian foreign residents were serving in the military as draftees or volunteers.[80] A few of these started applying for naturalization.[81] John B. Zabriskie, a judge of the Court of Common Pleas in Bergen County, New Jersey, sent a telegram on July 6, 1918, to the Department of Justice: "I construe naturalization law of May Ninth nineteen eighteen to permit the naturalization of Chinese and Japanese in military service. Please wire at once if this agrees with your ruling. Am naturalizing soldiers at Camp Merritt." He was told that Chinese were not eligible for citizenship and that "courts almost uniformly hold Japanese not eligible for naturalization."[82] On December 4, 1918, federal district court judge Horace W. Vaughan of Honolulu, who had refused to naturalize Ozawa, said that he would naturalize Japanese, Chinese, and Korean soldiers: "We had drafted them into our service and they had thought enough of us to be willing to serve, to risk their lives in our service."[83] The next month, in January 1919, Judge Vaughan naturalized more than one hundred Japanese and several Koreans. The Bureau of Naturalization was split on the issue between Campbell, who favored maintaining the exclusion of Asians, and Crist, who believed that Asian soldiers were entitled to naturalization. Crist wrote to Campbell that he "believed the law is as Judge Vaughan has construed it, whether it was the intention of Congress or not. The language seems to me to be perfectly clear."[84]

It fell to the courts to decide. Campbell wanted one of these cases to reach the Supreme Court. He decided to submit the case of Kinichiro (Henry)

Nagao, who had been naturalized on April 25, 1919, for the institution of a cancellation proceeding. But Nagao was serving as a cabin steward on the *Mayflower*, the president's yacht, and the Department of Justice asked Campbell to choose another case.[85] Hidemitsu Toyota was his next choice. Born in 1888 in Japan, Toyota had served continuously in the U.S. Coast Guard since 1913, and had received eight honorable discharges.[86] Nevertheless, the Supreme Court ruled in *Hidemitsu Toyota v. United States*[87] that the act of 1918, which allowed aliens who had served in the war to become naturalized, did not evince any intention to eliminate from eligibility to naturalization "the distinction based on color or race."

Naturalization of Japanese, Malays, and Chinese was halted. But the status of the hundreds of Asians soldiers naturalized American by courts all across the country since 1918 was at stake.[88] Very rapidly their service in the U.S. army prevented the Naturalization Bureau from acting against Japanese, Chinese, and Koreans already made American by some courts.[89]

The bureau did not feel the same compunction when acting against the naturalized South Asians, whom the Supreme Court had declared ineligible for American citizenship. The Supreme Court had already cancelled the naturalization of an Indian Asian who had served in the military during the war. But Baghat Singh Thind did not base his claim on the application of the 1918 act. He argued that as an Indian Asian he could be naturalized under the law, even if the U.S. government had officially interpreted the act against Indian Asian naturalization since 1907. That year, the U.S. attorney of the Northern District of California, Robert T. Devlin, had written to Attorney General Bonaparte. In a few months, he wrote, "several natives of British India have applied for declarations of intention to become citizens of the United States. The clerks of the local superior courts have refused to issue such papers without the advice; i.e. the opinion, of the Attorney General." In his reply to Devlin's letter, Bonaparte reasoned: "it seems to me clear that under no construction of the law can natives of British India be regarded as white persons within the meaning of section 2169 R.S."[90] This became the official position of the Justice Department.

But some local courts continued to naturalize South Asians, considering them to be white. In 1922, in *United States v. Thind*,[91] the Supreme Court held that a Hindu, being neither white nor African, could not be naturalized. To reach that conclusion the Supreme Court turned its reasoning in *Ozawa*, (where it found it legitimate to justify exclusion on the basis of a "scientific definition" of race) on its head. Even though immigrants from western and southern Asia, such as Syrians or Indians, could well be classified as Caucasian by anthropologists,[92] the Court held that the words "free white persons" were "words of common speech, to be interpreted in accordance with the understanding of the common man." As so understood and used, added the Court, "whatever may be the speculations of the ethnologist,"[93] the category did not include "the body of people" to whom Thind belonged.[94]

After the *United States v. Thind* case, U.S. attorneys brought the cases of naturalized South Indians to the courts. Among them was Vaishno Das Bagai. He had arrived in the United States from Calcutta in 1915 and became a successful merchant. He was naturalized on March 7, 1921, by a federal court in San Francisco, together with his wife and three minor children. In 1923, the bureau of naturalization initiated the proceedings and Das Bagai was denaturalized by the same court on May 5, 1925.[95] For two years, he refused to give up his certificate of naturalization, and then committed suicide in 1928. In the note he left, he wrote: "But now they come to me and say, I am no longer an American citizen. . . . What I have made of myself and my children? We cannot exercise our rights, we cannot leave this country. Humility and insults, who are responsible for all of this? I do not choose to live a life of an interned person. . . . Is life worth living in a gilded cage? Obstacles this way, blockades that way, and the bridges burnt behind."[96] The consequences of the denaturalization were particularly dramatic in the case of Vaishno Das Bagai.

However, in 1924, a district court dismissed the suit against Sakharam Ganesh Pandit, a high-caste Hindu. The Ninth Circuit Court of Appeals supported the district judge on the grounds that at the time of Pandit's naturalization the court determined he was a white person. For the court, because the United States had not appealed that finding, it was *res judicata*.[97] On December 7, 1926, Senator David A. Reed of Pennsylvania introduced a resolution in the Senate to confirm the naturalization of seventy-five persons of "the Hindu race," but failed to have it adopted.[98] It was backed by Chief Justice Taft but defeated in an effort led by Rep. Albert Johnson (R-Wash.), a former member of the Asiatic Exclusion League and chairman of the House Immigration Committee and the California Immigration Committee, a successor organization to the Asiatic Exclusion League.[99]

Yet, on April 2, 1927, the Supreme Court declined to grant certiorari and Pandit remained a citizen.[100] Following that decision, the U.S. government dismissed the cancellation proceedings of the fifteen Hindu Americans who had not yet been denaturalized.[101] By 1928, however, fifty Hindus had had their citizenships revoked by federal courts, rendering most stateless.[102] This is what

82 A Conditional Citizenship

happened to Vaishno Das Bagai's family. Several years after his death, Das Bagai's wife and son were told that despite "the denial by the U.S. Supreme Court of a writ of certiorari to the govt. in the case of U.S. vs. Pandit in 1927,"[103] the cancellation of Vaishno Das Bagai's naturalization divested them of any claim they "might have had to United States Citizenship through such naturalization."[104]

Another case of an attempted cancellation of naturalization was that of Sheriarki Maneck, born in India in 1869 of Parsee parents. He moved to the United States in 1893 and married Claire Irene Flynn. He was naturalized in 1903, and in 1919 he moved to the Hague, Netherlands, to represent the Allen Typewriter Company. He applied for a passport in 1923 but, at the request of the consul in the Hague, an investigation began.[105] His son, Eugene E. Maneck, living in New York, testified on December 20, 1925, that his father in various conversations with him had said that "he is a full blooded Parsee and a Zoroastrian by religion."[106] More than one year later, on January 26, 1927, Eugene was asked to testify again. He said that he was unable to very definitely describe his father's complexion, "that is to say, the color of his skin. He is unquestionably of a dark complexion, bordering on brown, but since I have no standard for comparison," he added, "I cannot make any more definite statement."[107] All three departments involved—State, Labor, and Justice—recommended that a cancellation suit be instituted on the basis that "by construction of the Supreme Court in the *Thind* case, a Hindu is no more entitled to naturalization than a Chinaman."[108] On February 28, 1927, Maneck was informed of this action. But on January 10, 1929, the U.S. attorney for the Southern District of New York received a request to discontinue the cancellation of Maneck's citizenship.[109]

Sheriarki Maneck was doubly lucky. He benefitted from the Supreme Court decision to decline certiorari on Pandit. Additionally, since Maneck was also a naturalized citizen living abroad, he could have been denaturalized if a stricter interpretation of the statute had prevailed. But denaturalization for living abroad had long been a ground of intense conflict—between the courts and the government and between the State and Justice Departments. Maneck had the good fortune to benefit from this conflict.

As cataclysmic as they were for the individuals concerned, from 1906 until the end of the 1930s, denaturalizations for political or racial reasons numbered fewer than one hundred. The majority of cases continued to revolve—at a pace of hundreds some years—around foreign-born Americans residing abroad. Until 1940, these were perceived to be a very different category of denaturalization case.

CHAPTER 6

In the Largest Numbers:
The Penalty of Living Abroad

One provision of the 1906 Act had already addressed the issue of a naturalized citizen taking up permanent residence in another country in the five years following naturalization. This would serve "as 'prima facie' evidence of a lack of intention . . . to become a permanent citizen of the United States."[1]

At the request of the State Department, but over the objection of the majority of the Purdy Commission, which was unwilling to foster statelessness,[2] if newly naturalized citizens took up residence abroad within five years of becoming citizens, this would be considered evidence of a lack of intention. Many newly naturalized citizens, as successive presidents had argued, returned to their native countries and established residence after securing U.S. citizenship, enjoying the best of both allegiances.[3] Since 1906, in the absence of countervailing evidence, foreign residence by a naturalized citizen was "sufficient in the proper proceeding to authorize the cancellation of his certificate of citizenship as fraudulent."[4]

Since the end of the Civil War, the United States stood in sharp contrast to the growth of compulsory military service in Europe. It was suspected that some European immigrants came to the United States to escape conscription. Once Americans, they could return to Europe protected by American consulates and laws in their countries of origin.[5] The records from the Passport Bureau of the State Department showed that approximately 16 percent of the naturalized citizens who applied for passports had been naturalized less than six months earlier. They were presumably avoiding and abusing the duties and responsibilities of their native countries while living as foreigners in the United States, and then benefiting from citizenship protection provided by U.S. consulates as needed in their birth countries.[6] In the State Department's view, the 1906 provision was insufficient. Secretary of State Elihu Root, stopping in Morocco on his way back from the 1906 Algeciras conference, commented on American citizens living in Morocco: "[They] were all those who had come over to get the cloak of American naturalization and then returned to take advantage of a privileged status in their native home. There was not one native-born citizen of the United States there. Fifty percent had returned within three months of naturalization."[7]

This was justification enough, in Root's view, for new provisions, even if he had to admit the advantage the United States enjoyed from this "tenuous thread": the presence in Morocco of U.S. citizens explained its participation in the conference and gave it "an opportunity to do what the Open Door did— preserve world peace because of the power of our detachment."[8] A few months after the passage of the 1906 Naturalization Act, on March 2, 1907, the next session of Congress passed the Expatriation and the Protection of Citizens Act. The new law expanded the previous provision: at any time— the five-year limit was abolished—a residence of two years in the original foreign state of a naturalized citizen or of five in any other foreign state would allow the government to assume that he or she "has ceased to be an American citizen."[9]

This provision was hotly debated on the House floor, not only because there was no longer a time limit to the penalization of a residence abroad but also because the provision transformed denaturalization from a judicial to an administrative procedure. "Under section 15 of the bill passed at the last session, the party in whose favor the naturalization certificate has been issued is given an opportunity to be heard before his certificate is cancelled," argued Representative Robert W. Bonynge, who opposed the bill. "The bill as now presented . . . provides simply that if he has been living abroad permanently for five [or two] years, without any sort of proceedings been instituted, the American consul abroad shall have the right to cancel the judgment of a court issued in the United States."[10]

Yet the expansion of the scope of denaturalization was approved by Congress. Together with the provision concerning American women marrying foreign men and Americans pledging allegiance abroad, the new act gave the term *expatriation* a new meaning.[11] When Congress passed the Expatriation Act in 1868,[12] it ensured the freedom of an immigrant to the United States to be naturalized as an American and to have his or her naturalization recognized by his or her country of origin—a German state or the United Kingdom. Suddenly in 1907, it meant denationalization and the possibility that the United States could exclude Americans from their citizenship against its will.

On April 19, 1907, the State Department issued a circular which specified how naturalized citizens could overcome the presumption that they were no longer citizens because they lived abroad. The exceptions were limited. They included being a representative of American trade and commerce, having reasons of health or education, or intending to return to the United States permanently.[13] In 1908, Attorney General Charles J. Bonaparte urged Congress to enact a law "providing for the cancellation of certificates of persons who by reason of the expatriation act of March 2, 1907, were no longer citizens of the United States."[14]

However, in 1910, Bonaparte's successor, George Wickersham, took the opposite stance. Wickersham held that the new laws had been enacted not to deprive the naturalized American abroad of his or her citizenship, but only to relieve the State Department of the burden of protecting them after an extended stay abroad.[15] He based his interpretation on the congressional debates leading up to the law's passage, and more precisely on the answer provided by Congressman Edgar D. Crumpacker to his colleague Congressman Bonynge during the debates. Crumpacker recognized that the law said "that one ceases to become an American citizen by simply residing abroad," but argued that its intention was not to "decitizenize them, but to withdraw from them the ordinary protection of a citizen if they have become permanent residents abroad."[16] In a letter to Charles Nagel, the secretary of commerce and labor, Wickersham asserted, "The purpose of this act is, I think, simply to relieve the Government of the obligation to protect such citizens residing abroad after the limit of two or five years."

Wickersham's interpretation of the 1907 statute—that it was relevant only to protection and not to citizenship[17]—prevailed, despite the opposition of the State Department.[18] In the years following the Wickersham opinion, under the Taft and Wilson administrations, the Department of Justice expanded the interpretation of the 1907 Expatriation Act to include cases of naturalized citizens who had left U.S. territory to live abroad within the five-year period following their naturalization, and could thereby violate the standards set by the 1906 act. On July 12, 1911, for example, the State Department called on the Department of Justice to open proceedings to cancel the naturalization of fifteen Americans, "natives of the Azores, who, after becoming naturalized in this country, returned to their native land and established therein permanent residences."[19] Despite the fact that their return to the Azores occurred within the five-year time limit set by the 1906 statute, the attorney general refused to denaturalize these citizens.[20]

The State Department retaliated against the Department of Justice's interpretation. It started denaturalizing by a de facto administrative decision—simply by refusing to deliver a passport. For example, Joseph Streda was denied a passport by the American Embassy in London in April 1912. Both the Division of Naturalization and the State Department thought that the fact that Streda had obtained his certificate of naturalization in 1904, before he had resided in the United States five years, "knowingly and willfully in violation of the law," was sufficient to decline his passport request even if no court had decided to denaturalize him. The fact that he had resided abroad ever since was only an "additional reason."[21]

The power to commence a denaturalization proceeding was, in fact, quite discretionary. It became, perhaps as an inevitable result, a highly political, often symbolic tool of the U.S. government and within it of the State Department. One particularly striking example is the U.S. government's decision not to act on the denaturalization requests made by the Cuban descendants of two naturalized American citizens, despite strong evidence and sound legal arguments in their favor.

Tirso Mesa y Hernandez was born in Cuba in 1847, naturalized in the United States on June 23, 1900, and died in Cuba on November 29, 1908.[22] In a letter three years after Mesa's death, New York attorney Charles Stewart Davison laid out the case of his client, Mesa's son, to Wickersham.

According to the letter, Mesa was "a well-known Cuban, who at the time of his death had been offered the position of Minister of Agriculture in the Republic of Cuba." In fact, all of Mesa's business interests were in Cuba, where he was engaged in the sugar business and was the president or director of two railway companies.[23] Mesa married in 1881, had three children, and had never left Cuban territory until 1888, when, on his doctor's orders, he went to Saratoga, New York. He subsequently visited the United States frequently, but only briefly on each occasion: "He never stayed within the United States except at a hotel or as a guest at a private home. . . . No attribute of his life bore any relation to American citizenship." Apparently, Mesa only sought U.S. citizenship "for the purposes of protection in their Cuban lives" due to the "troubled times in Cuba."[24]

Mesa's nationality would become directly relevant at the time of his death. Davison explained that under Cuban inheritance law, on the death of a husband and a father, his wife would receive one-third, and the children two-thirds, of any inheritance. The complication revolved around the fact that Mesa, on one of his visits to the United States, had drawn up an American will. Mesa's family sought to have his American naturalization overturned so that Cuban law would again take primacy, and so that they could reclaim the portion of the inheritance that had been taken by the American executors.

In a letter dated November 24, 1911, when Wickersham was attorney general and had imposed his policy of enforcement restraint, Assistant Attorney General W. H. Harr responded to Mesa's situation on behalf of the U.S. government: "Aside from the question whether cancellation proceedings under some circumstances are authorized by law, the Department does not think it advisable to undertake such proceedings in this case, because it does not appear that the Government now has any interest in the matter; that is, it is not perceived that any good purpose whatever of the Government would be subserved thereby."[25] As a result, Mesa was not posthumously denaturalized.[26]

Eleven years later, in 1922, in a comparable case, at a time when the Wickersham policy had been reversed and many denaturalizations occurred on grounds of residence abroad, the decision was similar. This case involved Antonio Gonzalez Curquejo, who was naturalized in New York Supreme Court on July 29, 1903. A man of considerable wealth, residing in Havana, Cuba, for many years, Gonzalez was a well-known member of the community who had run a local pharmacy.[27] Gonzalez was brought to the government's attention by his grandson, Marcus Gonzalez, who testified that his grandfather never had a bona fide residence in the United States, but came to New York from Cuba on business trips only prior to his naturalization and that his purpose in acquiring American citizenship was to defeat his children in their desire to inherit his property.

Marcus' father and grandmother were both deceased, leaving him a potential heir to his grandfather's fortune. He provided a biography of his grandfather, who was born in Spain in 1847, emigrated to Cuba in 1859, and became a pharmacist in 1868. Marcus said that his grandfather was born Spanish, but "after the war of independence in Cuba in 1898, automatically became a citizen of Cuba."[28] The younger Gonzalez said that his grandfather must have remained a Cuban citizen, because the laws of Cuba require a pharmacist to live in his store, and since his grandfather continued to be a pharmacist, he must have maintained Cuban residency and citizenship. The grandson estimated that his grandfather spent a total of eleven months in the United States

during this mandatory five-year period and returned immediately to Cuba
after his naturalization.

The grandson then explicitly laid out the reason for his attempts to have
his grandfather denaturalized: "According to the Spanish Civil Code, still ad-
hered to in the courts of Cuba, a citizen is compelled to leave his entire fortune
excepting one-eighth thereof to his lineal descendents; Dr. Antonio Gonzalez
having become a citizen of the United States is not bound by the aforesaid
provisions of the Civil Code." With his grandmother and father deceased, the
younger Gonzalez (along with a possible aunt referenced in the documents)
would have been the sole heir to the Gonzalez fortune, but only if his grandfather were to lose his American citizenship and again become a Cuban national. In affidavits submitted to the court, the grandson included testimony
to back up his case. He cited the elder Gonzalez's son-in-law, who said that
"he has many times in the past heard the [second] wife of Dr. Gonzalez, Mrs.
Amelia Valdes, declare that her husband had become an American Citizen
for the sole object of disposing freely on his property without being obliged
to leave any bequests to his children." The grandson concluded his case by requesting that his grandfather's American citizenship be retroactively cancelled
"as of July 29th, 1903 on account of the property rights involved."

In an internal memo dated March 12, 1923, the commissioner admitted
that the facts of the case seemed to justify Gonzalez's denaturalization. But
it was, by law, the duty of the State Department to initiate the cancellation
proceedings. Since the department did not, Gonzalez's citizenship was never
revoked.[29]

In parallel, the interdepartmental battle was evolving toward a workable, if
temporary consensus. In 1913, the Supreme Court in *Luria v. United States*[30]
upheld the retroactivity of the provision of the act of 1906 permitting denaturalization on the grounds of George A. Luria's permanent residence abroad.[31]
In its opinion, the Court asserted:

> It is true that §4 of the Act of 1906 exacts from the applicant a declara-
> tion of his intention to reside in the United States, and it is also true
> that the prior laws did not expressly call for such a declaration. But
> we think it is not true that, under the prior laws, it was immaterial
> whether the applicant intended to reside in this country or presently
> to take up a permanent residence in a foreign country. On the con-
> trary, by necessary implication, as we think, the prior laws conferred

the right to naturalization upon such aliens only as contemplated the continuance of a residence already established in the United States. Citizenship is membership in a political society, and implies a duty of allegiance on the part of the member and a duty of protection on the part of the society. These are reciprocal obligations, one being a compensation for the other.[32]

But *Luria* had not convinced the Justice Department to depart from its position that both the 1906 and 1907 Acts concerned the protection of naturalized Americans abroad, not the maintenance of their citizenship. Several years later, the Republican presidents of the 1920s and a Republican Congress enacted very restrictive immigration policies and became more restrictive in denaturalization matters as well. The Department of Justice, in a break with the Wickersham approach, agreed to resume denaturalization proceedings for residence in the country of origin within five years of naturalization as determined by the 1906 Act. Bernard Lazar, for example, was naturalized on June 12, 1906 and was stripped of his citizenship on March 2, 1922, for having resided in Poland since 1907.[33] Patrick Kelly, who was naturalized before the Court of Common Pleas at Bridgeport, Connecticut, on October 18, 1894, took up residence in Ireland within five years. He was stripped of his citizenship at the request of the State Department by the U.S. District Court in New Haven on November 5, 1923.[34]

But the two departments continued to have opposing stances regarding how to interpret the 1907 act. Joseph George Aboumossa, for example, who was naturalized in 1894 and returned to his native Syria in 1913 did not make it back to the United States until nine years later in 1922. The chief examiner of the Naturalization Service in St. Louis confirmed Aboumossa's citizenship on the basis of the attorney general's opinion, despite the Immigration Service's attempt to cancel it.[35] The consequences of such differences were reflected in the delivery of passports. On July 2, 1924, Secretary of State Charles Evans Hughes signed a memo ordering his employees not to deliver a passport to a naturalized citizen living abroad when the presumption arose under the statute "that he has ceased to be an American citizen." Until the question had been determined judicially, Hughes did not feel compelled to adhere to the opinion of the Department of Justice. In 1916, the same New York court had delivered opposing decisions on the interpretation of the 1907 clause.[36] And in the following years the courts remained split.[37] "In my opinion", Hughes asserted, "the mere fact of return without regard to other circumstances is not sufficient to rebut a presumption already risen."[38]

Yet, on March 26, 1926, his successor, Frank Kellogg, reversed the order. A Supreme Court decision from 1924 had endorsed the Department of Justice's approach and described the presumption of loss of citizenship based on foreign residence as a "presumption easy to preclude, and easy to overcome. It is a matter of option and intention."[39] The State Department subsequently decided to make peace –or at least to sign a truce - with the Department of Justice. The State Department asserted that "in view of the diversity of opinion of various Departments of this Government and because of certain decisions of courts which do not appear to accord entirely with the strict construction of the statute contained in the previous memorandum," it endorsed the Department of Justice's interpretation of the statute. The presumption that a naturalized American living abroad had ceased to be an American citizen would no longer exist "upon his return to the United States and his reestablishment here in good faith of a permanent residence."[40]

The State Department was temporarily satisfied with this agreement. Active cooperation with the Department of Justice to actively implement the 1906 Act (if not the 1907 Act as well)[41] had a big impact. Denaturalizations of naturalized citizens living in their countries of origin rose. By the mid-1930s they represented the majority of cases: of 6,631 revocations between 1937 and 1946, 5,086 occurred because the individual established permanent residence abroad within five years of naturalization.[42] However, the State Department was waiting for an occasion to go further, to expand by law the scope of denaturalization of foreign-born Americans residing abroad.

The occasion came at the end of the 1930s when Congress codified the provisions related to nationality. This work which had started in 1938 provided an opportunity to amend the statute. The Nationality Act was passed in October 1940, in a climate of fear caused by the outbreak of World War II in Europe. Congress expanded the scope of denaturalization: sections 404–406 applied automatic loss of citizenship to naturalized citizens residing three or even two years in their country of origin or five years in any other foreign countries, any time after their naturalization. [43] For Richard Flournoy of the State Department, it was "one of the most important changes effected by the Act."[44]

But Congress went far beyond foreign-born Americans by deciding to denationalize native-born Americans perceived to be un-American. In addition to foreign naturalization or allegiance, already included in the Expatriation Act of 1907—foreign military service or employment, voting in foreign elections—conviction for desertion from the armed forces of the United States or for committing treason would also become causes for the loss of citizenship.[45] President Roosevelt supposedly did not approve of these amendments to the code. But he was unable to convince Congress. He even unsuccessfully lobbied to get rid of a provision passed unanimously by the House that would expatriate any American "if he remains for six months or longer within any foreign state of which he or either of his parents shall have been a national."[46]

When the United States entered World War II after the attack on Pearl Harbor, the loyalty of foreign-born Americans residing on U.S. soil became a national security priority: naturalized citizens of enemy origin would become the target of government policy. They were joined by a new and important contingent of American-born citizens. This overlapping persecution would profoundly alter the destinies of both groups.

CHAPTER 7

The Proactive Denaturalization Program During World War II

On February 12, 1918, the chief examiner of the local Bureau of Naturalization in St. Paul, Minnesota, wrote the Washington office that a judge in Wisconsin had "informed him that he had a number of cases in his circuit of naturalized Germans who were known to be disloyal," and that he had "contemplated the practicability of making an order cancelling their naturalization on that ground." The bureau acknowledged that "thus far [it] has had only two or three cases of this kind reported by the Chief Examiners." Still, to the bureau, the danger was real: "Perhaps it may be of practical interest to you to know that in a recent letter addressed by the Attorney General to the Secretary of Labor the statement was made that the Dpt of Justice in its investigation has met with more trouble from naturalized Germans than from those who still remained subjects of the Emperor of Germany." And the respondent added: "What recourse then is there to correct this manifest danger to the peace and security of this country? Obviously in the first instance the *affirmative action of the Executive government* through its representatives, in this case peculiarly the naturalization examiners, to bring every such case before the court where the person who is to affected will have the opportunity to vindicate himself from the charge of disloyalty if he is innocent" (emphasis added).[1] The "affirmative action" that the Bureau of Naturalization sought during World War I was finally implemented in World War II.

Denaturalization played only a marginal role in the Department of Justice's management of national security during World War I. It faced resistance from the Department of Labor, which as the home of the Division of Naturalization was in charge of collecting evidence. In March 1942, denaturalization became part of a larger national security program at the instigation of Attorney General Francis Biddle.

The Deutschamerikanische Volksbund (German American National League), generally referred to as "the Bund," was a notorious Nazi organization founded in 1936. Its rallies at Madison Square Garden presented a familiar picture of brown-shirted Nazis with swastika flags spouting racist rhetoric. The leader of the Bund, Fritz Julius Kuhn, had immigrated to the United States in 1927. His followers tended to be other recent immigrants who had not experienced the wave of anti-German sentiment during World War I. On December 19, 1938, a complaint was filed in Los Angeles against Herman Schwinn, founder and leader of the Western German-American Bund. His certificate of citizenship was cancelled in 1939 on the ground that he obtained his papers by fraudulently misrepresenting the length of his residence in the United States.[2] The Bund suffered a major setback on May 26, 1939, when Kuhn himself was arrested for embezzling funds from his organization and sentenced on December 5, 1939, to three to five years in prison.[3]

But this focus on individual cases did not please Attorney General Robert Jackson. In July 1940 Jackson wanted a new provision in the law that would create a "rebuttable presumption that a citizen recently naturalized, who is a member of an organization such as the German-American Bund" did not naturalize in good faith, justifying the cancellation of naturalization on the ground of fraud.[4] It was not a propitious time for Jackson to get approval for developing denaturalization, however. His initiative conflicted with President Roosevelt's aversion to expanding the grounds for nonvoluntary expatriation.

So for the time being, the attorney general had to remain within the framework of the existing law. On December 20, 1940, he sent a memo to Major Lemuel Schofield, special assistant to the attorney general in charge of the Immigration and Naturalization Service, calling attention to the records of the German-American Bund seized in Chicago. These records indicated that between fifteen hundred and two thousand members were in U.S. military or naval service. He asked Schofield to designate a representative at once to "determine whether persons have become naturalized within the past few years while members of the Bund, or have taken out Bund membership after naturalization. Such persons should be made defendants in proceedings to cancel their naturalization. Unquestionably citizenship is obtained in such circumstances without a true renunciation of allegiance [to Germany] and is subject to cancellation for misrepresentation."[5]

In January 1941 Major Schofield, by then immigration commissioner within the Justice Department, launched an investigation. Nine months later, on October 4, 1941, his 702-page report, together with a special report on

Fritz Kuhn, concluded that an adequate basis existed for the revocation of the naturalization of all members of the German-American Bund who were naturalized citizens.

According to the report, these members had as their only aim to support and assist the Nazi government in Germany, opposition to democratic government, and adherence to the Fuhrer Principle. There were two distinct grounds for denaturalization: (1) an alien could not in good faith take the oath to the United States and at the same time have allegiance to the Bund, whose character, precepts, and activities were contrary to democratic principles; and (2) this new citizen "had not been, for the five years previous to his naturalization, attached to the principles of the Constitution" if he was a member of the Bund, a group that backed the Fuhrer Principle.[6]

All through 1941, the denaturalization initiative proceeded slowly. On September 5, 1941, the Immigration Service examined cases of seven naturalized citizens of German origin and two of Lithuanian origin, who had been classified as class A suspects.[7] The government had a choice between revoking their citizenship on the ground of disloyalty and revoking it because it was "illegally procured," that is, they had failed to comply strictly with statutory requirements. The former would depend on the evidence obtained, so the latter would be a more secure way of obtaining a favorable decision in the courts. If the option were available, it would still be more efficient to go to court on the ground of illegality than to risk the pursuing someone on the shakier terrain of disloyalty.

In January 1941, an assistant to the attorney general, Forrest R. Black, had criticized the *indirect* method of cancellation where disloyalty was involved: "Some of these cases seem rather far-fetched in their reasoning because of the interval of time elapsing between the date of the certificate and the date of the disloyal utterance or act. . . . While we can understand the patriotic motives of the judges in these wartime cases, we cannot endorse the legal doctrine utilized to reach the desired result. In the absence of Congressional action, which would affirmatively make disloyalty a ground for revocation, it is not a legitimate function of the courts to resort to this kind of chicanery."[8] Black suggested that a *penalty* section be added to the federal criminal code providing that any naturalized citizen convicted of treason, inciting rebellion or insurrection, criminal correspondence with foreign governments, seditious conspiracy, or recruiting or enlisting for service against the United States would have his or her certificate of citizenship cancelled.[9]

Instead, the Justice Department followed another path. On December 6, 1941, it submitted to Congress an amendment to the Nationality Act of 1940 to permit the revocation of citizenship for conduct that established a foreign allegiance, focusing on naturalized citizens after their naturalization.[10] Since 1930, the Bureau of Naturalization had unsuccessfully proposed amending the law so as to permit the denaturalization of citizens for acts committed postnaturalization. The U.S. entry into the war seemed to offer a window of opportunity.[11] The bill, introduced by Rep. Samuel Dickstein (D-N.Y.), passed the House, and hearings were held in the Senate on February 17, 1942.[12] The House version would have permitted the expatriation of a naturalized American "on the ground that his utterances, writings, actions, or course of conduct, establishes that his political allegiance is to a foreign state or sovereignty."

The bill faced strong opposition from the American Civil Liberties Union and the Federation of Constitutional Liberties. When the bill reached the Senate, the Subcommittee of the Committee on Immigration approved it but its chairman, Senator Francis Maloney (D-Conn.), expressed concerns that the new provision would lead to the same kind of excesses as had occurred during World War I.[13] The bill was never brought to a vote in the Senate and "at the end of the year the issue was dead."[14]

With no new legislation, the Justice Department had to turn to the courts, where there was great uncertainty. As a previous commissioner described his work in a March 1939 letter to a U.S. senator:

As you know, . . . the burden is upon the Government to establish that fraud or illegal procurement obtains in any particular case in which it proceeds to review the action of the court admitting the alien to citizenship. In a case where it may be alleged that a naturalized person is or was an adherent of Communism or Nazism, it may be anticipated that such person would not admit the charge. It would therefore become necessary, in order to divest him of his status of American citizenship, to prove by evidence which would meet the approval of the court hearing the case that such person may be now or was actually a Communist or a Nazi during the five years antedating the naturalization, and as a consequence thereof did not, when he was naturalized, in good faith take the oath of allegiance to the United States prescribed by law.[15]

By the end of 1941, nothing had happened except the review of individual cases sent by the FBI or the INS to the Criminal Division of the Justice Department. The first impulse to initiate cases had come from Jackson. Yet transforming this idea into a more collective effort took the lobbying of the Immigration Service, strong pressure on Biddle (who had succeeded Jackson as attorney general), and a window of opportunity seized by the assistant to the attorney general to launch a coordinated and affirmative program that was also a political coup.

On February 26, 1942, Schofield wrote to Biddle, reminding him that Jackson had ordered an investigation to consider whether or not adequate basis existed for the revocation of the naturalization of all the members of the German-American Bund who were naturalized citizens. A case-by-case examination would be impracticable; the procedure in equity permitted numerous defendants to be joined as proper or permissible parties where, as here, the complaints were based on the same series of acts. At least, Schofield suggested, all the officers of the Bund, past and present, including the leaders of the Eastern, Midwestern, and Western Divisions and the local branch leaders, should be named as defendants.[16]

But Schofield recommended going further: simultaneous proceedings should be instituted in which all naturalized members of the Bund should be joined as defendants in one suit, together with naturalized citizens who, while not members of the Bund, participated in its activities. Already the Special Defense Unit had identified eight hundred naturalized American members of the Bund, and additional facts were gathered on another two thousand.[17]

The 702 pages of evidence gathered by the INS, including testimonies from former members, translations of articles in German, and the status of local organizations, would be enough "to show the un-American character of the German-American Bund as a national organization."[18]

Biddle did not answer. Since the attack on Pearl Harbor on December 7, 1941 and the entry of the United States into World War II, he could no longer resist the pressure of President Roosevelt, War Secretary Henry Stimson, or public opinion to reduce civil liberties for Americans and aliens of enemy origin or nationality in the name of national security. But he was balancing their decisions by implementing his own actions. On the night following Pearl Harbor 736 Japanese aliens and a small number of Germans and Italians were arrested. During the first year of the war, 12,000 enemy aliens were taken into custody.[19] On December 22, 1941, Biddle created the Alien Enemy Control Unit as a new division in the Department of Justice and in early 1942 a network of Alien Enemy Boards was established to protect aliens from abuses and discrimination.[20] On December 13, Biddle had announced the postponement for ninety days of the pending applications for naturalization of Germans and Italians with the purpose to weed out the relatively few enemy aliens of the subversive class. But he insisted that citizens of enemy countries would not be mistreated if they were loyal to the United States.[21]

Yet in mid-January 1942, all aliens of enemy nations—600,000 Italians, 300,000 Germans, and 90,000 Japanese—were required to reregister and to carry at all times new identification certificates.[22] On February 19 an executive order signed by Roosevelt authorized Secretary of War Stimson to exclude "any or all persons from specific areas" within the continental United States. Biddle exempted Austrians, Austro-Hungarians, and Koreans from alien enemy registration[23] and decided to accelerate the procedures of naturalization of alien residents, including those of alien enemy nationality.[24] In mid-March 1942, at the request of Tom C. Clark, then a civilian coordinator for the forced relocation of Japanese Americans, James Rowe Jr., the new assistant to the attorney general, and Schofield agreed to send out a special squad of naturalization examiners to the West Coast to "speed up the naturalization hearings before the courts, so that Germans and Italians, who have been prevented from becoming citizens through no fault of their own but because of the bottleneck in naturalization proceedings, would become citizens after the usual investigations and would not have to be evacuated."[25]

But Rowe, sent by Roosevelt to assist Biddle just before Pearl Harbor, still had his eyes and ears on the presidency and was worrying about the bad mood he was sensing there.[26] "You and the Department are 'on the spot' on the grounds of not being tough enough" he wrote to Biddle few days later.[27] This negative atmosphere was spreading within the department itself. Joseph Savoretti, deputy commissioner to Schofield, had blocked on his own initiative the program of naturalizing Germans and Italians with the comment that "the Attorney General might be criticized on the ground he was attempting to evade the purpose of the military authorities of evacuating alien enemies." Rowe decided to hold up the program "because of the growing criticism that you have been too lenient," he wrote to Biddle.[28] An envoy of Roosevelt in Biddle's office, "on close and easy terms" with the President,[29] yet faithful to his new boss, Rowe was looking to reestablish Biddle's reputation and perhaps save his position.

Suddenly, denaturalization seemed like an opportunity, "one way to get off."[30] On March 11, 1942, Rowe wrote to Biddle:

I have been hearing a great deal of discussion about the denaturalization cases with what I confess has been some disinterest. It has
suddenly occurred to me that I have been completely asleep on this
matter. It is obvious, not only from our personal discussions before I
came to the Department, but also from the administrative set-up of
the Department, that this sort of problem is peculiarly my responsibility and no one else's, subject of course to your review. . . . I am
amazed that neither you nor I have even thought of it. The hour is late,
but I still think it should be rectified.[31]

Within two days, a conference was convened, composed of representatives of the Criminal Division, the INS, and Special Defense Unit, all within
the Justice Department. Its object was to institute proceedings to revoke the
naturalization of leading members of the German-American Bund and of
additional persons whose subversive activities strongly indicated a "mental
reservation in their oath of allegiance."[32]

On March 16, 1942, Assistant Attorney General Wendell Berge, the head
of the Criminal Division, announced to Biddle that he had selected a group
of six experienced attorneys to work under his direction "exclusively on
this matter, relieving them of all other duties. The men selected are vigorous and enthusiastic U.S. Attorneys to be chosen for the program based on
their knowledge of subversive activities as well as their Criminal Division
experience." During the previous days—over a full weekend—this team had
reviewed FBI and Special Defense Unit files, and selected 120 individuals as
possible subjects for cancellation proceedings, among them 30 "for the most
immediate attention and which will serve to place the program in operation."
In addition, Berge called for the assembly of a team of attorneys to study all
the legal precedents and procedures on denaturalization, including liaisons
from the INS and special agents from the FBI.[33]

But Berge's approach provoked reluctance and concern. The first issue at
stake was the scope of the target: whether to focus only on the leaders of the
Bund or on all its individual members.

In a March 18, 1942, memorandum to Lawrence M. C. Smith, chief of the
Justice Department's Special Defense Unit, Joseph Prendergast, one of his dep-
uties, pointed out that "the Attorney General has repeatedly gone on record to
the effect that he would not permit a repetition of the raids and persecutions of
innocent minority groups that occurred in the last war." The need to establish a
general policy and standards was for Prendergast even more apparent

when one realizes the difference between a proceeding to revoke citizenship and a criminal prosecution. The former is a proceeding in equity, with none of the safeguards of criminal trial, strong rules of evidence, and other constitutional requirements. Furthermore, the question in a criminal trial is whether an individual has or has not committed an act which the law defines to be a crime. In a proceeding for the cancellation of a certificate of citizenship, the question is whether the acts charged are sufficiently grave to show that the individual did not pledge true allegiance. The law defined no standards for such acts. The case existing precedents under the present law permitted the cancellation of a certificate for fraud on the basis of practically any type of conduct or utterance, however slight, that can be related back to the naturalization proceedings, even though those proceedings may be as long ago as 35 years. In other words, if the Department does not set up some standards of self-restraint, but approaches the situation as a criminal matter, there is a serious possibility of a repetition of the persecution of the last war.[34]

Prendergast's concern—backed by Smith—was that the U.S. attorneys should not begin proceedings without prior authorization from Washington. "As I pointed out to you, this problem occurred in the last war," Prendergast recalled.[35]

The Department of Justice was divided, and Biddle could not decide his own stance. On March 23, 1942, Rowe wrote him an important personal and confidential memo, within which was a highly unusual warning.

Dear Francis:

I write this memorandum more as a friend then a subordinate. I have now been in the Department of Justice for approximately three months. I think I have begun to get the "feel" of the Department.

I am seriously disturbed about the Department both from the short range point of view and from a long-range point of view.

There is instilled in the public mind a belief that you and the Department are "civil liberties boys" and "softies." I believe strongly the verdict of history will bear you out. In this memorandum, I am not interested in the intrinsic merits of our point of view. For this present discussion, they are irrelevant. I want to talk about tactics. This public belief grew, first of all, from our handling of the alien enemy

problem. We emphasized that most alien enemies are loyal. We soon
found we had to change our tune, play down the loyalty of the many
and emphasize how tough we were on the disloyal few. Unfortunately,
our change in tactics was "too little and too late."[36]

Rowe further described how there was "constant needling going on": from
Walter Winchell, the gossip columnist, who "has been doing it for weeks,"
from the commentator Walter Lippmann, and from Anna Rosenberg, to
whom "the President listens entirely too much."[37] "I am convinced a great
deal of it is planted by the Army. I am also convinced much of this is being
presented exparte to the President," he told Biddle. "The question is what
should be done *immediately* about it. In the next two weeks we can strike in
two places. It is more important to strike dramatically than anything else."
The first proposal Rowe then made is about "*the denaturalization cases.*" "The
cumbersome machinery cracked and groaned while Smith and Berge politely
bickered about whether the cases were any good or not. The fact is we aren't
getting anywhere!" Rowe proposed that the big German Bund cases be taken
over by Mathias Correa, U.S. attorney of the Southern District of New York:
"the important thing is that we emphasize we are using our crack prosecutor
to go after the Nazis." In the rest of the letter, Rowe proposes to create a war
division within the department of Justice.[38] He concluded: "I believe, Francis,
that we are up against the gun! We had better get moving fast and set up some
machinery that can *move fast.*"[39]

Within two days, Francis Biddle launched the first and only federal program of denaturalization in U.S. history. Circular No. 3663, sent on March 25,
1942, by the Attorney General to all U.S. attorneys, opened with a statement
that the Department of Justice had been studying cases of disloyalty among
naturalized citizens whose "conduct, activities and sympathies indicate mental reservation amounting to fraud in naturalization," which if established
would appear to be grounds for denaturalization. The circular informed the
U.S. attorneys that cases would be forwarded to them to institute proceedings
for the cancellation of subjects' naturalization certificates on the ground of illegality or fraud. And he added: "Cancellation of naturalization is a most important weapon in dealing with organized subversive and disloyal activities
and will be fully utilized. At the same time the greatest care will be exercised
to avoid those cases involving mere thoughtless expressions of sympathy for
the subject's former homeland and to bring proceedings only against those
whose persistent course of conduct, activities and utterances unmistakably

show their true allegiance and fidelity to be to a foreign country rather than to the United States."[40]

Rowe wanted Biddle to make the denaturalization program an instrument of public relations: "This problem must be handled not only competently but with a 100% performance and a big press campaign,"[41] Rowe wrote to Biddle on March 21.[42] Biddle did not need to be convinced. On March 25, the same day he signed the circular, Biddle mobilized the media. He publicly announced the beginning of the program: "We are now ready to shoot and we are going to shoot very quickly."[43] Biddle explained the logic of attacking members of Nazi organizations: "This is a matter of loyalty; membership in such societies makes loyalty to any other country impossible."[44]

For Biddle, the denaturalization program was a way of looking tough and and winning Roosevelt's confidence—the president had made him wait six months as acting attorney general before confirming him as the full attorney general. It was also a way of appearing fair by demonstrating an apparent equality of treatment of Japanese and German Americans. The treatment was in fact completely unequal: Japanese Americans could not be American except by birth on U.S. territory, as they were banned from naturalization. On the West Coast, they were interned even if they were citizens. German Americans could only be interned if they had first been denaturalized. Internment was in fact the main objective of the cancellation procedure. Appeal did not suspend the effect of a decree to revoke citizenship—it took effect immediately upon its entry, and the defendant was divested of his citizenship "until an appellate court reverses the judgment of the trial court."[45] It was perhaps also a way of saving face as a defender of civil liberties. After all, Biddle could argue that the decision to denaturalize was not administrative; it belonged to the courts which preserved the rights to a defense.

Rowe had provided good advice to Biddle in that process and had created a strong and trusting relationship with him, which is reflected in Biddle's portrait of Rowe in his memoirs:

He knew the setup, knew everyone in the government, on the Hill. He was aggressive, and could stand up and fight. He was a Catholic—and recognized and respected power. He had imagination and employed it. He had a sense of humor that was wry and idiomatic. . . . He was interested in government on two levels: that of efficient administration, which he believed possible within unavoidable human limits: and in the play of politics, which he took to like a gull to water. He . . .

believed that his chief should be permitted to deal with policy and that he, the Assistant Attorney General, should run the Department; knew the necessity of publicity, had friends everywhere; was partisan; had strong likes and dislikes. Ever since he came to work with me he has proved a devoted and delightful friend.[46]

Very soon, Biddle would become a proactive advocate of the Denaturalization Program, almost obsessive in his quest for results. But he first had to select who would run the program. Rowe thought it "need[ed] vigorous leadership." On March 11 he indicated Gerhard A. Gesell was "a natural." But unable to convince Gesell, "despite tremendous pressure applied by Bill Douglas, Dean Acheson and myself," Rowe suggested Mathias F. Correa, a "really top-notcher," in his March 23 memo. But it would be "breaking a lot of precedents" to recruit a U.S. attorney to do the job. Rowe did not care about this rift with tradition, but the senior staff attorneys of the department did. Finally, Biddle chose to promote Dewey Balch, a Minnesota attorney at the head of the program within the Criminal Division.[47] But in parallel, on March 26, Biddle designated Correa to handle the cancellation of naturalization of leading members of the German-American Bund residing in his New-York district and to guide the other attorneys on how to proceed with their own German Bund cases.[48]

How cooperation between the different divisions within the department should be organized was the next issue. "The Immigration and Naturalization service has proved over the years an effective means of investigation,"[49] Clarence Goodwin, special assistant to the attorney general, wrote, and claimed to run the program. Originally, the FBI was not even at the first meeting convened by Rowe. On March 26, 1942, however, Biddle and Rowe decided that it should play a key role in the Denaturalization Program. But it took a few weeks—until April 24—to make the operating agreement clear and workable between INS and FBI agents.[50] The FBI conducted the investigations in the Denaturalization Program, which focused on Bund members and sympathizers;[51] the other denaturalization suits remained the responsibility of the INS.[52]

A couple of weeks later, the agreement achieved its first successes: all INS districts were mobilized to supply the Criminal Division with a summary of the evidence appearing for each case in their records.[53] The INS also sent a representative of each immigration district to assist U.S. attorneys in the preparation and prosecution of the cases. Soon each was "devoting his entire time to that purpose, if necessary."[54] The INS established lists of naturalized citizens for whom records indicated a basis for proceedings.[55] Cooperation with the INS was working well on the ground,[56] and would continue to work well until the end of the war.[57]

But the development of the program was delayed by another obstacle. Despite the active cooperation of the INS,[58] Correa was lagging behind in New York. In fact, what was required from him was not only to initiate proceedings against the leader of the Bund but also to set the legal principles and reasoning that would permit the Denaturalization Program to be implemented successfully by all U.S. attorneys. On May 13, 1942, Goodwin visited Correa and reported that he had not really started studying the cases.[59] Balch noted the impact on other U.S. attorneys who did not "feel justified in filing complaints against other subjects referred to them until the most notorious Bund leaders are the subjects of complaints."[60]

On May 20, Biddle became impatient: "Is it going as vigorously as possible? Should not there be some central organization of the technical material prepared in the report of the Immigration Service which can cooperate with the U.S. Attorneys?"[61] U.S. attorneys did not want to start any trials before Correa started his trials against the leaders of the Bund. While waiting for Correa, the officials involved in the Denaturalization Program discussed its scope.

In his May 13 memo to Berge, Goodwin had emphasized the priority and legal possibilities of denaturalizing all naturalized Germans who were members of the Bund at the time of their naturalization.[62] Harry Hopkins, a friend of Roosevelt who was working at the White House, also backed the same policy. He asked Biddle: "Why should we not proceed against every former member of the Bund who is a naturalized citizen to strip him of his naturalization?"[63] Biddle was convinced and asked Berge for a memo about it.[64] Rowe investigated and came back to Biddle with the opinion of the Criminal Division: "membership alone in this organization is not sufficient as a general rule to warrant denaturalization."[65] People who joined for social or business reasons only, people who may have joined under some coercion, and people who did not spend long enough in the organization or were "too disinterested to learn what it stood for" had to be excluded from denaturalization. The strategy chosen would therefore be to file complaints against national and local officers and other active leaders when their "Bund activities are not too far removed in date from the time of their naturalization."[66] The courts would also be asked in each district to permit the consolidation of the cases insofar as proof was concerned, in order to obviate the necessity of introducing the proof of the un-American character of the Bund in each case.[67]

Biddle was getting impatient again. On August 10, 1942, he wrote to each U.S. attorney to request the status of denaturalization proceedings in their districts "in regard to accelerating the present cancellation program:"[68] "I would like to express to you my personal interest in this program and reiterate my desire that cancellation cases receive your personal and prompt attention."[69] The distinction between the different kinds of members of the Bund was produced in August 1942 by lawyers in Correa's office, as they prepared to file complaints against the leaders of the organization.[70]

Another issue concerned the many German Americans who had returned to Germany. In a memo of September 10, 1942, J. Edgar Hoover concluded after an investigation that one-third of the ten thousand purchasers of the so-called German Rueckwanderer marks had returned to Germany.[71] Berge was ready to launch trials against them, even if they were not a priority in comparison to naturalized citizens who were free in the United States, and would be jailed after denaturalization.[72] In addition there were legal difficulties: the need for evidence and the notice to the defendant.

On December 17, Hoover again raised the issue with Berge and asked for the outlines of a policy related to these cases.[73] On February 13, 1943, the U.S. attorney for the District of New Jersey informed Berge that he could not introduce civil actions against 109 naturalized Germans: "The countries where they are now living are either belligerent or occupied by enemy forces and, therefore, the United States Attorney cannot comply with the rules . . . [which] require that notices be mailed to the defendants or served upon them personally."[74] Earl Harrison, head of the INS, considered the issue and agreed that there was nothing more to do than what the U.S. attorney suggested: to render the cases inactive "until the facilities for mailing letters to foreign countries have been restored."[75] This approach was confirmed later in correspondence in May 1943 between Berge and Correa.[76]

For the members of the Bund still in the U.S., Balch still depended on Correa and his team for a general statement on how to handle the cases. On October 4, Attorney General Biddle issued a public statement illustrating just how confident the Department of Justice felt about its ability to denaturalize Bundists:

The aims and purposes of the Bund are wholly inconsistent with American citizenship. Loyalty to one excludes loyalty to the other. It therefore follows that those Germans who became naturalized American citizens and at the same time turned actively to the affairs of the

Bund are guilty of fraud. Their oaths of allegiance were not honestly taken.

We are moving at once to clean out this source of danger to our national security. The courts will be asked to denaturalize these disloyal Bundists. Deprived of their citizenship, they automatically become alien enemies. As such I shall order them interned for the duration of the war.[77]

Yet, on October 7, 1942, Balch reported on a trip to Chicago and Milwaukee for the purpose of consulting with U.S. attorneys and the FBI "in order to arouse additional interest and enthusiasm in the rather concentrated work which is required to put the program over."[78] All the pending cases in Chicago were being reviewed. Milwaukee, a city with a large German population, lacked the resources to conduct a review: an attorney was sent from Washington to do the work.

One month later, on November 23, 1942, Biddle wrote a personal letter to all U.S. attorneys who he felt were dragging their feet on the Denaturalization Program. He started his letter to Frank J. Hennessy in San Francisco with the following words: "The records of the Department reflect that there has not as yet been a single 'denaturalization' case filed in your district. The Criminal Division has had correspondence with you concerning a large number of cases and has files on approximately one hundred subjects under investigation in the Northern District of California, reports on all of which cases should be in your files."[79] On December 11, Rowe sent a telegram to several U.S. attorneys (including Hennessy): "The Denaturalization Program throughout the Country is regarded as of utmost importance by the Attorney General and first matter of business by all United States Attorneys; I am told this program is proceeding very unsatisfactorily in your district. Please airmail report immediately." On December 12, Berge sent a letter to the U.S. attorney in Indianapolis: "In your district it appears that only two cases have been filed. As you know the department has asked that 'denaturalization' cases be given special attention. It would appear that there is probably a sizable number of persons against whom action should be considered in your district, and I would like to have a report on the progress which has been made in the 'denaturalization' program." In addition, Berge informed him that he would be sending an inspector from the INS who was specially trained in denaturalization work.[80]

Every week, Biddle asked Rowe what was happening in New York in the cases concerning the leaders of the Bund.[81] Correa, after another visit from Balch in December 1942, finally delivered material on how to pursue the denaturalization cases, and on January 5, 1943, the Criminal Division sent to all U.S. attorneys a brief of evidence consisting of five hundred pages in three volumes including witnesses, exhibits, and articles from Bund newspapers.[82]

Finally, two months later, on March 10, 1943, a 158-page memo was delivered to the attorney general. It explained how to handle the cases legally in front of the court, comprising developments on theories and precedent, pleadings and practice, policy and procedure.[83] A few days earlier, on March 6, one year after the launch of the Denaturalization Program, Balch had completed a report assessing its implementation: in his view, things had not turned out as well as they might have hoped.

Of course, by February 1, 1943, fifty-seven denaturalizations had been obtained for three hundred complaints, and five hundred additional cases were pending, for a total of eight hundred cases.[84] But Balch reported numerous difficulties. Delays were mostly due to a lack of human resources: "A complete denaturalization investigation requires the full time of one man for at least a month." In addition, there was still no body of policy defining with any degree of precision the types of activities that fall within the scope of denaturalization proceedings: the vagueness of the law, the limited accumulation of court decisions, and the changing and complex social and political circumstances surrounding the Denaturalization Program rendered the task of formulating such policy difficult:[85] "disloyal acts or utterances" were for Biddle vague guides and they and related criteria needed to be more precisely defined.[86]

Legal staff had asked for investigations by the FBI in many different cities, "throwing its work into disarray."[87] The FBI was responsible for the surveillance of individuals considered a threat to national security. For instance, it gathered evidence on enemy aliens to determine their possible custodial detention. But, Hoover noted, "while hearsay evidence and the statements of confidential informants may be acceptable in enemy alien detention hearings, they cannot be introduced in a court of law. Specific acts or utterances rather than conclusions as to the Fascist or undemocratic character thereof are required."[88] Sometimes the FBI had general information on the type of evidence the prosecutor was looking for but not enough detail to merit action. For example, "the FBI is advised that detailed information on the purchase of Rueckwanderer Marks is pertinent; but the FBI is not advised that the purchase of such Marks is not significant when the action was taken for the purpose of supporting parents or relatives in the mother country."[89]

Nevertheless, "one of the essential requirements for a large number of de-naturalization proceedings is presentation to the courts of evidence related to the character of various fascist organizations." But the FBI had only started gathering evidence on the German Americans workers' organization DAB (Deutsch-Amerikanische Berufsgemeinschaft) or on other organizations linked to the Bund. They were not yet available for use in court.[90] Additionally, the U.S. attorney's office was subjected to "a tremendous increase in duties and work."[91] The office received assistance from the INS, but this help was not enough to compensate for the attrition of some of the office's best and most ex-perienced employees, attracted by the high salaries paid by such newly created agencies as the Office of Price Administration, the War Production Board, the Office of War Information, and the Selective Service Board.[92]

To resolve these problems, Balch proposed the creation of an Internal Se-curity Division. Denaturalization was only one among many activities carried out by the Justice Department "for the protection of internal security." It also prosecuted people for sedition and for sabotage under the Foreign Agents Registration Act; it arranged for the freezing of funds or for the denial of the use of the postal service; it handled alien enemy detention; and so on. These activities were scattered among two distinct divisions and three units of the department.[93] As Balch explained,

> In many cases the form of internal security action to be taken is not finally determinable until a complete assembly and review of the evi-dence. An espionage case may ultimately turn out to be a denatural-ization case or it may be that the only action which can finally be taken is a denial of the use of the mails. An alien enemy investigation may develop into a sabotage case. In one instance, an alien enemy investigation developed evidence on the alien's husband which might be used for denaturalization proceedings against the latter. This inter-relationship of the various internal security activities in the Depart-ment indicates strongly the need for a coordinated direction of these activities within a single organization unit in the Department.[94]

After reading the report and its proposals, Rowe annotated it on the front page and ordered: "Hold until Schneiderman decision."[95] Indeed, the U.S. government's denaturalization proceedings against William Schneiderman, an official of the California Communist Party, would soon redefine the terms of the debate.

PART III

War in the Supreme Court

Surely the Congress has the right to exact from aliens, to whom the privileges of citizenship are granted, attachment to the principles of the Constitution of the United States as much as the USSR has the right to exact, and has exacted, devotion to its principles from Russian citizens.

—Felix Frankfurter to Harlan Stone, March 31, 1943

Section 1 of the Fourteenth Amendment that confers citizenships and narrows a person born here with citizenship also provides that no state shall make or enforce any law which shall abridge the privileges or immunities of citizens of the United States; nor shall any state deprive any person of life, liberty or property without due process of law. The first of these two clauses plainly makes privileges and immunities of United States citizenship free from abridgment by a state. The Amendment then goes on to recognize a power in states to deprive all persons including citizens of "life, liberty or property" if they are afforded "due process of law." But even if afforded due process of law the state is granted no power under the fourteenth amendment to "deprive any person" of the citizenship granted by the Fourteenth Amendment.

—Draft of Hugo Black's concurring opinion in *Nishikawa*,
March 3, 1958

CHAPTER 8

Schneiderman:

A Republican Leader Defends a Communist

On June 21, 1943, three months after Dewey Balch submitted his report on internal security measures to James Rowe Jr., the U.S. Supreme Court handed down a five-to-three decision in the case of *Schneiderman v. United States.*[1] Born in Russia in 1905, William Schneiderman came to the United States when he was three years old. In 1922, he became a charter member of the Young Workers (later Communist) League in Los Angeles. He served as educational director of the League from 1922 to 1925 and became its official spokesman in 1928. In 1924, at the age of eighteen, Schneiderman filed his declaration of intention to become a citizen, and, later that same year, he became a member of the Workers Party (the predecessor to the Communist Party of the United States). In addition to his day job as a bookkeeper, he attended night classes at the University of California at Los Angeles.

Schneiderman's certificate of naturalization was issued on June 10, 1927, by the U.S. District Court for the Southern District of California. Now an American citizen, Schneiderman proceeded to serve as the organizational secretary of the Communist Party in California, then in Connecticut, and eventually in Minnesota, where he ran unsuccessfully as the party's candidate for governor in 1932, receiving a half percent of the vote.[2] In 1935, he spent a year in the USSR.

On June 30, 1939, the U.S. government initiated a denaturalization proceeding against him, arguing that his naturalization had been illegally procured because Schneiderman was at the time of his naturalization an active member of the Communist Party, "whose principles were opposed to the principles of the Constitution . . . and [who had] advised, advocated and taught the overthrow of the United States by force and violence."[3] In

response, the District Court for the Northern District of California nullified Schneiderman's citizenship,[4] and the Ninth Circuit Court of Appeals
affirmed that judgment.[5] The Supreme Court then granted certiorari on October 13, 1941.[6]

In the circuit court, Schneiderman had been represented by Carol King.
Early in 1921, after graduating from New York University Law School in 1920,
she applied for a job at Hale, Nelles & Shorr, a law firm involved in fighting
the Palmer Raids. Though it lacked the resources to hire her, the partners
offered to let her rent a room in their suite where she could start her own
office.[7] She soon became a prominent human rights lawyer, participating in
the landmark defenses of Ben Gitlow (a Communist leader), the Scottsboro
Boys (nine young black men unjustly charged with raping two white women),
and Angelo Herndon (an African-American labor organizer arrested and
convicted of insurrection). With Walter Nelles she would create and run the
ACLU *Law and Freedom Bulletin*, the first continual effort to collect state and
federal cases raising constitutional issues involving civil liberties.[8] In addition
to the ACLU, one of her clients was the American Committee for the Protection of Foreign Born, which is how King met Schneiderman after a Harry
Bridges deportation hearing. Since 1939 King had been working in California
on the defense of Bridges against deportation charges. Bridges, an immigrant
from Australia, was a leader in the International Longshore and Warehouse
Union and served as the California regional director of the Committee for
Industrial Organization.

Schneiderman, impressed by King, asked her to be one of his lawyers in
the circuit court.[9] When they lost, she decided to write to Wendell Willkie,
the Republican Presidential candidate who received nearly 45 percent of the
vote in the November 5, 1940, election. King was a personality "defying clas-
sification."[10] She had always proceeded in this way:[11] she wanted to work with
the lawyer who would best improve her client's chances before the Supreme
Court—believing that she herself would have little luck because she was a
woman.[12] In 1935 she had pursued a similar strategy in the *Herndon*, case,
which involved the constitutional guaranty of freedom of assembly.[13] In that
case she convinced Whitney North Seymour to pen the legal briefs and Herbert Wechsler to argue the case. Her strategy paid off when they won.[14] And
for Harry Bridges, she would go to the Supreme Court with Nathan "Nuddy"
Greene, and they would win again.[15]

Willkie originally attracted King's attention after he wrote an article in
the *New Republic*[16] that criticized the House Committee on Un-American

Activities and concluded that Earl Browder, then head of the Communist Party, was jailed "not for a violation of passport law, but for politics."[17] Although a lawyer, Willkie had never represented a client before the Supreme Court. King sent him the brief, without any preface or introduction, together with the writ of certiorari in which the Supreme Court had agreed to review the case.[18] "I read it on a Saturday morning," Willkie said. "I reread it. After that I could not with my beliefs ha[ve] been satisfied with myself if I refused to accept the case, if two conditions were true—(1) that Schneiderman was a decent fellow personally, and (2) that the record sustained the brief. That was the reason for my making inquiries about Schneiderman and asking you to send me the record," he explained to King.[19]

Willkie had asked a California colleague, Bartley Crum, to investigate Schneiderman, and Crum reported that he was a citizen of good reputation. Willkie made clear to King that the case involved the individual liberties of an American citizen, and not a Communist. With that understanding, he would agree to represent Schneiderman without fee from "the Communist party or anyone else."[20] Carol King agreed with these conditions, and Willkie announced that he was taking the case on November 29, 1941, with King remaining as associate counsel.[21]

Schneiderman met with Willkie on December 7, 1941, at his office on 15 Broad Street in front of the New York Stock Exchange. He was probably the first Communist Willkie had ever met. In the midst of a flurry of significant political events and activities—Pearl Harbor, the fight for control of the Republican Party—Willkie submitted to the court his personal brief on January 16, 1942.[22]

On May 6 the Court postponed oral arguments until the fall:[23] acting on the initiative of Undersecretary of State Sumner Welles, Charles Fahy, the solicitor general had, on April 11, 1942, on behalf of the government, requested this postponement in a letter to the Chief Justice.[24] Welles had followed the recommendation of Green H. Hackworth, the legal adviser of the state department; he wished to obtain a stay of the proceedings for the duration of the war, to save the government from embarrassment. The Justices, disconcerted by the request and leaning toward maintaining their calendar, finally opted for the short postponement proposed by Fahy.[25] In actuality, President Roosevelt seemed unconcerned with the potential political effects of the case. *Schneiderman* was one of the few cases Solicitor General Fahy discussed personally with the president prior to argument before the Supreme Court. Yet Roosevelt gave no special instruction to Fahy.[26] And when the case was finally argued before the Court on November 9, 1942, Fahy felt free to "wage a vigorous legal battle on behalf of the government."[27]

Two days before the arguments, Willkie returned from a trip to the Soviet Union and China, where he was acting as a special envoy for Roosevelt.[28] He buried himself in the Carlton Hotel with "a large slice of his law library, an assistant from his office, and his secretary."[29] King, at some point, joined him. "He knew what he wanted to say," King's biographer, Ann Fagan Ginger, notes. "The process of preparation was one of working out ways and means."[30]

Two days later, the 220 seats in the red-curtained courtroom were packed. King was seated beside Willkie. But only seven justices appeared that day to hear him. Justice Robert Jackson recused himself because he had been attorney general when the case was first tried,[31] and Justice James F. Byrnes had just resigned.[32]

In the brief he submitted a few days before, Fahy had argued that the Communist Party advocated the forceful overthrow of the government and asserted that Schneiderman believed in the principles of the Communist Party. One of the conditions of naturalization at the time was that "the alien be and behave as a person attached to the principles of the Constitution and well disposed to the good order and happiness of the United States."[33] Furthermore, the alien "should not be a disbeliever in, or opposed to organized government."

Ultimately, Willkie argued from the heart and not from his notes. He talked of Schneiderman as a young boy from Stalingrad to whom it was unfair to impugn the views of other Communists. Schneiderman, he argued, had not lied: he had not been asked during the naturalization process if he was a Communist. Schneiderman had told the lower court he had not read the acceptance speech of William Z. Foster, a former Communist Party candidate for the presidency, but the court was not convinced. Willkie commented: "I doubt that any Presidential candidate's acceptance speeches are ever read." He added that the Communist Manifesto of 1848 "recommended such terrible things as a progressive income tax and universal education."[34] Then he said: "This country, with its institutions, belongs to the people who inhabit it. Whenever they shall grow weary of the existing government, they can exercise their constitutional right of amending it, or their revolutionary right to dismember or overthrow it." He paused and added, "This is from the founder of my party (Lincoln's second inaugural address)." And he continued: "The tree of liberty should be refreshed from time to time with the blood of patriots and tyrants." He paused again: "That is from Thomas Jefferson, the founder of the party of many of you gentlemen—the Democratic Party."[35]

Willkie then asked, "Would you take away from such a youth the right he had thirteen years ago to become an American citizen—which now makes him subject to the draft—just because he had such ideas?"[36]

On November 14 the Supreme Court met in conference briefly to discuss the case and then met again on December 5 and 12 to discuss it in greater depth.[37] In the December 5 conference, Justice Felix Frankfurter spoke at length: "None of you has had the experience that I have had with reference to American citizenship. I was at college when my father became naturalized and I can assure you for months preceding it was a matter of moment in our family life, and when the great day came it partook for me of great solemnity."[38] He added, "as one who has ties with no formal religion, perhaps the feelings that underlie religious forms for me run into intensifications of my feelings about American citizenship."[39] In other words, for him, "American citizenship implies entering upon a fellowship which binds people together by devotion to certain feelings and ideas and ideals summarized as a requirement that they be attached to the principles of the Constitution." He added, "I have known the Schneidermans and a good many of them since my college days. . . . They are the salt of the earth so far as character and selflessness goes. But they are devoted to a wholly different scheme of things from that of which this country, through its Constitution, is committed. He is not an ordinary member of the Communist Party but an active organizer. If the same case had come before the Court, with the same record, from an applicant who has been denied citizenship, would you cancel?" Frankfurter adjured his brethren to follow the lower courts and warned them that "our decision will bind us if a Nazi case comes to our court."[40]

Despite Frankfurter's personal pleas, it appeared that there was a majority to reverse in the Schneiderman case. And when the December 12 meeting came around, a majority of the justices registered their intention to do so. For Justice William Douglas, "Schneiderman himself was not guilty of any disobedience to the law" and "did not collect funds to incite against the overthrown of the Government."[41] "His conduct," Justice Hugo Black added, "was exemplary. He never did an act of violence."[42]

Despite this majority, Douglas felt uncomfortable delivering such a critical decision with only seven justices voting. So, the Court, led by Black, decided to hold the case for reargument before a fuller court. This would allow it to produce a more authoritative decision at a time when, Douglas realized, a number of cases were pending in district courts for revocation of naturalization.[43] After the confirmation of the new justice, Wiley Rutledge, on February

8, 1943, the Court ordered a rehearing of the arguments by Willkie and Fahy, which took place on March 12.[44]

Willkie called it preposterous to convict Schneiderman on the basis of his membership in the Communist Party: "to my mind guilt in America is personal."[45] "Gesturing vigorously," Willkie characterized the 1848 Manifesto as "one of the great historical documents of all time,"[46] which, he told the Court, he had read before he was twenty-one years old. Yet despite these rhetorical flourishes, Fahy later recalled that "Willkie's performance was far more 'lawyer-like' on re-argument and, therefore, far more effective."[47] Fahy himself repeated that the Communist Party "advocated the complete destruction of the existing form of government in the United States." He added that Schneiderman's Communist beliefs "were contrary to the principles of the United States Constitution."[48]

On March 15 the Court met in conference to discuss the case once again.[49] Chief Justice Harlan Stone delivered a long, passionate plea—for which he received congratulations from Frankfurter the following day.[50] Stone argued that "Congress has broad plenary power on aliens," that the "Bill of Rights, form of governments are the fundamental principles of our Constitution." Stone reviewed the life of Schneiderman, whom he saw as "intimately associated with the Party, its principles and its policies,"[51] and who, in his view, favored the overthrow of government "by force"—and not by "moral force but by guns and bullets."[52]

Black replied that the lower courts had no basis to make such assertions against Schneiderman, as his conduct had been "exemplary." The doctrine of imputed guilt, Black declared, is "offensive to me."[53] Black's position carried the day, and Rutledge joined the four other justices who had previously favored reversal. Black, as the senior member of the majority, assigned the opinion to Murphy, while it was agreed that Stone would write the dissent.[54]

Frankfurter strongly encouraged Stone to include in his dissent a paragraph the former had written describing his views on American citizenship: "Surely the Congress has the right to exact from aliens, to whom the privileges of citizenship are granted, attachment to the principles of the Constitution of the United States as much as the U.S.S.R. has the right to exact, and has exacted, devotion to its principles from Russian citizens."[55]

But the chief justice did not incorporate Frankfurter's comparison of citizenship in the United States and the USSR, which he probably disagreed with. Instead, Stone fell back on the history of the statute: "The Congress of 1795, which passed the statute requiring an applicant for naturalization to establish that he has 'behaved as a man . . . attached to the principles of the constitution,' evidently did not doubt that there were. For some of its members had sat in the Constitutional Convention." Stone assumed that there were such principles and listed some of them: "the principles of constitutional protection of civil rights and of life, liberty and property, the principle of representative government, and the principle that constitutional laws are not to be broken down by planned disobedience." He added, "I assume that all the principles of the Constitution are hostile to dictatorship and minority rule; and that it is a principle of our Constitution that change in the organization of our government is to be effected by the orderly procedures ordained by the Constitution and not by force or fraud." Stone then argued that the facts of the case, as determined by the lower courts, were unequivocal: Schneiderman was an active member of the Communist Party, the Communist Party advocated the overthrow of the American government, and, therefore, when Schneiderman was naturalized, he lacked attachment to the principles of the U.S. Constitution as required by U.S. naturalization law.[56]

Meanwhile, it took two months for Murphy to write the first draft of his majority opinion, which he circulated to just a few of the other justices forming the majority. His approach was result-oriented.[57] Indeed, according to Frankfurter, only a few days before the delivery of the opinion, Murphy told him, "My instincts are satisfied with the result. . . . The faith of my whole life is wrapped up in support of Liberty."[58] Murphy was primarily concerned with the sociopolitical consequences of denaturalization:

> We are a heterogeneous people. In some of our larger cities a majority of the school children are the offspring of parents only one generation, if that far, removed from the steerage of the immigrant ship, children of those who sought refuge in the new world from the cruelty and oppression of the old, where men have been burned at the stake, imprisoned, and driven into exile in countless numbers for their political and religious beliefs. Here they have hoped to achieve a political status as citizens in a free world in which men are privileged to think and act and speak according to their convictions, without fear of punishment or further exile so long as they keep the peace and obey the law.

For Justice Murphy, the central issue implicated by the *Schneiderman* case was free speech: "We brought this case here because of its . . . possible relation to freedom of thought." And he constructed the first draft of his majority opinion around the idea that denaturalization based on advocacy for and participation in the Communist Party would violate First Amendment protections.[59]

But one of the few justices who received Murphy's draft—the identity of the justice is unknown—reacted immediately by characterizing this approach as a non sequitur, a Latin expression to mean that a stated conclusion is not supported by its premise.[60] While Murphy's unnamed colleague on the Court recognized that freedom of thought was constitutionally protected, he also believed that when an immigrant "wants to become a citizen . . . he may be required to meet such conditions as the Congress deems necessary."[61] Schneiderman, for instance, was not, strictly speaking, being denaturalized for the exercise of freedom of thought either before or after his naturalization but for not having been attached to the principles of a free government at the moment of naturalization. So he urged Murphy to view the Communist Party's support for overthrowing the U.S. government as "theoretical and not intended as a call to action"[62]—similar to Jefferson's belief that revolution could be justified when other means to change an inefficient or unjust government have failed.[63]

Murphy was enthusiastic about this approach and endorsed it. And he finally circulated a draft among all the Justices rewritten on that basis. But Frankfurter reacted strongly. On May 31, 1943, he caustically wrote to Murphy: "Thorough and comprehensive as your opinion in Schneiderman is, you omitted one thing that, on reflection, you might want to add. I think it is only fair to state, in view of your general argument, that Uncle Joe Stalin was at least a spiritual co-author with Jefferson of the Virginia Statute for Religious Freedom."[64] Two days later, Frankfurter, proposed to Murphy the following headnote for his opinion: "the American Constitution ain't got no principles. The Communist Party don't stand for nuthin'. The Soopreme Court don't mean nuthin'. Nuthin' means nuthin' and ter Heil with the U.S.A. so long as a guy is attached to the principles of the U.S.S.R."[65]

Until the very day that the decision was delivered, Frankfurter tried to convince Justice Stanley Reed and then Justice Murphy to switch sides. But Frankfurter's influence on the Supreme Court was waning. He had been elevated to the Court on January 1939, with a reputation for possessing a formidable intellect and, importantly, a desire to lead the Court in the direction of judicial restraint at a time when the legislative branch wanted to implement a series of economic regulations. He had found a majority for that agenda. Yet many of the very same liberal colleagues (e.g., Black, Douglas, and Murphy) who had initially followed Frankfurter on his first decision involving civil liberties, the *Gobitis* case, which dealt with the flag salute,[66] were now moving in another direction.[67] Strong public reaction against the decision which upheld the government's power to impose a flag salute on Jehovah's Witnesses, despite their claim that it violated their religious beliefs, had affected his leadership.[68] On June 14, 1943, three years after it was decided, one week before *Schneiderman*, *Gobitis* was reversed in *West Virginia v. Barnette*.[69]

Yet even Murphy's more sympathetic colleagues thought his draft opinion required improvement. Douglas, for one, advised him to carefully read again the statute. It did not request that the applicant be attached to the principles of the Constitution but that the applicant to citizenship demonstrates in the five years preceding the naturalization that "he has *behaved* as a man of good moral character, attached to the principles of the Constitution of the United States, and well disposed to the good order and happiness of the same."

That was the approach George Wickersham had adopted in 1912, with the government arguing before a federal district court for the restoration of the American citizenship of Oleson, a socialist union leader for whose denaturalization the local U.S. attorney was responsible. But nobody on the Court had a memory of this case.[70] Murphy could rely also on Justice Oliver Wendell Holmes dissenting opinion in a previous important Supreme Court case, *United States v. Schwimmer*. In that case, the majority had found that the government possessed the right to consider in their entirety the opinions, beliefs, and behavior of an applicant for naturalization and, in that particular case, to deny citizenship to a fifty-year-old woman committed to pacifism who refused to bear arms in defense of the Constitution. Holmes, on the other hand, maintained that "if there is any principle of the Constitution that more imperatively calls for attachment than any other it is the principle of free thought—not free thought for those who agree with us but freedom for the thought that we hate. I think that we should adhere to that principle with regard to admission into, as well as to life within this country."[71] Murphy would quote this excerpt in his majority opinion.

Thus, if it was only Schneiderman's behavior at stake (and not the Communist Party's), Schneiderman stood on firm ground. He had "never been arrested, or connected with any disorder, and not a single written or spoken statement of his, during the relevant period from 1922 to 1927 or thereafter, advocating violent overthrow of the Government, or indeed even a statement, apart from his testimony in this proceeding, that he desired any change in the Constitution has been produced."[72] The sole possible objection, Murphy added, "is petitioner's membership and activity in the League and the Party, but those memberships *qua* memberships, were immaterial under the 1906 Act." After all, when Schneiderman was naturalized in 1927, the applicable statutes did not proscribe Communist beliefs or affiliation as such. They forbid only anarchists, polygamists, and advocates of political assassination. If attachment to the principle of the Constitution was the relevant issue, Congress could not have meant to restrict "doctrinal utterances and academic or theoretical exhortations; otherwise one must conclude that Jefferson and Lincoln had not behaved as one attached to the Constitution."[73]

Furthermore, according to Murphy, even if the decision to denaturalize was based on the beliefs espoused by the Young Workers League and Communist Party, groups to which Schneiderman belonged, it could hardly be shown that these groups' views were fundamentally at variance with the U.S. Constitution. "Said to be among those Communist principles in 1927 are," Murphy enumerated, "the abolition of private property without compensation; the erection of a new proletarian state upon the ruins of the old bourgeois state; the creation of a dictatorship of the proletariat; denial of political rights to others than members of the Party or of the proletariat; and the creation of a world union of soviet republics. . . . Those principles and views are not generally accepted—in fact they are distasteful to most of us—and they call for considerable change in our present form of government and society."[74]

But for Murphy, it reminded the government that "under our traditions beliefs are personal and not a matter of mere association" and that here were different possible interpretations of the Communist program: "the Constitutional fathers, fresh from a revolution, did not forge a political straitjacket for the generations to come. Instead, they wrote Article V, and the First Amendment, guaranteeing freedom of thought, soon followed. Article V contains procedural provisions for constitutional change by amendment without any present limitation whatsoever, except that no State may be deprived of equal representation in the Senate without its consent. This provision and the many important and far-reaching changes made in the Constitution since 1787 refute the idea that attachment to any particular provision or provisions is essential, or that one who advocates radical changes is necessarily not attached to the Constitution."[75] He wrote on behalf of the majority, "We do not think the government has carried its burden of proving by evidence which does not leave the issue in doubt that petitioner was not, in fact, attached to the principles of the Constitution and well disposed to the good order and happiness of the United States when he was naturalized in 1927."[76]

Finally for Murphy, there was also a decisive point suggested by Douglas: the *Schneiderman* case did not concern "a naturalization proceeding in which the Government is being asked to confer the privilege of citizenship upon an applicant. Instead, the Government seeks to turn the clock back twelve years after full citizenship was conferred upon petitioner by a judicial decree, and to deprive him of the priceless benefits that derive from that status. In its consequences, it is more serious than a taking of one's property, or the imposition of a fine or other penalty."[77] This does not mean that, once granted to an alien, citizenship could never be revoked or canceled on legal grounds when there existed sufficient and appropriate proof. But such a right, once conferred, should not be taken away without the clearest sort of evidence.[78] After the *Schneiderman* opinion, the United States would still be entitled to attack a claim of attachment based on a charge of illegality, but it now had to meet a very heavy burden to prove lack of attachment by "clear, unequivocal, and convincing" evidence that does not leave the issue in doubt.

Murphy's opinion was solid but ponderous and long-winded, the product of many amendments to a first draft that had needed improvements. When one reads the two concurring opinions of Douglas and Rutledge, who also helped Murphy finalize the majority opinion, one finds a more concise and clear summary of the beneficial consequences the *Schneiderman* decision might have for naturalized Americans.

In his concurrence, Justice Douglas insisted that a distinction had to be made between naturalization and denaturalization proceedings. Douglas reiterated that, in the latter, a lack of attachment to the principles of the Constitution had to be shown by "clear, unequivocal, and convincing" evidence. The United States when it seeks to deprive a person of his American citizenship carries a heavy burden of showing that it was procured unlawfully.

Justice Rutledge based his concurring opinion on the principle of equality of all citizens: "We are concerned with only one man, William Schneiderman. Actually, though indirectly, the decision affects millions. If, seventeen years after a federal court adjudged him entitled to be a citizen, that judgment can be nullified and he can be stripped of this most precious right, by nothing more than reexamination upon the merits of the very facts the judgment established, no naturalized person's citizenship is or can be secure."[79] He added:

No citizen with such a threat hanging over his head could be free. If he belonged to "off-color" organizations, or held too radical or, perhaps, too reactionary views, for some segment of the judicial palate, when his admission took place, he could not open his mouth without fear his words would be held against him. For whatever he might say or whatever any such organization might advocate could be hauled forth at any time to show "continuity" of belief from the day of his admission, or "concealment" at that time. Such a citizen would not be admitted to liberty. His best course would be silence or hypocrisy. This is not citizenship. Nor is it adjudication. It may be doubted that the framers of the Constitution intended to create two classes of citizens, one free and independent, one haltered with a lifetime string tied to its status.

This affirmation of the equality of all citizens with respect to freedom of thought was not the primary or most convincing argument for preserving Schneiderman's citizenship. But endorsed in the majority opinion, it was a clear reversal of the jurisprudence of the lower courts, which, up to 1943, had used the concept of "mental reservation" as means for denaturalizing foreign-born citizens for acts committed and speech uttered after their naturalization proceedings.

The *Schneiderman* decision provoked both relief and strong emotion among the militants and lawyers who had backed Schneiderman. A few days after the decision was delivered, in a meeting held at the City Auditorium in New York, Schneiderman told the eight thousand attendees: "The Supreme Court in their decision acted in the best traditions of Jefferson and Lincoln. What was at stake in this case was not only the rights of citizenship for Communists. There are eight million naturalized Americans who know now that their citizenships rights are inviolate, that no arbitrary court or authority can re-examine their citizenship status at any time, years after they were naturalized, that they are not in probation. Thus in reaffirming the fundamental American right of freedom of political opinions and free political association, the Supreme Court has done a great service to our country."[80] For Carol King there was one sentence that crystallized the importance of Murphy's opinion: "The constitutional fathers, fresh from a revolution, did not forge a political straitjacket for the generations to come."[81]

In the course of working on the case, King and Willkie had built a close friendship. But that relationship was cut short when on October 8, 1944, Willkie died suddenly. King wrote in the *New Masses,* a prominent American Marxist publication:

Willkie dead. It is unbelievable, as if the light had suddenly gone out of the sun. His handshake was so warm, his laugh so full of fun; he had been so very much alive and loved living. His death was a great personal loss to me. Even now it is hard to write of him. But I found in the few days after the public learned of his death how personal this loss was not only to me but to people who had just met him, or seen him, or even to those who only knew there was a Willkie, a great democratic American with a love for humanity and for the principles in which he believed. . . . Willkie helped unify the country, Republican and Democrat alike, behind the broad vision which made him see contending international forces as "One World."[82]

But the battle was far from over. On June 21, the very same day that the *Schneiderman* decision was to be announced, Frankfurter wrote a letter to Stone: "Dear Chief, you must let me tell you how you deserved especially well of the Republic today–both for your Schneiderman opinion and for the impressive oral delivery." One month later, on July 19, he wrote from New Milford, Connecticut: "I am glad to hear that editorial writers went to your Schneiderman dissent. Retrospect makes it steadily worse."[83] For Frankfurter the battle, in fact, had just begun.

CHAPTER 9

Baumgartner:
The Program Ends, but
Denaturalization Continues

Schneiderman v. United States was the first case in which the Supreme Court ruled on a charge that a naturalized American lacked attachment to his or her new country. The decision was a blow for the government and for the Denaturalization Program, and Dewey Balch, the head of the program within the Criminal Division, was pessimistic: "I believe that we cannot escape the fact that the Supreme Court has clearly shown a reluctance to cancel naturalization and has imposed a burden upon the government which will make it difficult, if not impossible, to prevail in a very large number of our cases."[1]

On August 20, 1943, Balch had assessed the program: 515 complaints had been filed, 155 had been completed, and 115 had ended with a denaturalization decision (38 in contested cases, 77 by default or consent decrees)—22 judgments went for defendants and 18 ended because of deaths or withdrawals. Ninety-one cases were still pending. In the two months following the *Schneiderman* decision, the government had won only one case on appeal (*Krause*, Seventh Circuit Court), had won no case in District Court, and had lost seven.[2]

Balch warned: "If we do not face it now and salvage as much of the program as we can, I am afraid that we may get enough unfavorable lower court opinions so that the precedent that we have been relying upon will be pretty largely overcome by others to the contrary."[3] But Balch had to acknowledge that, "at the same time, the policy has been laid down by the Attorney General and is being followed, namely, to go ahead with the program without retrenchment."[4]

In fact, *Schneiderma*n had done little to weaken the "determination" of the attorney general. Francis Biddle had decided to continue to fight. First, Solicitor General Charles Fahy was ordered to file a petition for rehearing, which he did on July 15, 1943.[5] At the same time, lawyers in the Justice Department carefully studied the decision in order to develop a narrower but still proactive strategy for denaturalization. In a circular sent on September 4, 1943, Biddle instructed all U.S. attorneys to give the closest possible attention to the denaturalization cases in order "to make sure that they are thoroughly investigated and prepared and so that the strongest cases may be heard in court and decisions obtained at an early stage."[6]

Biddle insisted that, to meet the new burden of proof imposed by the *Schneiderman* decision, "the government must produce 'clear, unequivocal and convincing' evidence 'which does not leave the issue in doubt.'"[7] In cases involving activity in a subversive organization, it became "important clearly to prove, by overt acts if possible, that the defendant knew the subversive aims and doctrines of the organization and agreed with them."[8]

Biddle emphasized that three distinctions could be made between the *Schneiderman* case, dealing with a Communist, and the denaturalization of Nazis, the main target of the program started in March 1942:

Illegality Versus Fraud: The government proceeding in the Supreme
   Court against William Schneiderman was based on the charge of
   illegal procurement, not on fraud,[9] which remained a ground for
   complaint against the Bund members.
Lack of Attachment Versus Lack of Allegiance: The complaint charged
   that Schneiderman was not a person attached to the principles
   of the Constitution of the United States or "well disposed to the
   good order and happiness of the United States." But another legal
   ground of denaturalization—lack of allegiance—was not an issue
   in the case. On the contrary, Justice Frank Murphy's opinion had
   "called attention to the fact that Schneiderman 'would bear arms
   against his native Russia if necessary.'"[10]
Nazism Versus Communism: Precisely on the ground of allegiance,
   an "important distinction" could be made between the *Schneiderman* case and Nazi cases: "the element of ambiguity which the
   Supreme Court found to inhere in communist doctrines is clearly
   not present in the case of Nazi aims and doctrines. . . .which have
   been recognized, without dissent, to be diametrically opposed to
   the principles of the Constitution."[11]

After the instructions of September 4 were sent out, good news arrived from the courts. Balch's pessimistic forecasts about the lower courts were proved to be wrong. In the large majority of the cases before them, courts held in favor of the United States. That being said, some courts had become reluctant to accept even the most obvious evidence. For example, in four cases tried in the Northern District of Ohio, the defendants had signed statements admitting mental reservation at the time of the naturalization, or had recognized facts expressing it.[12] The court decided in favor of the United States in only one of the cases, where a large number of witnesses confirmed the signed defendant's statement.[13] In another case, the court construed the defendant's admission as "expressions of temporary emotion and not of an obdurate and continuing view."[14] The court considered that the last two defendants had limited legal ability and that "their conduct should be interpreted as a sign of nostalgia rather than lack of allegiance."[15] But Judge Frederick H. Bryant in Syracuse, New York, ordered the denaturalization of five members of the Bund on the basis that membership and participation in the activities of the Bund with knowledge of its aims and purposes, and work for their fulfillment, demonstrated "a strong enough adherence to the German Reich to prove non-existence of full allegiance at the time of taking the oath." Bryant distinguished the case, *United States v. Max Oscar Haas*, from *Schneiderman*: "The issues are different. Here the issue is legal fraud. In the *Schneiderman* case, the issue seems to have been illegal procurement in the absence of fraud."[16]

In California, on January 10, 1944, Judge Louis E. Goodman denaturalized seven members of the Bund based on the fact that the "principles and purposes of the German American Bund and its predecessors were of a different character entirely" from the beliefs at stake in the *Schneiderman* case. "Allegiance to the Fuhrer and the leadership and blood doctrine implied and convincingly connoted allegiance to the Fatherland."[17] In another Californian case, Arnold Wilhelm Johannes Wolff, the local secretary of the German American Bund, was denaturalized on February 4, 1944.[18] Carl August Vogl was denaturalized on January 27, 1944, on the ground that a member of the Bund at the time of naturalization who had knowledge of the organization's objectives and program could not have taken a valid oath.[19]

Another six members of the Bund were denaturalized in Michigan on March 10, 1944, on the grounds that "persons having become informed of the nature of the Bund could not continue their association with it and be in fact loyal citizens of the United States." Biddle immediately transmitted the good news of these cases to all U.S. attorneys.[20] But the victories were tenuous. Cases in the circuit courts multiplied as *Schneiderman* encouraged denaturalized former citizens to appeal. And on June 12, 1944, in a unanimous decision, the Supreme Court took things further, and reversed the denaturalization of a Bund member.[21]

Carl Baumgartner was born in Germany in 1895. He fought in the German Army in World War I before being captured and imprisoned by the British for two years. After receiving an electrical engineering degree, he moved to the United States in 1927. From the moment of his arrival, Baumgartner expressed pro-Nazi, pro-Hitler sympathies.

Justice Felix Frankfurter had warned his colleagues during the discussion of the *Schneiderman* case: "I cannot deal with this case any differently than I would deal with a case involving a Bundist."[22] The opinion of the Court was assigned to him and he stood with the outcome of *Schneiderman*. The case was even simpler: in 1932, when he took the naturalization oath, Baumgartner was pro-Hitler and pro-Nazi, but at the time of taking the oath and foreswearing allegiance to any other country, Germany was still governed by the Weimar Republic, which Baumgartner opposed. Therefore he could not be accused of keeping allegiance to a foreign ruler at the time of his naturalization. The case also involved a man whose militancy was not proven, and had it been proven, his activity was at the lowest level of the organization.

Subsequently, after his naturalization, Baumgartner deserved the same amount of freedom of speech as any American citizen. Frankfurter asserted:

> American citizenship is the right to criticize public men and measures—and that means not only informed and responsible criticism, but the freedom to speak foolishly and without moderation. Our trust in the good sense of the people on deliberate reflection goes deep. For such is the contradictoriness of the human mind that the expression of views which may collide with cherished American ideals does not necessarily prove want of devotion to the Nation. It would be foolish to deny that even blatant intolerance toward some of the presuppositions of the democratic faith may not imply rooted disbelief in our system of government.[23]

A few days later (with Murphy writing a concurring opinion) Baumgartner's denaturalization was cancelled unanimously. Philip Elman, Frankfurter's clerk on the Supreme Court from 1942 to 1943, who had just joined the office of the solicitor general, immediately wrote him:

> The decision is right, of course; the evidence of Baumgartner's allegiance or the lack of it, in 1932, was of the most evanescent character. I worked on the brief briefly and without enthusiasm. . . . . The difficulty was that the Dpt. regarded this as a very important case, testing whether the denaturalization program was to be continued. The people who initiated the program, and whose working lives were devoted [to its continuation], made it impossible to assume a more judicious, less contentious position in this case. Anyway, I'm glad that the final chapter of the Baumgartner case was a happy one. And I hope it means the end of the Dept's denaturalization program which is 98% stupidly conceived and sloppily executed.[24]

Elman was right. The Denaturalization Program would soon be declared dead. When the decision was announced, more than half the complaints filed within the program had been disposed (311 out of 544). Citizenship had been cancelled in 182 cases, judgment was for the defendant in 43, and 86 ended mainly because of death or withdrawals.[25] In the weeks preceding the *Baumgartner* decision, many appeals courts had reversed denaturalization decisions made by the trial courts.[26] This tendency would only accelerate after *Baumgartner.*[27]

But Elman's assessment was a legal, not a political one. Tom C. Clark, now the head of the Criminal Division, in charge of the program on Biddle's staff, had a more positive opinion concerning its impact: "In appraising the results of the denaturalization program as a whole, probably more important than the tangible results in terms of persons denaturalized, has been the intangible effect the program has had in informing the public about the activities of the Bund and similar activities, and also in discouraging persons of German extraction from openly manifesting any disloyalty to the United States that they might have felt."[28]

For Clark, one important question remained: What would the Department of Justice, in the aftermath of the *Baumgartner* decision, do with the two hundred remaining cases instituted by the government? Clark's June 17, 1944, memorandum set new requirements:

1. Naturalization had to have occurred after January 30, 1933, after Hitler came to power.

2. There was a need for clear and compelling evidence of disloyalty prior to or practically contemporaneous with naturalization.

Clark had no illusions regarding the outcome of the pending cases. He recognized that "the *Baumgartner* decision was controlling in a large number" of them.[29] But he still proposed action, however, and his memo studied these cases one by one. He found that in the eleven cases against German American Bund leaders under advisement in Buffalo, New York, seven involved evidence he believed was clearly distinguishable from the Baumgartner case while three others were possibilities. In ten cases of a similar nature under advisement in Milwaukee, he thought three could be distinguished from the *Baumgartner* case, "while two additional cases involve evidence which may possibly be distinguishable."[30]

Biddle asked Fahy, the solicitor general, to go over the program with Clark and to advise him: "1.What cases should be abandoned in the CCA's. 2. In the District Courts. 3. Should a General 'Policy' letter be sent to US. Atty's? 4. Or specific letters in each district. 5. Or both."[31]

J. Edgar Hoover of the FBI preferred general instructions,[32] but Fahy rallied Clark and chose a case-by-case approach under his direct, personal control. On June 29, Fahy wrote to Biddle: "several cases which have been acted on promptly have already been acted upon by me as to their further prosecution or the dismissal."[33] Simultaneously, the FBI was ordered to continue the program as before and was continuing to open new cases when some basis appeared to exist for the cancellation of citizenship on the ground of fraud.[34]

But many U.S. attorneys did not want to file a petition, or at least decided to wait for a decision from the department that did not come. On May 23, 1945, an annoyed Hoover asked for a clear instruction from the department as to whether the FBI should "continue, modify or terminate its denaturalization program."[35] At that point, twenty-eight denaturalization cases were still pending on the court dockets. After further review, sixteen were ordered dismissed, while twelve remained under investigation.

The end of the Denaturalization Program was formally pronounced on August 21, 1945: "new cases should not be opened except in exceptional instances where there is evidence of disloyalty approximating in time the date of naturalization, or where there may be evidence of fraud or disloyalty related to some other requirement for valid naturalization."[36] Other cases not in the above category were ordered to be closed without prior approval of the Justice Department.[37]

After *Baumgartner* and as World War II was ending, the Justice Department had to resolve another complicated question: how to deal with the appeals of the previously denaturalized German American internees who claimed "that they would not have been denaturalized, had the *Baumgartner* case been decided at the time their cases were heard and decided."[38]

The internees requested that the Department of Justice vacate their decrees of denaturalization. "Perhaps half of the cases" previously decided in favor of the government would have been lost "if either *Schneiderman* or *Baumgartner* opinions had governed their disposition."[39] On September 5, 1944, Elman wrote a memo to the solicitor general:

> A judgment cannot be set aside merely because it is inconsistent with subsequent appellate decisions—at least, not without the consent of the successful party. It seems to me, however, that serious questions of policy may be involved. The Supreme Court has determined that the denaturalization program followed by the Department has collided, to a very considerable extent, with the minimum standards of proof required by law in order to deprive one of the valuable privilege of citizenship. In obedience to the Supreme Court's definitive exposition of the law, the Department has in a sense confessed error in every pending case, which does not meet the evidentiary tests defined by the Court. Is it fair that the Department's expiation should be merely prospective? Would it be practical and just to reexamine all of the denaturalization cases, including those which are legally dead, with a view to remedying that which the Supreme Court would say was a wrong?[40]

Elman himself was "inclined to let sleeping dogs lie." Fahy had previously asked that the matter regarding the inequality in the application of the law[41] be taken up in conference with the attorney general. On September 26, 1944, Clark refused any change in the legal situation of that "fair percentage of the cases won prior to the Baumgartner decision [that] might have resulted otherwise had they been tried subsequently." Legally, he argued, "they were not entitled to the retrospective application of the *Baumgartner* principles." Further, he did not believe "there is one among them who did not grossly abuse his citizenship, nor any who have since experienced such a change of views as would permit present loyalty." If there was, he concluded, "there is open to them the expedient of a new application for naturalization."[42] Months after the end of the war many of these denaturalized German Americans were removed from the United States and sent back to Germany.[43]

Four years after the beginning of the Denaturalization Program, at the end of World War II, the *Baumgartner* decision seemed to have terminated or at least suspended the practice of political denaturalization. The unanimity of the Supreme Court in *Baumgartner* had convinced the majority of commentators and legal scholars that *Schneiderman* and *Baumgartner* were of the same ilk. The *New York Times* reported the day after the *Baumgartner* ruling, recalling the split in *Schneiderman*, that Frankfurter now spoke for the unanimity of the Court.[44] Harry Kalven was struck by the change of tone between the Frankfurter who dissented one year before in *Schneiderman* and the one who delivered the majority opinion in defense of the right of naturalized citizens in *Baumgartner*. He attributed it to Frankfurter's anti-Communism.[45]

It was a false impression. The best readers of *Baumgartner* understood it reflected tensions and divergences within the Court. Murphy had written a concurring opinion, but civil rights attorney Thurgood Marshall remembered it as a dissent, in which Murphy made it clear that "his views were even broader than those expressed in the *Schneiderman* case."[46] John P. Frank also viewed Murphy's opinion in *Baumgartner* as a dissent, and thought the majority opinion had "departed from the *Schneiderman* principles."[47] Both Marshall and Frank were right.

After the *Schneiderman* decision, Frankfurter was waiting for a case involving a member of the Bund to reach the docket of the Court. When Baumgartner was given certiorari in January 1944, he was without funds and without counsel, interned at the alien enemy internment camp in Bismarck, North Dakota. Chief Justice Harlan Stone proposed to assign him a counsel and ask his brethren of the Court for suggestions.[48] Frankfurter urged Stone to assign Baumgartner "not some junior lawyer but a senior, well known, highly competent lawyer."[49] Frankfurter's assignment to deliver the opinion of the Court in *Baumgartner* would permit him to elaborate his own approach on denaturalization. In the first draft of his opinion, Frankfurter did not quote the *Schneiderman* decision, a choice encouraged by the chief justice. "Dear Frankfurter," he wrote, "I am with you in No. 439, *Baumgartner*, notwithstanding Murphy's lament that you do not cite the *Schneiderman* case, or, if it would appease I would not object to saying that there was a lack in *Baumgartner* of the clear and convincing evidence which some members of the Court thought was present in the *Schneiderman* case."[50]

Not only Stone's approach would have infuriated Murphy, it could provoke the loss of a majority for Frankfurter. Murphy was circulating a draft of his concurring opinion, referring to *Schneiderman* as "a rule of law governing denaturalization proceedings . . . equally applicable whether the citizen against whom the proceeding is brought is a Communist, a Nazi or a follower of any political faith."[51] Black and Rutledge joined him. So did Douglas, who wrote him, "I hope you get 5."[52] Frankfurter backpedaled in response. On May 17, he announced to his brethren he was going to cite *Schneiderman* in his opinion, referring to the importance of "clear, unequivocal, and convincing" proof.[53] The day after, on May 18, in a memo to his colleagues he added a second quotation from *Schneiderman v. United States*.[54] Two weeks later, he wrote to Murphy that he was "truly sorry to have occasioned difficulty by my Baumgartner opinion. . . . For no time did the thought ever enter my head of disrespecting the Schneiderman decision or questioning its authority. But that case never involved for me any question as to the measure of proof required for invalidating a judgment. That fraud requires convincing proof is one of the commonplaces of the law—and hardly seemed to me in question. And so the *Schneiderman* case seemed to present very different questions from those at stake in *Baumgartner* and such still seems in fact, as much as Mortensen raised different questions from *Caminetti* and so did not call for citation of latter. Even two as great judges as the Court has ever had, Holmes and Brandeis, helped decide *Caminetti*."[55] But he added: "Of course I would have promptly referred to Schneiderman at the slightest suggestion. I think I am most amenable to meeting any Brethren's wishes when I write for the court. And I responded to the desire as soon as I knew it. That's all . . . and that's the whole truth: Take it or leave it that's the whole truth."[56]

Murphy knew the quotation of *Schneiderman* was diplomatic, necessary for preserving Frankfurter's majority. Elman understood that very well too. In his letter sent to Frankfurter after *Baumgartner* was decided, he said, "I'm glad that *Baumgartner* was assigned to you and that you took full advantage of the opportunity to slough off the silly formalism in which *Schneiderman* was crookedly enveloped. You've done a really good job of removing all the confusion resulting from the use of legal mumbo-jumbo; and the Department will be free to apply the denaturalization statute in those relatively few cases where it should be applied."[57]

Elman was right. Frankfurter used the majority opinion to set a standard for preserving the use of denaturalization within the authority of Congress.[58] That is why Murphy, backed by three other justices, wrote a concurring-dissenting opinion, concurring on the outcome of the conclusion but not on its reasoning.

Even if a higher standard had to apply for denaturalization than for refusal of naturalization, Frankfurter construed the right given to Congress " 'to establish a uniform Rule of Naturalization" as a power to "alone" "give or withhold naturalization."[59] Frankfurter was deferential to Congress. He distinguished between cases where "non-fulfillment of specific conditions, like time of residence or the required number of supporting witnesses, are easily established, and when established leave no room for discretion because Congress has left no area of discretion" and those where "the claim of 'illegality' really involves issues of belief or fraud, proof is treacherous, and objective judgment, even by the most disciplined minds, precarious." In these latter cases, denaturalization "calls for weighty proof, especially when the proof of a false or fraudulent oath rests predominantly not upon contemporaneous evidence, but is established by later expressions of opinion argumentatively projected, and often through the distorting and self-deluding medium of memory, to an earlier year when qualifications for citizenship were claimed, tested and adjudicated."[60]

Murphy refused these distinctions. He believed that a naturalized citizen had as much rights as the natural-born citizen. For him "the requirement that the Government prove its case by 'clear, unequivocal, and convincing' evidence transcends the particular ground upon which the Government seeks to set aside the naturalization certificate."[61] In all denaturalization cases, it was thus incumbent on the government to meet the standard of proof laid down by the Court in *Schneiderman*.

Schneiderman and *Baumgartner* had ignited a new battle over the role of the Supreme Court in protecting rights of American citizens. On one side, Frankfurter, the great defender of judicial deference to Congress; on the other were Black, Douglas, Murphy, and Rutledge, advocates of the intervention of the Court to safeguard individual rights. The battle would soon expand to expatriation cases, last twenty-seven years, and involve at least twenty-five Supreme Court decisions. From 1944 to 1971, the Supreme Court would remain harshly and roughly evenly divided.

CHAPTER 10

A Frozen Interlude in the Cold War

The Supreme Court would soon confirm that, in spite of its vastly diminished impact, denaturalization was still dividing the court. On the one end, it was still possible to be denaturalized. In 1943, the U.S. government had filed a suit against Paul Knauer, a German American member of the Bund.[1] Born in 1895, Knauer had fought for the German Empire in World War I. He came to the United States in 1925 and became a citizen in 1937, at a time when Hitler was already ruling Germany. In contrast to Baumgartner, Knauer was an active pro-Hitler leader before his naturalization. He had met him personally in Germany, and was supposedly offered a job by him. Knauer had solicited donations for the German Winter Relief Fund, joined the German-American Bund, and sent his daughter to the Youth Movement of the Bund summer camp. He infiltrated and tried to take control of older and less Nazi-friendly German American organizations, and later helped form and served on the executive committee of a new pro-Nazi association.

Justice William Douglas delivered the majority opinion. He concluded that there was "convincing evidence that Knauer, before the date of his naturalization, at that time, and subsequent[ly] was a thorough-going Nazi and a faithful follower of Adolph Hitler." Membership in the Bund was not in itself sufficient to prove fraud, "otherwise, guilt would rest on implication." In this case, however, the conclusion was "irresistible . . . that when he forswore allegiance to the German Reich he swore falsely." Hugo Black, "troubled by the idea that a man who is naturalized can be denaturalized,"[2] hesitated to join the majority, but finally did. Frank Murphy was afraid that the case would be used "to oust all naturalized citizens."[3] Wiley Rutledge, followed by Murphy, dissented on this ground. He thought that denaturalization was unconstitutional: "[We] can't allow it unless we create 2nd class citizenship."[4] Murphy and Rutledge were a minority, but their defeat in *Knauer* did not mean that the door of denaturalization had been reopened. Two years later on January 17, 1949, in *Klapprott v. United States,* Frankfurter could not keep a majority on his *Baumgartner* interpretation of denaturalization. August Klapprott had been denaturalized in 1942 for his disloyalty to the United States, as a leader and a member of the German American Bund and other subversive organizations. He was served with notice, but seven days before expiration of the sixty-day delay, he was arrested on federal criminal charges. Klapprott was confined in a New York jail, where he claimed that he was unable to appear in court and to pay for a lawyer. Without hearings or evidence, the court entered a default judgment canceling his certificate of naturalization. The Supreme Court reversed the judgment and remanded the case to the district court with instructions to grant the petitioner a hearing on the merits of the issues raised by the denaturalization complaint.[5] Frankfurter dissented, arguing that Congress never indicated that a certificate of naturalization could not be annulled by default and that the Court was not justified in adding any requirement.[6] Black delivered the opinion of the Court. Quoting *Schneiderman,* he reminded the government that it had the burden to prove its charges in *all* denaturalization cases, including in the absence of the defendant, by clear, unequivocal, and convincing evidence.[7] For him, denaturalization could only happen on this heavy burden of proof.[8]

The iron curtain had already descended across Europe, and anti-Communism peaked in a context of economic dislocation and high tensions in U.S.-Soviet relations.[9] The Republican Party had a sweeping victory in the midterm election of 1946, during which the New Deal was associated with Communism by the newly elected Congressman Richard Nixon and Senator Joseph McCarthy.[10] Reacting to this, President Harry S. Truman tried to preempt the anti-Communist hysteria. He established a temporary Committee on Employee Loyalty in November 1946, and set up a full-scale employee loyalty checkup the following year.[11]

These efforts were not enough for the new Republican majority. The Labor–Management Relations Act (the Taft-Hartley Act), which prohibited jurisdictional, wildcat, solidarity, or political strikes, and monetary donations by unions to federal political campaigns, also required union officers to sign non-Communist affidavits with the government. It was adopted by Congress on June 23, 1947, overriding Truman's veto.[12]

The House Un-American Activities Committee set investigators in search of Communists. Truman was reelected in 1948, campaigning at the same time against the Republican Thomas E. Dewey on his right and the Progressive Party candidate Henry Wallace on his left. But the fall of China, the explosion of the first Soviet atomic bomb in 1949, and the outbreak of the Korean War in 1950 kept giving momentum to strong anti-Communist campaigns in domestic politics. As Senator McCarthy started his crusade, Congress passed the McCarran Act in 1950,[13] which authorized the president to detain in time of war or insurrection all people believed to be participating in "acts of espionage or sabotage," with no provision for judicial review. Truman vetoed a bill that "would greatly weaken our liberties and give aid and comfort to those who would destroy us," but again his veto was overridden.[14]

The McCarran Act also included a new statutory presumption: affiliation within five years of naturalization with an organization that, at the time of naturalization, would have precluded citizenship was made prima facie evidence of an *earlier* lack of attachment to the principles of the Constitution and so of fraud.[15] The 1952 Immigration and Nationality Act (the McCarran-Walter Act, on which Truman's veto was also overridden)[16] added a new ground for the revocation of citizenship: refusing within ten years of naturalization to testify before a congressional committee concerning one's subversive activities.[17]

It had been a long time since the Naturalization Service had tried to pass provisions permitting denaturalization for actions committed after naturalization and not before. With this legislation now on the books, on the eve of the 1952 presidential election, the last Truman administration attorney general, James McGranery, launched a campaign to deport alien racketeers and to denaturalize those who "have taken out citizenship."[18] Organized criminals were the main target, especially Frank Costello, one the chiefs of the mafia. Communists, however, were a major aim as well.[19]

On December 15, 1952, McGranery ordered that denaturalization proceedings be instituted against a presumed Communist, Constantine Radzie,[20] and a left-wing union leader, James J. Matles.[21] Three months later, Herbert Brownell Jr., who succeeded McGranery as President Dwight D. Eisenhower's first attorney general, declared that ten thousand naturalized Americans were under investigation for possible deportation as subversives.[22] Nearly every three months or so, he made headlines by announcing denaturalization proceedings against presumed Communists: on August 25, 1953, against fifty-six-year-old Paul Novick, a founder and longtime editor in chief of a left-wing Yiddish daily, *The Morning Freiheit*, and an active Communist; on October 12, 1953, against Sam Sweet, a forty-two-year-old native of Poland, based on charges of Communist Party activities.[23] Despite the mobilization of Ernie Goodman, his courageous Detroit lawyer, one of the rare attorneys who defended presumed Communists throughout the 1950s,[24] Sweet was denaturalized in 1954 together with Nicholai Chomiak and George Charnowola, all three from Detroit, on the ground that his naturalization, obtained on February 5, 1946, was fraudulently and illegally procured. The government claimed that Sweet had concealed the fact that he was for some time during the ten-year period prior to his naturalization a member of the Communist Party.[25] Michael Chruszczak, naturalized in 1941, was sued by the government for not having declared a previous membership in the Communist Party. The Northern District Court of Ohio found on July 9, 1954, that "the evidence of defendant's membership in the Communist Party in 1943 subsequent to his admission to citizenship in 1941, although not controlling on the issues here," gave support to and was persuasive "as to his activities and participation in the years in question prior to his admission." And it revoked Chruszczak's citizenship.[26]

On June 8, 1955, Sam Title also was denaturalized. Born Teitelman, in Romania, in 1907, he had been in the United States since 1923. In his petition for naturalization by reason of marriage to an American citizen, and in his testimony before the naturalization examiner on July 30, 1941, he did not mention his membership in the Communist Party.[27]

Yet Brownell announced on October 7, 1956, that not ten thousand but seventy suits had been filed for denaturalization since he took office in January 1953.[28] And at the end, less than half of them—thirty-one—had been successful.[29] Why?

First, *Schneiderman* and *Baumgartner* had the deterrent impact of limiting the scope of governmental action. Naturalization officers faced some reluctance from U.S. attorneys and judges. For example, Anthony Scariano, an assistant U.S. attorney in Illinois from 1949 to 1954, refused to initiate proceedings for denaturalization requested by the INS against a German-born American who had neglected to declare on his application for naturalization that he was reading *The Masses*, a fact discovered by a search of his mail deliveries.[30]

Second, lower courts did not always follow the government's wishes. In New York, on June 23, 1954, the district court refused to consolidate action to denaturalize ten Americans suspected to be Communists,[31] on the ground that they were naturalized at very different dates between January 26, 1927, and January 8, 1945, that their presumed membership in the Communist

Party of the United States ranged from 1919 to 1937, and that therefore "the result would be most prejudicial to each defendant."[32]

Again, in a new case against Harry Bridges, after having lost two times in the Supreme Court, the government attempted to revoke Bridges's naturalization through a civil procedure, arguing that under the 1940 act Bridges had illegally procured citizenship by falsely stating that he was not and had not been a member of the Communist Party. The federal district court, however, ruled for Bridges and the government did not appeal.[33]

The Supreme Court, in contrast, "got caught up in the anticommunist fever of the times,"[34] especially when free speech was stake, a domain where its jurisprudence was not sturdy.[35] Yet during the hottest period of the anti-Communist campaign, between 1950 and 1955, the Supreme Court kept silent in denaturalization cases involving Communists.[36] Was it a matter of respect for very recent and ultimately quite convergent precedents (*Baumgartner* and *Schneiderman*) in cases not involving constitutional issues but only interpretations of statutes? Was it the fact that Frankfurter's reluctance to attack civil liberties was more influential in denaturalization cases because of these precedents than on other cases related to Communists? Between 1949 and 1953, when the intensity of the second Red Scare was at its peak, Frankfurter often stood with his traditional opponents Black and Douglas in cases involving civil liberties, and against their restriction. For example Black, Douglas, and Frankfurter lobbied, unsuccessfully, to hear the Rosenberg case.[37] In his thorough study of the Vinson Court, John P. Frank shows that between 1946 and 1953, in the non unanimous civil right cases, Frankfurter stood in the majority of the cases on behalf of claimed rights, though less often than Black and Douglas.[38] All three were in opposition to the bloc constituted by the four Truman nominees around Vinson, which with the addition of Stanley Reed most often constituted the majority of five.

There were two reasons for the almost general silence of the Court.[39] First, the government did not appeal when it lost cases in lower courts. Second, the Supreme Court most often refused certiorari when the government faced appeal in the cases where the lower courts had denaturalized Communists.

In 1949, the most liberal members of the Court, Murphy and Rutledge, died and were replaced by Sherman Minton and Harold Burton, who "shared Truman's worldview."[40] Together with Frankfurter, Robert Jackson, Reed, and the new chief justice, Vinson,[41] these justices defended classical judicial restraint, especially when national security was at stake. Black and

Douglas, sometimes joined by Jackson, alone voted for certiorari, produc-
ing an opposing bloc short of the minimum of four set by the rule of the
Court.[42]

The consequences of the court's new, more conservative composition is
best illustrated by several emblamatic cases. Sam Sweet, Nicholai Chomiak,
and George Charnowola, who had all had their denaturalizations confirmed
at the circuit court level,[43] were also denied in their 1954 petitions for certiorari.[44] These three cases, as noted earlier, concerned naturalized American
who were members of the Communist Party before their naturalization and
after the passage of the 1940 Nationality Act. This act prohibited the naturalization of those who in a ten-year period before naturalization believed in
the violent overthrow of the government or were members of organizations
that advocated such action. In all three cases, the petitioners, relying on the
reasoning that had led to the *Schneiderman* decision, pleaded that they had
never personally advocated the overthrow of the government.

The case of Charnowola was, for Douglas's clerk James F. Crafts Jr., the
most outrageous of the three. Charnowola was over sixty years old when he
was naturalized in 1946. During his naturalization examination, he had denied having ever been a member of the Communist Party. The district court
found the petitioner had been a party member from 1925 to 1932, years prior
to the ten-year period during which party membership was a bar to naturalization under the 1940 act. His citizenship was nevertheless cancelled on the
basis of fraud. The court thought that the petitioner's misrepresentation had
been material, even if "when [the] petitioner was naturalized, the government
had produced before the naturalization court the same evidence upon which
denaturalization has now been ordered, there would have been no statutory
grounds for denying naturalization and the evidence might well have been
excluded as immaterial."[45]

When the second Red Scare declined, and a few years after Earl Warren succeeded Vinson (1953) and John Harlan succeeded Jackson (1954), the Court
started granting certiorari again, and cancelling denaturalization decisions of
the lower courts on a precise, narrow, and applicant-rights-oriented interpretation of the naturalization statute, thus not involving constitutional issues.
This was an approach Frankfurter had to back to appear publicly coherent in
light of his *Baumgartner* opinion.[46]

Ettore Zucca, a Communist, was naturalized on January 4, 1944. In 1954,
he was denaturalized by the Southern District of New York, on the ground

that, during his naturalization process, he had falsely sworn "that he did not belong to and was not associated with any organization which teaches or advocates the overthrow of existing government in this country, as he was a member of the Communist Party or of other organizations affiliated with it from 1925 to 1947."[47] On April 30, 1956, the Supreme Court invalidated the denaturalization because the U.S. attorney did not file an affidavit showing good cause.[48] The term "good cause" refers to showing of substantial facts and evidence, required by law, in the affidavit the U.S. attorney files with the court. Otherwise, unfounded denaturalization complaints might tarnish the reputation of American citizens even if they ultimately prevailed in court.[49]

The next case concerned Stanley Nowak, a former state senator in Michigan defended by Ernest Goodman.[50] Together with George Crockett, the African American colleague with whom Goodman formed in 1951 the first integrated law firm in Michigan, he was Sweet's lawyer. He had lost the case when his petition for certiorari was rejected. Raised in Detroit's old Jewish ghetto, Goodman did not attend college. He earned his law degree in a non-accredited night school.[51] He was also a social activist, and from the 1930s until his death in 1997 he fought for labor and civil rights. He would plead for three of the four denaturalization cases that would reach the Supreme Court in the following years.

Nowak had arrived in the United States at the age of ten in 1912, and was naturalized in 1938. In the 1930s, he was a United Auto Workers organizer in Detroit.[52] In 1938, he was elected a state senator of Michigan, a position that provided a better way to communicate with Ford workers in Dearborn, where free speech was not easy for union organizers.[53] He was reelected four times consecutively and remained a member of the Michigan legislature until 1948. On March 9, 1952, during his hearing before the House Un-American Activities Committee, he was denounced as a member of the Communist Party by an informer. He refused to confirm that information, invoking his constitutional right against self-incrimination.[54] Following the passage of the 1952 Immigration and Naturalization Act, the U.S. government sued him for having been fraudulently naturalized in 1938 because he lied in answering "no" to question 28 of his application: "Do you belong to or are you associated in any organization which teaches anarchy or the overthrow of the existing government in this country?"

On July 13, 1954, eighteen months after having been notified of the government action,[55] he stood trial in front of Judge Frank Picard of the U.S. Eastern District Court of Michigan. Government witnesses testified that he had been a member of the Communist Party, but they stumbled during cross-examination.[56] One professor, more convincingly, testified that, during the 1930s, Nowak had collected his dues for the Communist Party of the USA. On July 15, 1955, Nowak was stripped of his citizenship. The following year, the court of appeals upheld the judgment,[57] but the Supreme Court decided to review the case. For Goodman it indicated "that the events of the 14 years since it decided the *Schneiderman* case makes it necessary to re-examine the legal basis upon which so many hundreds have already lost their citizenship."[58]

On May 26, 1958, Justice Harlan delivered the opinion of the Court. He stood on the same reasoning as the Court in *Schneiderman* and *Baumgartner*: to be naturalized under the 1906 act, an alien had to be "attached to the principles of the Constitution of the United States" for at least five years preceding his application for citizenship. The fact that Nowak had been a member of the Communist Party—the Court found that the record contained adequate proof of that fact—did not prove, under the standard required in denaturalization cases that Nowak had known of the party's advocacy of forcible governmental overthrow. The question was ambiguous. Nowak could have thought it was related solely to anarchy.[59] His denaturalization, together with that of Rebecca Maisenberg, another Detroit left-winger, was cancelled.[60]

These decisions were a blow to many pending cases in the federal courts. Katherine Kemenovich, born in Austria-Hungary, came to the United States in 1921 and was naturalized in Ohio in 1941. In 1954, the Immigration and Naturalization Service instituted proceedings to revoke Kemenovich's citizenship, alleging that she concealed at the time of her naturalization her membership in the Communist Party. After *United States v. Zucca*, the *Kemenovich* case was dismissed without prejudice, the government having failed to file the required affidavit. The proceeding could not be reinstituted, because of the *Nowak* and *Maisenberg* decisions that required proof of knowledge on the part of the defendant that the Communist Party advocated the overthrow of the government by force and violence, something the government could not provide in Kemenovich's case.[61] On the basis of these two decisions, pending cases of naturalized Communists that had been initiated by the government, including the first case launched by McGranery against union leader James Matles in December 1952,[62] were cancelled or abandoned.[63] This provoked the ire of the House Un-American Activities Committee.[64]

Later, in 1960 in *Chaunt*, a case resembling *Charnowola*, the Court cancelled a denaturalization on the expansive interpretation of the requirement of "clear, unequivocal, and convincing evidence."[65] Peter Chaunt had not mentioned some facts on his naturalization application: on July 30, 1929, he was arrested for distributing handbills in New Haven, Connecticut, in violation of an ordinance. On December 21, 1929, he was arrested for violating the park regulations in New Haven by making "an oration, harangue, or other public demonstration in New Haven Green, outside of the churches." And on March 11, 1930, he was arrested again in New Haven and this time charged with "General Breach of the Peace." He was found guilty by the City Court and fined $25. He appealed, and the records show that the charges were "nolled" on April 7, 1930. In conference, Frankfurter voted against certiorari and therefore to let the denaturalization proceed.[66] After certiorari was granted with the votes of Black, William Brennan, Douglas, and Warren, Frankfurter joined them to reverse the denaturalization. The evidence was clear and unequivocal. But for the Chief Justice and the Supreme Court, these facts were "immaterial and minor"[67] facts that, if known at the moment of the naturalization decision, would not have led to denial of citizenship.[68] With the assessment of the "materiality" (i.e., the real importance) of concealed or misrepresented facts that could lead to denaturalization, the *Chaunt* decision opened the way for another reduction of the number of denaturalizations.[69]

Denaturalization cases for American living in the United States were in the hundreds per year in the 1930s. Their number was around fifteen per year in the 1950s.And in 1960, the campaign against the Communists was over. In fact, since *Schneiderman* and *Baumgartner*, the divergences between justices had narrowed, and the scope of executive action had been hugely limited, with even the interest of the executive branch itself in pursuing denaturalization substantially diminished because of the extent to which it had managed to make the naturalization procedure administrative.

In contrast, denaturalizations for residence abroad, already the majority just before World War II, were rising again. There were hundreds per year, and they represented 90 to 98 percent of all denaturalizations. They had declined during the war because it was difficult to initiate them from the United States, especially in enemy countries. As the war had ended in Europe, U.S. attorneys and J. Edgar Hoover had pressed the attorney general to resume them.[70] The first aim would be German Americans who had stayed abroad during the war. Then, very soon, the government targeted all naturalized Americans abroad.[71] As noted earlier, sections 404–406 of the 1940 Nationality Act applied automatic loss of citizenship to naturalized citizens residing three or even two years in their country of origin or five years in any other foreign countries, any time after their naturalization.

Table 1. Citizenship Certificates Revoked Due to "Living Abroad," 1950–1954

	Total Revoked	Revoked Due to Living Abroad	
1950	415	392	(94.46 percent)
1951	403	384	(95.29 percent)
1952	279	275	(98.57 percent)
1953	335	327	(97.61 percent)
1954	165	150	(90.91 percent)

The first targets of these new provisions in 1940 were "these Zionists," as Richard Flournoy from the State Department would call them, "principally Russian and German Jews who were naturalized in this country and later went to Palestine."[72] Earlier in 1949, the Supreme Court left Louis Bernard Lapides, born Austrian and naturalized in 1928, stateless. In 1934 he went to Palestine and remained there until 1947. Upon his return to the United States on July 3, 1947, he presented his certificate of citizenship and sought his admission as an American citizen. On July 8, 1947, a Board of Special Inquiry of the INS excluded him on the ground that his residence in Palestine has made him lose his American citizenship. He brought his case in federal court, lost, appealed, and lost again despite the backing of the ACLU, the American Jewish Committee, and the American Jewish Congress, who filed three different *amicus curiae*.[73] The District of Columbia Circuit Court affirmed that the Naturalization Act had as its purpose dealing with international affairs, and it did not arbitrarily impose a loss of citizenship: "It deals with a condition voluntarily brought about by one's own acts, with notice of the consequences."[74] Judge Henry W. Edgerton dissented, finding the act unconstitutional on two grounds: "Congress may not discriminate against naturalized citizens. Arbitrary discrimination is not due process of law."[75] But on October 24, 1949, a writ of certiorari was denied by the Supreme Court.[76]

Yet naturalized Americans living abroad who had risked losing their citizenship since 1906 had been joined since the 1940 Act by several new categories of American-born citizens: those who engaged in foreign military service or employment, who voted in political elections in foreign states, or who were convicted of desertion from the armed forces of the United States or treason.[77]

During the Cold War, the Supreme Court had confirmed or declined to confront these different provisions. In 1950, in *Savorgnan v. United States*, an American woman who took Italian citizenship before her marriage to an Italian diplomat in the United States claimed that her intent was not to lose American citizenship. As soon as the intent for foreign naturalization existed,[78] and she did not deny such intent, the Court judged this ground sufficed to confirm her loss of citizenship.[79]

Together with denaturalization for residence abroad, which only concerned naturalized Americans, the courts were stripping citizenship from native-born Americans at a dramatic pace. In 1949, a total of 8,575 Americans were expatriated. In 1953, the number was 8,350, of which 32 percent were for having voted in foreign elections, 32 percent for being naturalized Americans living abroad, 20 percent for undergoing naturalization in a foreign country, and 8 percent for serving in a foreign army.[80] In 1951, the District Court of Hawaii had declared unconstitutional the 1940 expatriation provision that imposed loss of citizenship on Kiyokuro Okimura, a dual Japanese and American citizen, for serving in a foreign army.[81] But the Supreme Court implicitly rejected this conclusion by vacating the order and remanding for finding whether Okimura had served voluntarily or under duress.[82] Black was at that moment the only justice who backed the unconstitutionality of the expatriation clause, while Douglas was in favor of recognizing that Okimura had served under constraint.[83] In 1952, the District Court of Hawaii confirmed Okimura in his American citizenship.[84] In 1953, the same District Court of Hawaii affirmed that the provision imposing loss of citizenship for voting in foreign elections was also unconstitutional.[85] The number of cases in the courts was rising.[86] Pressure was mounting on the Supreme Court to deal with these denationalization provisions.[87]

CHAPTER 11

Nishikawa, Perez, Trop:
"The Most Important Constitutional
Pronouncements of This Century"

Just when the Cold War was at its coldest, a battle exploded in the Supreme Court soon after Earl Warren was appointed chief justice.[1] In 1955, in a unanimous *per curiam* decision,[2] the Court for the first time applied to denationalization cases the heightened standard of proof required in every denaturalization case since *Schneiderman*.

The case concerned Daniel Gonzales, born in New Mexico in 1924 to two Mexican citizens. When he reached the age of two, Gonzales was taken by his parents to Mexico, where he lived until 1946. Although Gonzales did not remember living in America as an infant, his parents informed him of his U.S. citizenship after he turned twelve. And in 1945, the now twenty-one-year-old Gonzales returned to the United States, but not before he registered for the Mexican draft. Soon after his arrival in 1945, he also registered under the U.S. selective service law.

But the damage was done, and the United States declared that Gonzales had voluntarily renounced his American citizenship by signing up for a foreign country's draft during a time of war. The government also introduced a transcript of Gonzales's hearing before an immigration board, in which he purportedly testified that he had remained outside the United States in order to avoid serving in its military. At trial, however, Gonzales denied ever having made statements to that effect. Because the government was unable to back up its claims, the Supreme Court found that the United States could not meet the heavy burden required for depriving the American-born Gonzales of his citizenship.[3]

The *Gonzales* case, however, was just the beginning. Only a few months later, the Supreme Court agreed to hear three more cases—*Nishikawa*, *Perez*, and *Trop*—which involved attempts by the U.S. government to expatriate native-born Americans. Each of the three revolved around a different provision of the 1940 Nationality Act.[4]

The first concerned Mitsugi Nishikawa, an American citizen of Japanese origin. Born in California in 1916, he went to study in Japan in August 1939, just as World War II was beginning. And in March 1941, he was drafted into the Japanese army. After the war Nishikawa applied for a U.S. passport with the intention of returning to the United States, but his application was denied. The government argued that Nishikawa voluntarily renounced his American citizenship under section 401(c) of the Nationality Act of 1940 for "entering, or serving in, the armed forces of a foreign state" (unless expressly authorized by the laws of the United States). Nishikawa claimed, however, that he had been forced to serve.

Clemente Martinez Perez was born in El Paso, Texas, in 1909. At the age of ten or eleven, Perez followed his parents to Mexico and, eventually, married a Mexican national. In 1928 Perez was informed that he was born in the United States and, as a result, held American citizenship. In 1943 and then again in 1944, he was admitted to the United States as an alien railroad laborer, on a temporary basis. In 1947, however, Perez applied in El Paso for admission to the United States as an American citizen. At a hearing before a board of special inquiry, Perez admitted to remaining outside of the United States to avoid military service and to voting in political elections in Mexico. He was ordered excluded on the ground that he had expatriated himself; this order was affirmed on review by the assistant commissioner of the INS and the Board of Immigration Appeals. Perez brought a new suit in 1954, requesting a judgment that declared him to be a national of the United States. But the district court and Court of Appeals for the Ninth Circuit confirmed his expatriation.

Private Albert L. Trop, born in Ohio, was serving at Casablanca in French Morocco in 1944. On May 22, he escaped from a U.S. Army stockade, where he had been confined for a breach of military discipline. He was gone less than a day and willingly surrendered to an officer in an Army vehicle while he was walking back toward his base.[5] Yet a court-martial convicted him of desertion and sentenced him to three years of hard labor, forfeiture of all pay and allowances, and a dishonorable discharge. At the time, he did not realize that he had also lost his American citizenship. In 1952, Trop applied for a passport in New York. The State Department checked Trop's background and informed him that he has lost his nationality according to section 401(g) of the Nationality Act of 1940 on the grounds that he had deserted the military in wartime.[6]

The debates and decisions on these three cases would provoke one of the most vigorous battles of the era within the Supreme Court. As *Time* magazine reported, the justices—writing twelve separate opinions over just these three cases—split with a "fundamental bitterness unknown since 1946, when Justice Robert Jackson began feuding in public with Justice Hugo Black."[7]

Dallin H. Oaks was one of Chief Justice Warren's clerks in 1957 and 1958. He recorded in his journal the scene in the courtroom on March 31, 1958, when the decisions in the three cases were announced at 1:50 P.M. At that time Felix Frankfurter

> stated the facts and issue without giving away the disposition, bringing the whole thing to a climax just at 2:00 P.M., when the court went to lunch. They returned at 2:30, as usual, and Frankfurter finished his discourse. When he was through the Chief began to read his dissent. He prefaced his remarks by stating that his dissent had been prepared with respect to the written opinion of Justice Frankfurter, which differed materially from the declarations he had just given from the bench. The Chief submitted that FF's statement was not necessarily the view of the Court, and stated that it was not as well supported by authority "as he would have you believe." Then the Chief read his Perez opinion. The afternoon wore on as each justice droned through the full text of each opinion. In all, twelve opinions were read. Every justice but Burton and either Clark or Harlan was heard: Chief and FF three times, and Brennan twice. Douglas broke the monotony when delivering his opinion in Perez. He announced, "These are the most important constitutional pronouncements of this century." Douglas' delivery and remarks were easily the most forceful of the afternoon. His statement about the cases' importance was dramatic. The courtroom was charged with an electric air of importance from that time forward.[8]

Warren and Frankfurter were emerging from a battle that was uncertain until the very end. Eleven months prior, Warren had seemingly pieced together a majority in the three cases and was on track to deliver all three opinions of the Court. Yet by November, Warren had lost his majority, and

Frankfurter was assigned to deliver the three majority opinions. But in the previous month Warren had made an unusual and unexpected comeback. On this day he had delivered two majority opinions, in *Trop* and *Nishikawa*. In the most important case of the day, *Perez*, however, he was defeated. Not to be outdone, Chief Justice Warren delivered a notable dissenting opinion, which he hoped, would forge a path for battles still to come. As Frankfurter himself acknowledged, this would not be the end of the fight, but its beginning.

Oral arguments in the three cases were first heard by the Supreme Court on May 1–2, 1957. When the justices decided to hear the cases together, the Chief Justice scribbled his view in a bench memorandum:[9]

> Reverse: I would reverse all three of these cases but in . . . Nishikawa, I would remand it for determination as to whether he voluntarily joined the Japanese army in which event I would consider it a voluntary expatriation. But in that proceeding I would put the burden on the government to establish that the conscription did not amount to coercion.
>
> In the other two cases, Congress has to my mind made the loss of citizenship punishment for doing certain acts. I do not believe that Congress has any such power. It can punish—even to death for wartime crimes, but I know of no power to add loss of citizenship. Banishment too is cruel and inhuman punishment. The thought of making stateless an American boy of 18 years who "goes over the hill" in a training camp is repulsive. The government concedes that could be the results. The desertion in 710 (Trop) approximates that situation (3 yrs). The govt has the right to provide for denaturalization when the individual makes the choice under dual citizenship or voluntary relinquishment as necessary in external affairs.[10]

On the first page of this handwritten memo, Warren penciled regarding the *Trop* case: "This is one of the series of cases depriving native born Americans of citizenship. This is an important case, because there was no renouncing here nor adhering to any foreign government. This was a case of simple desertion from the army in wartime. Does Congress have power thus to deprive citizens of their nationality?"[11]

In the justices' conference meeting a few days later, on May 4, Warren cobbled together a bare majority for reversing the decisions of the lower courts in all three cases, effectively reestablishing the citizenship of Nishikawa, Perez, and Trop.[12] Warren assigned the opinions to himself. On June 5, he circulated draft opinions,[13] but the *Perez* and *Trop* cases, which, unlike *Nishikawa*, raised constitutional rather than simply statutory issues, immediately attracted the attention of the rest of the Court. Upon receipt of Warren's drafts, Frankfurter found himself unwilling to sign on;[14] instead, he announced his decision to write his own opinion expressing the "views upon the denationalization powers of Congress." But he requested time for it, since "the issues at stake are too far reaching and the subject matter calls for too extensive an investigation."[15] A reargument was approved and the three cases were reheard at the beginning of the 1957 term, on October 28.[16] The next day, the justices met in conference to discuss the cases.

Frankfurter's position was apparently convincing to the other justices. At the October 29 conference, Justice John M. Harlan, who had previously declared his intention to vote with Warren to reverse, announced that he was switching sides and would now join an affirmance with Frankfurter in *Perez* and *Trop*.[17] Frankfurter had already convinced Justice William Brennan, admitting to him at length how foolish Congress was in enacting the Expatriation Act, but insisting there was nothing in the Constitution prohibiting Congress from "making a damn fool of itself."[18] Now Brennan was with Frankfurter on *Perez* and with Warren on *Trop*. Initially, Justice Charles Whittaker intended to join Frankfurter's group to affirm in *Perez*, but he shifted toward Warren's opinion, reversing in *Trop*. The effect of these shifting alliances caused Warren to lose his majority in *Perez*[19] while barely hanging on in *Trop*—with Whittaker replacing Harlan as the fifth member of the majority.

Yet in the following weeks, Whittaker, bowing to Frankfurter's influence, moved back to his previous position in *Trop*.[20] Together with Burton and Brennan he also joined Frankfurter in a middle-of-the-road position—to remand—in *Nishikawa*, a position Warren had decided to rally.[21] This meant that Frankfurter would now deliver the opinion of the court in all three cases, in *Nishikawa* because Warren assigned it to him[22] and in the two others because Warren was now in the minority.

The whole result was a blow to the chief justice: Warren had lost his majority partly because his opinions were not very convincing, lacking sufficient theoretical grounding.[23]

*　　*　　*

Warren's initial set of draft opinions in *Perez* and *Trop* begin by quoting the first sentence of the Fourteenth Amendment: "All persons born or naturalized in the United States, and subject to the jurisdiction thereof, are citizens of the United States and of the State wherein they reside."[24]

But in the *Perez* draft, after solemnly announcing that U.S. citizenship is a "petitioner's constitutional birthright as it is that of every person born in this country," the rest of the document is a laborious effort to find a path somewhere between a bold declaration of constitutional rights and a more restrained reliance on jurisdictional precedents that had permitted expatriation on two provisions of the 1907 Expatriation Act.

Under the Expatriation Act any American naturalized in or who took an oath of allegiance to a foreign country was considered to have voluntarily renounced and abandoned his American citizenship. Indeed, this was the fate of American women who married foreigners from 1907 until 1922—as noted earlier, this provision applied longer still, until 1931, if an American woman's husband belonged to a race ineligible for U.S. citizenship. Such marriages to foreigners were considered a "condition voluntarily entered into with notice of the consequences."[25] But because these marriages differed from an express renunciation, in a 1915 case, *Mackenzie v. Hare*, the Supreme Court justified the Expatriation Act's marriage provision by referencing Congress's authority to avoid international "embarrassments" and "controversies."[26]

In both categories of cases—foreign naturalization and marriage—the Court held that Congress could expatriate someone to prevent the acquisition of a dual nationality. That was how Warren's first draft approached the issue. But because neither Clemente Perez nor Albert Trop had accepted another country's citizenship, under this view, they could not be expatriated. Furthermore, because Trop, whose proceedings were based entirely on his desertion from the U.S. military (and not on any supposed allegiance to a foreign power), had no other citizenship, denationalization would render him stateless. As a result, Warren's draft in *Trop* timidly evokes the possibility that such a consequence would be considered a violation of the Eighth Amendment's prohibition on cruel and unusual punishment.[27]

But the position that expatriation was acceptable for avoiding international "embarrassments" and "controversies" made Warren's reasoning fragile: where should one place the limits on the right to expatriate for "international embarrassment"? Could not voting in foreign elections be understood as creating "embarrassments" and "international controversies"?[28]

In Frankfurter's view, inherent in Congress's power to declare war and to regulate foreign affairs is a responsibility "to reduce to a minimum the frictions which inevitably result from the coexistence of sovereigns, sensitive in matters touching their dignity and interests."[29] As a result, Congress can define acts [for] which volunteer accomplishment can lead to expatriation.[30] This might include the act of voting in foreign elections. If voluntarily accomplished, it could result in the loss of citizenship, "so long as Congress, in establishing this relationship between conduct and consequence, acts reasonably within the framework of its express and implied powers, and so long as no person loses his citizenship unless he enters upon an expatriation course of conduct on his own free will." If so, there was no problem of constitutionality.[31]

Between the proclamation of the amendment and reference to precedents, Warren's draft opinion lacked theoretical heft. This is probably why Warren, now forced to reframe his majority opinions as dissents, asked one of his clerks to compose a new draft of a single combined opinion for the *Perez* and *Trop* cases.[32]

It started by defining "the nature of nationality" as "the most basic right man can possess."[33] Established as a sovereign state, the United States of America "was endowed with those implied powers that are essential to the proper functioning of a sovereign in the community of nations, under the label of foreign affairs."[34] But a vague and undefined need to reduce international tension cannot endow the government "with limitless powers to regulate all conduct on the pretext of aiding our foreign relations."[35] The power to take away nationality arises "from the inherent power of a sovereign state to deal with a particular problem of sovereignty, namely—the avoidance of the international conflicts that result when an individual pl ace himself in a position calling for allegiance to more than one nation."[36] This power of denationalization "is a special attribute of sovereignty, available only to deal with problems incidents to the protection of sovereignty,"[37] not to improve foreign relations. He concluded that neither Clemente Perez nor Albert Trop had committed acts that demonstrated allegiance to a foreign state.

After receiving the new draft, Warren handwrote five pages of notes and comments on long, brown strips of paper, which he tore out of a stenographer's notebook. The scraps contained seventeen different points in total:

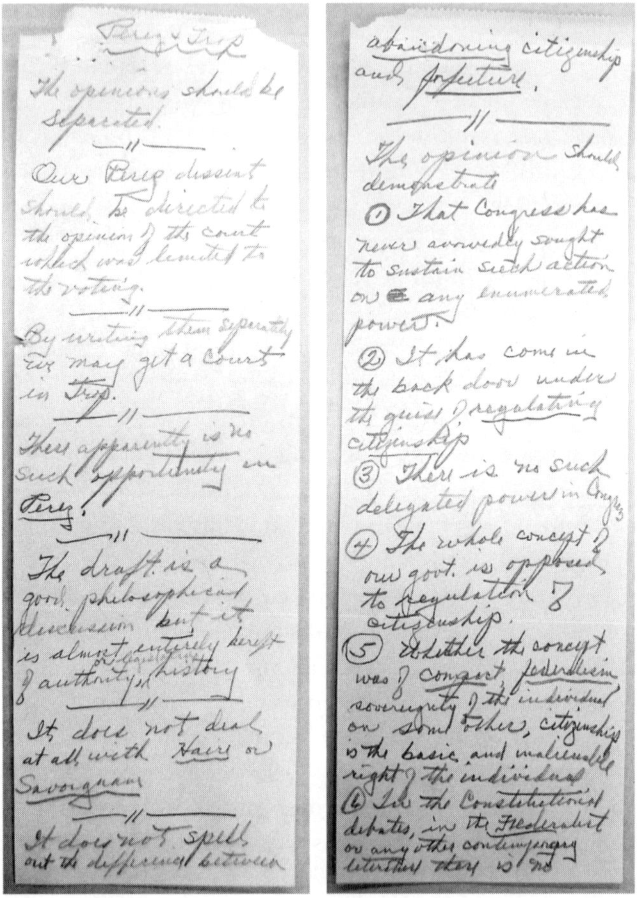

Figure 3. Chief Justice Earl Warren's handwritten notes on pages from a stenography pad, probably written between December 31, 1957, and February 5, 1958. Box 582, Warren Papers, Manuscript Division, Library of Congress, Washington, D.C.

suggestion that Congress be given the right to denaturalize citizens.

⑦ I am convinced that such a suggestion would have been shocking to the Founding Fathers and the American people.

⑧ It should still be shocking.

⑨ It was not, even conceded, for many years that a citizen could divest himself of citizenship.

⑩ Only our historical background and conflict with other nations led to that conclusion.

⑪ The legislative history of the statutes

on the subject does not lead to a contrary conclusion.

⑫ Congress has never directly asserted such a right.

⑬ Neither has this court recognized it.

⑭ Hall and Savorgnan show how cautious the court was in permitting expatriation.

⑮ In Perez we should say that we are not dealing specifically with the right of Congress to punish in this manner because the court has chosen to deal solely with the voting issue, and not the draft dodging (clearly

punishment) We will deal with that in Trop.

⑯ The majority opinion finds justification in the fact that the petitioner has refused to perform one of the basic responsibilities of govt. There are others — to pay taxes — to protect the purity of elections — to defend honesty of public officials — the involvement of this country in foreign difficulties. (Only a few days ago some men were arrested in Fla. who were preparing a ship for armed revolutions in Cuba)

⑰ Facts of case.

Perez + Trop

The opinions should be separated.

Our Perez dissent should be directed to the opinion of the Court
  which was limited to the voting.

By writing them separately we may get a court in Trop.

There apparently is no such opportunity in *Perez*.

The draft is a good philosophical discussion but it is almost entirely
  bereft of authority, or legislative history[.]

It does not deal at all with *Hare* and *Savorgnan*[.]

It does not spell out the difference between *abandoning* citizenship
  and *forfeiture.*

The opinion should demonstrate

1. That Congress has never avowedly sought to sustain such action on
   any enumerated power.
2. It has come in the back door under the guise of *regulating citizenship*[.]
3. There is no such delegated power in Congress[.]
4. The whole concept of our government is opposed to regulation of
   citizenship.
5. Whether the concept was of compact, federalism, sovereignty of the
   individual or some other, citizenship is the basic and inalienable right
   of the individual.
6. In the constitutional debates, in the Federalist or any other contemporary literature[,] there is no suggestion that Congress be given the
   right to denaturalize citizens.
7. I am convinced that such a suggestion would have been shocking to
   the Founding Fathers and the American people.
8. It should still be shocking.
9. It was not even conceded for many years that a citizen could divest
   himself of citizenship[.]
10. Only our historical background and conflict with other nations led to
    that conclusion[.]
11. The legislative history of the statutes on the subject does not lead to a
    contrary conclusion[.]
12. Congress has never directly asserted such a right.
13. Neither has this court recognized it.
14. *Hare* and *Savorgnan* show how cautious the court was in permitting
    expatriation[.]

15. In Perez we should say that we are not dealing specifically with the right of Congress to punish in this manner because the court has chosen to deal solely with the *voting* issue and not the draft dodging (clearly punishment)[;] we will deal with that in *Trop.*
16. The majority opinion finds justification in the fact that the petitioner has refused to perform one of the basic responsibilities of govt. There are others—to pay taxes—to protect the purity of elections—the honesty of public officials—the involvement of this country in foreign difficulties. (Only a few days ago some men were arrested in Florida who were preparing a ship for arming revolutionists in Cuba[.])[38]
17. Facts of case[.]

At first blush, Warren's extraordinary notes appear to be a reaction to a draft written by a clerk with novel ideas and new instructions on where and how to go next. They are not. Jon O. Newman, who was the senior clerk that year for Warren, never saw these notes. Although Newman did not write this second draft, he would ultimately write the drafts of Warren's final opinions in *Perez* and *Trop.*[39]

Indeed, Warren already had his own ideas and convictions regarding the expatriation provisions. Two years earlier, in a meeting of the justices to discuss *Gonzales v. Landon,* Warren, joined by Black,[40] had taken the position that the expatriation provisions of the Nationality Act were "unconstitutional."[41] Roger K. Newman, Hugo Black's biographer, notes that "Warren instinctively understood what was at stake in a case; what was significant and why." But he also adds that usually "he didn't think or care about the intellectual process."[42] Norman Dorsen, who clerked with Justice Harlan the year these cases were decided, emphasizes, "Warren's tendency to react to a case viscerally, without probing legal subtleties."[43] And after serving with Warren for fourteen years, Black similarly admitted, "I wish he knew a little more about law."[44]

Yet Chief Justice Warren's notes suggest a different view. Not only do they show Warren's deep interest in the expatriation cases, his belief in their importance as well as his will to win back a majority,[45] they also reveal sophisticated legal reasoning and convincing justifications for why certain parts of the Nationality Act were unconstitutional. The notes provide a framework for a solution to the problem that Warren had been trying to resolve since the fall.

After being shown Warren's written observations, Warren clerk Jon Newman reacted with surprise, "These notes are astonishing. I have never seen notes like these before."[46] Newman, now a senior judge on the U.S. Court of Appeals for the Second Circuit, hypothesizes that the notes might have been jotted down during a conversation with another justice: "The Chief may have been sitting down with another justice. And when the other made some points, the Chief made notes for himself about what the other justice was saying."[47] These notes could also have been written *after* a conversation with another justice.[48] Frankfurter, for one, would later share with Justices Brennan and Harlan his conviction that Warren was influenced by Black and Douglas in writing his opinions in these cases.[49]

Some conversations do seem certain, but it was more likely that Black (and not Douglas) had influenced the chief justice. The historical record shows that Black discussed the expatriation opinions with Warren at a later stage of the drafting process, and other evidence suggests that the two justices may have exchanged thoughts from the beginning.[50] Warren had a habit of entering Black's chambers, where they would discuss the cases and share ideas.[51] "I could never forget the sixteen years *that I sat by his side on the Court and the strength I felt because of his presence,*" Warren would write to Hugo Black's widow after his passing.[52] These were not empty words. Black was generous in providing ideas for opinions he would not sign. Now a senior judge on the U.S. Court of Appeals for the Second Circuit, Guido Calabresi clerked for Black during the October 1958 term and confirms this description of their relationship:

> The important thing is that there was this kind of communication between Black and the Chief. And that the Chief very often did take Black's views of how a case should go and made it his own. Because of their particular relationship, the Chief didn't resent it; the Chief resented it when Frankfurter, early on, started teaching him like a school boy and telling him what to do. But Black had enormous respect for the Chief, in his sense of fairness, his command of the Court, any number of other things which Black coming out of politics just like Warren and also [being] that kind of person thought the Chief was an extraordinary person and thinker. And so the Chief with somebody like that didn't mind using Black's ideas, because he knew that Black was in fact something like a genius in his ideas about law. He wanted the law to be right but he didn't care at all whether it was associated with him or with somebody else. If people accepted his ideas it was fine. In that respect, he was much more a judge than an academic.[53]

Black had been a diligent student of the Fourteenth Amendment. Since 1947, in his notable dissent in *Adamson v. California*,[54] Black had interpreted the amendment through a lens that was simultaneously originalist and textualist. Given these circumstances, Black could very well have furnished Warren with ideas.

In fact, Black had already developed his personal views in what was, at the end of 1957, a draft dissenting opinion in *Nishikawa*—Black's opinion eventually evolved into a concurrence when a majority of the court coalesced around his proposed result.[55] Even then, however, Black and Douglas were the lone justices to base their reversal on the unconstitutionality of denationalization and not, as the majority of the Court ultimately would, simply on the involuntariness of Nishikawa's membership in the Japanese army. In writing his opinion in *Nishikawa*, Black would have the opportunity to elaborate in broad strokes on the application of the Fourteenth Amendment to the practice of expatriation.[56] Although it has received little attention in recent years, Black's concurrence is significant; in it, Black lays out for the first time reasoning that would form the foundation for the Court's approach to denationalization for years to come.

Indeed, several of the ideas outlined in Warren's seventeen points can be traced back to Black's opinion in *Nishikawa*:

- "The Fourteenth Amendment declares that 'All persons born or naturalized in the United States and subject to the jurisdiction thereof are citizens of the United States and of the State wherein they reside.' Nishikawa was born in this country while subject to its jurisdiction; therefore American citizenship is his constitutional birthright."[57]
- "What the Constitution has conferred neither the Congress, nor the Executive, nor the Judiciary, nor all three in concert, may strip away. Congress . . . cannot involuntarily expatriate any citizen. . . . This results not only from the provisions of the Fourteenth Amendment, but from the manner in which the Government of the United States was formed, the fundamental political principles which underlie its existence, and its continuing relationship to the citizenry who erected and maintain it."[58]
- "In my view, the notion that citizenship can be snatched away whenever such deprivation bears some 'rational nexus' to the implementation of a power granted Congress by the Constitution is a dangerous and frightening proposition. By this standard, a citizen could be transformed into

a stateless outcast for evading his taxes, for fraud upon the Government, for counterfeiting its currency, for violating its voting laws and on and on *ad infinitum*."[59]

The similarities suggest that Chief Justice Warren's scribblings might have been notes taken during or after a conversation with Justice Black. Both were, perhaps, reacting to the new draft opinion that they found overly "philosophical" and, in the process, developing fresh ideas. For example, the terms "sovereign" and "sovereignty" are used thirteen times in the ten pages of the draft opinion to impress the idea that citizens submit to the sovereignty of the state. This may have pushed Black and Warren after reading it to reply, by turning this relationship on its head, and to proclaim, instead, that citizens are themselves sovereign, and that no organ of the government can strip an American of her citizenship. Warren would express this very idea in his *Perez* dissent where, following these notes, he would focus on the issue of voting in foreign elections.

Whatever the circumstances surrounding them, the seventeen points that Warren listed in his notes undoubtedly served as basis for his strategy in the following weeks and as a guide for his new senior clerk, Newman, to follow when redrafting the decisions in the expatriation cases.

So in *Perez*, Warren would say, as in *Trop*: "Citizenship *is* man's basic right, for it is nothing less than the right to have rights. Remove this priceless possession and there remains a stateless person, disgraced and degraded in the eyes of his countrymen. He has no lawful claim to protection from any nation, and no nation may assert rights on his behalf. His very existence is at the sufferance of the state within whose borders he happens to be."[60]

This definition of citizenship as "the right to have rights"—initially mentioned in one of Hannah Arendt's books—made its way to the Supreme Court in the *Perez* dissent and *Trop* decision along an interesting path. Jon Newman, who drafted Warren's opinions, borrowed the words "right to have rights" from Chief Judge Charles E. Clark's dissent from the Second Circuit's decision in *Trop*.[61] In that decision, Clark quoted from, and highly praised, a note on "The Expatriation Act of 1954," published by the *Yale Law Journal* in 1955, which mentioned Arendt as its origin.[62]

Yet defining citizenship as "the right to have rights" might protect Albert Trop, who was at risk of becoming stateless, it could not prevent the expatriation of Clemente Perez. Unlike Trop, Perez was also recognized as a citizen in a second country: Mexico. Even if he were expatriated, as a Mexican he could continue to enjoy "the right to have rights." Therefore this rights-centered conception of citizenship could not be the basis of the complete security of American citizenship. Another idea, "sovereignty of the individual," was mentioned in Warren's notes. In the new draft of his *Perez* opinion, the "sovereignty of the citizen" set a threshold high enough to protect each citizen against involuntary expatriation and came to form the basis of Warren's understanding of citizenship.

Warren described the idea as a founding principle of the American Republic:

> What is this Government, whose power is here being asserted? And what is the source of that power? The answers are the foundation of our Republic. To secure the inalienable rights of the individual, "Governments are instituted among Men, deriving their just powers from the consent of the governed." I do not believe the passage of time has lessened the truth of this proposition. It is basic to our form of government. This Government was born of its citizens, it maintains itself in a continuing relationship with them and, in my judgment, it is without power to sever the relationship that gives rise to its existence. I cannot believe that a government conceived in the spirit of ours was established with power to take from the people their most basic right . . . with power to decree this fate. The people who created this government endowed it with broad powers. They created a sovereign state with power to function as sovereignty. But the citizens themselves are sovereign, and their citizenship is not subject to the general powers of their government. Whatever may be the scope of its powers to regulate the conduct and affairs of all persons within its jurisdiction, a government of the people cannot take away their citizenship simply because one branch of that government can be said to have a conceivably rational basis for wanting to do so.[63]

Sovereignty, instead of serving as "the supreme power of the State on individuals within its Jurisdiction,"[64] had become something like a shared quality attributed to all citizens, with each benefitting from its character of inalienability and permanency. Therefore, for Warren, citizenship was not something that could be stripped away by a government. Only voluntary expatriation was acceptable. In the past, the Court did not impose expatriation on its citizenship. To demonstrate his point, Warren cleverly argued that marriage between an American woman and a foreign male did not, in the 1915 *Mackenzie v. Hare*[65] decision, terminate the American's citizenship. It merely suspended it for the duration of her marriage. Although the statute provided that "any American woman who marries a foreigner shall take the nationality of her husband," it continues, "at the termination of the marital relation, she may *resume*[66] her American citizenship." Warren concluded: "Her citizenship was not taken away, it was held in abeyance."[67]

Frankfurter thought Congress possessed the statutory authority to declare that, if an American citizen performs certain prescribed acts in a voluntary manner—for example, by voting in a foreign election—she can lose her citizenship.[68] Warren thought it was only if you perform an act that objectively means a change in citizenship—such as acquiring a foreign nationality —that it was constitutional to be judged as having lost your citizenship.[69] For Black, however, the threshold was even higher: a person needed to *knowingly* give up American citizenship for it to be lost.[70]

The new Warren draft opinion was stronger, and its conclusions were much clearer than in the initial draft. Rooted in America's founding principles and based on the citizenship clause of the Fourteenth Amendment,[71] Warren was able to anchor his otherwise revolutionary conception of citizenship in the historical jurisprudence of the Supreme Court. Warren's opinion was an important one, but its true significance would not be realized until several years later, because Chief Justice Warren was and would remain in the minority in *Perez*.[72] Ultimately, a majority of justices would endorse the loss of citizenship for voting in a foreign election, based on Congress's authority to manage the nation's foreign affairs.[73]

Yet in *Trop*, foreign relations were not involved. Instead, the principal question was whether deprivations of citizenship upon convictions for desertion during a time of war violated the Eighth Amendment by rendering American citizens stateless.[74] Warren and Black thought they could rally a majority of the justices around the affirmative view.

The application of the Eighth Amendment to the expatriation context was initially suggested in the unsigned *Yale Law Journal* note mentioned above.[75] The unlisted author was, in fact, Stephen Pollak, who was a Yale Law School student when it was published. The article's topic, the Expatriation Act of 1954, which stripped violators of the Smith Act of their nationality, was suggested to Pollak by his professor, Myres S. McDougal. The article required an entire year to complete. Norbert A. Schlei, the editor of the *Yale Law Journal* and, eventually, Harlan's clerk in 1956, provided important editorial work.[76]

In his dissent to the Second Circuit's decision in *Trop*, Chief Judge Clark said he agreed with the *Yale Law Journal* note's "masterful analysis of expatriation legislation," as well as "with the author's documented conclusions therein that punitive expatriation of persons with no other nationality constitutes cruel and unusual punishment and is invalid as such."[77]

In the nineteenth century, the Supreme Court's application of the "cruel and unusual punishment" clause[78] was limited exclusively to the criminal law context as well as to punishments that involved excessive bodily harm.[79] In 1910, for the first time, "cruel and unusual punishment" was extended to cover punishments beyond injury to an individual's person.[80]

To convince a majority of the Court that the *Trop* case involved a violation of the Eighth Amendment, Newman suggested to Warren that he reply to Frankfurter's position by arguing that, although denationalization took the form of a regulatory provision, it was in fact a "punishment." According to the Frankfurter view, denationalization was within the scope of Congress's war power, consistent with a "non-penal" purpose to regulate the military forces, especially in time of war.[81]

So Newman composed a draft for Warren's new opinion:

> In form, at least, the statute is set up to appear to be a regulation of the status of nationality. But surely form alone cannot provide the answer to our inquiry. A statute punishing robbery would not cease to be penal simply because the legislation read, "A person shall lose his liberty by committing robbery." Nor would the statute become a regulation by force of the argument that there is a rational connection between preventing robbery and imprisoning robbers. The inquiry must be directed to substance. . . . It cannot be denied that Congress's power to raise and maintain armies necessarily includes the power to make necessary and proper regulation for the service of soldiers in wartime. . . . But is it a *regulation* of the armed forces to prescribe what consequence will befall one who fails to abide by these regulatory provisions? Plainly legislation prescribing imprisonment for desertion is penal in nature. If loss of nationality is substituted for imprisonment, can it fairly be said that the use of this particular sanction transforms the fundamental nature of the statute?[82]

In the final version of the opinion, in which the later paragraph was minorly amended, Warren added stronger language:[83] "The basic concept underlying the Eighth Amendment is nothing less than the dignity of man. While the State has the power to punish, the Amendment stands to assure that this power be exercised within the limits of civilized standards." And he added: "The provisions of the Constitution are not time-worn adages or hollow shibboleths. They are vital, living principles that authorize and limit governmental powers in our Nation."[84]

On February 8, the redrafted Warren opinion in *Trop* was sent around to at most a few of the justices and, perhaps, only to Black. On February 26, Warren then circulated to several members of the Court—Black, Brennan, Douglas, and Whittaker—a draft amended by Black that would conclude the opinion with a proclamation of the superiority of the civil power over the military power:

> I deny that any power to denationalize may constitutionally be exercised by the military authorities. If the priceless right of citizenship is ever to be forfeited in a trial, it should be in a civilian court of justice, where all the Bill of Rights protections guard the fairness of the outcome. Military courts are to try soldiers for military crimes and impose punishments that do not encroach on purely civilian rights. Who is worthy of continued enjoyment of citizenship is not the constitutional concern of the Army. Its business is to fight wars.[85]

Justice Brennan, who was a deciding vote in both *Perez* and *Trop*—voting with Warren in *Trop* and with Frankfurter in *Perez*—probably asked Warren to suppress the passage proposed by Black. Warren first replaced the Black amendment he had included on February 27 with another paragraph that read: "Guarding against the encroachment of military jurisdiction upon civilian affairs must be a continuing concern of a democratic people. It is with this concern that I approach the constitutional questions raised by a statute that gives the military authorities discretion to send American servicemen back to civilian life stripped of their fundamental right of United States citizenship." But Brennan reacted to this paragraph by scrawling a big "NO!" on the margin and adding that: "It is what Congress has provided not what the military do [*sic*] that brings expatriation about."[86]

In response, the concluding reference to military power was stripped from the opinion.[87] Instead, a new passage, which may have been a suggestive repudiation of the *Korematsu* decision, now figured in a concurring opinion written by Black. In Warren's majority opinion, however, the military references were replaced by international law-related notions suggested by Newman that were not present in the draft circulated on February 26.[88] For Brennan, this would bring some of the conceptual coherence he was looking for. *Perez* was justified in his eyes, in the name of the international regulation of citizenship. *Trop* could be justified too on the same grounds, as statelessness was becoming a great concern internationally, even if this resulted in diverging outcomes for the expatriation defendants: Clemente Perez would lose his American citizenship, and Albert Trop would keep it.

With Whittaker and Brennan's backing, Warren would now deliver the opinion of the court in *Trop*. In response, Frankfurter, who was relegated to the *Trop* dissent, insisted on the duty of the Court to exercise judicial restraint,[89] while in his *Perez* majority opinion he waxed on the authority of Congress to manage foreign affairs. To create some coherence between the Court's decisions, Chief Justice Warren declared in *Trop* that "desertion in wartime, though it may merit the ultimate penalty, does not necessarily signify allegiance to a foreign state. Section 401(g) is not limited to cases of desertion to the enemy, and there is no such element in this case. This soldier committed a crime for which he should be and was punished, but he did not involve himself in any way with a foreign state."[90]

And then, just before the decisions were about to be announced, Warren regained a majority for reversing and remanding the decision to denationalize in the third case before the Court, *Nishikawa*. The government, the Court ruled, had not proven "by clear, convincing and unequivocal evidence" that Nishikawa was voluntarily conscripted and thus had, thus, joined the Japanese Army of his own free will. Interestingly, while *Trop* and *Perez* left Warren and Frankfurter strongly divided, in *Nishikawa* they were not in complete disagreement. Originally, in June 1957, Warren had put together a majority for reversing the lower court's decision to expatriate Mitsugi Nishikawa, and he circulated a draft opinion to the other justices. Yet in November 1957, a shift by Brennan and Whittaker forced Warren, in order to keep a majority, to join Frankfurter's opinion in favor of remanding the case to a lower court for a reassessment of the facts.[91] Warren then assigned to Frankfurter the task of writing the opinion for the Court, and Frankfurter composed his own draft opinion.

But by the end of March 1958, Whittaker changed his mind a second time and Warren, joined also by Black, Douglas again commanded a majority for reversal and remand and decided to write a new opinion himself. Brennan wrote to Frankfurter on March 26, five days before all three cases were announced, stating that he would join Warren. Brennan also encouraged Frankfurter to abandon the latter's opinion in favor of remand as Brennan believed "strongly that there should not be two opinions stating virtually the same rule governing burden of proof."[92] But out of bitterness against not only Warren but also against Brennan,[93] Frankfurter decided to publish a concurring opinion in *Nishikawa* rather than joining Warren's majority.

Explaining his reasons to Brennan, Frankfurter wrote:

> The Chief assigned the writing of the Nishikawa opinion to me. He himself told me that his view and mine are very close together. In so far as they are not, I should suppose that the ordinary course of judicial administration is to ask the fellow who wrote the opinion for the Court to make whatever accommodations others may desire. It does seem odd that the fellow to whom an opinion was assigned and wrote it four months ago should throw his opinion in the wastebasket for another formulation that is deemed to be substantially the same. The Chief Justice, I should suppose, is the last person who should cause the ordinary course of procedure to stand on his head. . . . You may well say that I am personally touchy, and I won't argue the matter except to say that this Court was here before we came and will be, I hope, after every one of us is gone, and I for my part, will discharge what I regard as a post of trusteeship, not least in keeping the Chief Justice in his place, as I am around.[94]

By the time the decisions in the expatriation cases were announced, the atmosphere in the Court had grown noticeably tense. When he delivered his majority opinion in *Trop,* Earl Warren mentioned the eighty-one times the Supreme Court had declared acts of Congress unconstitutional. That, replied Felix Frankfurter, ad libbing in his opinion, was not much to boast about—especially since a good many of those decisions had later been reversed by the Court itself.[95] The Justices' remarks in the courtroom "verged on the bitter, even waspish" noted Anthony Lewis in the *New York Times,* adding that the Court was now "divided in a way reminiscent of the early Nineteen Thirties, when four justices repeatedly stood together in an assertive view of the court's role and invalidated a handful of New Deal statutes."[96] Warren still lacked the majority that he needed to proclaim that expatriation by congressional action was unconstitutional, and the future was uncertain. But with the help of Justice Black and, his talented young clerk, Jon Newman,

Chief Justice Warren was not only able to limit some of the damage posed by the triumvirate of expatriation case,[97] but also able to use them to lay the foundations for a new approach to denationalization. From then on, the "sovereignty of the citizen" formed the basis for a revolution in America's conception of citizenship.

CHAPTER 12

American Citizenship Is Secured:
"May *Perez* Rest in Peace!"

There would be no break in the battle brewing on the Supreme Court. On April 7, 1958, one week after deciding *Trop* and *Perez*, the Court remanded another expatriation case—*Mendoza-Martinez*—for reconsideration in light of *Trop*.[1] Francisco Mendoza-Martinez was born in the United States in 1922 "and therefore acquired American citizenship by birth."[2] Under Mexican law, he was also a Mexican citizen, and in 1942, Mendoza-Martinez moved there in order to avoid serving in the U.S. military during World War II. In November 1946, he returned to the United States, was convicted by a federal court in 1947 of evading the draft, and served the imposed sentence of a year and a day. He remained in the United States without issue until 1953 when he was arrested and ordered deported by the Department of Justice based on a provision in section 401(j) of the Nationality Act of 1940 stripping draft dodgers of their American citizenship.[3]

After the Board of Immigration Appeals rejected his appeal, Mendoza-Martinez filed a new suit asking that a federal court find him to be an American citizen and declare section 401(j) unconstitutional. The court rejected Mendoza-Martinez's suit, but he appealed, eventually reaching the Supreme Court, which, sent the case back down to the district court to be reconsidered in light of the Supreme Court's recent decision in *Trop*. On September 24, 1958, the district court declared on remand that section 401(j) was unconstitutional.[4]

The Mendoza-Martinez case was debated again in conference on December 11, 1959, and six of the justices indicated that they would join an opinion to declare him expatriated. Justice Felix Frankfurter, as the senior member of the majority, assigned the majority opinion to Justice Potter Stewart, who sent around to the other justices a proposed opinion that argued that the military draft was a vital objective in a time of war and evading it should be interpreted as a voluntary expatriation. Justice William Brennan indicated that he would side with the majority in expatriating Mendoza-Martinez, but declined to join the court's opinion, relying instead on Mendoza-Martinez's status as a dual citizen as the basis for expatriation.[5] Meanwhile, Chief Justice Earl Warren, together with Justices William O. Douglas and Hugo Black, strongly opposed the majority's holding. Warren questioned why, if the federal government considered Mendoza a foreigner, it could have him condemned as a draft evader, as foreigners are not subject to the draft.

But Stewart's majority opinion was never issued. Instead, the Court once again sent the case back down to the trial court, this time to consider whether Mendoza-Martinez's conviction for draft evasion—a crime that is only applicable to American citizens—prevented the government from now claiming that Mendoza-Martinez lacked American citizenship. The trial court rejected this argument but also reaffirmed its previous conclusion regarding the unconstitutionality of Section 401(j). The government appealed and, eventually, the case again reached the Supreme Court for a third time.

Brennan had at this point shifted his position to oppose expatriation and now tried to delay what he feared would be an unfavorable decision.[6] On October 5, 1961, Brennan raised with the other justices an issue that he maintained should justify a third remand: could a declaratory judgment that a federal law was unconstitutional be issued by a single judge, as had happened in the *Mendoza-Martinez* case, or was a three-judge panel required? But the rest of the Court declined to send back down a case that they already perceived to have been unduly delayed. By October 13, 1961, a five-justice majority still favored reversal of the lower court decision (Frankfurter, Harlan, Whittaker, Stewart, and Clark), and Stewart was again assigned to write the majority opinion. In January 1962 Stewart circulated another draft which justified the constitutionality of Mendoza-Martinez's expatriation under the war power: Congress had legitimately exercised this power "to recognize an abandonment of citizenship by those who have abandoned this nation to avoid defending it in time of war."[7] But this time Whittaker reacted to the Stewart draft opinion by declaring that he would concur only in the result. He refused to agree with Stewart that war power "authorizes Congress to divest one born in this country of his United States citizenship."[8] But at the end of February, Whittaker fell ill and did not sit again on the Court, ultimately stepping down from the bench on March 31, 1962. In April 1962, *Mendoza-Martinez* was assigned for reargument for the end of that year and consolidated with *Cort*—another expatriation case that had wound its way up to the Supreme Court.

Joseph Cort was born in Boston in 1927 but, unlike Mendoza-Martinez, possessed solely American citizenship.[9] After receiving a medical degree from Yale in 1951, he moved to England to serve as a research fellow at Cambridge University. That same year, he refused to comply with the instructions of the American Embassy in London requesting that he send in his passport so that it could be altered to be "valid only for return to the United States." He had been a member of the Communist Party when he was at Yale and stated that he "did not wish to subject myself to this and similar forms of political persecution then prevalent in the United States."[10]

In 1952, although he was still in England, Cort accepted a position at Harvard Medical School for the following year. Even though Cort was not able to secure a deferment from military, he refused requests from his local draft board that he report for service, and, for this, was indicted under section 12(a) of the Selective Service Act. When the British Home Office refused to renew his residence permit, Cort moved with his American wife and children to Prague, Czechoslovakia, where he worked as a scientist at the Cardiovascular Institute. In April 1959, when Cort applied at the American Embassy in Prague for a new passport, he was informed that he had lost his American citizenship under section 349(a)(10) of the Immigration and Nationality Act of 1952—the successor provision to section 401(j).

By the time the Court met again in December 1962 to decide *Cort* and *Mendoza-Martinez,* former Deputy Attorney General Byron White had replaced Whittaker. But Whittaker's seat was not the only change to the Court's composition. Frankfurter suffered a stroke, and he resigned on August 28, 1962. He was replaced by Arthur Goldberg, President Kennedy's Secretary of Labor. At a December 1962 conference following reargument, White supported upholding the constitutionality of 401(j). Goldberg, on the other hand, opposed it, shifting the majority to favor striking it down.[11] Warren assigned the opinion to Goldberg, who delivered it in the name of this new majority.

"Goldberg had a very different view of the law and the process than Frankfurter," explained Peter Edelman, Goldberg's clerk the year that Mendoza-Martinez was decided, "He thought the purpose of the Court was to do justice. Legal theories were tools to find . . . justice. He came up with the due process idea that was involved in this case."[12] Goldberg asked Edelman to write a draft on this basis, and the two of them worked paragraph-by-paragraph to produce the majority opinion. On February 18, 1963, the Court issued a single decision in *Mendoza-Martinez* and in *Cort*,[13] declaring unconstitutional section 401(j) of the Nationality Act of 1940 and section 349(a)(10) of the Immigration and Nationality Act of 1952.[14] The penalty of denationalization "cannot be imposed without a prior criminal trial and all its incidents, including indictment, notice, confrontation, jury trial, assistance of counsel, and compulsory process for obtaining witnesses."[15]

Even if Goldberg's "mediating way" had adjourned the "apocalyptic debate" between "the ultimates of judicial assertion or denial of governmental power,"[16] it was clear that the practice of forced expatriation was losing ground. In a concurring opinion written on the day's two cases, Justice Brennan asserted that, "Congress is constitutionally debarred from so employing the drastic, the truly terrifying remedy of expatriation, certainly where no attempt has been made to apply the full panoply of protective safeguards which the Constitution requires as a condition of imposing penal sanctions." Perhaps even more significantly, he expressed "some felt doubts of the correctness of *Perez*, which I joined."[17] Picking up on his equivocation, the *Washington Post* added that Brennan's doubts "may be resolved in favor of a higher regard the rights of nationality in the constitutional scale when a comparable issue arises in the future."[18]

But the triumph of Warren and Black's expatriation position would not advance free from any setbacks. Just a few months after it issued its judgment in *Mendoza-Martinez*, the Court heard the case of Angelika L. Schneider,[19] which brought the Supreme Court face-to-face with the country's oldest denaturalization provision, on the books since 1906. The Court would now get to consider whether the United States could strip the citizenship of a naturalized American citizen who moved back to her country of origin.

Angelika Schneider was a twenty-nine-year-old native of Germany. She had immigrated to the United States as a five-year-old, and when Schneider turned sixteen she and her mother were naturalized. After earning a degree at Smith College, she won a scholarship to study abroad in Paris, where in 1956 she met a German lawyer, whom she married and, afterward, lived with in Cologne, Germany. In 1959, the U.S. consulate refused to issue Schneider an American passport on the grounds that she was no longer a citizen and requested that she surrender her naturalization certificate, which she did under protest.[20] She received the status of stateless in Germany, where she was still living.[21]

After an initial set of appeals ultimately brought Schneider's case to the

Supreme Court in 1963, the Court remanded it to a three-judge panel on the federal district court in Washington, D.C.[22] Judge Charles Fahy, the former solicitor general who had argued in 1943 in favor of the denaturalization of William Schneiderman, now found himself in the minority, pleading vigorously for the unconstitutionality of the provision authorizing the denaturalization of naturalized American citizens who moved abroad. In his opinion, Fahy agreed with Schneider's arguments that the law discriminated against naturalized citizens, noting that "no comparable choice is required of a national born on American soil who lives abroad in like circumstances."[23]

Judge Fahy distinguished Angelika Schneider's background from the plaintiff in *Perez*. In the latter case, the Supreme Court found that dual citizens who participated in foreign elections manifested "some elements of an allegiance to another country."[24] But Schneider was not accused of being a draft dodger—like Joseph Cort or Francisco Mendoza-Martinez—or a military deserter—like Albert Trop. Her only offense was to have met and married a man making his living in Germany. This, unfairly, Fahy maintained, "put [Schneider] in the choice of abandoning either her husband or her nationality."[25] Nevertheless, the majority of the panel upheld the denaturalization, relying primarily on the *Perez* case: Congress possessed the authority to pass legislation whose aim it is to avoid "embarrassment and controversies in the relations between the United States with other Countries."[26]

Schneider successfully petitioned for certiorari to the Supreme Court. One year later, on May 1, 1964, the Court held unconstitutional the statute providing for loss of citizenship by naturalized Americans for residing in a foreign country. Justice Douglas, who delivered the opinion of the Court, noted that "a native-born citizen is free to reside abroad indefinitely without suffering loss of citizenship." By contrast, "The discrimination aimed at naturalized citizens drastically limits their rights to live and work abroad in a way that other citizens may. It creates indeed a second-class citizenship." This distinction, Douglas maintained, was untenable: "Living abroad, whether the citizen be naturalized or native born, is no badge of lack of allegiance, and in no way evidences a voluntary renunciation of nationality and allegiance. It may indeed be compelled by family, business, or other legitimate reasons."[27] Douglas concluded that this provision was contrary to the Fifth Amendment, which forbids discrimination that is "so unjustifiable as to be violative of due process."[28]

The significance of the Court's decision in *Schneider* is hard to overstate. Residence in the country of origin in the five years following the naturalizations had served as the basis for the majority of denaturalizations since 1906—in all, approximately 14,000 of the 22,000 Americans denaturalized in the twentieth century. In addition, under section 404 of the Nationality Act of 1940, 23,366 new Americans lost their citizenship for residing three or even two years in their country of origin or five years in any other foreign countries, any time after their naturalization.[29] It had been declared unconstitutional. The impact was both immediate and concrete: in 1963 a total of 1,089 naturalized Americans lost their citizenship for living in the nation of their birth or of their former nationality; in 1964 the number decreased to 618; and by 1965 it became zero.

But on the same day that it decided *Schneider*, in a different case an evenly split Supreme Court confirmed the loss of American citizenship for an American man who had joined pro-Castro forces in Cuba, effectively rendering him stateless.[30]

Herman F. Marks was an American citizen born in 1921 in Milwaukee, Wisconsin. In 1958, he traveled to Cuba and "joined Fidel Castro's revolutionary forces fighting in the Sierra Maestra Mountains to overthrow the government of Fulgencio Batista."[31] After a break of two months in Florida following the revolution's January 1959 triumph, Marks returned to Cuba to serve as a captain in Castro's army. In May 1960 Marks quit Cuba entering the United States again in July. In January of the following year, he was arrested by the INS, and the Justice Department commenced his deportation proceedings, arguing that, by serving voluntarily in a foreign army, Marks had given up his citizenship. The Board of Immigration Appeals upheld Marks's deportation.[32] But Marks filed a separate suit in federal court, and the U.S. District Court for the Southern District of New York granted his habeas corpus petition. On cross appeals, the Second Circuit Court decided to reverse the judgment of the district court and confirmed the government's position that Marks had indeed surrendered his American citizenship.[33]

The *Marks v. Esperdy* case divided the Supreme Court. In conference Brennan provided the all-important fifth vote for reversing the Second Circuit but admitted to his fellow justices that he was not "sure how he will finally retreat from *Perez*."[34] In the end, however, Brennan's vote would be irrelevant: due to a late-discovered conflict of interest, Brennan declined to participate in the *Schneider* and *Marks* cases.[35] This left the Court with four justices in favor of upholding the deportation of Herman Marks, with another four opposed. The effect of the dead-center split was to affirm the Second Circuit's finding that Marks had renounced his citizenship—without creating any precedent that might bind the Court in future cases.

The government argued to the Court that serving in a foreign army is "an outward manifestation of allegiance to the foreign state." Marks, on the other hand, responded that "he never renounced or intended to renounce his American citizenship" and, additionally, that denationalization leading to statelessness is precisely the same form of cruel and unusual punishment that the Court condemned in *Trop*.[36] Yet, as Justice Tom C. Clark noted, unlike *Trop*, the *Marks* case implicated foreign affairs and, therefore, Congress was justified in intervening.[37]

But despite these thin logical distinctions, to many the Court's expatriation jurisprudence appeared to be confusing, relying on reasoning that was strained at best and contradictory at worst. In 1958, Albert Trop's American citizenship was saved because, despite his desertion of the army (for twenty-four hours), statelessness was considered a cruel and unusual punishment and thereby contrary to the Eighth Amendment. But only six years later, Herman was not permitted to retain his citizenship even though, like Albert Trop, the consequence of denationalization would be statelessness. In 1958 the Court determined that Clemente Perez, a dual citizen who voted in foreign elections, could be deprived of his American citizenship on the basis of Congress' authority over foreign affairs. But in *Schneider v. Rusk*, the Court limited the congressional expatriation authority in instances when statutes treated native-born and naturalized Americans differently. Noting "the lack of continuity in the Court's opinion" in expatriation cases, Philip Kurland mockingly wrote in his review of the Supreme Court's 1963 term for the *Harvard Law Review*, "I[t] would be interesting to know what the 'law of the land' is on the subject of expatriation."[38]

The contradictions between the *Trop* and *Marks* decisions cast doubt on the relevance of the Eighth Amendment to expatriation and obscured the reasoning behind the Court's progression of decisions. As Black would soon write, "Since *Perez*, this Court has consistently invalidated on a case-by-case basis various other statutory sections providing for involuntary expatriation." Yet the Court acted without "finding it necessary to confront the fundamental issue of whether Congress can constitutionally deprive a person of his citizenship against his will."[39] Black's position had remained unchanged since *Nishikawa*. In *Mendoza-Martinez*, even while the majority sided with the Francisco Mendoza-Martinez on narrow due process grounds, Black continued to argue that the expatriation of individuals in his position ran contrary to the Fourteenth Amendment.[40] The Court finally reached this conclusion three years later, in *Afroyim v. Rusk*,[41] when it reconsidered its holding in *Perez*.[42]

Beys Afroyim was a Jewish painter who was born in Poland in 1893. He emigrated to the United States in 1912 and was naturalized as an American in 1925. Twenty-five years later, in 1950, Afroyim left the United States for Israel and, the following year, voted in an election for the Israeli Knesset.[43] In 1960 Afroyim decided to return to the United States, but the State Department refused to renew his passport, according to the same provision of the 1940 Nationality Act that the Supreme Court upheld in *Perez*.[44] Afroyim contested the State Department's decision, but his position was rejected by both the trial court and the court of appeal.[45]

The Supreme Court remained as divided as ever over the extent of the elected branches' expatriation power—but the Court's 5-4 majority in *Perez* was now flipped. Brennan's ideological change of heart and the Court's new composition proved essential to this shift. The triumvirate of stalwarts— Black, Warren, and Douglas—were joined by Brennan who was now able to complete the shift to the anti-expatriation camp that had previously been stalled by his recusals in *Mendoza-Martinez* and *Schneider*. Meanwhile, Frankfurter's replacement Arthur Goldberg had joined Warren's group in *Mendoza-Martinez*, writing the majority opinion in that case, only to be replaced himself by Abe Fortas.[46] But Abe Fortas took up Goldberg's mantle on the expatriation cases and provided the necessary fifth vote for overturning *Perez*.

On May 29, 1967, the Court announced the *Afroyim* decision. Writing for the majority, Justice Black proclaimed, "The Constitution, of course, grants Congress no express power to strip people of their citizenship, whether, in the exercise of the implied power to regulate foreign affairs or in the exercise of any specifically granted power."[47] Black's reasoning relied in part on the concept of "citizen sovereignty" that had previously been articulated by Warren in *Trop*: "In our country the people are sovereign and the Government cannot sever its relationship to the people by taking away their citizenship. Our Constitution governs us and we must never forget that our Constitution limits the Government to those powers specifically granted or those that are necessary and proper to carry out the specifically granted ones."[48]

Black couched his interpretation of the proper relationship between the sovereignty of the American people, on the one hand, and Congressional authority, on the other, largely in the language of the Fourteenth Amendment.

Although Black believed history bore out his views, he conceded that prior "legislative and judicial statements may be regarded as inconclusive" with respect to the expatriation power.[49] However, "the unequivocal terms of the Amendment itself" left little room for doubt. As Black explained, the citizenship clause "provides its own constitutional rule in language calculated completely to control the status of citizenship: 'All persons born or naturalized in the United States . . . are citizens of the United States.'" The significance of Black's statement in *Afroyim* that "Our holding, we think, is the only one that can stand in view of the language and the purpose of the Fourteenth Amendment" is perhaps best illuminated by an unpublished draft of Black's *Nishikawa* opinion:

> Section 1 of the Fourteenth Amendment that confers citizenship and narrows a person born here with citizenship also provides that "no state shall make or enforce any law which shall abridge the privileges or immunities of citizens of the United States; nor shall any state deprive any person of life, liberty or property without due process of law." The first of these two clauses plainly makes privileges and immunities of United States citizenship free from abridgment by a state. The Amendment then goes on to recognize a power in states to deprive all persons including citizens of "life, liberty or property" if they are afforded "due process of law." But even if afforded due process of law the state is granted no power under the fourteenth amendment to "deprive any person" of the citizenship granted by the Fourteenth Amendment.[50]

Unlike the Fourteenth Amendment's due process clause, which permits life, liberty, or property to be deprived as long as the government follows a certain set of procedures, Black believed the language of the citizenship clause gave absolute protection to the basic right of citizenship.[51]

Black concluded his opinion forcefully and by building on Warren's *Perez* dissent and the Court's prior precedent in *Trop*:

> Citizenship is no light trifle to be jeopardized any moment Congress decides to do so under the name of one of its general or implied grants of power. In some instances, loss of citizenship can mean that a man is left without the protection of citizenship in any country in the world—as a man without a country. Citizenship in this nation is a

part of a cooperative affair. Its citizenry is the country, and the country is its citizenry. The very nature of our free government makes it completely incongruous to have a rule of law under which a group of citizens temporarily in office can deprive another group of citizens of their citizenship. We hold that the Fourteenth Amendment was designed to, and does, protect every citizen of this Nation against a congressional forcible destruction of his citizenship, whatever his creed, color, or race. Our holding does no more than to give to this citizen that which is his own, a constitutional right to remain a citizen in a free country unless he voluntarily relinquishes that citizenship. *Perez v. Brownell* is overruled. The judgment is *Reversed.*[52]

At long last, *Perez* and its expansive interpretation of the expatriation power were no more. But the preceding nine years of battles over cases like *Schneider* and *Marks* had only enlarged the determination of the judicial opponents of expatriation. The solidification of the Warren-Black position was reflected in the *Afroyim* holding, which was, in the end, even more protective of American citizenship than Warren had been in his *Perez* dissent. Whereas Warren conceded in *Perez* that performing an act that objectively signified a change in citizenship—such as naturalization in a foreign nation—was a sufficient basis for losing American citizenship, Black's opinion on behalf of the court in *Afroyim* required that an individual voluntarily relinquish American citizenship.

For the five justices in the *Afroyim* majority, at least, the atmosphere on the Court was triumphant. Nine years after his vote in *Perez*, Brennan had Black remind readers in a footnote that in his concurring opinion in *Kennedy v. Mendoza* in 1962, Brennan had already expressed "felt doubts of the correctness of Perez."[53] Later, Brennan congratulated Black for "a really magnificent opinion." Chief Justice Warren gloated over the imminent *Afroyim* decision. On April 13, 1967, he sent a note to Justice Black to tell him he agreed with his opinion in the case. At the end of this note, he typed the epitaph, "May *Perez* rest in peace!"[54]

Conclusion

The *Afroyim* decision marked Chief Justice Earl Warren's victory in an expatriation battle that had lasted almost ten years. But Warren's legacy would fall on the shoulders of Justices Hugo Black and William Brennan—an increasingly unlikely set of allies—to resist a spirited set of challenges.

In 1968 Warren decided to resign before the end of President Lyndon Johnson's term so that Johnson could name his successor. But Johnson's nominee, Abe Fortas, who had served on the Court as an associate justice since 1965,[1] failed to win Senate approval, and it fell to President Richard Nixon to choose the next chief justice. His choice, Warren Burger, took office on June 23, 1969. Burger had only been on the Court for a few months when it first considered on direct appeal the expatriation case of Aldo Bellei.[2] Bellei was born in Italy in 1939 to an American mother and an Italian father and was a dual citizen of both countries. In order to preserve his American citizenship under the laws then in effect, Bellei was required to satisfy a five-year continuous residency requirement between the ages of fourteen and twenty-eight. But Bellei, who was raised in Italy and spent time only intermittently in the United States, had not done so. When he applied for an American passport in 1966, he was notified by the American consul in Rome that he had lost his U.S. citizenship according to Section 301(b) of the Immigration and Nationality Act of 1952. Bellei filed suit in response, requesting that the court invalidate Section 301(b) and declare him an American citizen. In 1969, a three-judge district court panel sustained Bellei's claims and, citing *Afroyim v. Rusk* and *Schneider v. Rusk*, held his expatriation to be unconstitutional.[3]

The government appealed directly to the Supreme Court, and the case was heard on oral arguments on January 15, 1970. In conference, Black found himself as part of a five-to-three majority favoring the view that Bellei had been properly deprived of his American citizenship, and Burger assigned him the opinion.[4] But a few weeks later, Black wrote to his colleagues that "the difficulty of the task of a reversal finally appeared to me to be insurmountable." Black ultimately decided to write a memo arguing the opposite position, leaving the Court equally divided.[5] The case was reargued on November 12, 1970, and the opinion was assigned to Harry Blackmun, who had just joined the Court to fill Abe Fortas' vacant seat after the latter's retirement following a scuttled chief justice nomination and ethics scandal. In a memo composed a few days before the case was reargued, Blackmun stated his inclination for overturning the Court's *Afroyim* and *Schneider* holdings: "I would like to be able to reverse. The two cases, however, give me great difficulty. I am not at all sure that they are correctly decided. Yet, there they stand. I shall necessarily be interested in Mr. Justice Harlan's reaction to this."[6]

But, although John M. Harlan's sympathies lay with the majority, he had already expressed his distaste with using the *Bellei* case as a vehicle for overturning *Afroyim*. Harlan's jurisprudential philosophy was to follow precedents,[7] and he felt "bound to bow"[8] to even to those "he most disapproved."[9] As a result, Harlan sought to ensure that his vote was "wholly consistent with bowing to the basic holding in *Afroyim*."[10] This meant that Blackmun lacked the majority necessary for reversing *Afroyim*. But, as a consolation, he was able to muster five votes in favor of reading it narrowly, effectively restricting the protections offered by the citizenship clause of the Fourteenth Amendment.

In response, Black asserted that the term *naturalization* as it was used in the first sentence of the Fourteenth Amendment should be construed to include American citizens born abroad and, furthermore, that Bellei had never voluntarily relinquished his citizenship.[11] Black was defeated on that point. Bellei would lose his American citizenship, but the decision would *not* reverse of *Afroyim*.

Thus, Blackmun's opinion for the majority in *Bellei*, finally decided on April 5, 1971, could be seen as a reaffirmation of *Afroyim* construction of the Fourteenth Amendment. But, at the same time, the decision excluded American born outside of the physical borders of the United States from the Fourteenth Amendment's benefits and protections:

> The central fact, in our weighing of the plaintiff's continuing and therefore current United States citizenship, is that he was born abroad. He was not born in the United States. He was not naturalized in the United States. And he has not been subject to the jurisdiction of the United States. All this being so, it seems indisputable that the first sentence of the Fourteenth Amendment has no application to plaintiff Bellei. He simply is not a Fourteenth-Amendment-first-sentence

citizen. His posture contrasts with that of Mr. Afroyim, who was naturalized in the United States, and with that of Mrs. Schneider, whose
citizenship was derivative by her presence here and by her mother's
naturalization here.[12]

The Court under new Chief Justice Burger had worked, as noted scholar
of constitutional law Gerald Gunther immediately comprehended, with no
"inclination to overturn clear, carefully explained precedent," but simply to
narrow its reading.[13] Later, in *Vance v. Terrazas* (1980), the Court again confirmed—unanimously, this time—the key holding of *Afroyim v. Rusk* that
Fourteenth Amendment citizenship was safeguarded and could not be taken
away, though an act of Congress, from a person who did not desire to give it
up.[14]

Nevertheless for a few years, uncertainty existed about what exactly was
meant by a "voluntary" relinquishment of one's citizenship.[15] Congress decided in the 1986 Immigration Reform and Control Act that an American
would lose his citizenship only "by voluntarily performing" some acts like obtaining naturalization in a foreign state upon his own application or serving
in the armed forces of a foreign state engaged in hostilities against the United
States "with the intention of relinquishing" his United States nationality.[16]
And in 1990 the State Department declared that individuals will be presumed
to intend to retain U.S. citizenship even when they obtain naturalization in a
foreign state or accept a "non policy level employment with a foreign government."[17] From then on denationalization could only result from the express
will of an American citizen.

The story of denaturalization, which can still be imposed even today, is a
little different.[18] Although its use has been substantially reduced, since 1967
denaturalization is still available on two basic grounds.[19]

The first of these grounds applies to individuals who have committed
gross violations of human rights. In 1979, the U.S. government created an Office of Special Investigation (OSI) in the Department of Justice whose task it
was to deport, often after their denaturalization, formerly naturalized Americans who had not disclosed their Nazi past when applying for citizenship. Between 1979 and 2012, the OSI and its successor the Human Rights and Special
Prosecutions Section,[20] pursued the denaturalization or deportation of 137
individuals on the basis of participation in Nazi-sponsored acts of persecution. 86 such persons have been denaturalized (the last one in 2007) and 67
have been removed.[21]

In contrast to judicial skepticism of expatriation in the 1960s and 1970s, courts have not challenged the authority of the government to denaturalize individuals responsible for committing human rights violations. In *Fedorenko v. United States*, the Supreme Court backed the government in the denaturalization of a man who had willfully misrepresented his past as a concentration camp guard when trying to gain admission into the United States as an "eligible displaced person."[22] Yet in *Kungys v. United States*,[23] the Court refused to uphold the denaturalization a man because the government had not shown that Juozas Kungys's lies concerning the date and place of his birth were facts that, if known, would have warranted denial of citizenship.[24]

In 2004, the competence of the Office of Special Investigation was extended beyond the Nazis to include naturalized Americans who participated in acts of genocide, torture or extrajudicial killings anywhere in the world.[25] Jadranko Gostic, a Serbian American, was stripped of his U.S. citizenship and deported to Serbia in May 2010 for hiding his role the 1995 Srebrenica massacre.[26] In September 2010 Gilberto Jordan, a former Guatemalan soldier, was stripped of his American citizenship and sentenced to ten years in prison in the United States for concealing his participation in the 1982 massacre of at least 162 villagers during the Guatemalan civil war.[27] Nowadays, denaturalization is largely a tool for targeting the perpetrators of crimes against humanity.

The second modern ground for denaturalization is for fraud or misrepresentation committed during the naturalization process. But even this justification for denaturalization is employed only rarely. When the Immigration Act of 1990 transferred the power to naturalize from the courts to the attorney general, another provision of the same act transferred to the attorney general the power "to correct, reopen, alter, modify, or vacate an order naturalizing the person."[28] But in 2000 the Ninth Circuit Court of Appeals in *Gorbach v. Reno* affirmed the exclusive statutory competence of the judiciary to revoke American citizenship. Since this decision, the secretary of the Department of Homeland Security, which took over naturalization responsibilities from the Department of Justice, has not attempted to resume the use of this administrative denaturalization.

Very recently, only a few dozen naturalized Americans have lost their citizenship, largely because they committed various types of fraud during the naturalization process.[29] The numbers speak for themselves: between 1907 and 1967, a total of 22,000 denaturalizations were concluded. Since 1968, there have been fewer than 150. There were as many as a thousand denaturalizations in some years during the 1930s, but denaturalization has been

imposed on fewer than a half-dozen people per year since 1968, many for
having camouflaged crimes against humanity prior to their immigration to
the United States. Although denaturalization has largely become a thing of
the past, it retains an important symbolic function: all naturalized citizens are
secure in America except those who have committed the very worst crimes
against their fellow human beings.

Even while America's practice of expatriation on a massive scale fades into
history, the Supreme Court's expatriation decisions continue to be critically
relevant to a number of issues of contemporary significance, including the
rights of Americans suspected of committing acts of terror to their citizenship and—even more pertinent at the current moment—the debate on the
constitutional status of the children of undocumented immigrants. In 1982,
Justice Brennan asserted in footnote 10 of his opinion for the Court in *Plyler
v. Doe*[30] that "no plausible distinction with respect to Fourteenth Amendment 'jurisdiction' can be drawn between resident aliens whose entry into
the United States was lawful, and resident aliens whose entry was unlawful."
Professor Peter Schuck, an advocate of an interpretation of the Fourteenth
Amendment that would permit Congress to limit the right of children born
in the United States to undocumented parents to become American citizens,[31] recently argued in a *New York Times* op-ed column that the Supreme
Court has never, except in this "brief 1982 footnote" mentioned above, asserted "that the American-born children of illegal immigrants were constitutional citizens."[32]

But the *Plyler* footnote may be more strongly embedded in the Supreme
Court's historical jurisprudence than Schuck leads one to believe.[33] Brennan
opened the footnote by glancing backward: "Although we have not previously
focused on the intended meaning of this phrase, we have had occasion to examine the first sentence of the Fourteenth Amendment, which provides that
'[a]ll persons born or naturalized in the United States, and *subject to the jurisdiction thereof*, are citizens of the United States'" (emphasis added). Brennan
then recalled Justice Horace Gray's lengthy discussion in *United States v. Wong
Kim Ark* of the history of the citizenship clause and of the "predominantly
geographic sense in which the term 'jurisdiction' was used" in the Fourteenth
Amendment.[34] In other words, according to Brennan (and to Justice Gray),
by being born within the territorial boundaries of the United States, even the
children of undocumented immigrants meet the requirements of geographic
jurisdiction. Thus, the historical development of the Fourteenth Amendment

does not permit the government to distinguish between the American-born children of resident aliens whose entry into the United States was lawful and those of resident aliens whose entry was unlawful.

Justice Brennan declined to develop the other part of the footnote's introductory sentence where he asserts, "We have had occasion to examine the first sentence of the Fourteenth Amendment." Nevertheless, Brennan's decades-long involvement in cases and debates concerning the constitutionality of expatriation might provide some clues as to his meaning. During the early part of his long career as a jurist, Brennan opposed using the citizenship clause to protect American-born citizens from involuntary expatriation. Indeed, it was this position that forced Warren into the minority in *Perez v. Brownell* in 1958. But prior chapters chronicled the shift in Brennan's views of expatriation. Many years, after it occurred, he would later call his vote in *Perez* "the biggest mistake of his entire tenure."[35] Yet Brennan would have the opportunity to correct his error. In 1963, five years after *Perez*, Brennan would announce in chambers his support of Warren and Black in *Kennedy v. Mendoza-Martinez* to oppose the denationalization of a U.S. citizen who fled the country to avoid the draft. Although Brennan was ultimately forced to recuse himself in *Schneider v. Rusk* and *Marks v. Esperdy*, this would only delay the eventual triumph of Black and Warren's position until the three justices could join together in the *Afroyim* majority just a few short years later.

Having cast votes during the span of his term from 1956 to 1980 on both sides of cases dealing with the constitutionality of expatriation, Brennan was well aware that many of the defendants were born in the United States to foreign parents: *Gonzales* in 1955 (decided just before Brennan became an associate justice) as well as *Nishikawa* and *Perez* in 1958 and *Mendoza-Martinez* in 1962 (all decided after his elevation to the bench). These cases were among the Court's most divisive and, as this book has shown, each spurred a fierce debate between opposing camps of justices.

Surely, then, if the justices vigorously opposed to placing limits on the government's twin powers of denaturalization and expatriation believed that the words "subject to the jurisdiction thereof" might possibly limit the protections afforded by the citizenship clause to the children of undocumented immigrants, they would have raised this position at least once during oral arguments and in their opinions. But none ever did.

In *Perez v. Brownell*,[36] Felix Frankfurter delivered the opinion of the Court, which he began by recounting Clemente Perez's history: "Petitioner was born in Texas in 1909. He resided in the United States until 1919 or 1920, when he

moved with his parents to Mexico, where he lived, apparently without inter-
ruption, until 1943. In 1928, he was informed that he had been born in Texas.
At the outbreak of World War II, petitioner knew of the duty of male United
States citizens to register for the draft, but he failed to do so."[37] Frankfurter
made no mention of the relevance of Perez's parents' immigration status to
Perez's own citizenship. And, notably, in his dissent Chief Justice Warren asserted that "United States citizenship is thus the constitutional birth-right of
every person born in this country."[38]

In *Nishikawa*, Warren wrote on behalf of the majority: "Petitioner was a
native-born citizen of the United States and he was considered by Japan to
be a citizen of that country because his parents were Japanese citizens."[39] In
the same case, Frankfurter begins his concurring opinion: "this case involves
a native-born citizen of Japanese parentage who has been declared to have
lost his citizenship by virtue of §401(c) of the Nationality Act of 1940."[40] Four
years after *Nishikawa* and *Perez*, in *Mendoza-Martinez*, Justice Arthur Goldberg delivered the opinion of the Court, which began: "Mendoza-Martinez,
the appellee in No. 2, was born in this country in 1922, and therefore acquired
American citizenship by birth."[41]

The legality of parental residence status was never raised as an issue either in majority or in dissenting opinions despite numerous opportunities
presented to the different Justices. Implicitly if not explicitly, the Supreme
Court unanimously recognized that being born in the United States meant
being American, independently of the status an American-born individual's
parents. Brennan knew the facts surrounding all these cases and participated
in the deciding of most of them. They still were surely in his memory when
he drafted *Plyler* footnote 10 and extended Justice Gray reasoning in *United
States v. Wong Kim Ark* to the children of undocumented immigrants.[42]

In his memoirs, Earl Warren described the differences between the political
process that he was familiar with as the governor of California from 1943 to
1953 and the judicial process that he came to run as Chief Justice. Politics
was for Warren the "art of the possible," where "progress could be made and
most often was made by compromising and taking half of the loaf when the
whole loaf could not be obtained."[43] The opposite is true, Warren writes, for
the judicial process, particularly on the Supreme Court. Through it, "the basic
decision is principle, and should not be compromised and parceled out, a
little in one case, a little more in another, until eventually someone receives
the full benefit." Rather, "If the principle is sound and constitutional, it is the

birth-right of every American, not to be accorded begrudgingly or piecemeal to special groups only, but to everyone in its entirety whenever it is brought into play."[44]

To the specter of expatriation that cast a pall shadow over a great many American citizens, the United States Supreme Court, under Warren's leadership, responded by embracing the innovative concept of citizen sovereignty. Nowhere else in the democratic world has a court of law defined so smartly and with such novelty the complexity of the link between the individual and the nation-state. The right to have rights, of which Emma Goldman and Hannah Arendt both spoke of from their position of statelessness, requires governments both to take care of the stateless and to prevent the creation of additional stateless people. But citizen sovereignty goes further than this by protecting citizens from unwilling expatriation even if they also possess another nationality. The Supreme Court has understood and reinforced the dual nature of citizenship: it is both a club that limits entrance from outsiders and a public good that places no inherent limits to the secured rights of its members.[45]

But, even if the American approach was ultimately unique, the Supreme Court wrestled with the rights of American citizens against the backdrop of a worldwide movement to shape and define a set of international citizenship rights. In 1948 the founders of the United Nations drafted the Universal Declaration of Human Rights, which recognized that everyone has the right to a nationality.[46] The international approach to citizenship issues was refined further when the Convention Relating to the Status of Stateless Persons and the Convention on the Reduction of Statelessness were adopted in 1954 and 1961, respectively. These international efforts to prevent statelessness were rooted in an understanding that citizenship guarantees the right to have other rights. As many nations have reduced through domestic laws or international conventions[47] the risk of losing one's nationality by marriage or forced denationalization, the protections afforded through the idea that citizens are themselves sovereign has expanded well beyond the jurisprudence of Supreme Court and the borders of the United States.

For all of the benefits of this reconceptualization of citizenship, some have questioned: is this approach, and its favouring of multiple citizenships, ultimately a dangerous one? Legal scholar Peter Spiro, for instance, has warned that the acceptance of multiple citizenship implied in Warren's dissent in *Perez* and Black's majority opinion in *Afroyim* have caused a decline in attachment to a unique national citizenship.[48]

Multiple citizenships have increased not only in the United States but also throughout much of the world. In a sense, then, the Supreme Court's monumental decision in *Afroyim* was as much a product of global social changes as it was the cause of a changing understanding of citizenship. For instance, as we have seen, in the early part of the twentieth century American women who married foreign men were losing their citizenship. But laws— in the United States and in other countries—that provided women and men with different rights to possess citizenship became increasingly untenable in the face of movements advocating for gender equality.[49] Now, in most countries, a woman who marries a man of another nationality no longer loses her nationality; she transmits it to her children, just as her husband does.

While multiple citizenship may be a relatively recent accepted in the United States, in many countries it has older roots. Since the beginning of the twentieth century France and the United Kingdom have been indifferent to the multiple citizenship status of their naturalized citizens. For them, it was a matter of sovereignty, in its old meaning, an attribute of the state. As a French minister of justice put it in 1915, "our law cannot bow before foreign legislation and give up viewing as French those individuals upon whom it has deemed it appropriate and in our interest to confer this title every time it pleases foreign law to keep them in bonds of allegiance."[50] But for France and the United Kingdom, this stance reflected also the confidence of these states in the capacity of their bodies politic to attract and integrate new citizens.

In the nineteenth and early twentieth centuries, the United States was a fledgling nation, uncertain around more established European powers, and still dependent on immigration and naturalization to develop and occupy vast and underpopulated lands. In these earlier decades, American institutions were young, perceived as fragile, and thought to be imperiled by ideologies or ethnicities construed or constructed as foreign. But the time where exclusion and expulsion, together with legally enforceable domestic segregation, were the laws of the land is now past.

It was also this message that the Warren Court wanted to transmit, its strong confidence in the United States. When the Court chose to protect American citizens against the actions by an increasingly federalized government, it was also betting that a state that guarantees basic and fundamental rights to its citizens is more likely that one that acts primarily through threats and punishment to secure the attachment and fidelity of the modern citizen.[51] By saying to each American that, as a citizen you are a part of the sovereign, independent of your age and your country of origin, the Supreme Court provoked a silent revolution in the relationship between the American people and their government. By tracing the stories of the engineers of America's de-naturalization machinery, by following the journeys of those threatened with loss of citizenship, and by detailing the thirty-year battle of ideas between the Supreme Court justices who eventually rejected contingent citizenship, this book has sought to describe the tremendous impact that the practice of expatriation has had, through the years, on the development and transformation of American citizenship.

APPENDIX 1

A Woman Without a Country

This version was published in *Mother Earth* 4, no. 3 (May 1909).

The United States government in a mad chase after Emma Goldman.

What a significant title for a funny story. What rich material for a cartoon!

By the decision of the Federal government, Emma Goldman, the terrible, may now be deported. Well, serves her right. What on earth made her select our dear country, anyway? It's different with us Americans. We are here through no fault of ours. But for her to come voluntarily, to live here twenty-five years, and to go on as if she were at home—that is strong, indeed.

What didn't our government do to get rid of her?! For seventeen years the police have camped on her trail; her meetings were broken up; her audiences clubbed innumerable times, but that didn't seem to help. Then she was arrested again and again—not for what she did but for what she was going to say. Why, she was actually sentenced to Blackwell's Island penitentiary once, for inciting to riot which didn't take place, but which might have taken place. Well, what happened? When she came out, she was worse than ever. In 1901 she was held under twenty thousand dollar bail, while our poor government spent thirty thousand dollars to connect her with McKinley's death. In short, every conceivable method was used to relieve the anxiety of the United States government. But that woman simply sticks and sticks. However, if there is anything Uncle Sam cannot do, we should like to know it. Hasn't he men in the secret service patriotic enough to do any kind of dirty job for money? Well, we sent some of them to a city called Rochester, where, many years ago, a man had the misfortune to marry that there Emma Goldman. He was a good man, you know; for no American citizen can be a very bad man. But the marriage was a blotch on his citizenship. So, out of Christian kindness and American loyalty, his naturalization papers were annulled. Wasn't that a clever idea? Of course, it cost quite a lot. Some people in Rochester had to be cajoled, intimidated, threatened, frightened, and possibly bribed. But it was done all right, and the country might now breath easy if—but there is Emma Goldman, still enjoying *our* air, looking at *our* sky, counting *our* stars, basking in *our* sun and dreaming un-American dreams,—can there be a greater indictment against any human being? Not enough of that, she actually disbelieves in our or any government, and insists that they are only here to divide human interest. She attacks the entire system; she will have it that it is a life-and-soul-destroying mechanism, and that it strips man of the finest and best in him. Did anyone ever hear of such treason?

Were she an American citizen, we might some day hang or electrocute her. But an alien—what's left for us to do but to deport her. The trouble is, where, oh where can we send her?

Poor, poor United States Government! Yours is, indeed a difficult task. True, your hard, persistent labors have been crowned with some success. You have Emma Goldman's citizenship. But she has the world, and her heritage is the kinship of brave spirits—not a bad bargain.

Emma Goldman

A Woman Without a Country

"A Woman Without a Country" was published in *Free Vistas* (ed. Joseph Ishill) in 1933. It was reprinted as a stand-alone pamphlet, under Goldman's name, by Cienfuegos Press in 1979.

The title is perhaps misleading because in a technical sense, I am not without a country. Legally I am a "subject of his Britannic Majesty." But in a deeper, spiritual sense, I am indeed a woman without a country, as I shall try and make plain in the course of this article.

To have a country implies, first of all, the possession of a certain guarantee of security, the assurance of having some spot you can call your own and that no one can alienate from you. That is the essential significance of the idea of country of citizenship. Divested of that, it becomes sheer mockery.

Up to the World War citizenship actually did stand for such a guarantee. Save for occasional exceptions in the more backward European countries, the native or naturalized citizen had the certainty that somewhere on this globe he was at home, in his own country, and that no reversals of personal fortune could deprive him of his inherent right to have his being there. Moreover, he was at liberty to visit other lands and wherever he might be he knew that he enjoyed the protection of his citizenship.

But the War has entirely changed the situation. Together with countless lives it also destroyed the fundamental right to be, to exist in a given place with any degree of security. This peculiar and disquieting condition of affairs has been brought about by a usurpation of the authority that is quite incredible, nothing short of divine. Every government now arrogates to itself the power to determine that a person may or may not continue to live within its boundaries, with the result that thousands, even hundreds of thousands, are literally expatriated. Compelled to leave the country in which they happen to live at the time, they are set adrift in the world, their fate at the mercy of some bureaucrat vested with authority to decide whether they may enter "his" land. Vast numbers of men and women, even of children, have been forced by the War into this terrible predicament. Hunted from place to place, driven hither and thither in their search for a spot where they might be permitted to breathe, they are never certain whether they may not be ordered at any moment to leave for other parts—where the same fate is awaiting them. Veritable Wandering Jews, these unfortunates, victims of a strange perversion of human reason that dares question any person's right to exist.

From every "civilized" country men and women may now be expelled any time it suits the police or the government. It is not only foreigners who are thus virtually driven off the face of the earth. Since the World War citizens are also subject to the same treatment. Citizenship has become bankrupt: it has lost its essential meaning, its one-time guarantee. Today the native is no more safe in "his own" country than the citizen by adoption. Deprivation of citizenship, exile and deportation are practiced by every government; they have become established and accepted methods. So common are these proceedings that no one is any more shocked by them or made sufficiently indignant to voice effective protest. Yet, for all their "legality" denaturalization and expatriation are of the most primitive and cruel inhumanity.

The War has exacted a terrific price in this stupendous number of human lives lost, men maimed and crippled, countless hearts broken and homes destroyed. But even more fearful is the effect of that holocaust upon the living. It has dehumanised and brutalised mankind, has injected the poison of hatred into our hearts, has roused man's worst instincts, made life cheap, and human safety and liberty of the smallest consideration. Intolerance and reaction are rampant, and their destructive spirit is nowhere so evident as in the growing

despotism of official authority and in its autocratic attitude toward all criticism and opposition. A wave of political dictatorship is sweeping Europe,
with its inevitable evils of irresponsible arbitrariness and oppression. Fundamental rights are being abolished, vital ethical conceptions scorned and
flouted. Our most precious possession, the cultural values which it has taken
centuries to create and develop, are being destroyed. Brute force has become
the sole arbiter, and its verdict is accepted with the servile assent of silence,
often even with approval.

Till 1917 the United States had fortunately not become affected by the in-
ternecine madness which was devastating the Old World. The idea of war
was very unpopular, and the American sentiment was virtually unanimous
against mixing up in the European imbroglio. Then, suddenly, the entire situation changed: a peace-insisting nation was transformed, almost over night,
into a martial maniac run amuck. A study of that strange phenomenon would
no doubt be an interesting contribution to our understanding of collective
psychology, but the subject is outside the present discussion. Here it must
suffice to recollect that, after having elected Woodrow Wilson president because he "had kept them out of war," the American people were somehow
persuaded to join the European war. The President's decision, very unwill-
ingly concurred in by a no-war Congress, had the effect of changing the entire psychology of the United States. The tranquil country became a land of
flaming jingoism, and deluge of intolerance and persecuting bigotry overwhelmed the people. The vials of mutual suspicion, of hatred and compulsion
were poured out from North to South and from East to West, setting man
against man, and brother against brother. In the halls of legislation the spirit
of the new militarism manifested itself in draconic law passed against every
critic and protestant.

The sanguine European struggle for territory and markets was proclaimed a holy crusade on behalf of freedom and democracy, and forcible
conscription was hailed as "the best expression a free citizenry." The war
orgy evidenced a psychosis on a nation-wide scale never before witnessed
in the United States. Compared with it the temporary American aberration
that followed the violent death of President McKinley, in 1901, was a mere
flurry. On that Occasion, as will be remembered, the Federal Government
rushed through special legislation outlawing everything that indicated the
least symptom of non-conformism or dissent. I am referring to the notorious
anti-anarchist law, which for the first time in the history of the United States
introduced the principle of government by deportation. Persons suspected of

anarchist tendencies, disbelievers in the organized government, were not to be allowed entry to the United States, the land of the free; or if already there could be sent out of the country within a period of three years. According to that law men like Tolstoy and Kropotkin would have been refused permission to visit the United States, or deported if found within its boundaries.

That law, however, product of a short lived panic, virtually remained a dead letter. But the war-time psychosis revived the forgotten anti-anarchist statutes and broadened them to include everyone who was persona non grata to the powers that be, without the benefit of time limitations. There began a national hunt for "undesirables." Men and women were gathered in by the hundred, arrested on the street or taken from their work-benches, to be administratively deported, without hearing or trial, frequently because of their foreign appearance or on account of wearing a red shawl or necktie.

The war cyclone, having swept Europe, gained increased momentum in America. The movement to make the world safe for democracy and liberty, solidly supported by the "liberal" intelligentsia of the press and pulpit, made the United States the most dangerous place for democrat and libertarian. An official reign of terror rules the country, and thousands of young men were literally driven into the army or navy for fear of their neighbours and of the stigma of "slacker" cast upon everyone in citizens dress—cast mostly by idle ladies of fashion who paraded the street to aid the cause of "humanity." Everyone who dared raise his voice to stem the tide of the war-mania was shouted down and maltreated as an enemy, an anarchist and public menace. Jails and prisons were filled with men and women ordered deported. Most of them were persons that had lived many years in their adopted country, peacefully following their vocations; some of the others had spent almost their entire lives in America. But length of sojourn and useful occupation made no difference. The great Government of the United States stooped even to the subterfuge of secretly depriving naturalized citizens of their citizenship, so as to be able to deport them as "undesirable foreigners."

Future historians will wonder at the peculiar phenomenon of American war psychology: while Europe experienced its worst reaction as a result of the war, the United States—in keeping with its spirit of "get there first"—reached its greatest reactionary zenith before entering the war. Without warning, as it were, it forswore all its revolutionary traditions and customs, openly and without shame, and introduced the worst practices of the Old World. With no more hesitation than necessary it transplanted to America methods of autocracy which had required centuries of development in Europe, and it initiated expatriation, exile and deportation on a whole scale, irrespective of any considerations of equity and humanity.

To be sure, the pacifist intellectuals who prepared America for war solemnly insisted that the summary abrogation of constitutional rights and liberties was a temporary measure necessitated by the exigencies of the situation, and that all war-legislation was to be abolished as soon as the world would be made safe for democracy. But more than a decade has passed since, and in vain I have been scanning American newspapers, journals and magazines for the least indication of the promised return to normalcy. It is easier to make laws than abolish them, and oppressive laws are particularly notorious for their longevity.

With its habitual recklessness it has outdone the effete Old World in "preparedness." The former great democracy of Thomas Jefferson, the land of Paine and Emerson, the one-time rebel against State and Church, has turned persecutor of every social protestant. The historic champion of the revolutionary principle, "No taxation without representation," compelled its people to fight in a war waged without their consent. The refuge of the Garibaldis, the Kossuth and Schurzes practices deportation of heretics. America, whose official functions always begin with a prayer to the Nazarene who had commanded "Thou shalt not kill" has imprisoned and tortured men who scrupled to take human life, and has hounded those who proclaim "peace and good will on earth." Once a haven for the persecuted and oppressed of other lands, the United States has since shut its doors in the face of those seeking refuge from the tyrant. A new twentieth-century Golgotha for its "foreign" Saccos and Vanzettis, it silences its native "undesirables," its Mooneys and Billingses, by burying them alive in prison. It glorifies its flying Lindberghs, but damns their thinking fathers. It crucifies manhood and expatriates opinion.

The practice of deportation places America, in a cultural sense, far below the European level. Indeed there is less freedom of thought in the United States than in the Old World. Few countries are as unsafe for the man or woman of independence and idealism. No offence more heinous there than an unconventional attitude; every crime may be forgiven but that of unapproved opinion. The heretic is anathema, the iconoclast the worst culprit. For such there is no room in the great United States. In a singular manner that country combines industrial initiative and economic self-help with an almost absolute taboo against ethical freedom and cultural expression. Morals and behavior are prescribed by draconic censorship, and woe to him who dares step out of the beaten path. By substituting rule by deportation for its fundamental law, America has recorded itself thoroughly reactionary, it has erected formidable barriers against its cultural development and progress. In the last analysis such policies are a means of depriving the people of the finer value and higher aspirations. The great body of labor is, of course, the most direct victim of this menace. It is designed to stifle industrial discontent, to eliminate the spokesmen of popular unrest, and subjugate the inarticulate masses to the will of the masters of life.

Unfortunately it is the workers themselves who are the main bulwark of reaction. No body of any toilers in any country is as mentally undeveloped and as lacking in economic consciousness as the American Federation of Labor. The horizon of their leaders is sadly limited, their social shortsightedness positively infantile. Their role in the World War days was most pitiful and subservient in their vieing to outdo each other as trade drummers for the Moloch of slaughter. They championed the most reactionary measures too fatuous to understand that the same will remain a post-war weapon in the hands of the employers of labor. They learned nothing from past experience and have forgotten the lesson of the Sherman Law, passed by the efforts of the workers to check the industrial trust but since applied by the American courts to weaken and emasculate the organizations of labor. As was to be foreseen, the "temporary" war legislation, sponsored by the American Federation of Labor, is now being used in the industrial struggles against the toilers.

It was Fridjof Nansen, the famous explorer, who was one of the first to realize the far-reaching effects of the war psychosis in relation to these expatriated. He introduced the special passport that bears his name and which is designed to insure at least a modicum of safety to the increasing number of refugees. Because of Nansen's great services in organizing the millions of homeless and parentless children during the war, the League of Nations was induced to approve his project and established the so-called Nansen passport. Few countries, however, recognized its validity, and that half-heartedly, and in no case does it guarantee its holder against exile and deportation. But the very fact of its existence goes to prove the havoc wrought by the post-war developments in the matter of citizenship and the utterly wretched situation of the thousands of expatriated and countryless.

It should not be assumed that the latter consists mostly of political refugees. In that huge army of exile there are great numbers of entirely a-political people, of men and women whom territorial rapacity and the Versailles "peace" have deprived of their country. Most of them do not even get the benefit of the Nansen passport, since the latter is intended only for the political refugees of certain nationalities. Thus thousands find themselves without legal papers of any kind, and in consequence may not be permitted to stay anywhere. A young woman of my acquaintance, for instance, a person who has never been interested in any social or political activities, is at this very moment adrift in this Christian world of ours, without the right of making any country her home, without fatherland or abode, and constantly at the mercy of the passport police. Though a native of Germany, she is refused citizenship in that country because her father (now dead) was an Austrian. Austria, on the other hand, does not recognize her as a citizen because her father's birthplace, formerly belonging to Austria, has by the terms of the Versailles treaty become part of Rumania. Rumania, finally, declines to consider the young woman as a citizen on the ground that she is not a native, and never lived in the country, does not speak the language and has no relatives there. The unfortunate woman is literally without a country, with no legal right to live anywhere on earth, save by the temporary toleration of some passport officials.

Still more hazardous is the existence of the vast army of political refugees and expatriated. They live in ever-present fear of being deported, and such a doom is equivalent to a sentence of death when these men are returned, as is only too often the case, to countries ruled by dictatorships. Quite recently a man I know was arrested in the place of his sojourn and ordered deported to his native land, which happened to be Italy. Had the order been carried out, it would have meant torture and execution. I am familiar with a number of cases of political refugees not permitted to remain in the countries where they had sought refuge and deported to Spain, Hungary, Rumania or Bulgaria, where their lives are in jeopardy. For the arm of reaction is long. Thus Poland has on several occasions lately decreed the deportation of Russian political refuges to their native country, where the Tcheka executioner was ready to receive them. It was only through the timely intercession of influential friends abroad that the men and their families were saved from certain death. European despotism reaches even across the sea, to the United States and South America; repeatedly politicals of Spanish and Italian descent have been deported to their native lands as an act of "courtesy" to a friendly power.

These are not exceptional instances. Large numbers of refugees are in a similar position. Not to speak of the thousands of non-political, denaturalized and expatriated and despoiled of abode. In Turkey and France, to mention two countries only, there are at present over half a million of them, victims of the World War, of Fascism, of Bolshevism, of post-war territorial changes and of the mania for exiling and deporting. Most of them are being merely tolerated, for the time being, and are always subject to an order to "move on"—somewhere else. Lesser but still very considerable numbers are scattered throughout the world, particularly in Belgium, Holland, Germany and in the various countries of Southern Europe.

There is nothing more tragic than the fate of those men and women thrown upon the mercy of our Christian world. I know the mercy of our Christian world. I know from personal experience what it means to be torn out of the environment of a lifetime, dug out by the very root from the soil you have had your being in, compelled to leave the work to which all your energies have been devoted, and to part from those nearest and dearest to you. Most disastrous are the effects of such expatriation particularly on persons of mature age, as were the great number of those deported by America. Youth may adapt itself more readily to a new environment and acclimatize itself in a strange world. But for those of more advanced age such transplantation is a veritable crucifixion. It requires years of application to master the language, custom and habits of a new land, and a very long time to take root, to form new ties and secure one's material existence,—not to speak of the metal anguish and agony a sensitive person suffers in the face of wrong and inhumanity.

As for myself, in the deeper significance of spiritual values, I feel the United States "my country." Not to be sure, the United State of the Ku Kluxers, of moral censors in and out of office, of the suppressionists and reactionaries of every type. Not the America of Tammany or of Congress, of respectable inanity, of the highest skyscrapers and fattest moneybags. Not the United States of pretty provincialism, narrow nationalism, vain materialism and naive exaggeration. There is fortunately another United States—the land of Walt Whitmans, the Lloyd Garrisons, the Thoreaus, the Wendell Phillipses. The country of Young America of life and thought, or of art and letters; the America of the new generation knocking at the door, of men and women with ideals, with aspirations for a better day; the America of social rebellion and spiritual promise, of the glorious "undesirables" against whom all the exile, expatriation and deportation laws are aimed.

It is to that America that I am proud to belong.

Chiefs of Naturalization Bureau and Evolution of Departmental Responsibilities

---

1903: Bureau of Immigration under the Department of Commerce and Labor

U.S. Commissioner General of Immigration:

1. Frank P. Sargent: June 26, 1902–September 4, 1908
   Richard K. Campbell: Chief of Naturalization Division, 1906
2. Daniel J. Keefe: July 1, 1909–May 31, 1913
   Richard K. Campbell: Chief of Naturalization Division, 1906

1913: Bureau of Immigration under the Department of Commerce and Labor

U.S. Commissioner General of Immigration:

1. Anthony J. Caminetti: June 1, 1913–March 13, 1921
2. William W. Husband: March 15, 1921–May 15, 1925
3. Harry E. Hull: May 13, 1925–April 26, 1933
4. Daniel W. MacCormack: April 27, 1933

1913: Bureau of Naturalization under the Department of Commerce and Labor

U.S. Commissioner of Naturalization:

1. Richard K. Campbell: March 4, 1913–December 21, 1922
2. Raymond F. Crist: January 1, 1923–August 9, 1933

1933: Immigration and Naturalization Service under the Department of Labor

U.S. Commissioner of Immigration and Naturalization:

1. Daniel W. MacCormack: August 10, 1933–January 1, 1937
2. James L. Houghteling: August 26, 1937–July 31, 1940

1940: Immigration and Naturalization moved under the Department of Justice

U.S. Commissioner of Immigration and Naturalization:

1. Lemuel B. Schofield: October 1, 1940–July 19, 1942
2. Earl G. Harrison: July 20, 1942–July 20, 1944
3. Ugo Carusi: January 9, 1945–August 26, 1947
4. Watson B. Miller: August 27, 1947–June 9, 1950
5. Argyle R. Mackey: April 23, 1951–May 23, 1954
6. Joseph M. Swing: May 24, 1954–January 5, 1962
7. Raymond F. Farrell: February 5, 1962–March 31, 1973

Naturalization Cancellations in
the United States, 1907–1973

Year	Count	Year	Count	Year	Count
1907	86	1930	412	1953	335
1908	457	1931	384	1954	165
1909	921	1932	562	1955	197
1910	397	1933	522[b]	1956	288
1911	225	1934	682[b]	1957	269
1912	212	1935	864	1958	176
1913	414	1936	1,016	1959	154
1914	319	1937	991	1960	124
1915	184	1938	1,085	1961	44
1916	152	1939	882	1962	26
1917	154	1940	1,011	1963	7
1918	136	1941	1,055	1964	11
1919	115	1942	640	1965	2
1920	132	1943	373	1966	5
1921	150	1944	238	1967	8
1922	174	1945	165	1968	5
1923	182	1946	186	1969	0
1924	408	1947	94	1970	1
1925	448	1948	163	1971	3
1926	631[a]	1949	184	1972	4
1927	764	1950	415	1973	0
1928	621	1951	403	**Total**	**22,026**
1929	337	1952	279		

[a] For the year 1926, data of the Commissioner of Naturalization and of the Annual Reports of the Attorney General show a 5 percent difference: 631 vs. 672. This difference can be explained by a gap in the time of registration of the cases or by the nonregistration of some cases initiated directly by the Department of Justice, by the Bureau of Naturalization.

[b] For the years 1933 and 1934, the only available data come from the Annual Reports of the Attorney General.

Data compiled by Patrick Weil. Sources: the reports of the administration in charge of naturalizations since 1906: Annual Reports of the Commissioner General of Immigration, Annual Reports of the Commissioner of Naturalization, Annual Reports of the Secretary of Labor, and since 1940 Annual Reports of the immigration and naturalization service within the Department of Justice.

Americans Expatriated, by Grounds and Year, 1945–1977

Grounds for expatriation	1945	1946	1947	1948	1949	1950	1951	1952	1953	1954	1955	1956	1957	1958	1958*	1959	1960	1961	1962	1963	1964	1965	1966	1967	1968	1969	1970	1971	1972	1973	1974	1975	1976	1976	1977
Total number[a]	1936	1113	6758	6779	8575	5792	4443	3265	8350	6938	4202	4987	5564	5908	5865	2899	3374	3657	3212	3164	2321	2083	2010	1919	1400	450	2064	1618	1634	1250	1522	1843	1651	723	1503
Voting in a foreign political election or plebiscite[b]															473																				
Continuous residence in a foreign state of birth or former nationality[c]			4515	1693	1401	1186	2651	2222	1237	1436	1515	1748	1748	992	1239	1290	977	943	568	869	769	370	20												
Residence of a naturalized national in a foreign state (§404, Nationality Act of 1940)					694	1424	1084	711	2657	1557	1063	1776	2223	2592	2165	796	873	1027	1017	1089	618														
Continuous residence in a state by dual national who sought benefits of §335.1 and Nationality Act														55	33	21	52	29	23	30	31	22	42												
Continuous residence in a state by dual national who sought benefits of §350 Immigration and Nationality Act																									26		10								
Residence in a foreign state under treaties and conventions[d]																372	188	68	72	67	44	53	51	11	7	26	10	3	5	28	26	6	6		

Grounds for expatriation

Grounds for expatriation	1945	1946	1947	1948	1949	1950	1951	1952	1953	1954	1955	1956	1957	1958	1958*	1959	1960	1961	1962	1963	1964	1965	1966	1967	1968	1969	1970	1971	1972	1973	1974	1975	1976	1976	1977
Naturalization in a foreign state				754	1096	836	622	1677	1544	841	829	616	565	565	383	625	619	642	585	653	662	555	858	26	4	1537	955	1051	819	976	1238	1224	548		1183
Entering or serving in the armed forces of a foreign state				339																															
Renunciation of nationality				356	149	228	136	398	425	331	167	250	213	213	188	194	189	183	248	234	286	379	485	679	444										
Departing from or remaining away from the United States to avoid training and service in the land or naval forces				259	109	69	45	134	139	69	61	45																							
Taking an oath of allegiance in a foreign state				738	430	369	147	123	152	220	233	237	248	230	230	64	85	99	46	59	42	32	40	63	35	2	111	106	146	101	215	332	188	82	142
Accepting or performing duties under a foreign state				99	163	73	56	67	134	84	112	146	125	125	78	57	62	50	20	11	17	14	18	9	5	16	5	3	5	14	8	2	3		
By departing from or remaining outside the United States in time of war for purpose of avoiding U.S. military service, or deserting from armed forces of the United States				1																							4								
Desertion from the armed forces				41																															
Other grounds				5	64	38	2	3	6	5	2	3	7	5	12	6	10	38	14	19	20	22	18	41	22										

a Cases of 90 persons expatriated for departing from or remaining away from the United States to avoid military service, reported for 1958–1963, were not included because this statutory provision was ruled unconstitutional by the U.S. Supreme Court on February 18, 1963: *Kennedy v. Francisco Mendoza-Martinez* (372 U.S. 144) and *Rusk v. Joseph Henry Cort* (372 U.S. 224).

b The Supreme Court decision in *Afroyim v. Rusk* (387 U.S. 253, May 29, 1967), ruled as unconstitutional the law providing for a loss of citizenship by voting in a foreign political election

c The Supreme Court decision in *Schneider v. Rusk* (377 U.S. 163, May 18, 1964), ruled as unconstitutional statutory provisions that cause naturalized citizens to lose their nationality by extended residence abroad.

d Naturalized U.S. citizens expatriated in countries with which the United States has treaties or conventions providing on a reciprocal basis for loss of nationality through extended residence in the country of original citizenship.

APPENDIX 5

Supreme Court and Other Important Court Decisions Related to Denaturalization and Nonvoluntary Expatriation from *Schneiderman* and Participating Supreme Court Justices

Schneiderman v. United States, 320 U.S. 118 (1943): Argued November 9, 1942, reargued March 12, 1943, decided June 21 1943, opinion: Murphy, joined by Black and Reed. Douglas concurring, Rutledge concurring; Stone dissent, joined by Frankfurter and Roberts.

Baumgartner v. United States, 322 U.S. 665 (1944): Argued April 26, 1944. June 12, 1944, unanimous, opinion: Frankfurter joined by Jackson, Reed, Roberts, Stone. Murphy concurring, joined by Black, Douglas, Rutledge.

Knauer v. United States, 328 U.S. 654, (1946): Argued March 28, 29, 1946, decided June 10, 1946. Opinion: Douglas, joined by Black, Frankfurter, Jackson, Reed, Roberts, Stone. Rutledge, joined by Murphy, dissenting.

Klapprott v. United States, 335 U.S. 601 (1949): Argued October 20, 1948, decided January 17, 1949. Opinion: Black joined by Douglas, Murphy and Rutledge; Burton concurring. Reed, with Vinson and Jackson dissenting; Frankfurter dissenting.

Savorgnan v. United States, 338 U.S. 491 (1950): Argued November 7–8, 1949, decided January 9, 1950. Opinion: Burton joined by Clark, Jackson, Minton, Reed, Vinson. Frankfurter, joined by Black, dissented. Douglas did not participate.

Acheson v. Okimura and Murata, 99 F. Supp. 587, Supreme Court: 342 U.S. 899 (1951).

Bindczyck v. Funicane, 342 U.S. 76 (1951): Argued October 10, 1951, decided November 26, 1951. Opinion: Frankfurter joined by Black, Clark, Douglas, Jackson, Minton, and Vinson. Reed, joined by Burton, dissenting.

Gonzales v. Landon, 350 U.S. 920 (1955) *per curiam.*

United States v. Zucca, 351 U.S. 91 (1956): Argued January 24–25, 1956, decided April 30, 1956. Opinion: Warren, joined by Black, Douglas, Frankfurter and Minton. Clark, joined by Reed and Murton, dissenting. Harlan did not participate.

Perez v. Brownell, 356 U.S. 44 (1958): Argued May 1, 1957, reargued October 28, 1957, decided March 31, 1958. Opinion: Frankfurter, joined by Burton, Clark, Harlan, Brennan. Dissents: Warren, joined by Black and Douglas; Douglas, joined by Black; Whittaker.

Trop v. Dulles, 356 U.S. 86 (1958): Argued May 2, 1957 reargued October 28–29, 1957, decided March 31, 1958. Opinion: Warren, joined by Black, Douglas, Whittaker. Concurring: Black, joined by Douglas. Concurring: Brennan. Dissent by Frankfurter joined by by Burton, Clark, Harlan

Nishikawa v. Dulles, 356 U.S. 129 (1958): no. 19, argued May 1–2, 1957, reargued October 28, 1957, decided March 31, 1958. Opinion Warren, joined by Brennan, Whittaker: joining and concurring Black and Douglas. Concurring in the result: Frankfurter, joined by Burton. Dissent: Harlan, joined by Clark

Nowak v. United States, 356 U.S. 660 (1958), and *Maisenberg v. United States*, 356 U.S. 670 (1958), both argued January 28, 1958 and decided May 26, 1958. Justice Harlan delivered the opinion of the Court and was joined by Black, Brennan, Douglas, Frankfurter, Warren. Burton, Clark and Whittaker, dissenting.

Chaunt v. United States, 364 U.S. 350 (1960): no. 22, argued October 17, 1960, decided November 14, 1960. Opinion by Douglas, announced by Harlan, joined by Black, Brennan, Frankfurter, Warren. Clark, with Stewart and Whittaker, dissenting.

Polites v. United States, 364 U.S. 426 (1960): Argued October 18, 1960, decided November 21, 1960. Opinion: Stewart, joined by Clark, Frankfurter, Harlan and Whittaker. Brennan, joined by Black, Douglas, Warren dissenting.

Costello v. United States, 365 U.S. 265 (1961): Argued December 12, 1960, decided February 20, 1961. Brennan delivered the opinion of the Court joined by Clark, Frankfurter, Harlan, Stewart, Warren and Whittaker. Black and Douglas dissented. Harlan did not participate.

Mendoza-Martinez v. Mackey, 356 U.S. 258 (1958): Decided April 7, 1958, *Per Curiam.* followed by *Kennedy v. Mendoza-Martinez*, 372 U.S. (1963), and *Cort* 372 U.S. 144 (1963) Argued October 10–11, 1961, restored to the calendar for reargument April 2, 1962, reargued December 4, 1962, decided February 18, 1963. Opinion: Goldberg, joined by Black, Douglas, Warren, with Brennan concurring; dissent: Stewart, joined by Clark, Harlan White.

Schneider v. Rusk, 372 U.S. 224 (1963); decided February 18, 1963, *per curiam.*

Schneider v. Rusk , 377 U.S. 163 (1964), Argued: April 2, 1964, decided May 18, 1964. Opinion: Douglas, joined by Black, Goldberg, Stewart, Warren, Dissent: Clark, joined by Harlan, White.

Marks v. Esperdy, 377 U.S. 214 (1964): Argued April 2, 1964, decided May 18, 1964. 315 F. 2d 673, affirmed by an equally divided Court, four in favor of reversing the circuit court decision (Black, Douglas, Goldberg, Warren), four in favor of affirming (Clark, joined by Harlan, Stewart, White.

Afroyim v. Rusk, 387 U.S. 253 (1967): Black opinion joined by Brennan, Douglas, Fortas, Warren; Harlan dissenting opinion, joined by Clark, Stewart, White.

Rogers v. Bellei, 401 U.S. 815 (1971): Argued January 15, 1970, reargued November 12, 1970, decided April 5, 1971. Opinion: Blackmun joined by Burger, Harlan, Stewart and White. Black dissent joined by Douglas and Marshall, Brennan dissent joined by Douglas.

Vance v. Terrazas, 444 U.S. 252 (1980): Argued October 30, 1979, decided January 15, 1980. Opinion: White joined by Burger, Blackmun, Powell and Rehnquist. Marshall and Stevens concurred in part and dissented in part. Brennan dissented in Part II, joined by Stewart who filed a dissenting statement.

Fedorenko v. United States, 449 U.S. 490 (1981): no. 79–5602, argued October 15, 1980, decided January 21, 1981. Opinion of Marshall, joined by Brennan, Stewart, Powell, Rehnquist, concurrences of Burger and Blackmun; dissents of White and Stevens.

Kungys v. United States, 485 U.S. 759 (1988): no. 86–228, argued April 27, 1987, reargued October

13, 1987, decided May 2, 1988. Opinion: Scalia in which Rehnquist and Brennan, White and O'Connor joined with respect to Parts I, II-A, and III-A, and, with respect to Parts II-B and III-B, in which Rehnquist and Brennan and (as to Part III-B only) O'Connor joined. Brennan filed a concurring opinion. Stevens joined by Marshall and Blackmun concurred. O'Connor concurred in part and dissented in part, White dissented. Kennedy did not participate.

Gorbach v. Reno, 219 F 3d 1087 (9th Cir., 2000)

Participating Justices

Hugo Black: 1937–1971 (replaced by Lewis Powell)
Harry Blackmun: 1970–1994
William Brennan Jr.: 1956–1990
Warren Burger: 1969–1986
Harold Burton: 1945–1958 (replaced by Stewart)
Tom C. Clark: 1949–1967 (replaced by Marshall)
Wiliam O. Douglas: 1939–1975
Abe Fortas: 1965–1969 (replaced by Blackmun)
Felix Frankfurter: 1939–1962 (replaced by Goldberg)
Arthur Goldberg: 1962–1965 (replaced by Fortas)
John Marshall Harlan II: 1955–1971 (replaced by Rehnquist)
Robert Jackson: 1941– 1954 (replaced by Harlan)
Thurgood Marshall: 1967–1991
Sherman Minton: 1949–1956 (replaced by Brennan)
Frank Murphy: 1940–1949 (succeeded by Clark)
Sandra Day O'Connor: 1981–2006
Lewis Powell: 1971–1986
Stanley Forman Reed: 1938–1957 (replaced by Whittaker)
William H. Rehnquist: 1971–2005
Willey Rutledge: 1943–1949 (replaced by Minton)
Antonin Scalia: 1986–
John Paul Stevens: 1975–2010
Potter Stewart: 1958–1981 (replaced by O'Connor)
Fred Vinson: 1946–1953 (replaced by Warren)
Earl Warren: 1953–1969 (replaced by Burger)
Byron White: 1962–1993
Charles Evans Whittaker: 1957–1962 (replaced by White)

NOTES

Introduction

1. In *Knauer v. United States*, Justice William O. Douglas, who delivered the opinion of the Court, speaks about the "cherished status" of citizenship. *Knauer v. United States*, 328 U.S. 654 (1946), 658.

2. The 1922 Cable Act (42 Stat. 1021, Married Women's Independent Nationality Act) permitted American women to keep their citizenship when they married foreigners; except if they married Asians. The Act was amended in 1931 so as to suppress this discrimination.

3. A denaturalization proceeding is then considered "an action by the sovereign to nullify the status of a naturalized person that should never have been a citizen." See *Luria v. United States*, 231 U.S. 9, 24 (1913), and John P. Roche, "Statutory Denaturalization: 1906–1951," *University of Pittsburgh Law Review* 13 (1951–1952): 276.

4. On the denaturalization provisions in foreign laws during the interwar period, see Durward V. Sandifer, "Nationality at Birth and Loss of Nationality," *American Journal of International Law* 29 (April 1935): 248, 261.

5. A first version of "A Woman Without a Country" was published in the May 1909 edition of *Mother Earth*. The version I am quoting was published in the magazine *Free Vistas* (ed. Joseph Ishill) in 1933. It was reprinted as a stand-alone pamphlet, under Goldman's name, by Cienfuegos Press in 1979. The title surely refers to Edward Everett Hale's novella *The Man Without a Country*, "written during the Civil War and republished dozens of times since, especially during World War I and World War II, most recently shortly after 9/11." See Linda K. Kerber, "Presidential Address: The Stateless as the Citizen's Other: A View from the United States," *American Historical Review* 112 (February 2007): 11–12.

6. The majority of the publications reflect this association between war and denaturalization. See John L. Cable, *Loss of Citizenship, Denaturalization, the Alien in Wartime* (Washington, D.C.: National Law Book, 1943); Harry Kalven, Jr., *A Worthy Tradition: Freedom of Speech in America*, ed. Jamie Kalven (New York: Harper and Row, 1988); Geoffrey R. Stone, *Perilous Times: Free Speech in Wartime from the Sedition Act of 1798 to the War on Terrorism* (New York: W. W. Norton, 2004). Only Richard W. Steele, *Free Speech in the Good War* (New York: St. Martin's Press, 1999), bases his work on archival sources.

7. John P. Roche wrote the only comprehensive and the best legal history of denaturalization, his Ph.D. dissertation (Cornell University), published in three different articles. John P. Roche, "Prestatutory Denaturalization," *Cornell Law Quarterly* 35 (1949); "Loss of American Nationality: The Years of Confusion," *University of Pennsylvania Law Review* 99, no. 1 (October 1950); and

"Statutory Denaturalization: 1906–1951," cited earlier. But this remarkable study stops in 1954, is not based on archival sources, and relies mainly on the jurisprudence of the courts and on official publications of the government. Also useful is John L. Cable, *Decisive Decision of United States Citizenship* (Charlottesville, Va.: Michie, 1967).

8. Frank George Franklin, *The Legislative History of Naturalization in the United States from the Revolutionary War to 1861* (South Hackensack, N.J.: Rothman Reprints, 1981), 48.

9. On that history, see James H. Kettner, *The Development of American Citizenship, 1608–1870* (Chapel Hill: University of North Carolina Press, 1978).

10. See Rogers Smith, *Civic Ideals, Conflicting Visions of Citizenship in U.S. History* (New Haven, Conn.: Yale University Press, 1997), 313.

11. Selective Draft Law Cases, 245 U.S. 366 (1918)

12. "The dignity of citizenship" is mentioned in *Mandoli v. Acheson*, 344 U.S. 133, 139 (1952). Judith Shklar observes that "citizenship has a political and a social standing"; *American Citizenship: The Quest for Inclusion* (Cambridge, Mass.: Harvard University Press, 1991), 57.

13. Theodore Roosevelt, "Presidential Address, December 7, 1903," *New York Times*, December 8, 1903.

14. See Karen Orren and Stephen Skowronek, *The Search for American Political Development* (Cambridge: Cambridge University Press, 2004), 123.

15. Joseph Carens, *Culture, Citizenship, and Community: A Contextual Exploration of Justice as Evenhandedness* (Oxford: Oxford University Press, 2000), 166

16. Benedict Anderson, *Imagined Communities: Reflections on the Origin and Spread of Nationalism* (London: Verso, 1983).

17. Smith, *Civic Ideals*.

18. See Patrick Weil, "From Conditional to Secured and Sovereign: The New Strategic Link Between the Citizen and the Nation-State in a Globalized World," *The International Journal of Constitutional Law* (2011) 9(3–4): 615–635.

19. See István Szijártó, "Four Arguments for Microhistory," *Rethinking History* 6, no. 2 (2002): 209–215. The term "microhistory" refers to the program and the practices of a small group of Italian historians who began publishing in the 1970s, the best known of whom are Carlo Ginzburg, Edoardo Grendi, Giovanni Levi, Carlo Poni, and Jacques Revel. According to Levi, "Microhistory as a practice is essentially based on the reduction of the scale of observation, on a microscopic analysis and an intensive study of the documentary"; the unifying principle of all microhistorical research is the belief that microscopic observation will reveal factors previously unobserved. See Giovanni Levi, "On Microhistory," in *New Perspectives on Historical Writing*, ed. Peter Burke (University Park: Pennsylvania State University Press, 1992), 95. See also Jacques Revel, "Microanalysis and the Construction of the Social," in *Histories: French Constructions of the Past*, ed. Jacques Revel and Lynn Hunt (New York: New Press, 1995); Carlo Ginzburg, *Clues, Myths and the Historical Method* (Baltimore: Johns Hopkins University Press, 1989), 100, and "Microhistory: Two or Three Things That I Know About It," *Critical Inquiry* 20 (1993): 10, 21.

20. Orren and Skowronek. *The Search for American Political Development*, 6.

21. See Matti Peltonen, "Clues, Margins, and Monads: The Micro-Macro Link in Historical Research," *History and Theory* 40 (October 2001): 347, 357.

22. See Orren and Skowronek, *The Search for American Political Development*, 123. Orren and Skowronek refer to this phenomenon of competing authorities as an "intercurrence between multiples orders" or "problematic impingements." Ibid., 113.

23. Henry Hazard wrote in 1927 about a trend toward administrative naturalization, but the decisive role denaturalization played in this process has never been noted. See Henry B. Hazard, "The Trend Toward Administrative Naturalization," *American Political Science Review* 21 (May 1927): 346.

24. The concept of "conditional citizenship" is used by Roche, "Statutory Denaturalization: 1906–1951," 276, 303, but he applied it only to the specific provision added March 27, 1942, to the Nationality Act for the naturalization of aliens serving in the U.S. armed forces. This provision accelerated naturalization, but this naturalization could be revoked in the event of discharge from military or naval forces.

25. The most recent important case that reaffirmed the legality of the practice was *Fedorenko v. United States* 449 U.S. 490 (1981).

26. Box 582, Warren Papers, Manuscript Division, Library of Congress, Washington, D.C. Cf. Figure 2 in Chapter 11.

27. See Daryl J. Levinson, "Empire Building Government in Constitutional Law," *Harvard Law Review* 118 (2004–2005): 915, 928.

28. See the interesting argument of Bonnie Honig, "Decision: The Paradoxical Dependence of the Rule of Law," *Emergency Politics: Paradox, Law, Democracy* (Princeton, N.J.: Princeton University Press, 2009), 65.

29. The concept of "mental reservation" was borrowed from the pledge of judges and justices and was used to justify denial of naturalization: "The statement of facts justifying the Supreme Court decision may show . . . that she cannot take the oath of allegiance without a mental reservation." *United States v. Schwimmer,* 279 U.S. 644, 654 (1929). See Chapters 5 and 8 below.

30. A few years later, Wickersham would defend the right of the Japanese American Ozawa to be naturalized, despite a statute authorizing only the naturalization of people of white and African descent. And in 1931, the Wickersham Commission report had a special section on immigration which proposed significant and substantial improvements in the hearing procedures of aliens in front of administrative instances. Many of these proposals were translated into statutory commands by the 1952 Act. See Wickersham report, 29, quoted by Mae Ngai, "The Strange Career of the Illegal Alien: Immigration Restriction and Deportation Policy in the United States, 1921–1965," *Law and History Review* 21 (Spring 2003): 91. See also Laurence M. Benedict, "Grave Abuses Charged in Deportation System: Ruthless Treatment of Aliens by Immigration Officials Asserted in Wickersham Report," *Los Angeles Times,* August 8, 1931 and Will Maslow, "Recasting Our Deportation Law: Proposals for Reform," *Columbia Law Review* 56 (March 1956): 309–366.

31. Roosevelt was said not to like these amendments to the code. The president's views were, it seemed, that the law expatriating citizens who swear allegiance to a foreign state and join its armed forces should be amended so that citizenship under such circumstances is not lost. He was not successful. He even failed to remove a provision passed unanimously by the House expatriating any American "if he remains for six months or longer within any foreign state of which he or either of his parents shall have been a national." See Memorandum of Lemuel Schofield to the attorney general, September 16, 1940, Library of Congress, Jackson Papers, box 90, folder 4.

32. *Kungys v. United States,* 485 U.S. 759 (1988).

Chapter 1. Denaturalization, the Main Instrument of Federal Power

1. That year 58,000 aliens were naturalized in New York City from a population of 800,000; in 1902, for example, 11,177 aliens had been naturalized from an estimated population of 3.5 million. *Report of the Naturalization Commission to the President* (hereafter Purdy Commission Report), 59th Cong., 1st sess., November 8, 1905, H. 46, appendix E, extracts of the report of C. V. C. Van Deusen, special examiner of the Department of Justice, June 14, 1905, 82–83. This was seven times more than the median annual number of naturalizations in the ten previous years in the State of New York, the most populous state in the country. John I. Davenport, *The Elections and Naturalization Frauds in New York City, 1860–1870* (New York: Davenport, 1894), 115–156.

2. Congressional Globe, 41st Congress, 2nd sess. (May 25 and June 9, 1870), 3808, 4270.

3. See Nick Parrillo, *Against the Profit Motive: The Transformation of American Government. 1780–1940* (New Haven, Conn.: Yale University Press, forthcoming), ch. 4. In 1845, two bills dealing specifically with denaturalization, H.R. 575 and S. 99, were introduced in Congress. The Senate bill contained three major voter fraud provisions including one related to denaturalization, which provided that if fraud or irregularity in naturalization is revealed to a court, then it would be rescinded. Neither bill became law, but twenty years later, the scandals of the frauds in naturalization in the state of New York provoked another round of naturalization law reform.

4. On the importance of West-East sectional division on the issue, see Nicolas Barreyre, "Réunifier l'Union: Intégrer l'Ouest à la Reconstruction américaine, 1870–1872," *Revue d'Histoire Moderne et Contemporaine* 49, no. 4 (October–December 2002): 24. Only the criminalization of naturalization frauds was included in the second Enforcement Act (16 Stat. 254–255 [1870]), keeping fraud and illegality at a potential high level.

5. The act of February 1, 1876 (19 Stat. 2, chap. 5, U.S. Compiled Statutes [1901], p. 1331), states that the declaration of intention may be made before the clerk of any court having jurisdiction on naturalization. See Frederick Van Dyne, *Citizenship of the United States* (Rochester, N.Y.: Lawyers' Co-operative Publishing Co., 1904), 63, and Parillo, *Against the Profit Motive*, ch. 4.

6. See Michael Schudson, *The Good Citizen: A History of American Civic Life* (Cambridge, Mass.: Harvard University Press,1999), chapter 4.

7. Ibid., p. 20.

8. The St. Louis Court of Appeals had issued 496 certificates of naturalization in three days of October 1902; 400 were proven to have been issued fraudulently.

9. William Preston, Jr., *Aliens and Dissenters: Federal Suppression of Radicals, 1903–1933* (Urbana: University of Illinois Press, 1994), 66.

10. Act of March 3, 1903 (32 Stat. 1222, chap. 1012 §39). In proposing the bill in his first state of the union address in December 1901, Theodore Roosevelt called for: excluding "not only all persons who are known to be believers in anarchistic principles or members of anarchistic societies, but also all persons who are of a low moral tendency or of unsavory reputation." Roosevelt added that this goal required "a more thorough system of inspection abroad and a more rigid system of examination at our immigration ports."

11. Purdy Commission Report, appendix E, extracts of the report of C. V. C. Van Deusen, special examiner of the Department of Justice, June 14, 1905, 91–92.

12. Purdy Commission Report, 77–78. A list of 488 persons registered to vote in the county of New York for the general election of 1902 with alleged certificates of naturalization issued by the U.S. district courts of the Eastern and Southern Districts of New York: no record of them

in either court could be found. Report of C. V. C. Van Deusen, special examiner, NARA, RG 59, General Records of the Department of State, Records of the Passports Division, 1790–1917, Reports of Passports Issued Abroad, 1896–1913, entry 531, box 1. In addition, 550 persons had been naturalized in courts in the state of New York, in violation of the 1895 Naturalization Law of New York State, which prohibited all state courts except the Supreme Court and county courts to exercise naturalization jurisprudence or in violation of the Act of Congress of March 3, 1903 (idem). In the whole country, several thousand of certificate did not conform the requirements made by this act to the courts to check the belief of the applicant in organized government and the truth of every material fact requested for naturalization. (Sc 39, Act of March 3, 1903 [32 Stat. at L. 1222, chap. 1012]).

13. Purdy Commission Report, 78. By May 1905, there were 103 trials pending, and there had been only three acquittals in the state of New York. In addition, 1,916 fraudulently obtained certificates of citizenship had been cancelled in the same state, and various judges in other states had acted similarly to cancel certificates. Purdy Commission Report, appendix D, extracts of Joel Marx to the Attorney General, Department of Justice, May 29, 1905, 76–78.

14. Grand jury of New York, in *Annual Report of the Attorney General of the United States, 1903* (Washington, D.C.: Government Printing Office, 1903), exhibit 29.

15. Third Annual Message, December 7, 1903, http://www.presidency.ucsb.edu/ws/index.php?pid=29544#axzz1iuWhfMV1.

16. In his fourth State of the Union speech Roosevelt called for a comprehensive revision of the naturalization laws: "The courts having power to naturalize should be definitely named by national authority; the testimony upon which naturalization may be conferred should be definitely prescribed; publication of impending naturalization applications should be required in advance of their hearing in court; the form and wording of all certificates issued should be uniform throughout the country, and the courts should be required to make returns to the Secretary of State at stated periods of all naturalizations conferred." Roosevelt called also for an inquiry into the subjects of citizenship, expatriation, and protection of Americans abroad, with a view to appropriate legislation." President Benjamin Harrison had previously made statements encouraging Congress to enact legislation that dealt with naturalization in his first and second state of the union addresses in 1889 and 1890. Roosevelt had made similar appeals in his third address in 1903, and did so again in 1905 (www.presidency.ucsb.edu http://www.presidency.ucsb.edu/ws/index.php?pid=29545#ixzz1QloQA2eh).

17. Massachusetts was first to change to secret ballot in 1888. In 1889, nine states had done so, in 1892 thirty, and in 1896, thirty-nine; see Schudson, *The Good Citizen,* 169

18. Courts had started to accept jurisdiction earlier. The first recorded denaturalization occurred in 1868. *Commonwealth v. Paper,* 1 Brewst. 263, 266 (Pa. 1868). Successively in 1869, 1878, 1892, and 1898, federal and state judges had cancelled certificates of naturalization when fraud had been proven. See John P. Roche, "Pre-Statutory Denaturalization," *Cornell Law Quarterly* 35 (1949–1950): 130–131.

19. 2 Stat. 153, 153–154 (1802) §1.

20. Ibid., 154, §1, codified in USRS 2165.

21. 2 Stat. 153, 153 (1802) §1 (three years prior); 4 Stat. 69, 69 (1824), §4 (reduced period from three years to two years).

22. The so-called Minor's Act (§2167 of the Revised Statutes, act of May 26, 1824).

23. Parrillo, *Against the Profit Motive.*

24. Purdy Comission Report, 19. This first federal law was just the continuation of state laws by

which naturalization was effected "by taking an oath of allegiance before a State court or a justice of the peace."

25. It was not necessary that the court have all common-law jurisdiction but merely "that it exercise its power according to the course of common law." Van Dyne, *Citizenship*, 64.

26. Children and women not counted. Statement of Gaillard Hunt, *Hearings Before the Committee on Immigration and Naturalization, January 23, 1906, to March 6, 1906, on the Bill to Establish a Bureau of Naturalization and to Provide for an Uniform Rule for the Naturalization of Aliens Throughout the United States* (Washington, D.C.: Government Printing Office, 1906), 12.

27. Purdy Commission Report, 23.

28. Ibid., 20.

29. Ibid., 26. The constitutional clause the commission referred to was clause 4 of section 8 of Article 1.

30. Ibid., 28. Attorney General Charles J. Bonaparte wanted only federal courts to be given the power to naturalize. *Annual Report of the Attorney General, 1904* (Washington, D.C.: Government Printing Office, 1904), iv–v. The commission, however, had to acknowledge that "the issuance of certificates of citizenship by the courts has been so long the custom that to take it away would result in great disturbance and dissatisfaction. The present system is fixed and is supported by public opinion, and the wisest course is to regulate it and not destroy it." Purdy Commission Report, 19.

31. Purdy Commission Report, 25–26.

32. Ibid., 28.

33. Senator Thomas C. Platt of New York had proposed (58th Congress, 3rd sess., S. 6655) to create in the State Department a bureau of naturalization that would provide uniform documents and would receive returns of naturalization fees. Purdy Commission Report, 27.

34. Purdy Commission Report, 29.

35. Statement of Benjamin F. Howell, President of the Committee, *Hearings Before the Committee on Immigration and Naturalization*, January 30, 1906, 43.

36. 34 Stat. 599 (1906) §11.

37. 34 Stat. 601 (1906).

38. Testimony of Richard Campbell, *Hearing Before the Subcommittee of the House Committee on Appropriations in Charge of the Sundry Civil Appropriation Bill for 1908* (Washington, D.C.: Government Printing Office, 1907), January 25, 1907, 137.

39. *Annual Report of the Chief of Division of Naturalization, 1907* (Washington, D.C.: Government Printing Office, 1907), 16.

40. *Annual Report of the Commissioner General of Immigration, 1910* (Washington, D.C.: Government Printing Office, 1910), 212. The number of declarations of intention had doubled in two years: 73,323 were filed in 1907, there were 137, 229 in 1908, and there were 145,794 in 1909.

41. See Department of Commerce and Labor, Bureau of Immigration and Naturalization, *Directory of Courts Having Jurisdiction in Naturalization Proceedings*, 1st ed. (Washington, D.C.: Government Printing Office, 1908).

42. *Annual Report of the Chief of Division of Naturalization, 1907*, 3.

43. *Annual Report of the Commissioner General of Immigration, 1910*.

44. The appropriation was for necessary expenses in connection with naturalization proceedings. Act of March 4, 1907, *Annual Report of the Attorney General, 1907* (Washington, D.C.: Government Printing Office, 1907), 216.

45. The cities were Boston, New York, Philadelphia, Pittsburgh, Detroit, Chicago, St. Louis, St.

Paul, Denver, San Francisco, and Seattle. Each attorney had charge of a given territory surrounding his headquarters, and the entire country, except some portions of the southern states, was thus covered by a field force of examiners under the immediate supervision of assistant U.S. attorneys. *Annual Report of the Attorney General, 1909* (Washington, D.C.: Government Printing Office, 1909), 14. Upon the establishment of this service, a necessary deficiency appropriation of $93,000 was made for the fiscal year ending June 30, 1908.

46. Testimony of Campbell, January 9, 1908, *Hearing Before the Subcommittee of the House Committee on Appropriations in Charge of the Sundry Civil Appropriation Bill for 1909* (Washington, D.C.: Government Printing Office, 1908), 492. They were appointed through the Civil Service Commission.

47. *Annual Report of the Attorney General, 1907*, report of Hon. Alford W. Cooley, assistant attorney general of operations, under the Naturalization Law, exhibit 18, 217. The Department of Justice's hope was to appoint enough examiners for "preliminary investigation of all petitions filed in [those] judicial districts."

48. Testimony of Campbell, February 5, 1909, *Hearing Before the Subcommittee of the House Committee on Appropriations in Charge of the Sundry Civil Appropriation Bill for 1910* (Washington, D.C.: Government Printing Office, 1909), 914.

49. See, for example, letter of assistant U.S. attorney in Pittsburgh of August 19, 1908, to the chief of the Division of Naturalization. NARA, RG 85, entry 26, file 106972. See also the chart sent by William H. Lewis, assistant U.S. attorney in Boston to Campbell, which shows that five of the eight cancellations of naturalization were of witnesses on a petition. NARA, RG 85, entry 26, file 10672/10. See also *Annual Report of the Secretary of Commerce and Labor, 1908* (Washington, D.C.: Government Printing Office, 1908), 28.

50. Ibid.

51. *Annual Report of the Chief of Division of Naturalization, 1908* (Washington, D.C.: Government Printing Office, 1908), 15. The public-land laws furnish also occasion for correspondence with the General Land Office, of the Interior Department, sometimes in regard to the legality of acquired citizenship and more frequently with reference to the evidence required either in support of claims filed on the public lands or to sustain the ultimate transfer, after naturalization, of title to the claimants.

52. *Annual Report of the Chief of Division of Naturalization, 1907*, 17–18: "All cases of this sort are reported by the Department of State, and through the division an investigation is made," resulting either in confirmation of the legitimacy of naturalization or in action to denaturalize.

53. According to a later evaluation, one naturalization examiner could handle nine cases per day while a denaturalization case took one month.

54. *Annual Report of the Chief of Division of Naturalization, 1907*, 19.

55. Campbell sent a letter to all U.S. attorneys on August, 10, 1908, for example. NARA, RG 85, entry 26, file 10672/10. Archives show that many dozens of denaturalizations were decided in 1907, 1908, and 1909 by the Supreme Court of the state of New York, and many other dozens in Hudson County (N.J.) and in St. Louis, Mo., as if a systematic policy of revision of fraudulent naturalizations had been pursued by some U.S. district attorneys. NARA, RG 85, entry 26, file 1737/ 13, 23, 50, and 122.

56. *Annual Report of the Attorney General, 1908* (Washington, D.C.: Government Printing Office, 1908), 11. The attorney general added that in regard to the law's requirement that the department investigate "the qualifications of every applicant for citizenship" and challenge naturalization of those not qualified, "Experience has shown that it is impossible to carry out the duty thus cast upon the .department with the appropriation made by the Congress for the fiscal year 1909."

57. *Annual Report of the Commissioner General of Immigration, 1907* (Washington, D.C.: Government Printing Office, 1907) and testimony of Campbell, January 9, 1908, *Hearing Before the Subcommittee of the House Committee on Appropriations for 1909*, 492.

58. Bonaparte, *Hearing Before the Subcommittee of the House Committee on Appropriations for 1910* , February 5, 1909, 998. Under President Theodore Roosevelt, Bonaparte served as the Secretary of the Navy from 1905 until December 17, 1906, when he became Attorney General. During his tenure, Bonaparte proved instrumental in numerous antitrust lawsuits. In 1908, he established what would become the Federal Bureau of Investigation.

59. Alford W. Cooley, assistant to the Attorney General Charles J. Bonaparte, added: "The system uniformly followed in other departments of the government by which the preliminary investigations of fact are made by the department directly charged with the administration of the law has, on the whole, worked satisfactorily." *Annual Report of the Attorney General, 1907*, 217–218.

60. Letter of Oscar Straus to Bonaparte, January 20, 1909. Library of Congress, Manuscript division, Charles Bonaparte Papers, box 131.

61. Testimony of Bonaparte, *Hearing Before the Subcommittee of the House Committee on Appropriations for 1909*, March 24, 1908, 798.

62. Testimony of Campbell, March 25, 1909, *Hearing before the Subcommittee of the House Committee on Appropriations for 1908*, 797–798.

63. *Annual Report of the Chief of Division of Naturalization, 1910* (Washington, D.C.: Government Printing Office), 8, 10.

64. Letter, the attorney general to the secretary of commerce, November 2, 1909, NARA, RG 85, INS Records of the Central Office, Administrative Files Relating to Naturalization (hereafter Naturalization Files), 1906–1940, entry 26, file 19742/7.

65. *Annual Report of the Attorney General, 1910* (Washington, D.C.: Government Printing Office), 25.

66. *Annual Report of the Chief of Division of Naturalization, 1908*, 23.

67. *Annual Report of the Attorney General, 1908*, 11. He recommended also that Congress enact a law to denaturalize "persons who by reason of the Expatriation Act of March 2, 1907, are no longer citizens of the United States."

68. Letter of Campbell to William Harr, assistant attorney general, September 15, 1909. NARA, RG 85, Naturalization Files, 1906–1940, entry 26, file 19742/7.

69. During his time as attorney general (1909–1913), Wickersham was especially involved in the enforcement of antitrust laws, and in 1913 he helped draft the Sixteenth Amendment to the U.S. Constitution. When the United States entered World War I, President Woodrow Wilson appointed Wickersham to the War Trade Board. Wickersham was also head of the National Commission of Law Observance and Law Enforcement under President Herbert Hoover.

70. NARA, RG 60, General Records of the Department of Justice, Administrative Orders, Circulars, and Memoranda, 1856–1953, unnumbered files (1856–1903); 1–250 (1907–1911). Instructions as to Naturalization Matters, Department of Justice, Department Circular Letter No. 107.

Chapter 2. The Installment of the Bureau of Naturalization, 1909–1926

1. Morris Roscoe Bevington, May 28, 1913, memo on the *Pippert* case, NARA, RG 85, entry 26, file 1737/26.

2. On November 14, 1910, fourteen certificates of naturalizations delivered by the District Court of Logan County, North Dakota, had been cancelled because the court was without jurisdiction to grant naturalization. NARA, RG 85, INS Records, Naturalization Files, 1906–1940, entry 26, file 106972/11.

3. Letter of Richard K. Campbell to William Harr, assistant attorney general, September 15, 1909. NARA, RG 85, INS Records of the Central Office, Naturalization Fil s, 1906–1940, entry 26, file 19742/7. The 1909 circular from the Department of Justice acknowled ed that the law's provisions applied "to certificates issued under prior laws as well as under the present Act."

4. *Annual Report of the Commissioner of Naturalization, 1913* (Washington, D.C.: Government Printing Office, 1913), 15.

5. The wording of the memo did not limit the restriction to older cases, but the time of its implementation, only three years after the passing of the law, supports the interpretation of Campbell.

6. Memorandum of Campbell, for the acting secretary, April 27, 1915, NARA, RG 85, INS Records, Naturalization Files, 1906–1940, entry 26, file 19742/7.

7. The Bureau argued that though the Department of Justice "institute[ed] and conduct[ed]" cases, in most of them, examiners gathered evidence and brought the cases to U.S. attorneys. "Would it not be wise to have these officers who are in most instances, not only good lawyers but specialists in naturalization law, handle all denaturalization cases?" the bureau added. *Annual Report of the Chief of Division of Naturalization, 1914* (Washington, D.C.: Government Printing Office, 1914), 17–18.

8. *Annual Report of the Commissioner of Naturalization, 1917* (Washington, D.C.: Government Printing Office, 1917), 11.

9. 225 U.S. 277 (1912).

10. *Annual Report of the Commissioner of Naturalization, 1917,* 11.

11. Ibid.

12. See Adam Goodman, "Defining and Inculcating 'the Soul of America': The Bureau of Naturalization and the Americanization Movement, 1914–1919," University of Pennsylvania Program on Democracy, Citizenship, and ConstitutionalismWorkshop Draft, November 2009, 7, available at http://www.sas.upenn.edu/dcc/workshops/documents/Goodman_DCC09.pdf. This paragraph relies on this excellent article.

13. 65th Congress, sess. 2, chap. 69, 1918, 40 Stat. 544.

14. *Annual Report of the Commissioner of Naturalization, 1919* (Washington, D.C.: Government Printing Office, 1919), 9.

15. *Report of the Naturalization Commission to the President* (Purdy Commission Report), 59th Congress, 1st sess., November 8, 1905, H. 46, 19.

16. Lawrence Preuss, "Denaturalization on the Ground of Disloyalty," *American Political Science Review* 36 (August 1942): 705.

17. Isaac A. Mansour had been charged by the government with lying about the length of his American residency, a charge that, under the new law, could lead to his denaturalization. Mansour unexpectedly requested a jury trial in the case, which caught the government flat-footed; the denaturalization law itself did not specify how such requests were to be treated. In the end, the courts settled on a comparison between denaturalization and the process for the revocation of a patent, since both naturalization and the issuance of a patent have at their core credibility in information provided exclusively by the applicant. *United States v. Mansour,* 170 Fed. 671, 676 (S.D.N.Y. 1908); cf. NARA, RG 85, entry 26, file 106974/3. In his conclusion Judge Charles M. Hough asserted, "that a naturalized citizen is as much as any other, and to observe that the provisions of the Act regarding

the effect of five years residence abroad constitute as to naturalized aliens, an unconstitutional attack upon their rights as citizens." See Henry B. Hazard, "The Right of Appeal in Naturalization Cases in the Federal Courts," *American Journal of International Law* 21, no. 1 (January 1927): 40.

18. "Denaturalization and the Right to Jury Trial," *Journal of Criminal Law and Criminology* 71, no. 1 (Spring 1980): 47. In 1913, in its decision *Luria v. United States*, 231 U.S. 9 (1913), the Supreme Court confirmed this previous lower court ruling that denaturalization procedures were a "suit in equity" as opposed to a legal matter, and that therefore a jury trial would not be appropriate.

19. 225 U.S. 227 (1912).

20. 245 U.S. 319 (1917).

21. The Court did not apply the rule of *res judicata*. The only case where the Supreme Court seemed to apply the rule of *res judicata* was related to racial exclusion of a Hindu American. See Chapter 6 below.

22. *United States v. Ness*, 245 U.S. 319, 326 (1917). Eleven years later, after the Supreme Court had judged that naturalization proceedings were merely an instrument of granting a certificate of citizenship, it confirmed in *Maney v. United States,* 278 U.S. 17 (1928), that *res judicata* did not apply. Justice Oliver Wendell Holmes delivered the opinion of the Court and concluded: "As the certificate of citizenship was illegally obtained, the express words of §15 authorize this proceeding to have it cancelled. The judgment attacked did not make the matter *res judicata,* as against the statutory provision for review. . . .It hardly can be called special treatment to say that a record that discloses on its face that the judgment transcends the power of the judge may be declared void in the interest of the sovereign who gave to the judge whatever power he had. 278 U.S. 23 (1928)." See Henry B. Hazard, "The Doctrine of Res Judicata in Naturalization Cases in the United States," *American Journal of International Law* 23, no. 1 (January 1929): 50.

23. *Tutun & Neuberger v. United States,* 270 U.S. 568 (1926). Hazard, "The Right of Appeal in Naturalization Cases," 43.

24. John L. Cable, *Loss of Citizenship, Denaturalization, the Alien in Wartime* (Washington, D.C.: National Law Book, 1943), 6.

25. See the last sentence of Justice Brandeis's opinion in *Tutun & Neuberger v. United States*: "we answer that the circuit court of appeals has jurisdiction to review by appeal the order or decree of the district court denying the petition to be admitted to citizenship in the United States." 270 U.S. 580 and in *United States v. Ness*, 245 U.S. at 326, n. 9.

26. "Normally in equity proceedings the doctrine of 'laches' prevents the reopening of a question after a reasonable period has passed. . . . However it has been held that 'laches' is no defense against denaturalization as it may not be pleaded against the sovereign," says John P. Roche in "Statutory Denaturalization: 1906–1951," *University of Pittsburgh Law Review* 13 (1951–1952): 295, quoting *United States v. Richmond* 17 F.2d 28 (3d. Cir. 1927); *United States v. Spohrer*, 175 Fed. 440 (C.C.D.N.J. 1910); *United States v. Brass*, 37 F.Supp. 698 (E.D.N.Y. 1941). Appeal of a judgment of naturalization decided by a district court must be made within three months following the decision (in Shoemaker, "Judicial Review of Naturalization Cases").

27. Roche, "Statutory Denaturalization," 283–287 and 291–292.

28. See ibid., 277, and G. Fred DiBona, "Cancellation of Certificates of Citizenship for Fraud or Illegality in the Procurement Under Section 15 of the Naturalization Act of 1906," *University of Pennsylvania Law Review* 88, no. 7 (May 1940): 842.

29. See *Annual Report of the Commissioner of Naturalization, 1914* (Washington, D.C.: Government Printing Office, 1914), 23–25.

30. This court was the Federal Court in Massachusetts. Statement of Farrell, U.S. House of Representatives, 67th Cong., 1st sess., *Progress and Processes of Naturalization, Hearings Before the Committee on Immigration and Naturalization*, October 19, 1921, 1017.

31. In the same statement, Farrell testified that "the superior court throughout the State has no rule," he added, "but it is acting practically on the same basis." Then he mentions that the practice has developed also in New Hampshire; ibid., 1017.

32. Ibid.

33. On July 1, 1925, the Naturalization Service was divided into twenty-seven naturalization centers, or twenty-three main headquarters, of which four had substations. These new districts replaced the existing eleven centers. *Annual Report of the Commissioner of Naturalization, 1927* (Washington, D.C.: Government Printing Office, 1927), 7.

34. *Annual Report of the Commissioner of Naturalization, 1918* (Washington, D.C.: Government Printing Office, 1918), 31.

35. See John Palmer Gavit, *Americans by Choice* (New York: Harper, 1922), 264.

36. See Lucy E. Salyer, "Baptism by Fire: Race, Military Service, and U.S. Citizenship Policy, 1918–1935," *Journal of American History* 91, no. 3 (December 2004).

37. *Annual Report of the Commissioner of Naturalization, 1923* (Washington, D.C.: Government Printing Office, 1923), 26..

38. *Annual Report of the Commissioner of Naturalization, 1918*, 31.

39. The appropriation went from $675,000 in 1919 to $550,000 in 1920, then $534,500 in 1921, to $550,000 in 1922, and then to $600,000 in 1923 but would never go back to the level of 1919.

40. Testimony of Thomas B. Shoemaker, *Hearing Before the Subcommittee of the House Committee on Appropriations, Sundry Appropriation Bill, 1922*, 66th Cong., 3rd sess., December 10, 1920, 1718.

41. *Annual Report of the Commissioner of Naturalization, 1923*, 14.

42. Testimony of Thomas B. Shoemaker, December 10, 1920, 1718.

43. *Annual Report of the Commissioner of Naturalization, 1923*, 1.

44. Testimony of Raymond Crist, *Hearings Before the Subcommittee of the House Committee on Appropriations, Appropriation Bill, 1920*, 66th Cong., 2nd sess., December 29, 1919, 463.

45. Testimony of Shoemaker. *Hearing Before the Subcommittee of the House Committee on Appropriations, Appropriation Bill, 1923*, 67th Cong., 2nd sess., February 9, 1922, 818. During the 1920s denunciations became a means to control who became citizens. National Archives files contain examples of denunciations of foreigners accused of disloyalty or bad moral character; see, for example, for a district attorney and a minister accusing Russian immigrants of disloyalty for having spoken out against "our late president Harding." NARA, RG 85, entry 26, file 71/19,

46. Testimony of Crist, December 29, 1919, 464. After the reorganization of the bureau and its split into two separate agencies, Crist became the deputy commissioner of naturalization in 1913. In 1919, he became the director of citizenship at the bureau before being appointed commissioner of naturalization in 1923, a position he held until his resignation in 1933.

47. *Annual Report of the Commissioner of Naturalization, 1925* , 10.

48. Fred Schlotfeld, "Function and Duties of Clerks of Courts Exercising Naturalization Jurisdiction" (INS Lecture 11, Washington. April 16, 1934), 2. NARA, RG 85, entry 26, file 55475/7–11.

49. The Purdy Committee had proposed $11.

50. On November 23, 1917, Louis Post, assistant secretary of labor, approved a new regulation that permitted the bureau to calculate the amount of fees collected at the end of each year and not

by quarter, a system that was putting some clerks at a disadvantage. NARA, RG 85, INS Records of the Central Office, Naturalization Files, 1906–1940, entry 26, file 12.

51. In addition, in many states, where the clerks of the courts were salaried, the fees conferred by the federal statute would go to the state fisc. See Nick Parrillo, *Against the Profit Motive: The Transformation of American Government, 1780–1940* (New Haven, Conn.: Yale University Press, forthcoming).

52. See the question of Senator Selden P Spencer, Senate Committee on Appropriations, *Departments of State, Justice, Commerce and Labor Appropriation Bill, 1926, Hearings Before the Subcommittee on Appropriations on H.R. 11753, January 29, 1925*, 68th Cong., 2nd sess., 1925, 4.

53. Statement of Farrell, *Progress and Processes of Naturalization*, October 19, 1921, 1024. This phenomenon had already been mentioned in 1909 to explain the fluctuation of the number of courts engaged in naturalization proceedings: "Still another reason for such fluctuation is found in the attitude of clerks of courts, many of whom turn away applicants upon the ground that some other accessible court is transacting such business and that they have neither the time nor the inclination to undertake the business." *Report of the Secretary of the Department of Commerce and Labor and Reports of Bureaus* (1909) (Washington, D.C.: Government Printing Office, 1909), 289.

54. *Annual Report of the Commissioner of Naturalization, 1921* (Washington, D.C.: Government Printing Office, 1921), 9.

55. Senate Committee on Appropriations, *Departments of State, Justice, Commerce and Labor Appropriation Bill, 1926*, 3.

56. Ibid., 3.

57. Ibid., 6–8.

58. *Annual Report of the Commissioner of Naturalization, 1924* (Washington, D.C.: Government Printing Office, 1924), 8.

59. Calvin Coolidge Papers, Manuscript Division, Library of Congress, Washington, D.C. Series 1, 15-F.

60. Testimony of Crist, *Hearings Before the Subcommittee of the House Committee on Appropriations, Fiscal Year 1920*, 66 Cong., 1st sess., September 4, 1919, 822.

61. Ibid.

62. Testimony of Campbell, *Hearings Before the Subcommittee of the House Committee on Appropriations, Fiscal Year 1913*, 62nd Cong., 2nd sess., January 24, 1912, 750.

63. *Annual Report of the Commissioner of Naturalization, 1921*, 7–8.

64. In subsequent years the numbers were: 1924—501 (U.S. att.), 180 (DN); 1925—1,595 (U.S. att.), 53 (DN); 1926—1,000 (U.S. att.), 56 (DN); in 1927—549 (U.S. att.), 63(DN); in 1928—377 (U.S. att.), 24 (DN). In 1928, the Bureau of Naturalization recognized the shift back to its prior practice: "under the prevailing practice, it is customary for a suit to be recommended by the Commissioner or the deputy Commissioner to the department of Labor and by the latter submitted to the Department of Justice." The bureau submitted ninety cases that year; the Department of Justice did not act favorably on forty cases.

65. NARA, RG 85, INS Records of the Central Office, Naturalization Files, 1906–1940, entry 26, file 1737/53.

66. Ibid., file 15/8–102.

67. *Annual Report of the Commissioner of Naturalization, 1923*, 15.

68. *Annual Report of the Commissioner of Naturalization, 1926* (Washington, D.C.: Government Printing Office, 1926), 11–12.

69. Shoemaker, "Judicial Review of Naturalization Cases," 8–9. Shoemaker confirms in this

lecture that though the commissioner or deputy commissioner could legally institute cancelation proceedings, they were no longer instituting such proceedings.

70. In his testimony before a House committee, Chief Justice Taft later said, "When Judge Hand appealed to me about it, I took it up with the Labor Department. Judge Hand came here and had a conference with the officials of the Labor Department and agreed upon a bill which I think is the printed bill you have before you." House Committee on Immigration and Naturalization, *Statement of Honorary William Howard Taft, Chief Justice of the Supreme Court of the United States, Hearing No. 69.1.14 on Various Bills to Amend, Supplement the Naturalization Laws, and for Other Purposes, Relief of Judges in Naturalization Cases,* May 1, 1926, 4–5. On the judicial management of Taft, see Robert Post, "Judicial Management: The Achievements of Chief Justice William Howard Taft," *OAH Magazine of History* (Fall 1998): 24–29.

71. House Committee on Immigration and Naturalization, *Statement of Honorary William Howard Taft*, May 1, 1926, 4–5.

72. The act is entitled "An Act to Amend and Supplement the Naturalization Laws and for Other Purposes."

73. U.S. Department of Labor, *Historical Sketch of Naturalization in the United States* (Washington, D.C.: Government Printing Office, 1926), 14.

74. Since 1924, the Bureau of Naturalization had advocated the creation of naturalization courts, which would be administrative, rather than judicial, but "with the right of appeal to the appropriate United States court." The bureau added that "such courts have been urged for years by judges throughout the United States." *Annual Report of the of the Commissioner of Naturalization, 1924,* (Washington, D.C.: Government Printing Office, 1924), 18. This plea is repeated in 1925 (*Annual Report of the Commissioner of Naturalization, 1925* , 21) and endorsed in 1926 by the secretary of labor: "The ideal of absolute uniformity, in conformity with the mandate of the Constitution, would appear to be possible only in the event of the ultimate adoption of administrative naturalization, with a single source of interpretation and construction." *Annual Report of the Secretary of Labor, 1927* (Washington, D.C.: Government Printing Office, 1927), 151.

75. The Naturalization Act authorized proceedings to cancel certificates of naturalization fraudulently or illegally procured to be brought in state courts, but as noted in Chapter 1, in practice U.S. attorneys had been instructed by the attorney general (circular letter 107, September 20, 1909) to institute actions in the federal courts. One exception was *United States ex rel. Volpe v. Jordan,* 161 F. 2d 390 (7th Cir. 1947), in which a U.S. attorney requested a state court to set aside its own judgment. See Roche, "Statutory Denaturalization," 276.

76. See Interventions of M. Adolph Sabath, House Committee on Immigration and Naturalization, *Statement of Honorary William Howard Taft*, May 1, 1926, 9, 16.

77. Schlotfeld, "Function and Duties of Clerks of Courts,"16. The first year, the Federal courts were only 56 of the 238 exercising naturalization jurisdiction to adopt the new system; but the courts that adopted it rapidly dealt with the majority of applicants. *Annual Report of the Commissioner of Naturalization, 1927* (Washington, D.C.: Government Printing Office, 1927), 7.

78. *Annual Report of the Commissioner of Naturalization, 1930* (Washington, D.C.: Government Printing Office, 1930), 10..

79. In 1927, the number was 96,773 of 195,493, or slightly less than 50 percent. In 1928, the numbers were again lower, with 96,440 of 228,006, or 42 percent. In 1931, state courts These figures come from the *Annual Report of the Commissioner of Naturalization* for *1926,* 38; *1927,* 33; *1928,* 26; *1930,* 23; and *1931* (Washington, D.C.: Government Printing Office), 27; the applications denied

drop from 10 to 5 percent. In 1929, the power of naturalization examiners was reinforced by the the Registry Act of March 2, 1929 (45 Stat. 1512), which extended the possibility of an applicant to prove five years of residence anywhere in the United States, only six months being obligatory in the county of application. But in such a case, the naturalization examiner had exclusive competence to take and check the depositions. In 1940, the provision for the designated examiner was extended to state courts. Nationality Act of October 14, 1940, sec. 333, 54 Stat. 1154.

Chapter 3. The Victory of the Federalization of Naturalization, 1926–1940

1. NARA, RG 85, INS Records, Central Office, Naturalization Files, 1906–1940, entry 26, file 14–36. Among reasons the naturalization was considered illegal were that it did not include place of residence, occupation, date and place of arrival to the United States, or of declaration of intention.

2. NARA, RG 85, INS Records, Central Office, Naturalization Files, 1906–1940, entry 26, file 14-36.

3. NARA, RG 85, INS Records, Central Office, Naturalization Files, 1906–1940, entry 26, file 41–48.

4. This information was given to me by Zack A. Wilske, historian, Historical Library, Homeland Security Department.

5. Sam Bernsen, "Acquisition of Lawful Permanent Residence by Aliens in the United States," *Immigration and Naturalization Reporter* 7 (July 1958): 3–4.

6. *Annual Report of the Commissioner of Naturalization, 1925* (Washington, D.C.: Government Printing Office, 1925), 7.The Naturalization Act of 1906 had first required a record of lawful entry or admission as a prerequisite to naturalization. The effect of the new law became apparent five years later, in 1911, when numerous immigrants were unable to be naturalized because there was no record of their admission, or no such record could be found. These people could not be naturalized until Congress provided relief with the Registry Act of 1929. In the first "legalization program" authorized by Congress, immigrants subject to the certificate of arrival requirement for naturalization, but for whom no arrival record could be found, were allowed to have a record of their original arrival created. It applied in 1929 to immigrants who arrived before July 1, 1921. Later, with an amendment passed in 1939, Congress moved the ending date to July 1, 1924. On August 8, 1958, the ending date was moved to June 28, 1940. As a result of the 1958 changes, the registry mechanism became available to aliens who had entered the country illegally or who had overstayed, or violated the terms of a temporary period of entry. The registry date was subsequently changed to June 30, 1948, and then to January 1, 1972, where it stands today. Since 1985, approximately sixty thousand people have adjusted to lawful permanent residence under the registry provision.

7. Ibid., 7.

8. This act (40 Stat. 542, 1918) consolidated the previous statutes of July 17, 1862 (12 Stat. 597), which allowed waiver of the filing of a declaration if the applicant had a favorable discharge from the army, and of July 24, 1894 (28 Stat. 124), which extended this provision to applicants discharged from the navy or the marines.

9. *Annual Report of the Commissioner of Naturalization, 1919* (Washington, D.C.: Government Printing Office, 1919), 20–22.

10. *Annual Report of the Secretary of Labor, 1924* (Washington, D.C.: Government Printing Office, 1924), 130.

11. *Annual Report of the Secretary of Labor, 1930* (Washington, D.C.: Government Printing Office, 1930), 88, and *Annual Report of the Secretary of Labor, 1931* (Washington, D.C.: Government Printing Office, 1931), 71.

12. *Annual Report of the Secretary of Labor, 1931.*

13. Congress did appropriate extra money for the INS to increase its staff of naturalization examiners and clerks and thereby reduce the delays in processing citizenship applications. Mary Ann Thatcher, *Immigrants and the 1930s: Ethnicity and Alienage in Depression and Coming War* (New York: Garland, 1990), 187.

14. Ibid., 250.

15. *Annual Report of the Secretary of Labor, 1936* (Washington, D.C.: Government Printing Office, 1936), 101.

16. See *Annual Report of the Secretary of Labor, 1935* (Washington, D.C.: Government Printing Office, 1935), 81–82.

17. Dallas Hirst, "Is Citizenship a Fair Requirement in Old Age Assistance Acts?" *Social Forces* 11 (October 1932): 109–110.

18. Marietta Stevenson, "Old-Age Assistance," *Law and Contemporary Problems* 3, no. 2 (April 1936): 239.

19. Ibid., 239, 241–242.

20. Letter of J. L. Hugues, INS Philadelphia office, to Daniel W. MacCormack, commissioner of INS, Washington D.C., April 5, 1935, NARA, RG 85, entry 26, file 19742/1.

21. The persons involved were given certified copies of the judicial orders granting them citizenship, which they in turn presented to the local investigator of the Texas Old Age Assistance Commission and were certified as eligible for old age assistance. See Memo from the Chairman of the board of review approved by the deputy commissioner, November 17, 1938, NARA, RG 85, entry 26, files 41/49 to 41/53.

22. Harold Fields, "Where Shall the Alien Work?" *Social Forces* 12, no.2 (December 1933), 213-221.

23. Thatcher, *Immigrants and the 1930s*, 155–157.

24. Ibid., 167.

25. This provision allowed some flexibility, but nonetheless provided a clear sign to the WPA and to aliens that their hiring was perhaps soon to be restricted. In 1937, restrictions were indeed tightened further, this time excluding not only illegal immigrants but also those who had yet to apply for their "first papers." The "knowingly" and "prompt" language from the earlier bill carried over, but a failed effort to amend the bill to exclude aliens entirely kept immigrant advocates concerned for the future. Thatcher, *Immigrants and the 1930s*, 172, 175.

26. Thatcher, *Immigrants and the 1930s*, 183.

27. See, e.g., NARA, RG 85, INS Records, Central Office, Naturalization Files, 1906–1940, entry 26, file 1737/ 13.

28. *Annual Report of the Secretary of Labor, 1935*, 82.

29. *Report of the Attorney General, 1935* (Washington, D.C.: Government Printing Office, 1935), 65. Benjamin Bergman, alleged leader in an "extensive alien-smuggling and naturalization fraud ring," was found dead in a YMCA an hour and a half before he was scheduled to testify to Special Assistant Kaufman regarding his role in the racket. The specialty of Bergman's ring was to modify ships' manifests so as to provide proof of legal entry into the United States. His testimony was expected to result in charges against "a score of persons, including several government officials and clerks." Police ruled Bergman's death a suicide, since he was found with a two-thirds empty bottle

of white powder and a note reading "I took poison because of heart failure. No autopsy will be necessary." The newspaper article reporting his death notes that "Bergman never had complained of heart trouble, but often had indicated fear of gang reprisals to prevent his testimony." "Exposer of Racket Dies in a Mystery," *New York Times*, June 6, 1935.

30. *Annual Report of the Secretary of Labor, 1937* (Washington, D.C.: Government Printing Office, 1938), 94

31. Nationality Act of October 14, 1940, sec. 333, 54 Stat. 1154. In 1929, the power of naturalization examiners had been reinforced by the the the Registry Act of March 2,1929 (45 Stat 1512), which extended the possibility of an applicant to prove five years of residence anywhere in the United States, only six months being obligatory in the county of application. But in such a case, the naturalization examiner had exclusive competence to take and check the depositions.

32. Reorganization Plan No. V, 5 *Federal Register* 2223.

33. Bat-Ami Zucker, "Frances Perkins and the German-Jewish Refugees," *American Jewish History* 89, no. 1 (March 2001).

34. Robert W. Cherny, "Constructing a Radical Identity: History, Memory, and the Seafaring Stories of Harry Bridges," *Pacific Historical Review* 70, no. 4 (November 2001): 573.

35. Benjamin Welles, *Sumner Welles: FDR's Global Strategist* (New York: St. Martin's Press, 1997), 275.

36. Letter of Sumner Welles to Roosevelt, May 18, 1940, box 90, folder 6, Robert Jackson Papers, Manuscript Division, Library of Congress, Washington, D.C. At the end of January 1940, Attorney General Robert Jackson had heard about a rumor of a proposed transfer of the immigration service from the Department of Labor to his department. On February 1, 1940, he wrote to Judge Townsend: "If you hear something tangible about it, I should like to be advised." Memo from Jackson to Judge Townsend, February 1, 1940, box 90, folder 6, Jackson Papers Welles met him on May 14, 1940, and sent him a copy of the memos he was sending to Roosevelt. They emphasized that admission of aliens into the United States and their supervision were matters of increasing importance in light of existing world conditions. Welles also pointed defects in the existing system, particularly lack of control of entry and residence. Some aliens had not submitted to consular control before entry. Welles proposes in his letter to Franklin Roosevelt that the State Department coordinate all the departments in charge of the immigration issues a proposal Jackson then accepted. Letter of Jackson to Welles, May 15, 1940, box 90, folder 6, Jackson Papers.

37. After Roosevelt announced his decision to transfer the service, Republican Representative John Taber from New York declared: "We are going to vote for this reorganization plan because the President has not the patriotism nor the courage to remove the Secretary of Labor, a notorious incompetent, and one who for the last seven years has steadily and steadfastly failed and refused to enforce the Immigration Law, and continuously admitted and kept here those who were not entitled to stay." Perkins to Congressman John Taber, May 27, 1940, file: I-19, Perkins Papers, Connecticut College Library, New London, quoted in Zucker, "Frances Perkins and the German-Jewish Refugees," 59. Francis Biddle testified that "the secretary of labor acquiesced readily, as she had never relished its supervision. Miss Perkins had been neglecting the Service, and it had withered, as any human organization will, from lack of encouragement from the top." He adds: "The President had, it soon became apparent, decided that immigration control should be tightened." Francis Beverley Biddle, *In Brief Authority* (New York: Doubleday, 1962), 106.

38. Note of May 21, 1940, box 90, folder 6, Jackson Papers. On May 23, after the official announcement, Jackson announced that the INS would be maintained as a unit with an administrative

status similar to that of the FBI, the Bureau of Prisons, or the Bureau of War Risks Litigation. Department of Justice, news release, May 23, 1940, box 90, folder 6, Jackson Papers.

39. John P. Roche, "Statutory Denaturalization: 1906–1951," *University of Pittsburgh Law Review* 13 (1951–1952), 306.

40. The Alien Registration Act or Smith Act of 29th June, 1940 ((18 USC §2385), required all alien residents in the United States over 14 years of age to to register and fingerprint.

41. In 1941, 161 Examiners were added, 75 in 1942 (Memorandum of Lemuel B. Schofield for Francis Biddle, February 2, 1942, Box 31, Marshall Dimock Papers, Franklin D. Roosevelt Library).

42. Marian Schibsby, "New Developments and Procedures in the Field of Naturalization," *New Nationality Legislation and Administrative Procedure* (New York: National Council on Naturalization and Citizenship, 1944), 19.

43. Title X of the Second War Powers Act of March 27, 1942, ch. 199, 56 Stat. 176

44. President's Commission on Immigration and Naturalization, *Whom We Shall Become* (Washington, D.C.: Government Printing Office, 1953), 251.

45. See Edward Rudnick, "Trend Toward Uniformity in Naturalization Decisions," *Monthly Review, Department of Justice, Immigration and Naturalization Service* 5, no.1 (July 1947): 11.

46. In July 1947, over twenty-six thousand petitions had been reviewed. If the reviewing authority concurred in the proposed recommendation, the case was immediately presented to the court. In the event of disagreement, the field examiner was required to change his recommendation and to conform to that of the Central Office. See Rudnick, "Trend Toward Uniformity in Naturalization Decisions," 11, and Joseph Savoretti, "Administrative Changes in Naturalization Procedures," *New Frontiers in Nationality Problems* (New York: National Council on Naturalization and Citizenship, 1944), 9.

47. Internal Security Act of 1950, 64 Stat. 993.

48. See Rudnick, "Trend Toward Uniformity in Naturalization Decisions," 11.

49. 104 Stat. 4978 Charles Gordon, Stanley Mailman, and Stephen Yale-Loehr, "Immigration Law and Procedure" LexisNexis (96-01).

50. S. Rep. No. 101–55, 101st Cong., 1st Sess. 22 (1989), 3.

51. Miscellaneous and Technical Immigration and Naturalization Amendments of 1991, Pub. L. 102-232 §102, 105 Stat. 1733, 1734. Quoted in Gordon, Mailman, and Yale-Loehr, "Immigration Law and Procedure" (96-01).

52. For example, fraud accounted for only 382 cancellations of a total of 864 in 1935. *Annual Report of the Secretary of Labor 1935*, 92.

Part II. A Conditional Citizenship

Note to epigraph: U.S. Congress, House, Progress and Processes of Naturalization, Hearings *Before the Committee on Immigration and Naturalization*, 67th Cong., 1st sess., October 19, 1921, 1015.

Chapter 4. The First Political Denaturalization

1. There were 1,026,000 entries in 1905 and 1,100,000 in 1906. The population of the United States had reached 76,000,000 at the turn of the twentieth century. William Bernard, ed., *American*

Immigration Policy: A Reappraisal (New York: Harper, 1950). In the decade 1881–1890, northern and western European Immigration accounted for 3,778,000 immigrants compared to 958,000 from southern and eastern Europe. In 1890–1900 the numbers were 1,643,000 compared to 1,915,000. In 1901–1910, the numbers were 1,910,000 compared to 6,225,000. The quota system reestablished the numbers in favor of western and northern Europe: for 1921–1930, they were 1,284,000 compared to 1,193,000; this reversal was confirmed in 1931–1940, with 212,000 compared to 186,000. Bernard, *American Immigration Policy*, 300.

2. 34 Stat. 898. Section 39 of the act created a commission for the study of immigration composed of three senators, three representatives, and three presidential appointees. Known as the Dillingham Commission, named after its chairman, the commission delivered a report of forty-two volumes in 1911. Its main recommendation was to require passing a literacy test, which had been proposed by Senator Henry Cabot Lodge and the Immigration Restriction League since 1894. The concept of old vs. new immigrant was developed into a stereotype implying a value judgment: "the old immigrants were portrayed as hardy pioneers who had helped develop the United States and had become an integral part of the nation, while the new immigrants were viewed as cashing in on American prosperity and failing to assimilate." Robert A. Divine, *American Immigration Policy, 1924–1952* (New Haven, Conn.: Yale University Press, 1957), 4.

3. See Aristide R. Zolberg, *A Nation by Design: Immigration Policy in the Fashioning of America* (New York: Russell Sage Foundation, 2006), 214–216, and Son Thierry Ly and Patrick Weil, "The Anti-racist Origins of the American Immigration Quota System," *Social Research* 77, no. 1 (Spring 2010): 45–79.

4. Candice Lewis Bredbenner, *A Nationality of Her Own: Women, Marriage and the Law of Citizenship* (Berkeley: University of California Press, 1998), 8.

5. As noted earlier, the Cable Act in 1922, amended in 1934 to include American women marrying Asians, permitted American women to keep their citizenship when they married foreigners.

6. On April 29, 1915, the U.S. District Court of Seattle (Washington) cancelled the certificate of naturalization of Albert Dahlstrom for being "a man of bad moral character," because he held immoral views on marriage, had "illicit relations with various females," and advocated free love. NARA, RG 85, entry 26, file 037751/125.

7. *Turlej v. United States*, 31 F.2d 696 (8th Cir. 1929).

8. *United States v. Raverat*, 222 F. 1018, 1018 (D.C.Mont. 1915).

9. Geoffrey R. Stone, *Perilous Times: Free Speech in Wartime from the Sedition Act of 1798 to the War on Terrorism* (New York: W. W. Norton, 2004), 143.

10. On March 3, 1907 Oscar Straus sent circulars to all Commissioners of Immigration and supervising immigration inspectors advising them to cooperate with local police and detective forces in order to rid the country of alien anarchists and criminals falling under the provisions relating to deportation of the Immigration Act of 1907. NARA, RG 85, entry 9, subject and policy files, file 51924/30A.

11. Emma Goldman, *Living My Life*, vol. 1 (New York: Alfred Knopf, 1931), 404–410.

12. "Strictly confidential" telegram of Frank P. Sargent, commissioner general, Bureau of Immigration, Washington, D.C., to to the New York, Philadelphia, and Baltimore immigration offices, September 24, 1907, Department of Commerce and Labor, Emma Goldman Papers, University of California, Berkeley.

13. Letter of Joseph Murray, acting commissioner, New York, to Sargent, September 25, 1907, Department of Commerce and Labor, Emma Goldman Papers, University of California, Berkeley.

14. Goldman, *Living My Life,* 411.

15. Ibid.

16. Ibid.

17. Memorandum of the Bureau of Immigration to Straus, November 17, 1907, Department of Commerce and Labor, Goldman Papers.

18. Letter of Straus to Robert Watchorn, commissioner, Ellis Island, N.Y., November 19, 1907, Goldman Papers.

19. Letter from Sargent to the Chief of the Division of Naturalization, March 10, 1908, NARA, RG 85, INS Records, Central Office, Naturalization Files, 1906–1940, entry 26, file 1737/292.

20. Telegram of Palmer S. Chambers, to Richard K. Campbell, chief, Division of Naturalization., March 13, 1908, NARA, RG 85, Naturalization Files, 1906–1940, entry 26, file 1737/292.

21. Letter of Palmer S. Chambers, assistant U.S. attorney, Pittsburgh, to Richard K. Campbell, chief, Division of Naturalization [Bureau of Immigration], Department of Commerce and Labor, Washington, D.C., March 18, 1908, NARA, RG 85, INS Records, Central Office, Naturalization Files, 1906–1940, entry 26, file 1737/292.

22. Letter of John Gruenberg, immigrant inspector, Ellis Island, N.Y., to Sargent, May 27, 1908, Goldman Papers.

23. Ibid.

24. Letter of Straus to Campbell, May 29, 1908, NARA, RG 85, INS Records, Central Office, Naturalization Files, 1906–1940, entry 26, file 1737/292.

25. Letter of Campbell to Straus and Straus to Campbell, June 11, 1908, NARA, RG 85, INS Records, Central Office, Naturalization Files, 1906–1940, entry 26, file 1737/292.

26. *United States v. Jacob A. Kersner*: Bill of Complaint, September 24, 1908, issued by Lyman M. Bass, U.S. attorney, Goldman Papers.

27. Letter of Chambers to Charles J. Bonaparte, attorney general, January 16, 1909, Goldman Papers.

28. Ibid.

29. Memorandum of William R. Harr, assistant attorney general, to Bonaparte, February 2, 1909, Goldman Papers.

30. Letters of Bonaparte to Harr and to Straus, February 5 and 8, 1909, Goldman Papers.

31. Letter of Straus to Bonaparte, February 11, 1909, Goldman Papers.

32. Letter of Charles J. Bonaparte, Attorney General to Palmer S. Chambers, February 16, 1909, Goldman Papers.

33. *United States v. Jacob A. Kersner,* No 133149-1, Decree cancelling certificate of Naturalization, April 8, 1909, John R. Hazel, Judge, U.S. District Court of the Western District of New York, NARA, RG 85, INS Records, INS Central Office, Administrative Files Relating to Naturalization, 1906–1940, entry 26, file 1737/292.

34. Box 31, folder 9, Harry Weinberger Papers, Yale University Archives.

35. Memorandum of Charles Earl to Straus, March 21, 1908, NARA, RG 85, INS Records, Central Office, Naturalization Files, 1906–1940, entry 26, file 1737/292.

36. 152 F. 346 (3d Cir. 1907). NARA, RG 85, INS Records, Central Office, Naturalization Files, 1906–1940, entry 26, file 1737/292.

37. 232 U.S. 78 (1914). In this case, the Court held that it was satisfied that Congress expressed in the Immigration Act of 1903 and reiterated in the Immigration Act of 1907 that the law applied to the admission of aliens and mandated their deportation if they fell under any of the statutory

clauses, «irrespective of any qualification arising out of a previous residence or domicile in this country.» *Lapina v. Williams,* 91.

38. Harr wrote to Bonaparte that immigration authorities could determine Goldman was "not a citizen and was subject to exclusion on the ground of her anarchistic belief." The Supreme Court, he wrote, held that the immigration authorities could determine "the right of a person to enter" and "their decision is final unless an abuse of authority appears. The fact that their decision is wrong does not constitute ground for the interference of the courts (Chin Yow v. United States, 208 U.S. 8)." Harr assumed, he added, that immigration authorities would agree that "the cancellation of the husband's certificate of naturalization destroys the wife's citizenship." Memorandum of Harr to Bonaparte, February 2, 1909, Goldman Papers.

39. Quoted in letter of Herman F. Schuettler, assistant general superintendent, Anarchist Bureau, Chicago, January 1909 to Daniel D. Davies, Immigrant Inspector in charge, Bureau of Immigration, Chicago Goldman Papers.

40. "A Woman Without a Country," *Mother Earth* 4, no. 3 (May 1909).

41. Paul L. Murphy, *World War I and the Origins of Civil Liberties in the United States* (New York: W.W. Norton, 1979), 211.

42. Ibid., 212.

43. Alice Wexler, *Emma Goldman in Exile: From the Russian Revolution to the Spanish Civil War* (Boston: Beacon Press, 1989), 11.

44. Immigration Act of October 16, 1918, ch. 186, 40 Stat. 1012.

45. Letter of Harry Weinberger to the Commissioner General of Immigration, August 15, 1919, Box 30, folder 14, Weinberger Papers.

46. Louis F. Post, *The Deportation Delirium of Nineteen-Twenty, a Personal Narrative of an Historic Personal Experience* (Chicago: Charles H. Kerr, 1923), 14.

47. In the days leading up to Goldman's deportation, several of her American anarchist colleagues offered to marry her so as to provide her with a firm, unassailable claim on U.S. citizenship. Goldman considered the offers but, at the advice of legal counsel, turned them down. Her lawyer tried also to get the proof that her former husband was dead at the moment of his denaturalization (box 30, folder 11, Weinberger Papers), which did not seem to be the truth; a confidential memo from an immigration officer on May 3, 1909, indicated he had been located in Chicago working on his trade. Letter of Daniel D. Davies, immigrant inspector in charge, to Daniel J. Keefe, commissioner general of immigration, May 3, 1909, Goldman Papers. In a last letter to her friends before deportation, Goldman wrote: "If Emma Goldman can be deprived of her citizenship and deported, every other citizen of foreign birth is in similar danger. Therefore, she fights for her right of citizenship. If the guarantees offered by citizenship are delusion and a snare, if American citizenship in the United States is a mere scrap of paper, we shall put the government on record to that effect—for the enlightenment of people of America and of the world." Box 27, folder 18, Weinberger Papers.

48. Box 33, folder 3, Weinberger Papers. And she added: "I desire to go as soon as possible to Soviet Russia and I expect the Government to keep its promise to deport Berkman and myself as well as other Russians within ten days as promised to my attorney Harry Weinberger."

49. David Cole, *Enemy Aliens: Double Standards and Constitutional Freedoms in the War on Terrorism* (New York: New Press, 2003), 119.

50. Wexler, *Emma Goldman in America,* 268.

51. Letter of Goldman to Harry Weinberger, December 9, 1921, box 29, folder 11, Weinberger Papers.

52. "Nadan" seems to mean dowry.

53. Married Women's Independent Nationality Act, ch. 411, 42 Stat. 1021. See also Marian L. Smith, "'Any Woman Who Is Now or May Hereafter Be Married . . .': Women and Naturalization, Ca. 1802–1940," *Prologue Magazine* 30, no. 2 (Summer 1998).

54. It put an end to the provision of the 1907 Expatriation Act related to marriage. However, a clause of the Cable Act specified that if an American woman married a foreigner who was "ineligible for naturalization"—for example, an Asian—she would lose her American nationality for the duration of the marriage. She could recover it only by naturalization. This clause was abrogated in 1931.

55. This automaticity had been imposed since the act of February 10, 1855 (10 Stat. 604, chap. 71, Rev. Stat. §1994, U.S. Comp. Stat. 1901, 1268).

Chapter 5. Radicals and Asians

1. Letter of George Wickersham to Benjamin G. Humphrey, House of Representatives, June 14, 1912, citing note of Frederick William Lehmann, solicitor general to Wickersham, June 6, 1912. In his memo the solicitor general mentions that the only decided case he has found to sustain the Oleson decision is one from a district court of Texas in 1891 when Judge T.M. Paschal refused the naturalization of Richard Sauer an industrious German immigrant based on the fact he was a socialist. NARA, RG 60, file 162150-12 and Preston, *Aliens and Dissenters*, 63.

2. Copy of the judgment of the U.S. District Court, Western District of Washington Southern Division, No.1688, May 11, 1912, NARA, RG 60, file 162150.

3. Letter of Harr, for the Attorney General to W. G. McLaren, May 21, 1912, ibid., file 162150-1.

4. Letter of Wickersham to McLaren, Seattle, June 3, 1912, ibid., file 162150-2.

5. David M. Rabban, *Free Speech in Its Forgotten Years* (Cambridge: Cambridge University Press, 1997), 103–105.

6. Ibid., 105.

7. Ibid., 104.

8. Ibid., 105.

9. Letter of Wickersham to McLaren, June 17, 1912, NARA, RG 60, file 162150-10.

10. 34 Stat. 596 §4, par. 4.

11. Letter of Wickersham to McLaren, June 17, 1912, NARA, RG 60,file 162150-10.

12. Ibid.

13. Letters of Wickersham to Ira Benett, editor of the *Washington Post*, June 10, 1912, and to Melville Stone, general manager of the Associated Press, June 18, 1912, NARA, RG 60, file 162150-16.

14. Carlton H. Hayes and Edward M. Sait, "Record of Political Events," *Political Science Quarterly* 27, no. 4 (December 1912): 728–768.

15. H. 576, 62nd Cong., 2nd sess., June 7, 1912.

16. "Socialist Oleson Testified," *New York Times*, June 27, 1912. "The Detroit IWW (which became the WIIU) was the union branch of the Socialist Labor Party of America (SLP), which had helped to found the Industrial Workers of the World (IWW) in Chicago. The SLP withdrew from the IWW in 1908 and created with The Detroit IWW an industrial union structure that was similar to that of the IWW except that the Detroit IWW was referred to as socialistic while the Chicago IWW as quasi anarchistic. Robert Franklin Hoxie, Lucy Bennett Hoxie, Nathan Fine, *Trade Unionism in the United States* (New York: D. Appleton and Co., 1921), 49.

17. "Hanford Signs, No Impeachment," *New York Times*, July 23, 1912.

18. See "Federal District Judge Cornelius H. Hanford Resigns During Impeachment Investigation on July 22, 1912," http://www.historylink.org/index.cfm?DisplayPage=output.cfm&file_id=9547.

19. "Socialist Wins a Point," *New York Times*, February 13, 1913. Facing strong opposition from the district attorney on the government's analysis, Wickersham agreed on "a reversal for a new trial" and did not order the judgments to be set aside. See letters of McLaren to Wickersham, July 2 and October 1, 1912; letter of Wickersham to Clay Allen, October 10, 1912, NARA, RG 60, file 162150.

20. Letter of William Wallace, Jr., assistant attorney general, to Clay Allen, February 17, 1914, NARA, RG 60, 162150–37.

21. Letter of Wickersham to Nagel, Secretary of Commerce and Labor, June 17, 1912, and from Nagel to Wickersham, July 2, 1912, NARA, RG 60, 162150–10 and 152160–24.

22. Testimony of John Speed Smith, chief naturalization examiner for the Ninth District, Seattle, House of Representatives, *Progress and Processes of Naturalization, Hearings Before the Committee on Immigration and Naturalization*, October 21, 1921, 1151.

23. Lawrence Preuss, "Denaturalization on the Ground of Disloyalty," *American Political Science Review* 36, no. 4 (August 1942): 701–710.

24. In fact, the means for keeping German nationality while becoming American through naturalization did not exist. Theodore H. Thiesing demonstrates this quite convincingly in "Dual Allegiance in the German Law of Nationality and American Citizenship," *Yale Law Journal* 27, no. 4 (February 1918): 479–508.

25. Richard W. Flournoy, Jr., "Observations on the New German Law of Nationality," *American Journal of International Law* 8, no. 3 (July 1914): 478.

26. *Metropolitan Magazine* no. 2 (15 June 1915).

27. Letter of George A. Dew, to Thomas Gregory, July 31, 1916, NARA, RG 60, DOJ Files, file 182 473. On June 24, 1917, in the *New York Times*, a retired U.S. Navy rear admiral expressed his view that the German law called into question the validity of all naturalizations granted to Germans; he suggested annulling them all and refusing to grant American nationality until the Delbrück Law was abrogated. Casper F. Goodrich, "Why Stranger in Our Gates Remains an Alien; Among Causes Are Foreign Language Press and Delbrueck Law Enabling German-Americans to Continue Germans," *New York Times*, June 24, 1917.

28. Letter of Gregory to Dew, August 15, 1916, NARA, RG 60, DOJ Files, file 182 473.

29. Christopher Cappozola, *Uncle Sam Wants You: World War I and the Making of the Modern American Citizenship* (New York: Oxford University Press, 2008), 119–123.

30. Ibid., 182–183.

31. *Annual Report of the Attorney General, 1918* (Washington, D.C.: Government Printing Office, 1918), 39.

32. NARA, RG 85, INS Records, Central Office, Naturalization Files, 1906–1940, entry 26, file 3910/58.

33. In a June 25, 1918, in a letter to the Chief Examiner in St. Louis, the Office of the Commissioner of Naturalization responded, "Upon the facts submitted it appears that Mr. Weiler did not actually renounce his allegiance to Germany and accordingly you are directed to take appropriate steps looking toward the cancellation of the naturalization." Ibid., file 3910/58.

34. Ibid., file 3910/58.

35. Ibid., file 1737/62.

36. *United States v. Darmer*, D.C. Wash, 249 F. 989 (1918).

37. *United States v. Wusterbarth*, 249 Fed. 908 (D.N.J. 1918).

38. Ibid.

39. Circular No. 837, May, 22, 1918, *Annual Report of the Attorney General*, 1918, 747.

40. *United States v. Kramer*, 262 F. 395 (5th Cir. 1919).

41. *Schurmann v. United States*, 264 F. 917 (9th Cir. 1920).

42. Ibid., 921.

43. *United States v. Herberger*, 272 F. 278 (D.C.Wash. 1921).

44. Ibid., 281.

45. Ibid., 284.

46. Ibid., 290.

47. Ibid., 291.

48. *United States v. Woerndle*, 288 F. 47 (9th Cir. 1923), 48.

49. Ibid., 49.

50. *United States v. Swelgin*, 254 F. 884 (D.C.Or. 1918).

51. Ibid., 884.

52. NARA, RG 85, entry 26, File 3910-26.

53. Ibid.

54. Ibid.

55. *United States v. Stuppiello*, 260 F. 483 (D.C.N.Y. 1919).

56. *Glaser v. United States*, 289 F. 255 (7th Cir. 1923). The court ruled that the appellant had deceived the naturalization court with respect to his belief in organized government and his adherence to the principles of the Constitution. On April 26, 1921, Ole Christopher Olsen was denaturalized by the Western District Court of Washington, because the only witness present at his naturalization hearing testified that he was not worthy of becoming a citizen for having connections with members of the IWW. NARA, RG 60, entry 112, file 209 112-1.

57. 18 F.2d 246, 247 (9th Cir. 1927).

58. Letter of Louis Post, to Alexander M. Palmer, attorney general, August 12, 1920, NARA, RG 60, file 210791–49.

59. Memorandum of the Solicitor general William D. Mitchell for Mr. Oscar R. Luhring attorney general, June 7, 1927, NARA, RG 60, file 210791–49. In *FTC v. American Tobacco Co.*, 274 U.S. 543, decided on May 31, 1927, the Supreme Court decided that a judgment of an appeals court based on circumstances admitting different interpretations could not be revised by certiorari.

60. 1 Stat. 103, chap. 3.

61. 16 Stat. 256, chap. 254.

62. 22 Stat. 58.

63. NARA, RG 85, entry 26, file 1696/163.

64. NARA, RG 85, INS Records, Central Office, Naturalization Files, 1906–1940, file 1506/98.

65. NARA, RG 85, entry 26, file 1696/236.

66. Joan Jensen, *Passage from India: Asian Indian Immigrants in North America* (New Haven, Conn.: Yale University Press, 1988), 248.

67. All these examples are taken from Malcom Roy, *The Naturalization of the Japanese* (San Francisco: Japanese Association of American College Graduates, 1914).

68. NARA, RG 85, entry 26, INS Records, Central Office, Naturalization Files, 1906–1940, file 1506/98.

69. NARA, RG 85, entry 26, file 1696/221.

70. His application was directed to the governor-general of the Philippine Islands by Benedict's Manila-based attorney, perhaps because Benedict was living comparatively nearby in Hong Kong at the time.

71. NARA, RG 85, entry 26, box 1373, file 1696/232.

72. Memo from the Naturalization Service's Office of the Chief Examiner to the commissioner of naturalization, June 17, 1919, NARA, RG 85, entry 26, file 1696/232.

73. Letter of Post to Robert Lansing, secretary of state, July 25, 1919, NARA, RG 85, entry 26, file 1696/232.

74. *United States v. Charles Benedict*, District Court of the U.S. Southern District of Texas, Galveston Division, June 16, 1920, no. 36 in equity, NARA, RG 85, entry 26, file 1696/232

75. *Ozawa v. United States*, 260 U.S. 178.

76. Ian Haney-López, *White by Law: The Legal Construction of Race* (New York: New York University Press, 2006), 80.

77. *Ozawa v. United States*, 260 U.S. 178, 190.

78. Haney-López, *White by Law*, 81.

79. *Ozawa v. United States*, 260 U.S. 178.

80. Lucy Salyer observes that 1,313 Chinese and 83 Japanese "class I" aliens were eligible for the draft, many of them concentrated in Hawai'i. Lucy E. Salyer, "Baptism by Fire: Race, Military Service, and U.S. Citizenship Policy, 1918–1935," *Journal of American History* 91, no. 3 (December 2004): 847, 854.

81. A Chinese soldier was, for example, naturalized in the Naturalization District of St. Louis, Missouri. See the letter of Morris R. Bevington, Chief Examiner of the Naturalization Service in St. Louis to Campbell, June 19, 1918. NARA, RG 85, entry 26, file 106799/926.

82. Letter of Deputy Commissioner to John B. Zabriskie, July 8, 1918, NARA, RG 85, entry 26, file 106799/926.

83. *In re Ta* quoted by Salyer, "Baptism by Fire," 857.

84. Memorandum of Crist to Campbell, December 24, 1918, NARA, RG 85, entry 26, file 106799/926. Later he wrote again to Campbell that if Congress has had the intention to limit the application of the act of May 9, 1918, to aliens "who are themselves admissible to citizenship under the existing naturalization law, it could have made that provision" But, Crist added, "it did not do so." Memorandum of Crist to Campbell, January 22, 1919, NARA, RG 85, entry 26, file 106799/926

85. Letter of Campbell to the Secretary of Labor, August 17, 1921, NARA, RG 85, entry 26, file 106799/926.

86. Letter of James Farrell, Chief Examiner, Naturalization Service, Boston to Campbell, May 31, 1921, NARA, RG 85, entry 26, file 106799/926.

87. 268 U.S. 402 (1925), Chief Justice Taft dissenting.

88. They were more than seven hundred naturalizations of Asian (non-Filipino) soldiers. This estimation is based (1) on the memos sent by the chief examiners who have been asked by Campbell—two times at least, on June 13, 1919, and January 31, 1921—to report about the numbers of the naturalization of Asians having served in the U.S. military in their districts and (2) on the letter sent on January 26, 1927, by the U.S. attorney in Hawaii to the commissioner of naturalization mentioning that in his district "579 Orientals were naturalized after being drafted in and having served with the American forces during the World War." NARA, RG 85, entry 26, file 106799/926.

89. Cf. letter of James J. Davis to former Congressman John L. Cable, January 11, 1926, NARA, RG 85, entry 26, file 106799/926. Letter of Wickersham to John G. Sargent, Attorney General, February 21, 1927, NARA, RG 85, entry 26, file 106799/926. In this letter, George Wickersham wrote to his current successor that there was a "moral obligation" for Congress to "give official sanction to the promise it led out, and in the faith of which men devoted themselves to the military service and exposed their lives."

90. Letter of Devlin to Bonaparte, August 8, 1907, and Bonaparte to Devlin, August 14, 1907, NARA, RG 60, entry 112, file 97415.

91. 261 U.S. 204.

92. Haney-López, *White by Law,* 7.

93. *Thind,* 261 U.S. 204, 215.

94. To further justify its decision, the Supreme Court relied also on the intent of the Congress recently expressed in the act of February 5, 1917, 39 Stat. 874, c. 29, 3, which excluded from admission into the United States "all natives of Asia within designated limits of latitude and longitude, including the whole of India" (261 U.S. 204, 215).

95. U.S. Citizenship and Immigration Services, Washington, D.C., Naturalization Certificate File C1503240.

96. Cited in Haney-López, *White by Law.*

97. *United States v. Pandit,* 15 F.2d 285 (9th Cir. 1926). In view of the decision of the Supreme Court in the Thind case, the district court committed an "error" in holding that Pandit was a "free white person" but the circuit court argued that the contention that the certificate had been fraudulently or illegally obtained—the only causes for instituting cancellation proceedings—could not be sustained: when a court of competent jurisdiction grants a certificate of naturalization after hearing the objections of the government, the decision is final, subject only to the right of appeal, a right the government did not use. See J. W. Gardner, "Denationalization of American Citizens," *American Journal of International Law,* 21, no. 1 (January 1927): 106–107.

98. NARA, RG 60, Classified Subject Files, file 38–524.

99. Mae M. Ngai, *Impossible Subjects: Illegal Aliens and the Making of Modern America* (Princeton, N.J.: Princeton University Press, 2004), 49. The California Immigration Committee was an alliance of the American Legion, the California State Federation of Labor, the Grange, and the Native Sons of the Golden West. See Ngai, *Impossible Subjects,* 47.

100. *United States v. Pandit,* 273 U.S. 759 (1927). See John P. Roche, "Prestatutory Denaturalization," *Cornell Law Quarterly* 35 (1949): 291.

101. Letter of Robe Carl White, assistant secretary, Department of Labor, to John Sargent, attorney general, April 2, 1917, NARA, RG 60, Classified Subject Files, file 38–524.

102. Luella Gettys, *The Law of Citizenship in the United States* (Chicago: University of Chicago Press, 1934), 105–106.

103. Letter of Mr. Modi M. Bagai to the Commissioner of Naturalization, October 4, 1932, file C-1503240.

104. Letter of Earl Harrison, Commissioner of Immigration and Naturalization to Mr. Ram M. Bagai, June 26, 1943, file C-1503240.

105. Affidavit signed by the third secretary of the legation in The Hague, September 14, 1923, NARA, RG 85, entry 26, file 21/35.

106. Testimony of Eugene Maneck before the assistant district director of naturalization, on December 20, 1925, NARA, RG 85, entry 26, file 21/35.

107. Testimony of Eugene Maneck before the assistant district director of naturalization, January 26, 1927, NARA, RG 85, entry 26, file 21/35.

108. Note (signed AM) to Raymond Crist, commissioner of naturalization, September 22, 1926, NARA, RG 85, entry 26, file 21/35.

109. Letter from O. R. Luhring to James J. Davis, secretary of labor, January 10, 1929, NARA, RG 85, entry 26, file 21/35.

Chapter 6. In the Largest Numbers

1. 34 Stat. 601 (1906), carried forward into the Nationality Act of 1940 as §338, 54 Stat. 1158 (1940), and into the Immigration and Naturalization Act as §340(d), 66 Stat. 261, 8 U.S.C. §1451(d) (Supp. 1952).

2. Richard K. Campbell declared: "That was considered by the committee, and there was some objection to it. The most potent objection was that after a man had foresworn his allegiance to the country of his birth, if we were to undertake to deprive him of that citizenship, he would be divested of any allegiance to any country and of any claim on any country for his protection and the Commission left the matter in the status in which it is on that account." Statement of Campbell, *Hearings Before the Committee on Immigration and Naturalization, January 23, 1906, to March 6, 1906, on the Bill to Establish a Bureau of Naturalization and to Provide for an Uniform Rule for the Naturalization of Aliens Throughout the United States* (Washington, D.C.: Government Printing Office, 1906), 32–33.

3. In his first annual message in 1869 and his sixth annual message in 1874, President Ulysses S. Grant had expressed concern about the development of dual citizenship and of dual allegiance. Later, President Grover Cleveland not only addressed the issue on both grounds in its first annual message in 1885 but also on another ground, attacking those newly naturalized citizens who leave their new country after having been naturalized: Cleveland repeated his concern in his second (1886) and fourth (1888) annual messages.

4. Other sections within the act of 1906 addressed the administrative steps involved in a denaturalization decision—a sixty-day notice provision for those living in the United States, a publication requirement for those living abroad, and guidelines for courts involved in denaturalization procedures. Naturalization fraud remained explicitly criminalized, with both applicants (aliens) and administrators (court officials and clerks) singled out with a provision complementary to the 1870 provision: the denaturalization of the criminal naturalized citizen judged guilty. The last portion of the law applies the Naturalization Act of 1906 to all those naturalized under prior acts.

5. John P. Roche, «Loss of American Nationality: The Years of Confusion," *University of Pennsylvania Law Review* 99, no.1 (October 1950): 286. Except for persons coming from Prussia or other states with which the United States had signed treaties providing that naturalized American citizens who returned to their country of origin and stayed there for two continuous years would be presumed to have resumed their former nationality. The secretaries of states refused to implement this rule "as ironclad," interpreting it as establishing a presumption of expatriation and not an automatic loss See Roche, "Loss of American Nationality," 291.

6. *Report of the Naturalization Commission to the President* (Purdy Commission Report), 59th Congress, 1st sess., November 8, 1905, H. 46, 13.

7. Philip C. Jessup, *Elihu Root*, vol. 2, 1905–1937 (New York: Dodd, Mead, 1938), 59. The

conference, which took place in Algeciras, Spain, from January 16 to April 7, was convened to find a solution to a crisis between France and Germany over the control of Morocco. Twelve European countries participated, as well as the United States; President Theodore Roosevelt acted as a mediator.

8. Ibid.

9. At this time a Bureau of Citizenship was created within the Department of State, by order of Secretary Elihu Root, on May 31, 1907. It replaced the Passport Bureau created on July 3, 1902.

10. 59th Cong. Rec. H. (1907) 1465 (January 21, 1907).

11. Nancy L. Green, "Expatriation, Expatriates, and Expats: The American Transformation of a Concept," *American Historical Review* 114, no. 2 (April 2009): 316.

12. 15 Statutes at Large, Chapter 249 (section 1), enacted July 27 1868.

13. In addition, Root's instruction includes "some unforeseen and controlling exigency beyond his power to foresee has prevented his carrying out a bona fide intention to return to the United States within the time limited by law, and that it is his intention to return and reside in the United States immediately upon the removal of the . . . cause." Instruction of the Secretary of State to the Diplomatic and Consular Officers of the United States, April 19, 1907, NARA, RG 85, entry 19, Circulars, Forms, Instructions, 1913–1925.

14. In *Annual Report of the Attorney General of the United States, 1908* (Washington, D.C.: Government Printing Office, 1908), 11.

15. Georges Kearny and Emily Spilman, eds., *Digest of the Opinions of the Attorneys General of the United States (1906–1921)* (Washington, Government Printing Office, 1926), vol. 28, 504–510 (1910).

16. 59 Cong. Rec. H. 1465 (January 21, 1907). Crumpacker added that many such naturalized citizens had no intention of returning to the United States but planned to remain in another country." The act provided, he noted, that after five years, "the presumption shall arise that he intends to renounce his citizenship." 59 Cong. Rec., H. 1464 (January 21, 1907).

17. Roche, "Loss of American Nationality," 39.

18. To conform his department with the decision of the attorney general, the secretary of state sent on November 18, 1911, a general consular instruction (No. 77) that adds a fourth possibility to overcome the presumption of expatriation: that the citizen has made definite arrangements to return immediately to the United States for permanent residence. Upon evidence of such intent, the department could issue an emergency passport for the time of travel. NARA, RG 85, entry 19, Circulars, Forms, Instructions, 1913–1925.

19. See letter of the acting secretary of state to Wickersham, December 22, 1911, NARA, RG 60, Department of Justice entry 112, file 157793.

20. Letter of Wickersham to Philander C. Knox, secretary of state, August 8, 1911. NARA, RG 60, Department of Justice entry 112, file 157793. According to all sources, the number of naturalized Portuguese Americans living back in the Azores was significant. The census of 1930 evaluated them at 1,089. Another report put their number at 17,000. Naturalized or not, around World War I, almost all inhabitants of some of the Azores Islands were said to have been in the United States at least once. Leo Pap, *The Portuguese-Americans* (Boston: Twayne Publishers, 1981), 48.

21. NARA, RG 85, INS Records, Central Office, Naturalization Files, 1906–1940, entry 26, file 1506/470.

22. NARA, RG 60, entry 112, file 159462.

23. *In Re Estate of Mesa y Hernandez*, 87 Misc. 242, 243–254 (N.Y. Sur. Ct. 1914).

24. Letter of Charles Stewart Davison to U.S. Attorney General George Wickersham, November 24, 1911, NARA, RG 60, entry 112, file 159462.

25. Harr was here referencing a similar case the Department of Justice handled before.

26. In 1914, Davison filed a lawsuit in the Surrogate's Court of New York, objecting to the transfer tax appraiser's findings that Mesa was "at the time of his death a resident of the county of New York." Without reaching the question of Mesa's citizenship or nationality, the court found that "it is most obvious" that Mesa's last domicile was not in New York. Citing evidence of record in which Mesa was found to have only visited the United States for short periods, owned little American property and no real estate, and applied for naturalization just to protect his Cuban property, the court found that Mesa did not establish residency in New York by merely having the "intention" to do so. Therefore, the appraiser's report should be corrected accordingly. *In re Estate of Mesa y Hernandez,* 87 Misc. 242, 243–254 (N.Y. Sur. Ct. 1914). This decision was affirmed by the Appellate Division of the Supreme Court of New York, which further found that Mesa "never emigrated to this country, never resided continuously here for twelve years nor for ten years, and in fact never resided here at all." *In re Mesa's Estate,* 172 A.D. 467 (N.Y. App. Div. 1916). The court, operating under the assumption that Mesa's naturalization proceeding was valid, nonetheless found that he established his residence in Cuba upon his return. Therefore, the court held that the decree admitting his U.S. will to probate was not conclusive. The only other question involved was whether his widow was entitled to a one-half ownership of the joint estate under the law of Cuba, being the so-called gananciales. The court held that she was entitled to it. This order was further affirmed by the New York Court of Appeals without an opinion in In re Hernandez, 219 N.Y. 566 (N.Y. 1916).

27. Letter of the chief examiner of the Naturalization Service in New York City to Campbell, March 25, 1922, NARA, RG 85, file 1737/ 1055.

28. Testimony of Marcos Antonio Gonzalez, grandson of Antonio Gonzalez Curquero, February 6, 1923, NARA, RG 85, file 1737/ 1055.

29. Memorandum, Campbell, NARA, RG 85, file 1737/ 1055.

30. 231 U.S. 9 (1913).

31. On the policy of the State Department regarding the legal status of naturalized Americans who had established their domicile abroad before 1907, see I-Mien Tsiang, *The Question of Expatriation in America Prior to 1907* (Baltimore: Johns Hopkins University Press, 1942). In 1886, the State Department did not agree that a citizen's naturalization could be cancelled "solely by residence, however protracted, in the country of his origin." Instead, intent rather than just time of residence in the country of origin should determine. But the diplomatic agents considered often ipso facto a return to the native land as a prima facie evidence of the termination of American citizenship. See Tsiang, *Question of Expatriation,* 98–99.

32. 231 U.S. 10 (1913). A contradiction existed between the beginning of the paragraph related to denaturalization for residence abroad: "If any alien who shall have received a certificate of citizenship under the provisions of this Act shall, within five years" and its last: "The provisions of this section shall apply not only to certificates of citizenship issued under the provisions of this Act, but to all certificates of citizenship which may have been issued heretofore by any court exercising jurisdiction in naturalization proceedings under prior laws." 34 Stat. 601 (1906).

33. NARA, RG 85, INS Records, Central Office, Naturalization Files, 1906–1940, entry 26, file 14/01.

34. Ibid., file 1525/482.

35. Ibid., file 1525/562. The *Annual Report of the Commissioner of Naturalization* of 1925 shows

that at that date relations seem to have come back to normal: cases sent by the State Department have been transferred to Department of Justice and proceedings for denaturalization instituted. *Annual Report of the Commissioner of Naturalization, 1925* (Washington, D.C.: Government Printing Office, 1925), 3.

36. *United States ex rel. Anderson v. Howe*, 231 Fed 546 (S.D.N.Y. 1916), and *Stein v. Fleischmann Co.*, 237 Fed. 679 (S.D.N.Y. 1916).

37. In support of the State Department's interpretation: *Nurge v. Miller*, 286 Fed. 982 (E.D.N.Y. 1923); *Sinjen v. Miller*, 281 Fed. 889 (D. Neb. 1922). In support of Justice Department interpretation: *Camardo v. Tillinghast*, 29 F. 2d 527 527 (1st Circ. 1928); *Miller v. Sinjen*, 289 Fed. 388 (8th Cir. 1923); *Banning v. Penrose* 255 Fed. 159 (N.D. Ga. 1919).

38. Memorandum, Department of State, Office of the Secretary, July 2, 1924. NARA, RG 85, INS Records, Central Office, Naturalization Files, 1906–1940, entry 26, file 15 GEN.

39. *United States v. Gay*, 264 U.S. 353 (1924). See Roche, "The Loss of American Nationality," 25, 39.

40. Letter of Frank B. Kellogg, secretary of state, to James J. Davis, secretary of labor, March 26, 1926, NARA, RG 85, INS Records, Central Office, Naturalization Files, 1906–1940, entry 26, file 15 GEN.

41. See Chapter 2.

42. Gertrude D. Krichefsky, "Loss of the United States Nationality: Revocation of Nationalization," *Immigration and Naturalization Service Monthly Review* 4 (1946): 42. In 1935, of 864 cancellations, 45 were formal renunciations of U.S. citizenship, 413 came from informal renunciation, 382 were because of fraud, and 24 were due to other causes. *Annual Report of the Secretary of Labor, Fiscal Year Ended June 30, 1935* (Washington, D.C.: Government Printing Office, 1935), 92. In 1936, fraud in obtaining citizenship represented 351 of 1,016 cancellations. *Annual Report of the Secretary of Labor, Fiscal Year Ended June 30, 1936* (Washington, D.C.: Government Printing Office, 1936), 105.

43. Section 409 of the act gave naturalized Americans living abroad six years, until October 14, 1946, to get home. During that six-year period they were divested of U.S. protection under the 1907 act but not of U.S. citizenship under the 1940 act. See Roche, "Loss of American Nationality," 43.

44. Richard W. Flournoy Jr., *The Nationality Act of 1940*, Contemporary Law Pamphlets, series 5, number 4 (New York: New York University Law School), 8.

45. "These provisions had been inserted in the code at the request of the State Department and the Department of War. The army was said to have particularly advocated the one related to service in a foreign army, Lemuel Schofield reported in a memorandum, because "in the past . . . many Hawaiian citizens of the United States went to Japan and served in the Japanese Army. They were not required to take an oath of allegiance to the Emperor of Japan and, consequently, did not lose their American citizenship." His views were, it seemed, that the law should be amended so that citizens who join foreign armed forces lose their citizenship under such circumstances." Memorandum of Lemuel Schofield to the Robert Jackson, attorney general, September 16, 1940, box 90, folder 4, Jackson Papers, Manuscript Division, Library of Congress, Washington, D.C.

46. Sec. 402 of the Nationality Act of 1940, 54 Stat. 1169. See Memorandum of Lemuel Schofield to Robert Jackson, September 16, 1940, box 90, folder 4, Jackson Papers, Manuscript Division, Library of Congress, Washington, D.C.

Chapter 7. The Proactive Denaturalization Program During World War II

1. Letters from chief examiner, St. Paul, Minn., to Bureau of Naturalization, Washington, D.C., and from bureau to chief examiner, February 12 and February 19, 1918, NARA, RG 85, entry 26, file 3906.

2. "Acts Against Bund Chief, Government Attacks West Coast Leader's Citizenship Papers," *New York Times*, December 20, 1938.

3. "Fritz Kuhn Death in 1951 Revealed," *New York Times*, February 2, 1953. He was denaturalized together with nineteen other German Americans on March 19, 1943 (*United States v. Kuhn and nineteen other cases*, District Court, S.D. New York, 49 F. Supp. 407 [S.D. N.Y. 1943]), interned when he completed his sentence, and sent back to Germany in September 1945.

4. Memorandum of Alexander Holtzoff to Robert Jackson, attorney general, July 24, 1940, box 90, folder 4, Jackson Papers.

5. Memorandum of Clarence N. Goodwin, April 15, 1942, NARA, RG 60, DOJ Files, file 146-43-012.

6. The report of 702 pages comprised three volumes and four volumes of exhibits. The report on Fritz Kuhn conducted between April and September 1941 was 186 pages. Memorandum of Lemuel Schofield to Francis Biddle, attorney general, February 26, 1942,NARA, RG 85, entry 9, file 56056/49.

7. For example, Dr. Louis A. Ewald, naturalized on March 14, 1927, did not file his petition for naturalization for at least two years after his declaration of intention and had not resided continuously in the United States for five years immediately preceding the date of his petition. NARA, RG 60, file 146-43-012.

8. Forrest R. Black, "Disloyalty and Denaturalization," *Kentucky Law Journal* 29, no. 2 (January 1941): 143, 161. The assistant to the attorney general is the third-ranking officer in the Department of Justice and has charge of the general administration of the department, including questions of administration, personnel, and legislation.

9. This section would borrow from the British Law of 1918, adapting it to the American constitutional and jurisdictional context. As in the United Kingdom, which itself borrowed the relevant statutory language from France (see Patrick Weil, *How to Be French: Nationality in the Making Since 1789*, trans. Catherine Porter [Durham, N.C.: Duke University Press, 2008], 61), denaturalization would be explicitly permitted for actions committed after naturalization had occurred. Unlike in the United Kingdom, the American procedure would not be administrative. It would not even be included in the current frame of the denaturalization proceedings occurring for acts explicitly committed after naturalization. It would guarantee a jury, as provided for in criminal procedure.

10. The first ground for revocation in the proposed law would concern only naturalized citizens, who "within ten years [after naturalization], engage in a course of conduct which establishes that [their] true political allegiance is to a foreign state or sovereignty"; such conduct would be considered prima facie evidence that the person did not renounce allegiance to a foreign nation. The second ground of revocation would concern all citizens, and provided that in wartime, the government could "terminat[e] the citizenship . . . of any citizen who . . . has engaged in a course of conduct, which established that his true political allegiance is to [a] foreign state or sovereignty with which the United States is at war." NARA, RG 60, DOJ files, file 38-01-5.

11. On January 18, 1930, at the request of Congressman John L. Cable, Raymond Crist, commissioner of naturalization, had submitted a draft of legislation that would have permitted courts

to consider as *prima facie* evidence of fraud in the naturalization proceeding and of a lack of intention to become a permanent citizen of the United States at the time of the naturalization obtaining a foreign passport after naturalization or conviction of felonies or of acts of "moral turpitude." NARA, RG 85, INS Records, Central Office, Naturalization Files, 1906–1940, entry 26, file 20/GEN.

12. Amendment to Nationality Act of 1940, H. 6250, 77th Cong., 2nd sess., 1942. Senate Subcommittee of the Committee on Immigration, *Hearings on H.R. 6250 to Amend the Nationality Act of 1940*, 77th Cong., 2nd sess., February 17, 1942. In 1934, the House of Representatives had created the Special Committee on Un-American Activities Authorized to Investigate Nazi Propaganda and Certain Other Propaganda Activities. In May 1938, the House Committee on Un-American Activities was established as a special investigating committee. It was chaired by Martin Dies Jr., and its work was aimed mostly at German American involvement in Nazi activity.

13. Senator Maloney asked Lawrence M. C. Smith, chief of the Special Defense Unit of the Department of Justice, whether members of Congress who were naturalized citizens could be charged under the proposed amendment for criticizing "action or failure on the part of some of our allies in the war, in speeches outside Congress." Later Maloney asked, "You would not think that under the passage of this language . . . you would create the same kind of broad powers and the same kind of situation that prevailed in 1917 and 1918?" Senate Subcommittee of the Committee on Immigration, *Hearings on H.R. 6250*, 47–48. See http://www.loc.gov/law/find/hearings/pdf/00107800591.pdf.

14. Richard W. Steele, *Free Speech in the Good War* (New York: St. Martin's Press, 1999), 193.

15. Letter of James L. Houghteling, Commissioner of Immigration and Naturalization, to James J. Davis, U.S. Senator, March 29, 1939, NARA, RG 85, entry 26, file 71/49.

16. Memorandum of Schofield to Biddle, February 26, 1942, NARA, RG 85, entry 9, file 56056/49.

17. Ibid.

18. NARA, RG 85, entry 26, file 25/206, "German American Bund."

19. Mid-February 1942 not far off 10 percent of Japanese Aliens on the West Coast have been arrested. Peter Irons, *Justice at War* (Berkeley: University of California Press, 1993), 19.

20. Ibid., 23–24.

21. "Alien Curbs Aimed Only at Disloyal," *New York Times*, December 14, 1941, 9.

22. Roger Daniels, "Immigration Policy in Time of War: The United States, 1939-1945," *Journal of American Ethnic History*, Winter/Spring 2006, 108. See also David Cole, *Enemy Aliens: Double Standards and the Constitutional Freedoms in the War on Terror* (New York: New Press, 2003), 92–94.

23. "Biddle Exempts Two Aliens Classes," *New York Times*, February 10, 1942, 1.

24. See the exchange of memorandum between Biddle, Schofield, Joseph Savoretti, deputy commissioner, Andrew Jordan, chief supervisor of naturalization, W.W. Wiggins, assistant chief supervisor of naturalization, and Marshall Dimock, associate commissioner on suggestions for speeding up or shortening the naturalization process, from February 6 to February 13, 1942, Box 31, Marshall Dimock Papers, Franklin D. Roosevelt Library.

25. Memorandum of James Rowe Jr. for Biddle, "West Coast Naturalizations," March 21, 1942, Box 33, James H. Rowe Jr. Papers, Franklin D. Roosevelt Library.

26. On Roosevelt's frustration with Biddle lack of action against alien enemies, see Stone, *Perilous Times*, 256–258.

27. Memorandum of Rowe to Biddle, March 21, 1942, NARA, RG 60, DOJ Files, file 146-43-012.

28. Memorandum of James Rowe Jr. for Biddle, "West Coast Naturalizations," March 21, 1942, Box 33, James H. Rowe Jr. Papers, Franklin D. Roosevelt Library.

29. Irons, *Justice at War*, 32.

30. Memorandum of Rowe to Biddle, March 21, 1942, NARA, RG 60, DOJ Files, file 146-43-012.

31. Box 35, James H. Rowe Jr. Papers, Franklin D. Roosevelt Library.

32. Memorandum of Wendell Berge, Criminal Division, to Biddle, March 16, 1942, NARA, RG 60, DOJ Files, file 146-43-012 This conference is mentioned by Goodwin in his memorandum to Schofield, March 17, 1942, NARA, RG 60, DOJ Files, file 146-43-12.

33. Memorandum of Berge, March 16, 1942.

34. Memorandum from Joseph Prendergast to Lawrence M. C. Smith, March 18, 1942, box 35, Rowe Papers.

35. Memo from Lawrence M. C. Smith to James H. Rowe Jr., March 20, 1942, Box 35, James H. Rowe Jr. Papers, Franklin D. Roosevelt Library.

36. Memorandum of James Rowe Jr. for Biddle, "Personal and Confidential," March 23, 1942, Box 33, James H. Rowe Jr. Papers, Franklin D. Roosevelt Library.

37. Anna Rosenberg was a trusted adviser to Franklin Roosevelt and later to Harry Truman.

38. Consisting of the Special War Policies Unit, the Alien Property Unit, the Alien Enemy Control Unit, and later the War Frauds Unit, this division was created on May 19, 1942, and abolished on December 28, 1945.

39. Memo of Rowe for Biddle, March 23, 1942.

40. Circular No. 3663, March 25, 1942, NARA, RG 60, DOJ Files, 146-43-012.

41. Memorandum of Rowe to Biddle, March 21, 1942, NARA, RG 60 DOJ Files, file 146-43-012.

42. Lemuel Schofield was reluctant to receive too much publicity. In a letter to M. E. Gilfond, head of the Information Division of the Department of Justice, he wrote: "I hesitate however, without giving the matter considerable thought, to emphasize any particulars that I would wish to have published in *Time* magazine on this subject," March 14, 1942, NARA, RG 60, DOJ Files, file 38-012.

43. "Naturalized Foes to Lose Citizenship," *New York Times*. March 25, 1942, 25.

44. Ibid..

45. Letter of Biddle to Senator William Langer, January, 14, 1944, NARA, RG 60, DOJ Files, file 146-43-016. Biddle based his opinion on the position taken by Judge Merril H. Otis (Kansas City) in the case of *United States v. Carl Wilhelm Baumgartner* in remarks from the bench on November 18, 1942 and in an opinion rendered by Judge D. J. Bright in *United States v. Sotzek et al.*, on December 7, 1943.

46. Francis Biddle, *In Brief Authority* (New York: Doubleday, 1962), 254–255. A Montana native and Harvard Law School graduate, Rowe like Biddle has clerked with Oliver Wendell Holmes at the Supreme Court. After doing legal work in five New Deal agencies between 1934 and 1939 and campaigning for Roosevelt in 1936, he had joined the White House staff in 1939. See Irons, *Justice at War*, 32.

47. Steele, *Free Speech in the Good War*, 195.

48. Memorandum of Biddle to Schofield, April, 8, 1942, NARA, RG 60, DOJ Files, file 38-012.

49. Memorandum of Clarence N. Goodwin to Major Schofield, March 17, 1942, NARA, RG 60, DOJ Files, file 146-43-012.

50. On April 15, the deputy commissioner of the Immigration Service reported that the FBI informed his field officers that "all matters affecting cancellation of citizenship had been turned over to that unit." Memorandum of T. B. Shoemacker to Schofield, April 15, 1942, NARA, RG 60,

DOJ Files, file 146-43-012. On April 16, some immigration officers apparently asked the FBI to supply additional data on individuals against whom proceedings were contemplated. Instructions of Joseph Savoretti, deputy commissioner of the INS, to all districts directors, April, 26, 1942, NARA, RG 60, DOJ Files, file 38-012.

51. Memorandum of Berge to Biddle, April, 24, 1942, endorsed by a memorandum of Biddle to Schofield, April, 24, 1942, NARA, RG 60, DOJ Files, file 38-012.

52. The borders of this agreement tended to move: Schofield mentioned later to Biddle that the FBI mandate set by his April 24 memo which covered all naturalized persons "whose conduct and activities indicate disloyalty and lack of allegiance to the United States or lack of attachment to the principles of the Constitution" was "somewhat broader than the base originally contemplate[d] and the wording would cover naturalized citizens who are members of the Communist Party." Memorandum of Schofield to Biddle, May 7, 1942, NARA, RG 60, DOJ Files, file 146-43-012. In a memorandum of September 18, 1942, Schofield wrote that cases of communists would be dealt with by the Immigration Service, unless they were engaged in any disloyal activities which might be considered as being in opposition to the present war efforts of this country or which might be considered subversive." NARA, RG 60, DOJ Files, file 146-43-012.

53. See telegram of Savoretti to all INS districts, April 23, 1942, NARA, RG 60, DOJ Files, file 38-012.

54. Memorandum of Schofield to Biddle, May 7, 1942, NARA, RG 60, DOJ Files, file 146-43-012. See also Confidential Instruction to All District Directors of INS, Schofield, May 11, 1942, NARA, RG 60, DOJ Files, file 38-012.

55. For example, on May 7, 1942, a total of 367 names had been furnished.

56. Memorandum of Berge to Earl Harrison, commissioner of the INS, December 31, 1942. NARA, RG 60, DOJ Files, file 146-43-012. Berge acknowledged Harrison's "willingness to assist us whenever we have asked for help in the past" and requested the service of a special inspector in Kansas City to "assist us in the completion of a brief of law and policy which is to be furnished to all United States Attorneys for their assistance in this program."

57. At the end of the program, "recognition should be given to the fact that considerable Immigration and Naturalization Service personnel have been utilized. At times we have had as many as seventeen of their men on a full time basis, augmenting the Criminal Division staff and the investigation personnel of the FBI." Memorandum of Tom C. Clark, assistant attorney general, to Biddle, June 17, 1944, 7, NARA, RG 60, DOJ Files, file 146-43-012.

58. Schofield had made available a copy of the report of Inspector Charles G. Mulligan and other inspectors in New York City, prepared from January 2 to October 4, 1941. Memorandum of Schofield to Shoemaker, April 13, 1942, NARA, RG 60, DOJ Files, file 38-012. In addition, he provided Correa with assistants to prepare the cases.

59. Memorandum of Goodwin to Berge, May 13, 1942, NARA, RG 60, DOJ Files, file 146-43-012.

60. Memorandum of D. E. Balch to Berge, May 16, 1942, NARA, RG 60, DOJ Files, file 146-43-012.

61. Memorandum of Biddle to Rowe and Charles Fahy, May 20, 1942, NARA, RG 60, DOJ Files, file 146-43-012.

62. Ibid.

63. Memorandum of Harry L. Hopkins to Biddle, August 15, 1942, NARA, RG 60, DOJ Files, file 146-43-012.

64. Memorandum of Biddle to Berge, August 22, 1942, NARA, RG 60, DOJ Files, file 146-43-012.

65. Memorandum from Berge to Rowe, August 26, 1942, box 35, Rowe Papers. Rowe reported to Biddle: "As you know Harry [Hopkins] was probably bitten by a lawyer when he was young and doesn't think much of the breed except when they are 'yes' lawyers. I do not propose to argue the merits of his point of view; as a matter of fact I go about three-fourths of the same way with him. Unfortunately the judges don't, and they have the say, not you or Harry." Memorandum from Rowe to Biddle, August 26, 1942, box 35, Rowe Papers.

66. Memorandum from Berge to Rowe, August 26, 1942.

67. Ibid.

68. Memorandum of Biddle to Hoover, August 7, 1942, NARA, RG 60, DOJ Files, file 146-43-012, §6. In this memo, Biddle sent to Hoover a copy of the letter he would address three days later to all U.S. attorneys.

69. NARA, RG 60, DOJ Files, file 146-43-012, §2.

70. Memorandum of Balch to Mr. Barron, September 16, 1942, NARA, RG 60, DOJ Files, file 146-43-012.

71. The "emigrant" marks or Rueckwanderer marks were sold in the United States in exchange for U.S. dollars by five banks or agencies designated for this purpose by the German Gold Discount Bank. See Siegfried Stern, *The United States in International Banking* (New York: Columbia University Press, 1951), 237.

72. Memorandums of J. Edgar Hoover to Berge, and of Berge to Hoover, September 10 and September 28, 1942, NARA, RG 60, DOJ Files, file 146-43-12.

73. Memo of Hoover to Berge, December 17, 1942: NARA, RG 60, DOJ Files, file 38-012.

74. Memorandum of Berge to the INS, February 23, 1943, NARA, RG 60, DOJ Files, file 38-012.

75. Memorandum of Harrison to Berge, March 20, 1943, NARA, RG 60, DOJ Files, file 38-012. Cf. previous memorandum of Harrison to Berge on the same topic, February 17, 1943, NARA, RG 60, DOJ Files, file 38-012.

76. Letters of Correa to Berge and Berge to Correa, May 3 and May 8, 1943, NARA, RG 60, DOJ Files, file 38-012. Correa agreed with Berge's suggestion that in the case of a father no longer in the United States, his denaturalization would have the effect of cancelling that of his son, still in the United States and "whose sympathies and activities on behalf of Germany are similar to his father's."

77. "Bund Leaders Face Loss of Citizenship," *New York Times*, October 4, 1942, 28.

78. Memorandum of Balch to Baron, October 7, 1942, NARA, RG 60, DOJ Files, file 146-43-012.

79. Letter of Biddle to Hennessy, November 23, 1942, NARA, RG 60, DOJ Files, file 146-43-02.

80. Telegram of Rowe, December 11, 1942, Box 35, James H. Rowe Jr. Papers,. Letter of Berge to Howard Caughran, December 12, 1942, NARA, RG 60, DOJ Files, file 146-43-012.

81. Letter from Rowe to Howard Corcoran, assistant U.S. attorney, December 26, 1942, box 35, James H. Rowe Jr. Papers, Franklin D. Roosevelt Library.

82. Department of Justice, Criminal Division, Trial brief of evidence, January 6, 1943, 500 pages 3 volumes. Philip Strong papers, box 19, Mudd Manuscript Library, Princeton University.

83. On April 6, 1943, Biddle sent this memorandum dated March 10, 1943, "Theories and Precedent, Pleadings and Practice, Policy and Procedure," of 158 pages, signed by Berge, J. M. McInerney, Balch, and Marcia Maylott, as Supplement 9 to Circular No. 3663. NARA, RG 60, DOJ Files, file 146-43-02.

84. Report on the administration of the Denaturalization Program submitted by Balch to Rowe, March 6, 1943, NARA, RG 60, DOJ Files, file 146-43-012, §5, 1.

85. Ibid., §5, 5.

86. Ibid., §5, 4.

87. In a memorandum to Roosevelt on June 2, 1942, Hoover had to answer to accusations that the FBI neglected the task: "The President is reported to have expressed the opinion that the FBI is spending too much time in investigating suspected Communists in and out of the Government service, particularly in the Government service, and ignoring the Fascist-minded groups both in and out of the Government. This conclusion is not supported by the facts." Hoover mentioned all the groups that had been investigated, but added: "In connection with investigations conducted within the Government service, it is true that a larger number of such inquiries have been made concerning Communist activities than Nazi, Fascist or Japanese. However, this is directly attributable to the type of complaints received. A considerable number of these investigations were predicated upon a list of alleged Communists in the Government service which was supplied by Congressman Martin Dies. The FBI, in a great majority of these cases, has cleared the Government employee of Communist affiliation alleged by Congressman Dies." Memorandum from Roosevelt to Eleanor Roosevelt, President's Official File 10-B: Justice Department-FBI, 1941–42, box 11, Franklin Roosevelt Library.

88. Memorandum of Hoover to Berge, May 1, 1942, NARA, RG 60, DOJ Files, file 146-43-012.

89. The FBI had identified seventy-five hundred persons who had purchased or applied to purchase Rueckwanderer Marks. Ibid.

90. On March 2, 1943, Biddle sent Supplement 7 to the circular of March 25, 1942 including a ninety-page outline of evidence concerning the "silvershirt legion of America." NARA, RG 60, DOJ Files, file 146-43-02.

91. Memorandum of Walter Stein, special inspector, INS, to J. R. Espinosa, assistant commissioner for inspections, April 2, 1943, NARA, RG 60, DOJ Files, file 146-43-012.

92. Ibid.

93. The Special War Policies Unit, the War Fraud Unit, the Alien Enemy Control Unit, and the Criminal Division National Defense Section and the FBI.

94. Report submitted by Balch to Rowe, March 6, 1943, §5, 16.

95. Ibid.

Part III. War in the Supreme Court

Note to epigraphs: Felix Frankfurter to Harlan Stone, March 31, 1943, box 69, Stone Papers. Draft of Hugo Black's concurring opinion in *Nishikawa*, March 3, 1958, Box 333, Black Papers.

Chapter 8. *Schneiderman*

1. *Schneiderman v. United States*, 320 U.S. 118, 63 S.Ct. 1333, 87 L.Ed. 1796 (1943)

2. Biography of William Schneiderman, William Schneiderman Papers, San Francisco State University, http://content.cdlib.org/view?docId=tf109n97wg&chunk.id=bioghist-1.7.4&brand=oac.

3. 320 U.S. 121–122.

4. 33 F. Supp. 510 (N.D. Cal. 1940).

5. 119 F.2d 500 (9th Cir. 1941).

6. 314 U.S. 597 (1941).

7. Ann Fagan Ginger, *Carol Weiss King, Human Rights Lawyer, 1895–1952*, with a foreword by Louis H. Pollak (Niwot: University Press of Colorado, 1993), 6–7.

8. Ibid., 65.

9. Ibid., 366. William Schneiderman, *Dissent on Trial: The Story of a Political Life* (Minneapolis: MEP Publications, 1983), 85–93.

10. Howard Meyer quoted in Ginger, *Carol Weiss King*, 180.

11. Nathan Greene, a brilliant lawyer she recruited after he graduated from Harvard Law School, comments: "She made you feel that unless you took the case or wrote the brief, the guy would be deported and maybe killed in his home country. Once you grudgingly committed yourself, you got interested in the legal problems themselves and they kept you going and doing the best you could. I'm a lazy guy myself, but I really worked on cases Carol got me into." Ginger, *Carol Weiss King*, 149.

12. She herself made only one appearance before the Supreme Court, in *Butterfield v. Zydok* (342 U.S. 524 [1952]), a few weeks before she died without knowing she had lost. Ginger, *Carol Weiss King*, ch. 36.

13. *Herndon v. Georgia*, 295 U.S. 441.

14. Ginger, *Carol Weiss King*, 238–239. See also *Kessler v. Strecker*, 307 U.S. 22 (1939).

15. Ginger, *Carol Weiss King*, ch. 27, and *Bridges v. Wixon*, 326 U.S. 135 (1945). In 1934, immigration officials asked Secretary of Labor Frances Perkins to detain and deport Bridges on the basis of a supposed Communist Party affiliation. Under pressure from Congress, Perkins issued a warrant for the arrest of Bridges and he was tried in 1939. But the government's case fell apart at trial, as the government relied primarily on witnesses who had participated in a wide range of criminal and other illicit activities. At the end of the trial, the administrative law judge found that the government had failed to prove its case. The government again tried Bridges in 1941. This time the government was successful during the initial hearing, but the ruling was overturned by the Board of Immigration Appeals. Nevertheless, Francis Biddle, the attorney general, overruled the board, finding Bridges to be deportable. In 1945, however, the Supreme Court found in *Bridges v. Wixon*, 326 U.S. 135 (1945) that "since Harry Bridges has been ordered deported on a misconstruction of the term 'affiliation' as used in the statute and by reason of an unfair hearing on the question of his membership in the Communist Party, his detention under the warrant is unlawful" (156).

16. In "Fair Trial," published on March 18, 1940, Willkie wrote: "Equal treatment under the law means exactly what it says, whether the man before the tribunal is a crook, a Democrat, a Republican, a Communist, or a businessman; whether he is rich or poor, white or black, good or bad. You cannot have a democracy on any other basis. You cannot preserve human liberties on any other theory." Quoted in Joseph Barnes, *Willkie: The Events He Was Part of, the Ideas He Fought For* (New York: Simon and Schuster, 1952), 321.

17. Schneiderman, *Dissent on Trial*, 81.

18. Barnes, *Willkie*, 322.

19. Letter of Wendell Willkie to Carol King, December 18, 1942, partially quoted in Barnes, *Willkie*, 400, at greater length in Ginger, *Carol Weiss King*, 369.

20. Ginger, *Carol Weiss King*, 369.

21. Barnes, *Willkie*, 322.

22. Carol King had sent him a draft, but his brief did not include any of her thoughts. Ginger, *Carol Weiss King*, –371. His main point: the danger of government preserved by "totalitarian

methods" or by "freedom of political thought and belief." Willkie argued, "If Schneiderman, on the basis of views imputed to him, then a young man of 21, . . . can be deprived of his citizenship on the basis of these imputed views, the citizenship of every naturalized citizen in the United States is in danger." *New York Times*, January 17, 1942.

23. *New York Times*, January 17, 1942. Another version is in Jeffrey F. Liss, "The Schneiderman Case: An Inside View of the Roosevelt Court," *Michigan Law Review* 74, no. 3 (January 1976): 507.

24. Letter of Charles Fahy, Solicitor General to the Chief Justice of the United States, April 21, 1942 Box 53, Charles Fahy Papers, Franklin D. Roosevelt Library.

25. See Frank Murphy, Notes on the conference of April 22, 1942, roll 125, 402-414. Frank Murphy Papers, Bentley Historical Library, University of Michigan.

26. Liss, "The Schneiderman Case," 507, and Melvin I. Urofsky, *Division and Discord: The Supreme Court Under Stone and Vinson, 1941–1953* (Columbia: University of South Carolina Press, 1997), 52.

27. Liss, "The Schneiderman Case," 506–507, 500, 502.

28. Ginger, *Carol Weiss King*, 373.

29. Ibid., 375.

30. Ibid.

31. Jackson wished to record his reasons for not participating in the decision. Frank Murphy had been attorney general when the case was instituted. Jackson wrote a note to Murphy, now also a justice, two days before the decision came down: "As you know, I disqualified myself. . . . The inference from that is that this case was my responsibility. That is true to a very limited extent only, as you know." Note from Justice Robert Jackson to Justice Frank Murphy, June 19, 1943, quoted in Liss, "The Schneiderman Case," 621. See also John P. Frank, *Inside Justice Hugo L. Black: The Letter*, no. 2 of Tarlton Legal History Series (Austin: Tarlton Law Library, University of Texas School of Law, 2000), 63.

32. James Francis Byrnes was confirmed on June 12, 1941, and resigned on October 3, 1942.

33. Frederick R. Barkley, "Communist's Case Argued by Willkie, Supreme Court Is Asked to Bar Voiding of Naturalization for Party Membership," *New York Times*, November 10, 1942.

34. Ginger, *Carol Weiss King*, 377.

35. Ibid., 379.

36. Barkley, "Communist's Case Argued."

37. Sydney Fine, *Frank Murphy: The Washington* Years (Ann Arbor: University of Michigan Press, 1984), 410.

38. The following excerpts are from Joseph P. Lash, *From the Diaries of Felix Frankfurter* (New York: W.W. Norton, 1975), 211–214.

39. As Noah Feldman has noticed, Americanism had replaced Judaism in his spiritual life. Noah Feldman, *Scorpions: The Battles and Triumphs of FDR's Great Supreme Court Justices* (New York: Twelve Publishers, 2010), 227.

40. Frankfurter Conference Summary, December 5, 1942, box 218, Felix Frankfurter Papers, Harvard Law School Library.

41. *Schneiderman v. United States*. Summary of the discussion at Conference on December 12, 1942, box 218, legal files, Frankfurter papers, Library of Congress.

42. Murphy conference notes, quoted by Liss, "The Schneiderman Case," 509.

43. Lash, *From the Diaries of Felix Frankfurter*, 216.

44. Liss, "The Schneiderman Case," 503.

45. "Willkie Presses Argument for Red—He and Fahy Again Debate Before Supreme Court Case of Schneiderman Citizenship—Charge of Fraud Denied—Absence of Overt Act by His Client Is Stressed—Solicitor Points to Party Tenets," *New York Times*, March 13, 1943.

46. James W. Douthat, "High Court Hears Willkie on Marxism," *Washington Post*, March 13, 1945, 10.

47. Fahy quoted in Liss, "The Schneiderman Case,"503, n. 18.

48. Douthat, "High Court Hears Willkie on Marxism," 10.

49. See Douglas notes, Conference March 15, 1943, box 81, Douglas Papers, Library of Congress, Washington, D.C.

50. Frankfurter wrote: "Your exposition of Schneiderman was masterly. You must lay it out in your dissent with all the powerful detail with which you stated the case to us. The requirement of being 'attached to the principles of the Constitution of the United States' caries an historical meaning not lessened by time, to which you will, I know, give magisterial illumination and authority in your dissent." Letter of Justice Felix Frankfurter to Chief Justice Harlan Stone, March 16, 1943, box 73, Stone Papers, Library of Congress, Washington, D.C.

51. See Douglas notes, Conference March 15, 1943.

52. Ibid.

53. Fine, *Frank Murphy*, 411.

54. Liss, "The Schneiderman Case," 503.

55. Frankfurter added: "And since the Congress of the United States from the beginning of the country's history has exacted such attachment, it is the duty of courts entrusted with the enforcement of naturalization laws to observe obedience to the conditions imposed by the Congress in granting American citizenship." Frankfurter to Stone, March 31, 1943, box 69, Stone Papers.

56. In his dissenting opinion, Stone also argued: "It would seem passing strange that Congress—which authorized cancellation of citizenship . . . for failure to hold the naturalization hearing in open court instead of in the judge's chambers, or for failure to present the requisite certificate of arrival in this country—should be thought less concerned with the applicant's attachment to the principles of the Constitution and that he be well disposed to the good order and happiness of the United States." 320 U.S. 118, 171.

57. Liss, "The Schneiderman Case," 514.

58. Ibid., 513–514.

59. Memorandum, Frank Murphy Papers, University of Michigan Library, quoted by Fine, *Frank Murphy*, 412.

60. Liss, "The Schneiderman Case," 509.

61. Murphy Papers, quoted in Liss, "The Schneiderman Case,"509. In the majority opinion delivered on *United States v. Schwimmer*, 279 U.S. 644 (1929), Justice Pierce Butler had asserted that aliens "have no natural right to become citizens, but only that which is by statute conferred upon them. Because of the great value of the privileges conferred by naturalization, the statutes prescribing qualifications and governing procedure for admission are to be construed with definite purpose to favor and support the government. And, in order to safeguard against admission of those who are unworthy, or who for any reason fail to measure up to required standards, the law puts the burden upon every applicant to show by satisfactory evidence that he has the specified qualifications."

62. Unsigned memorandum to Murphy, undated, box 62, Murphy Papers.

63. Liss, "The Schneiderman Case," 510.

64. Note from Frankfurter to Murphy, May 31, 1943, General Correspondence 1878–1965, reel 85, Felix Frankfurter Papers, Library of Congress, Washington, D.C.

65. Note from Frankfurter to Murphy, June 2, 1943, General Correspondence 1878–1965, reel 85, Frankfurter Papers.

66. *Minersville School District v. Gobitis*, 310 U.S. 586 (1940).

67. His former clerk, Philip Elman, thought that Frankfurter had been "pushed into a corner by flag salute cases." And Elman adds, "he was slowly being pushed in that direction by these other cases in my two terms, the first being Bridges." *Bridges v. State of California*, 314 U.S. 252 (1941). Norman Silber, *With All Deliberate Speed: The Life of Philip Elman: An Oral History Memoir in Mr. Elman's Words* (Ann Arbor: University of Michigan Press, 2004), 106.

68. Gerald Gunther, *Learned Hand: The Man and the Judge* (New York: Knopf, 1994), 564.

69. *West Virginia State Board of Education v. Barnette*, 319 U.S. 624 (1943). Frankfurter lobbied intensively to have Roosevelt nominate Judge Learned Hand to the Supreme Court but failed. Rutledge, the nominee chosen in lieu of Frankfurter's choice, would help cause the majority to reverse *Gobitis*. See Gunther, "The Last Chance for a Supreme Court Appointment; The 1942 Vacancy," in *Learned Hand*.

70. See Chapter 5 above.

71. *United States v. Schwimmer*, 279 U.S. 644.

72. 320 U.S. 135. Murphy relied here on a previous district court decision refusing to denaturalize a Communist, *United States v. Rovin* 12 F.2d 94 (1926). The judgment declared: "The history of that great document and of the 19 important changes which have already been made in it, in accordance with its terms, should be a sufficient answer to any question as to whether a desire for such a change indicates opposition to, or absence of attachment to, the principles of our Constitution. There is no need to review the evidence in detail. While it tends to show that the defendant has on occasion expressed economic and political ideas with which the majority of our people (including myself) are not in accord, and the expression of which would probably be prohibited or punished by governments not enjoying the constitutional principle of freedom of speech, the careful consideration of the entire record to which I have already referred fails, in my judgment, to establish any of the charges of fraud here made. There is nothing in the record which would justify a finding that the defendant has ever advocated the overthrow or changing of our government by revolution or in any other manner except by constitutional methods."

73. Note from Murphy to John Pickering, May 22, 1943, box 62, Murphy Papers, quoted in Liss, "The Schneiderman Case," 510.

74. Ibid.

75. 320 U.S. 137.

76. Ibid., 118, 136.

77. Ibid., 120.

78. Ibid.

79. Ibid., 166.

80. Schneiderman, *Dissent on Trial*, 103.

81. U.S. Supreme Court, *The Schneiderman Case: United States Supreme Court Opinion: With an Introduction by Carol King* (New York: American Committee for Protection of Foreign Born, 1943), 5.

82. Carol King, "The Willkie I Knew," *New Masses*, October 29, 1944, 10–11. Harry Bridges declared: "Wendell Willkie was the only man in America who has proved that he would rather be

right than be President," in "Messages Extol Willkie as a Powerful Influence in Crusade to Form Better World Relations; Flood of Tributes Lauds His Service; Sorrow at Untimely Death of 1940 Nominee Expressed by Leaders of Many Groups," *New York Times*, October 9, 1944, 15.

83. Letters of Frankfurter to Stone, June 21 and July 19, 1943, box 69, Stone Papers.

Chapter 9. *Baumgartner*

1. Memorandum of Dewey E. Balch to Herbert Wechsler, assistant attorney general, July 23, 1943, NARA, RG 60, DOJ Files, file 146-43-012.

2. *United States v. Krause*, Seventh Circuit, 136 F.2d 935 (1943). Memorandum of Balch to Wechsler, August 20, 1943, NARA, RG 60, DOJ Files, file 146-43-012.

3. Memorandum of Balch to Wechsler, July 23, 1943.

4. Ibid.

5. Circular No. 3663, Supplement No. 11, September 4, 1943, NARA, RG 60,, DOJ Files, file 38-012. But the petition for rehearing was denied (320 U.S. 807 [1943]).

6. Circular No. 3663, Supplement No. 11, September 4, 1943, 6. Different drafts of the circular are in NARA, RG 60, DOJ Files, file 146-43-012, 6.0.

7. Circular No. 3663, Supplement No. 11, September 4, 1943.

8. Biddle adds, underlining it: "*Frequently this can be done only by developing the cooperation and using as government witnesses, one or more former local members of the organization.*" Ibid., 5.

9. The original complaint filed in the district court in 1939 had charged fraudulent procurement in that he concealed his Communist affiliation from the naturalization court, but Schneiderman testified that he was never asked by the district court about his affiliation.

10. Circular No. 3663, Supplement No.11, September 4, 1943, 2.

11. Ibid.

12. Letter of Tom C. Clark, assistant attorney general, to U.S. attorneys, December 9, 1943, Re: Denaturalization Program, of NARA, RG 60, DOJ Files, file 146-43-012.

13. Ibid. The case in question was *United States v. De Stefano*, District Court, N.D. Ohio, E.D., 54 F. Supp. 463; 1943 November 9, 1943.

14. Note Re: Denaturalization Program, Clark, December 9, 1943. The other case was *United States v. Class* (1943).

15. Note Re: Denaturalization Program, Clark, December 9, 1943. The last case was *United States v. Hilda and Emil Otto Heilman* District Court, N.D. Ohio, E.D., 54 F. Supp. 414 (1943).

16. *United States v. Max Oscar Haas et al.*, 51 Fed. Supp. 910 (1943). Circular No. 3663, Supplement No.13, October 2, 1943, NARA, RG 60, DOJ Files, file 146-43-02.

17. *United States v. Bruno Holtz, et al.*, 54 F. Supp. 63 N.D. Calif (1944). The federal government had filed a denaturalization action against twelve citizens. Judgment was awarded for the defendants in five cases.

18. *United States v. Arnold Wilhelm Johannes Wolff*, N.D. Calif. (1944).

19. *United States v. Carl August Vogl*, 54 F. Supp. 24 N.D. Ill. (1944).

20. Biddle to All United States Attorneys. Recent decisions in denaturalization cases. Circular No. 3663, Supplement No. 15, April 14, 1944, NARA, RG 60, DOJ Files, file 146-43-02.

21. *Baumgartner v. United States*, 322 U.S. 665 (1944).

22. Legal files, 1924–1963, box 218, Frankfurter Papers, Library of Congress.

23. *Baumgartner v. United States*, 674.

24. Letter of Philip Elman to Felix Frankfurter, June 13, 1944, Frankfurter Papers, Harvard Law Library, part III, reel 2.

25. "Denaturalization cases in court of which some disposition has been made." Memorandum of June 26, 1944, NARA, RG 60, DOJ Files, file 146-43-02.

26. See Fifth Circuit Court of Appeals: *Meyer v. United States*, rehearing denied, 141 F.2d 825 (1944); Forth Circuit Court of Appeals: *Orth et al. v. United States*, 142 F.2d 969 (1944); *Jogwick v. United States*, 142 F.2d 998 (1944).

27. See Ninth Circuit Court of Appeals: *Bergman v. United States*, 144 F.2d 34 (1944); Second Circuit Court of Appeals: *United States v. Rossler*, 144 F.2d 463 (1944); Second Circuit Court of Appeals: *United States v. Sotzek et al.*, 144 F.2d 576 (1944).

28. Memorandum of Clark to Francis Biddle, attorney general, June 17, 1944, 7, NARA, RG 60, DOJ Files, file 146-43-012. In 1945, after Franklin D. Roosevelt's death, new president Harry S. Truman appointed him attorney general. On the death of Justice Frank Murphy in July 1949, Truman appointed him to the Supreme Court, a position he resigned in 1967.

29. Ibid.

30. 34 Ibid., 3.

31. Memorandum of Biddle to Charles Fahy, solicitor general, handwritten on a Memorandum of Clark to Francis Biddle, attorney general, June 19, 1944, NARA, RG 60, DOJ Files, file 146-43-012.

32. Memorandum of J. Edgar Hoover, director of FBI, to Clark, July 6, 1944, NARA, RG 60, DOJ Files, file 146-43-012.

33. Memorandum of Fahy to Biddle, June 29, 1944, NARA, RG 60, DOJ Files, file 146-43-012. See also memorandum of Fahy to James M. McInerney, chief of the Internal Security Section, Criminal Division, July 11, 1944, NARA, RG 60, DOJ Files, file 146-43-012, §7: "I think you should continue, as I understand you will do, to let me go over individual cases in which you intend to take action at whatever stage that might occur; . . . whether they are to go to trial or whether appeals should abandoned, or error confessed etc. By working together this way the pending cases can be handled as well as we can manage and the program narrowed to the limits of the *Baumgartner* and *Schneiderman* cases."

34. Memorandum of Hoover to Clark, May 23, 1945, NARA, RG 60, DOJ Files, file 146-43-012.

35. Ibid.

36. Memorandum of Theron L. Caudle, assistant attorney general, Criminal Division, to Hoover, August 21, 1945, NARA, RG 60, DOJ Files, file 146-43-012.

37. Ibid.

38. Memorandum of K. D. Abbott to McInerney, July 24, 1944, NARA, RG 60, DOJ Files, file 146-43-012.

39. Ibid.

40. Memorandum of Elman, Office of the Solicitor General, to Fahy, September 5, 1944, NARA, RG 60, DOJ files, file 146-43-012.

41. Memorandum of Fahy to McInerney, August 11, 1944, NARA, RG 60, DOJ Files, file 146-43-012.

42. Letter of Clark to Edward J. Ennis, director, Alien Enemy Control Unit, September 26, 1944, NARA, RG 60, DOJ Files, file 146-43-012. Later on, a memo mentions that three procedures in the nature of bills of reviews had been filed in districts courts: *John H. Vogt v. United States*, and Civil #23541-R of Max Oscar Haas and Rudolf Simon, denaturalized in *Haas*, 51 Fed. Supp. 910.

43. See letter of Theron L.Caudle, assistant attorney general, November 13, 1946, rejecting a

request from Reverend John C. Fitting to reconsider the denaturalization of German Americans interned in Ellis Island, who had been ordered removed from the United States, NARA, RG 60, DOJ Files, file 146-43-012.

44. Lewis Wood, "High Court Upsets Conviction in Two Appeals on Civil Liberties," *New York Times*, June 13, 1944.

45. Harry Kalven, Jr., *A Worthy Tradition: Freedom of Speech in America*, ed. Jamie Kalven (New York: Harper and Row, 1988), 431–432.

46. Thurgood Marshall, "Mr. Justice Murphy and Civil Rights," *Michigan Law Review* 48, no. 6 (April 1950): 764.

47. John P. Frank, "Justice Murphy: The Goals Attempted," *Yale Law Journal* 59, no. 1 (December 1949): 8, n. 39.

48. Memorandum of Chief Justice Harlan Stone for the conference of January 29, 1944, dated January 20, 1944, part III, reel 4, correspondence with Stone, Frankfurter Papers, Harvard Law School Library.

49. Letter Re: No. 493 *Baumgartner v. United States* of Frankfurter to Stone, January 21, 1944, Stone Papers. Frankfurter had in mind "such lawyer as Marian Smith of Atlanta, or H. H. Phleger of San Francisco or William Mitchell of New York." Finally Harold Evans of Philadelphia was appointed. Under rule 53-7 of the Rules on the Supreme Court, the Court can appoint a member of the bar to serve as counsel for an indigent party. Robert L. Stern and Eugene Gressman, *Supreme Court Practice; Jurisdiction, Procedure, Arguing and Briefing Techniques, Forms, Statutes, Rules for Ppractice in the Supreme Court of the United States*, 4th ed. (Washington, D.C.: Bureau of National Affairs, 1969), 367, 749.

50. Letter of Stone to Frankfurter, May 16, 1944, part I, reel 11, Frankfurter Papers, Harvard Law Library. He added: "I think your reference on page 5 to 'almost compelling proof' goes too far. 'Clear and convincing' has been the test. I think we should stick to it."

51. Frank Murphy, Memorandum to the Court, May 17, 1944, Frank Murphy Papers, roll 126.

52. Handwritten note of Douglas to Murphy, May 17, 1944, Frank Murphy Papers, roll 126.

53. Letter of Felix Frankfurter to his brethren, May 17, 1944, Frank Murphy Papers, roll 128.

54. Memorandum of Felix Frankfurter to the conference, May 18, 1944, Frank Murphy Papers, roll 128.

55. Frankfurter appears to refer to the case of *Mortensen v. United States*, 322 U.S. 369 (1944), an opinion written by Murphy in which Frankfurter concurred, involving a conviction for transporting women for the purpose of prostitution; Murphy's opinion in *Mortensen* does not cite the leading case on the relevant statute, *Caminetti v. United States*, 242 U.S. 470 (1917), a case in which Holmes and Brandeis joined the majority opinion. Frankfurter seems to be saying that just as Murphy did not cite *Caminetti* in his *Mortensen* opinion, with no implied disrespect to Holmes and Brandeis, he did not cite Murphy's *Schneiderman* opinion in his first draft of the *Baumgartner* opinion.

56. Letter of Frankfurter to Murphy, June 1, 1944, part III, reel 2, Frankfurter Papers, Harvard Law Library.

57. Letter of Elman to Frankfurter, June 13, 1944, part III, reel 2, Frankfurter Papers, Harvard Law Library.

58. *Baumgartner.*

59. Ibid., 676.

60. Ibid.

61. Ibid., 679.

Chapter 10. A Frozen Interlude in the Cold War

1. *Knauer v. United States*, 328 U.S. 654 (1946).

2. Douglas's notes on the conference meeting of May 6, 1946, box 135, Douglas Papers.

3. Ibid.

4. Ibid. In his dissent, Rutledge wrote: "The power to naturalize is not the power to denaturalize. The act of admission must be taken as final for any cause which may have existed at that time. Otherwise, there cannot but be two classes of citizens, one free and secure except for acts amounting to forfeiture within our tradition; the other conditional, timorous and insecure because blanketed with the threat that some act or conduct, not amounting to forfeiture for others, will be taken retroactively to show that some prescribed condition had not been fulfilled and be so adjudged." *Knauer*, 328 U.S. 676.

5. *Klapprott v. United States* 335 U.S. 601 (1949) 6. 335 U.S. 601, 629.

7. 335 U.S. 613 Black was joined by only three other Justices: Douglas, Murphy and Rutledge. Burton, while agreeing that a judgment of denaturalization may be entered by default joined in the judgment of the Court as limited to the special facts of the case 335 U.S. 616.

8. In *Bindczyck v. Funicane*, 342 U.S. 76 (1951), two years later, the Court confirmed the denaturalization of Peter A. Bindczyck, a soldier in the U.S. Army who disclaimed loyalty to the United States and stated his desire to leave the country after the war, one day following his naturalization. Seven days afterward, the United States filed a motion to vacate and set aside the order of naturalization. Bindczyck admitted the charge of disloyalty and the court set aside the order .

9. Geoffrey R. Stone, *Perilous Times: Free Speech in Wartime from the Sedition Act of 1798 to the War on Terrorism* (New York: W. W. Norton, 2004), 323. Already before the war, in order to reduce the influence of the Communist Party, Congress had reenacted in March 1940 the Espionage Act of 1917 and passed in June 1940 the Alien Registration Act or Smith Act. But then during the war, the Soviet Union would become an ally of the United States, and the passion for anti-Communism subsided for a while.

10. Nixon was elected representative of the Twelfth District of California in the House and McCarthy was elected senator of Wisconsin.

11. Melvin I. Urofsky, *Division and Discord: The Supreme Court Under Stone and Vinson, 1941–1953* (Columbia: University of South Carolina Press, 1997), 160.

12. Labor–Management Relations Act, 61 Stat. 136, enacted June 23, 1947. Leaders of labor unions had to file an affidavit with the National Labor Relations Board affirming that they were not members of the Communist Party U.S.A. and did not advocate the violent overthrow of the federal government, otherwise that union would lose the protection of the board.

13. 64 Stat. 1014 (1950). Pat McCarran was a Democratic senator of Nevada and a fervent anti-Communist.

14. Stone, *Perilous Times*, 325. The act empowered a Subversive Activities Control Board to declare organizations to be Communist if they failed to register voluntarily as Communist. For the members of those declared as such, it meant being barred from government employment or employment in any private company engaged in government defense work.

15. See "Developments in the Law: Immigration and Nationality," *Harvard Law Review* 66, no. 4 (February 1953): 643, 723.

16. 66 Stat. 260 (1952). This act, which maintained the national origins quota as the main basis for immigration selection, faced strong opposition by Truman; after he vetoed it, he immediately

formed a presidential commission, whose report was delivered to him on January 5, 1953, a couple of weeks before he left office. The commission recommended among many other reforms that a naturalized citizen should not be subject to denaturalization for refusing to testify before Congress or for any conduct subsequent to his naturalization, unless the government could prove acquisition of citizenship by fraud or illegality. President's Commission on Immigration and Naturalization, *Whom We Shall Become* (Washington, D.C.: Government Printing Office, 1953), 238.

17. It was a ground for revocation "as having been procured by concealment of a material fact or willful misrepresentation." This legislation dropped illegal procurement and fraud as a basis for denaturalization, replacing them with the phrase just quoted. §340 (a), 66 Stat. 260. See "Developments in the Law," 643, 724.

18. "M'Granery Starts a Drive to Deport Aliens Racketeers—Campaign Includes Moves to Denaturalize Those Who Have Taken Out Citizenship,," *New York Times*, October 3, 1952.p.1.

19. Schneiderman was again on the list of targeted Americans. Lewis Wood, "U.S. Acts to Deport Reds and Bring Foster to Trial," *New York Times*, October 23, 1952.

20. Born in Vileika, Poland, in 1896, Radzie arrived in the United States in 1929, was naturalized in 1939, and was later accused of having been an active member of the Communist Party between 1919 and 1930. "Illegal Citizenship Is Laid to Red Here," *New York Times*, December 16, 1952.

21. When John L. Lewis set up the Congress of Industrial Organizations in 1935, Matles practically single-handedly converted his AFL-affiliated colleagues in the International Association of Machinists to a new union. As director of organization for the United Electrical, Radio and Machine Workers of America, one of the CIO's most influential arms, Matles gained a reputation as a left-leaning leader as well as an articulate, precise negotiator. *New York Times*, December 16, 1952. See also "Milestones," *Time*, September 29, 1975.

22. "Brownell Details Subversion Fights," *New York Times*, March 18, 1953.

23. "Denaturalization Suit Set," *New York Times*, October 13, 1953.

24. Stone, *Perilous Times*, 420–421.

25. These cases were *United States v. Sweet*, 106 F. Supp. 634; *United States v. Chomiak*, 108 F. Supp. 527; and *United States v. Charnowola*, 109 F. Supp. 810.

26. *United States v. Chruszczak*, 127 F. Supp. 743.

27. *United States v. Title*, 132 F. Supp. 185 (S.D. Calif. 1955). Eight years later Sam Title obtained a hearing from a federal court on the deportation decision by the INS, which had previously held that the hearing he received at the time of his denaturalization constituted the hearing procedure (*Title v. Immigration and Naturalization Service*, 322 F.2d 21 [9th Cir. 1963]). On May 26, 1958, Title claimed in front of the district court that in the judgment on his denaturalization, an affidavit showing good cause had not been filed by the government prior to the institution of the denaturalization proceedings, as required by 8 U.S.C. §1451(a) and by the Supreme Court in decisions rendered subsequent to the petitioner's denaturalization in *Zucca* (351 U.S. 93). On June 19, 1958, the district court denied appellant's motions. On appeal, the circuit court decided that a denaturalization judgment made in absence of an affidavit showing good cause could not be set aside, for it is not contrary to a fundamental jurisdictional element (*Title v. United States*, 263 F.2d 28 [9th Cir. 1959]). In considering his appeal, the circuit court recognized, however, that had the matter been brought to its attention on direct appeal, it would have reversed the denaturalization judgment: "Were Title's appeal presently before us, we would reverse the judgment of denaturalization rendered against him by the district court. But that appeal he has voluntarily failed to prosecute." 263 F.2d 30.

28. "Brownell Reports on Communists in U.S," *New York Times*, October 8, 1956.

29. Six in 1953, five in 1954, twelve in 1955, four in 1956, three in 1957, and one in 1958. Source: *Annual Reports of the Immigration and Naturalization Service, 1957* and *1958* (Washington, D.C.: Government Printing Office).

30. *Anthony Scariano Memoir*, vol. 1 of *Illinois General Assembly Oral History Program, 77*, Archives/ Special Collections, University of Illinois, Springfield.

31. The ten were Emmerich Lustig, Isaac Ronch, Constantine Radzie, Victor Jeremy Jerome, Louis Weinstock, Isidore Begun, Daniel Boanolouis, Jehuda Braverman, Paul Novick, and Sol Almazov Pearl.

32. *United States v. Lustig*, 16 F.R.D. 378 (S.D. N.Y., 1954).

33. *United States v. Bridges*, 133 F. Supp. 638 (N.D. Cal. 1955). Quoting Justice Frankfurter's decision in *Baumgartner*, judge Louis E. Goodman noted that to cancel the respondent's citizenship, after ten years of presumptively good citizenship, the government had to meet an "exacting standard." The judge ruled that it did not meet this standard by the kind of witnesses it produced, particularly after abortive efforts to prove the same issue in different proceedings over many years, *Bridges*, 133 F. Supp. at 644.

34. Urofsky, *Division and Discord*, 161.

35. In 1950, in *American Communications Assn. v. Douds*, the Court upheld section 9(h) of the Taft-Hartley Act. Chief Justice Vinson argued in his majority opinion that the abridgment of freedom of speech the act provoked had to be weighed against the government's power to regulate commerce and "that political strikes are evils of conduct which cause substantial harm to interstate commerce." *American Communications Assn. v. Douds*, 339 U.S. 382 (1950). Breaking with its First Amendment doctrine developed since World War I, the Court in *Dennis v. United States* (341 U.S.494 [1951]) affirmed the conviction of eleven leaders of the U.S. Communist Party under the Smith Act. Vinson, who delivered the plurality opinion, followed Chief Judge Learned Hand, who wrote the opinion of the circuit court (183 F.2d at 212). The most speech-protective interpretations of Justice Oliver Wendell Holmes's "clear and present danger" test were diluted, so as to imply that "in each case, [courts] must ask whether the gravity of the 'evil,' discounted by its improbability, justifies such invasion of free speech as is necessary to avoid the danger." Gerald Gunther, *Learned Hand: The Man and the Judge* (New York: Knopf, 1994), 599. For Vinson, "the mere fact that, from the period 1945 to 1948, petitioners' activities did not result in an attempt to overthrow the Government by force and violence is, of course, no answer to the fact that there was a group that was ready to make the attempt." *Dennis v. United States*, 341 U.S. 494.

36. *Bridges v. United States*, 346 U.S. 209(1953). Burton delivered the opinion of the Court, with Reed, Vinson, and Minton dissenting. On June 23, 1945, only five days after the Supreme Court ruled in his favor, Bridges began the naturalization process, becoming a citizen on September 17, 1945. In 1948, the government went after Bridges again, this time trying Bridges criminally, under 18 U.S.C. sections 371 and 1015(1), for fraudulently stating on his naturalization application that he was not and had never been a member of the Communist Party and for falsely stating the same under oath during his naturalization proceeding. A jury convicted Bridges, but the Supreme Court overturned its decision in this 1953 decision. The Court considered whether the Wartime Suspension of Limitations Act had extended the three-year statute of limitations for charging Bridges. In a decision delivered by Justice Burton, the Court ruled that it did not and that the charges against Bridges should have been dismissed by the district court because the government had failed to charge Bridges within the required three-year period.

37. Urofsky, *Division and Discord*, 178–189.

38. John P. Frank, "Fred Vinson and the Chief Justiceship," *University of Chicago Law Review* 21, no. 2 (Winter 1954): 212–246, particularly 228–229. For the cases of the period 1947–1953, Frankfurter stood on behalf of the claimed rights in 57 percent of the cases, with Black and Douglas standing in 81 and 83 percent of the cases respectively, while Jackson (27 percent), Burton (26 percent), Clark (25 percent), Vinson (17 percent), Reed (17 percent), and Minton (13 percent) would be on that side in the minority of cases. In the 1952 term, Frankfurter stood even more with both liberal justices in the non unanimous civil right cases, on behalf of claimed rights in 75 percent of the cases, Douglas in 85 percent, and Black in 95 percent. The turning moment was clearly the replacement of Murphy by Clark and of Rutledge by Minton in 1949: in the non unanimous civil right cases of the 1946–1948 terms, Murphy and Rutledge stood in 95 and 93 percent respectively of more than fifty cases on behalf of claimed rights.

39. Except when the case was procedural and where the matter was not directly denaturalization but a criminal charge in the naturalization proceeding.

40. Stone, *Perilous Times*, 410.

41. Vinson had replaced Chief Justice Harlan Stone, who died while delivering a dissenting opinion in Court in 1946.

42. See Joan M. Leiman, "The Rule of Four," *Columbia Law Review* 57, no. 7 (November 1957): 975–992.

43. *Sweet v. United States* (*Chomiak v. United States, Charnowola v. United States*), 211 F.2d 118 (6 Cir., 1954). See "Denaturalization Suit Set." Nicholai Chomiak was admitted to citizenship on August 7, 1945, and George Charnowola on January 28, 1946.

44. 348 U.S. 817. Black and Douglas were the only Justices who voted for certiorari on all the three cases. Burton, Clark, Frankfurter, Minton, Reed and Warren voted against on all. Jackson voted for certiorari only on Chomiak. See records of certiorari No.73, 74, 75, box 1155, Douglas Papers.

45. Memorandum of James F. Crafts, Jr. on *Charnolowa v. United States*, 1954 term, no. 75, August 13, 1954, box 1156, Douglas Papers.

46. Warren started his tenure standing on Felix Frankfurter's judicial restraint philosophy. He first reversed it in *Emspak v. United States*, where he joined Frankfurter in defense of a member of the Communist Party, investigated in 1949 by the Committee on Un-American Activities. *Emspak v. United States*, 349 U.S. 190 (1955). Julius Emspak, an official of the Electrical, Radio, and Machine Workers of America Union, during testimony was asked 239 questions about the union and its relationship with the Communist Party. He declined to answer 68 of these questions, citing "primarily the first amendment, supplemented by the fifth." A district court later held that Emspak's statement about his rights was insufficient; he needed specifically to invoke his right against self-incrimination under the Fifth Amendment. The Supreme Court decided that witnesses need only state their wish to be protected under the Fifth Amendment in a way that the court could "reasonably be expected to understand" and therefore set aside his fine and prison sentence. Frankfurter wrote to Justice Harlan, "I thought and think it was right to charge those loose-mouthed, loose mannered and loose-headed men on the Hill with a little more responsibility in the serious business of Congressional investigations." John Marshall Harlan Papers, Princeton University Archives.

47. *United States v. Zucca*, 351 U.S. 93 (1956).

48. *Zucca*, 351 U.S. 91. In another case decided a few months earlier, on January 16, *United States v. Minker*, 350 U.S. 179 (1956), the government had also lost. Abraham Minker, a naturalized citizen, was subpoenaed by an immigration officer to appear and give testimony as a "witness." The object

was to interrogate him to try to elicit information for proceedings to revoke Minker's naturalization. The Supreme Court decided that the word "witnesses" had to be construed so as not to include a citizen who is himself the subject of a denaturalization investigation.

49. Warren, backed by Douglas, Black, Frankfurter, and Burton, delivered the opinion of the Court. Harlan did not participate in the decision and Clark dissented, joined by Reed and Minton. One year later, Congress amended the statute to overrule the decision; see 66 Stat.163, 262, 8 U.S.C. §1451(j) (1952). See "Affidavit of Good Cause Prerequisite to Civil Denaturalization Proceeding," *Columbia Law Review* 55, no. 5 (May 1955): 751–754.

50. *Nowak v. United States*, 356 U.S. 660 (1958).

51. Steve Babson, Dave Riddle, and David Elsila, *The Color of Law: Ernie Goodman, Detroit, and the Struggle for Labor and Civil Rights* (Detroit: Wayne State University Press, 2010), 2.

52. See Margaret Nowak, *Two Who Were There: A Biography of Stanley Nowak* (Detroit: Wayne State University Press, 1989).

53. Babson, Riddle, and Elsila, *The Color of Law*, 265.

54. "Michigan Ex-lawmaker Named," *New York Times*, March 10, 1952.

55. On December 24, 1952. Babson, Riddle, and Elsila, *The Color of Law*, 267.

56. Nowak, *Two Who Were There*, 239–255.

57. 238 F.2d 282 (1956).

58. Nowak, *Two Who Were There,* 255.

59. Ibid., 273.

60. *Nowak*, 356 U.S. 660; *Maisenberg v. United States*, 356 U.S. 670 (1958). In both cases, Justice Harlan delivered the opinion of the Court and Justices Burton, Clark, and Charles Whittaker dissented.

61. House, *Problems Arising in Cases of Denaturalization and Deportation of Communists (Greater Pittsburgh Area—Part 3), Hearings Before he Committee on Un-American Activities*, 86th Cong., 1st sess., March 12, 1959.

62. *Matles v. United States*, 356 U.S. 256 (1958). The Court reversed the judgment of the circuit court (247 F.2d 378).

63. *Schwinn v. United States*, 112 F.2d 74 (9th Cir.), affirmed 311 U.S. 616, 61 S.Ct. 70, 85 L. Ed. 390; *United States v. Tuteur*, 215 F.2d 415 (7th Cir.); *United States v. Knight*, 291 F. 129 (D.C. Mont.), affirmed 299 F. 571 (9th Cir.); *United States v. Collins*, 131 F. Supp. 545 (S.D. N.Y.); *United States v. Shinkevich*, 131 F. Supp. 547 (E.D. Pa.); *United States v. Jerome*, 115 F. Supp. 818 (S.D. N.Y.); *United States v. Lustig*, 110 F. Supp. 806 (S.D. N.Y.); *United States v. Schuchhardt*, 48 F. Supp. 876 (N.D. Ind.); *United States v. Leles*, 227 F. 189, 236 F. 784 (N.D. Cal.); *United States v. Radzie*, 14 F.R.D. 151 (S.D. N.Y.); *United States v. Vavorito*, 7 F.R.D. 152 (N.D. Ohio).

64. House, *Problems Arising in Cases of Denaturalization*, March 12, 1959, 463.

65. *Chaunt v. United States*, 364 U.S. 350 (1960).

66. Box 1244, Douglas Papers.

67. Declaration of Warren in the Court Conference of October 21, 1960, Handwritten notes of Douglas, box 1244, Douglas Papers.

68. "The Government has failed to show by 'clear, unequivocal, and convincing' evidence either (1) that facts were suppressed which, if known, would have warranted denial of citizenship or (2) that their disclosure might have been useful in an investigation possibly leading to the discovery of other facts warranting denial of citizenship." *Chaunt*, 364 U.S. at 356.

69. In 1960 in *Polites v. United States* 364 U.S. 426, Gus Polites 's citizenship was revoked

because the District Court found that, within ten years preceding his petition for naturalization, he had been a member of the Communist Party. Polites had been naturalized under the Nationality Act of 1940, which, contrary to the 1906 act, explicitly excluded from naturalization an alien who, at any time within ten years preceding his application, had been a member of any organization that advocated the overthrow by force or violence of the government of the United States (which could be interpreted to include the Communist Party). His appeal was dismissed with prejudice. Four years later petitioner requested the judgment to be vacated, on the ground that it was void-able under the Supreme Court's decisions in *Nowak v. United States*, 356 U.S. 660, and *Maisenberg v. United States*, 356 U.S. 670. The Court decided that those decisions were not effective to alter the law controlling *Polites* case. Stewart, delivered the opinion of the Court, joined by Clark, Frank-furter, Harlan, Whittaker; Brennan dissented joined by the Chief Justice, Douglas and Black. And in 1961, Frank Costello was denaturalized for having indicated on his application for naturalization in 1925 that his occupation was "real estate." His true occupation was bootlegging and the Court considered that if known this misrepresentation would have prevented him to become a citizen. *Costello v. United States*, 365 U.S. 265 (1961) Brennan delivered the opinion of the Court. Harlan did not participate; Black and Douglas dissented. It would take until *Kungys v. United States*, 485 U.S. 759 (1988) to conclude this debate.

70. Memo of J. Edgar Hoover, director, FBI, to Tom C. Clark, assistant attorney general, September 7, 1944, NARA, RG 60, entry 60, DOJ Files, file 146–43 012.

71. A dozen cases were raised in the U.S. consulate in Cork, Ireland, on November 22, 1944. Airgram from the U.S. consul in Cork to the State Department, November 22, 1944, NARA, RG 60, DOJ Files, file 38–012. In April 1945, a total of 151 cases were sent from the district of New Jersey to U.S. consulates, mostly in Italy, but also in Germany, Poland, Ireland, and Greece. Letter of Clark to Thorn Lord, U.S. attorney, district of New Jersey, April 2, 1945, 3, NARA, RG 60, DOJ Files, file 8–012.

72. Richard W Flournoy Jr., *Hearings Before the Committee on Immigration and Naturalization on H.R. 6127 Superseded by H.R. 9980*, 76th Cong., 1st Sess., 409 (1940), 140–141. There was no section 404(c) in the Nationality Act proposed by experts from the State, Justice, and Labor Departments. Flournoy suggested it during his hearing. Later, in 1947, the assistant secretary of state wrote to the Senate Committee on the Judiciary asking for section 404(c) to be repealed "since it is believed in general to be disadvantageous to the United states, requiring it to withdraw citizenship from many persons who were naturalized in good faith in the U.S. and who while abroad have actively and substantially promoted the interests and prestige of the United States and leaving such person in the situation of being stateless." "Note: Citizenship Lost by Foreign Residence," *Stanford Law Review* 2, no. 3 (April 1950): 582, 586–587.

73. The decision of the Board of Special Inquiry of the I.N.S. was affirmed by the Commissioner of Immigration and on August 5, 1947, by the Board of Immigration Appeals acting for the Attorney General. Lapides then obtained a writ of habeas corpus from the District Court for the Southern District of New York but, on appeal, the order of that Court dismissing the writ was affirmed by the Circuit Court of Appeals for the Second Circuit *United States ex rel. Lapides v. Watkins* 165 F.2d 1017 (C.C.A, 1948). Thereafter, in March 1948, Lapides filed a complaint under section 503 of the Nationality Act of 1940 asking for a judgment declaring him a National of the U.S. See box 1492, folder Lapides, ACLU Papers, Mudd Manuscript Library, Princeton University. Not too much involved in denaturalization cases, the ACLU later handled the defense of two other de-nationalized Americans in front of the Supreme Court: Albert L. Trop and Angelika L. Schneider.

74. *Lapides v. Clark*, 176 F.2d 619 (1949).

75. Judge Edgerton added: "Congress may expatriate citizens on reasonable grounds. No doubt these may include five years residence abroad. But it does not follow that Congress may expatriate some citizens and not others on this ground." On *Lapides* and its unconstitutionality, see "Note: Section 404 (C) of the Nationality Act of 1940: Residence Abroad as Automatic Expatriation of the Naturalized American," *Yale Law Journal* 59, no. 1 (December 1949):139–151.

76. Writ of certiorari denied October 24, 1949, 338 U.S. 861 (1949). See Fowler V. Harper, "What the Supreme Did Not Do in 1949 Term—An Appraisal of certiorari (With A. S. Rosenthal)," 99 *Pennsylvania Law Review* 293 (1950), 305–307.

77. Memorandum of Lemuel Schofield to the Robert Jackson, attorney general, September 16, 1940, box 90, folder 4, Jackson Papers.

78. Willis B. Snell, "Citizenship: Intent Required for Expatriation," *Michigan Law Review 49*, no. 4 (February 1951): 595–605.

79. *Savorgnan v. United States*, 338 U.S. 491 (1950).

80. See Appendix 4.

81. *Acheson v. Okimura and Murata*, 99 F. Supp. 587 (D. Hawai'i 1951).

82. *Acheson v. Okimura*, 342 U.S. 899 (1952), 72 S.Ct. 293, 96 L. Ed. 674. Later in 1952, in *Mandoli v. Acheson*, 344 U.S. 133 (1952), the Supreme Court affirmed the citizenship of a dual citizen born in the United States but raised in Italy, who had served in the Italian Army, but the decision was based on an interpretation of a statute, not of the Constitution. Joseph Mandoli was born in the United States to Italian parents and was then a dual citizen of the United States and Italy. His parents had moved back to Italy when he was a child, and he had served briefly in the army in 1931. In 1937, he was denied a U.S. passport, on the ground that he had not return to the United States upon reaching the age of majority. The Supreme Court ruled that the law, as it then stood, did not permit natural-born U.S. citizens to be stripped of U.S. citizenship for failing to return to the United States upon reaching adulthood. Rather than base its ruling on constitutional arguments, the Court examined the legislative history of the relevant portions of U.S. citizenship law, and concluded that Congress had consciously chosen to make these provisions applicable only to naturalized U.S. citizens (see *Rogers v. Bellei* in the Conclusion). In particular, the Court noted that although U.S. law at that time required certain U.S. citizens with childhood dual citizenship (such as those born abroad to American parents) to make a specific "election" of U.S. citizenship (i.e., a declaration of allegiance followed by a return to the United States) upon reaching adulthood, no such requirement applied to a U.S. citizen having been born in the United States. The Court also decided that Mandoli's foreign military service did not warrant loss of his U.S. citizenship because, under Mussolini's Fascist government, he had had no choice but to join the Italian army.

83. See docket book, box 210, folder 1, no. 421, Douglas Papers.

84. *Okimura v. Acheson*, 111 F. Supp. 303 (D. Hawai'i 1952) and *Murata v. Acheson*, 111 F. Supp. 306 (D. Hawai'i 1952).

85. *Sakamoto v. Dulles*, 111 F. Supp. 308 (D. Hawai'i 1953).

86. See "'Voluntary': A Concept in Expatriation Law," *Columbia Law Review* 54, no. 6 (June 1954): 932.

87. §401, Nationality Act of 1940, 54 Stat. 1168, 8 U.S.C. 801. See Charles Gordon, "The Power of Congress to Expatriate," *I&N Reporter* 7 (July 1958).

Chapter 11. *Nishikawa, Perez, Trop*

1. "The most important constitutional pronouncements of this century" was in a note of Justice William O. Douglas's remarks, in Dallin H. Oaks's journal, entry of March 31, 1958, communicated by Oaks to the author.

2. *Gonzales v. Landon*, 350 U.S. 920, 921 (1955).

3. The Court reversed the lower courts' judgments without considering the constitutional question involved.

4. *Nishikawa v. Dulles*, 356 U.S. 129 (1958); *Perez v. Brownell*, 356 U.S. 44; *Trop v. Dulles*, 356 U.S. 86.

5. *Trop*, 356 U.S. 88.

6. Cf. Anthony Lewis, special envoy, "3 U.S.-Born Fight for Nationality to Test in High Court Power of Congress to Eliminate Their Citizenship," *New York Times*, November 11, 1957, at 24. Trop had submitted his case to ACLU in October 1954. On December 30, 1954, the ACLU Due Process Committee agreed to handle Trop's case. With the help of Herbert M. Levy, Osmond K. Fraenkel filed suit in federal court seeking declaratory judgment that Trop was a U.S. citizen. Letter of Trop to ACLU, October 20, 1954, Minutes of the Due Process Committee of ACLU, December 30, 1954, box 1740, ACLU Papers, Mudd Manuscript Library. On December 28, 1956, the United States Court of Appeals Second Circuit affirmed the judgment of the district court to deny Trop's claim. It did "not find enough doubt of the constitutionality of the statute." *Albert L. Trop v. John Foster Dulles*, 239 F.2d 527 (1956).

7. "The Supreme Court: The Judges or the Congress?" *Time*, April 14, 1958.

8. Oaks's journal, entry of March 31. The *New York Times* confirms that "the strongest oral statement" of the day" was by Justice Douglas, who bitterly described the majority view [on Perez] "as perhaps the most important pronouncement of this century," special envoy, "High Court Backs U.S. Expatriation; But Sharply Split Opinions Find Constitutional Limits in Citizenship Cases," *New York Times*, April 1, 1958, 22.

9. On the bench memorandums, see Bernard Schwartz, *Super Chief: Earl Warren and His Supreme Court, a Judicial Biography* (New York: New York University Press, 1983), 67.

10. Handwritten note on the bench memorandum related to *Trop*, box 181, Earl Warren Papers, Library of Congress, Washington, D.C.

11. Ibid.

12. On *Perez* and *Trop* his majority was composed of Black, Brennan, Douglas, and Harlan in addition to himself. See Schwartz, *Super Chief*, 314.

13. Warren's first draft on *Nishikawa* can be found in box 333, Hugo Lafayette Black Papers, Library of Congress, Washington, D.C.

14. Memorandum of Felix Frankfurter to the conference, June 7, 1957, Frankfurter Papers, Library of Congress.

15. Ibid.

16. The decision to reargue came on June 24. *Trop* and *Nishikawa* were on the summary calendar. The chief justice on September 12 granted a request for an additional thirty minutes on each side on *Perez*, which had the effect of removing this particular case from the summary calendar. Box 293, Harold Burton Papers, Library of Congress, Washington, D.C. On the summary calendar, see Robert L. Stern and Eugene Gressman, *Supreme Court Practice; Jurisdiction, Procedure, Arguing and Briefing Techniques, Forms, Statutes, Rules for Practice in the Supreme Court of the United States*, 4th ed. (Washington, D.C.: Bureau of National Affairs, 1969), §14.6, 489.

17. Schwartz, *Super Chief,* 316.

18. Seth Stern and Stephen Wermiel, *Justice Brennan: Liberal Champion* (New York: Houghton Mifflin Harcourt, 2010), 135.

19. He had only three votes (Black, Douglas, and himself).

20. Schwartz, *Super Chief,* 316.

21. In *Nishikawa,* a Brennan document shows Warren still having a majority in the vote of October 28, 1957, on this case for reversing (with Whittaker, Black, Douglas and Brennan), with Frankfurter in the minority for affirming. Box I-8-3, William Brennan Papers, Library of Congress, Washington, D.C. On Whittaker's shift to Frankfurter's opinion, backed by Burton, for remanding, see letter of Harlan to Justice Tom C. Clark, December 3, 1957, box 40, Harlan Papers. At that moment of the process, on *Nishikawa,* there were two dissenting groups: Black backed by Douglas wrote a dissent to reverse on the ground of unconstitutionality and Harlan and Clark wanted to affirm.

22. Frankfurter circulated a first draft of his *Nishikawa* opinion at the end of November 1957. See letter of Burton to Frankfurter, November 25, 1957, joining the opinion. Frankfurter Papers, Harvard Law School Library, part II, reel 32.

23. One of Harlan's clerks in a memo to his Justice writes about the opinion circulated by Warren as "a pretty poor job frankly," undated and unsigned memo, box 40, Harlan Papers.

24. Chief Justice Warren, Draft Opinion 710, *Trop v. Dulles,* June 5, 1957, Box 580 and Chief Justice Warren, Memorandum 572, *Perez v. Brownell,* June 5, 1957, Box 579 Warren Papers.

25. Memorandum 572, *Perez v. Brownell,* June 5, 1957, box 579, Warren Papers, 12.

26. Ibid. This draft was based on a Bench Memo written by William H. Allen, clerk for Chief Justice in the 1956 term. Cf. Bench Memo No. 572, 415, 710, box 180, Warren Papers, Manuscript Division, Library of Congress, Washington, D.C.

27. Ibid.

28. An additional and convincing argument—raised by Jerome A. Cohen—was that the Court could not have in *Mackenzie* upheld a statute denationalizing an American woman with the purpose to deal with dual nationality: many foreign laws did not "recognize as nationals women who married their nationals." Memorandum of Jerry Cohen to Felix Frankfurter, July 1957, No. 572 *Perez v. Brownell.* Frankfurter Papers, Harvard Law Library Part 2, reel 32.

29. Memorandum re No. 44 *Perez v. Brownell,* Nov. 1957, p. 24, Frankfurter Papers, Harvard Law Library, part 2, reel 32.

30. "Implicit," Frankfurter writes in his memorandum, "in the concept of expatriation is the requirement that loss of citizenship attach only in conduct engaged in voluntarily." Ibid., 17. See also " 'Voluntary': A Concept in Expatriation Law," *Columbia Law Review* 54, no. 6 (June 1954): 932.

31. Ibid.,17,

32. Nos. 44 and 70, ten pages, unsigned, undated, box 582, Warren Papers.

33. Ibid., 1, 2.

34. Ibid., 2, 4.

35. Ibid., 2.

36. Ibid., 4.

37. Ibid., 6.

38. These notes were probably written between December 31, 1957, and February 5, 1958, when another draft of a dissenting opinion of Warren, written by Jon Newman, appears in the archives. Box 582, annex X, Warren Papers.

39. Jon Newman was the law clerk who worked with Chief Justice Warren on the expatriation cases. A draft of the chief justice's opinion in *Trop* is in box 583 of the Warren Papers, with a clear indication on it that this draft was prepared by Newman. The final opinion in *Trop* includes much of the language from Newman's draft. In view of his role in drafting the opinion in *Trop* and of the testimonies of Oaks and of Norman Dorsen (Harlan's clerk), I have no doubt that Jon Newman played a similar role with respect to Warren's dissent in *Perez*, even though Newman, respecting a law clerk's obligation of confidentiality, declined to discuss his role in his interview with me on April 3, 2011.

40. Black stood alone a few years earlier in 1951 in *Acheson v. Okimura and Murata*, 99 F. Supp. 587 (D. Hawai'i), and agreed with the argument of unconstitutionality raised by the district court; he wanted to grant certiorari to the case. 342 U.S. 899. Note of Gerald Gunther on *Gonzales*, 350 U.S., box 1169, Douglas Papers. Warren joined the unanimity of the court on a narrower basis.

41. Handwritten note of Douglas, conference no. 111—*Gonzales v. Landon*, December 9, 1955, box 1169, Douglas Papers.

42. Roger K. Newman, *Hugo Black: A Biography* (New York: Pantheon Books, 1994), 566.

43. Norman Dorsen, *The Green Bag Almanac and Reader 2008*, edited by Ross E. Davies (Washington, D.C.: Green Bag, 2007), 93.

44. Ibid.

45. Roger K. Newman says of Warren: "Warren's mind worked like a dull knife, not a razor. He wasn't the type to reflect much, he admitted. Who won was more important than what the opinion said. He knew his limitations: his clerks wrote almost all his opinions, under his guidance and direction." Newman, *Hugo Black*, 566.

46. Jon Newman, interview, April 3, 2011.

47. Ibid.

48. Gerald Neuman, after having read the document, pointed out to me its strict organization and development of the notes and the use of the pronoun "I," both clues that make the hypothesis of Warren sitting *after* a conversation more plausible. But one other hypothesis is that he took notes under dictation.

49. First Frankfurter wrote to Brennan: "I think they [Black and Douglas] joined his opinion in *Nishikawa* because the whole atmosphere, if not the very words, represent their views." He added, "The overtones and the undertones are really the view which is explicitly spelt out by the Chief in *Perez*. I wonder if it is the fact that English is not my mother tongue that I cannot read the Chief's opinions no matter what he says in conversation about it, as being the kind of denial of power that Black and Douglas espouse. Look at the last page of his recirculation.*" The footnote read: "But every exercise of governmental power must find its source in the Constitution. The power to denationalize is not within the letter or the spirit of the powers with which the government was endowed." Letter of Frankfurter to Brennan, April 26, 1958, part II, reel 32, Frankfurter Papers, Harvard Law School Library. Under emotion, Frankfurter seems to make a lapsus (as he was mentioning the fact that English was not his mother tongue) by omitting a "not" between "as" and "being." This seems proven by the fact that at the same time he sends a letter to Harlan only composed of the page 17 of Warren dissent opinion. On this page he has annotated the paragraph he cited in the footnote of his letter to Brennan with this handwritten comment: "I cannot understand the English language if this does not mean what Black and Douglas believe—that there is no power to denationalize except by a citizen's abjuration, specific throwing of his citizenship. That is why they, Black and Douglas, agree with CJ's opinion. And that's the way, they and the bar will interpret it! FF." See letter of Frankfurter to Harlan, undated, box 42, Harlan Papers.

50. Later Black would write to Warren a handwritten letter: "In re Dissents in No 70-44. Dear Chief I have made a number of pencil . . . in your two dissents . . . I expect to come to the office & will see you then." Box 583 Warren Papers.

51. Newman, *Hugo Black*, 435–436, 471. Seth Stern and Stephen Wermiel, the biographers of Justice Brennan, note that later on, when Brennan replaced Black as "his chief unofficial adviser," the chief justice would each week enter Brennan's chambers unannounced "with his loose-leaf note book, in which he scribbled notes on the Court docket." See Stern and Wermiel, *Justice Brennan*, 183.

52. Letter of Warren to Elizabeth Black, September 27, 1971, box 347, Warren Papers, emphasis added.

53. Guido Calabresi, interview with the author, May, 26, 2011.

54. 332 U.S. 68.

55. The text of the dissenting opinion of Black in *Nishikawa* can be found in part II, reel 32, Frankfurter Papers, Harvard Law School Library. At the end of December 1957, the Court was divided into three groups: Harlan and Clark wanted to affirm the expatriation decided by the lower court; Black and Douglas were in favor of reversal for unconstitutionality of the statute; and Warren together with Whittaker, Burton, and Brennan had at that moment joined Frankfurter.

56. Symbolically, this case might have in addition presented a way to repair the damage from the *Korematsu* decision permitting the internment of Japanese Americans during World War II. His former clerk, Robert Girard, interview with the author, April 21, 2011. He didn't think Black ever felt very comfortable with the decision since the Supreme Court upheld the conviction of Fred Korematsu and the Japanese internment by 6-3 (*Korematsu v. United States*, 323 U.S. 214 [1944]). See David Cole, *Enemy Aliens: Double Standards and the Constitutional Freedoms in the War on Terror* (New York: New Press, 2003), 98. Black wrote a majority opinion relying on the findings of the military authorities, 323 U.S. 219.

57. 356 U.S. 139.

58. Ibid., 138.

59. Ibid., 139.

60. Ibid., 64.

61. *Trop*, United States Court of Appeals Second Circuit 239 F.2d 527 (1956).

62. "Comment: The Expatriation Act of 1954," *Yale Law Journal* 64 (1955): 1164, 1189–1199. The concept had been also evoked earlier by Emma Goldman in a "Woman Without a Country."

63. 356 U.S. 64.

64. Olivier Beaud, *La Puissance de l'Etat* (Paris: Presses Universitaires de France, 1994), 42.

65. 239 U.S. 299.

66. Emphasis added

67. This interpretation of *Mackenzie* v. *Hare* had been developed in a memo written to Warren on May 8, 1957 (memo on nos. 572, 415, and 710, May 8, 1957, box 181) Warren Papers, Manuscript Division, Library of Congress, Washington, D.C.; it was not included by Warren in the 1957 first version of its *Perez* opinion probably because it did not fit with its whole reasoning. Newman cleverly introduced it in its final version.

68. In a letter to Whittaker on March 5, 1958, Frankfurter writes: "To me the issue is clear and simple: once it is recognized, as I assume no one will deny, that Congress may attach the loss of citizenship to certain conduct that in the judgment of Congress may entail undesirable international consequences for the United States, the determination of a particular act, like voting in a serious

foreign election, entails such an undesirable consequence for this country is for Congress to make and for this Court not to disregard unless it can say in good conscience that Congress, in making such a determination, has really gone on a frolic of its own." Letter of Frankfurter to Whittaker, March 5, 1958, Frankfurter Papers, Harvard Law Library, Part2, reel 32.

69. "While the essential qualities of the citizen-state relationship under our Constitution preclude the exercise of governmental power to divest United States citizenship, the establishment of that relationship did not impair the principle that conduct of a citizen showing a voluntary transfer of allegiance is an abandonment of citizenship. Nearly all sovereignties recognize that acquisition of foreign nationality ordinarily shows a renunciation of citizenship. Nor is this the only act by which the citizen may show a voluntary abandonment of his citizenship. Any action by which he manifests allegiance to a foreign state may be so inconsistent with the retention of citizenship as to result in loss of that status." 356 U.S. 44.

70. Black and Douglas explain in their concurring opinion: "But whether citizenship has been voluntarily relinquished is a question to be determined on the facts of each case after a judicial trial in full conformity with the Bill of Rights. Although Congress may provide rules of evidence for such trials, it cannot declare that such equivocal acts as service in a foreign army, participation in a foreign election or desertion from our armed forces, establish a conclusive presumption of intention to throw off American nationality." *Nishikawa v. Dulles*, 356 U.S. 129 (1958), 139. Cf. *Tot v. United States*, 319 U.S. 463. Of course such conduct may be highly persuasive evidence in the particular case of a purpose to abandon citizenship. And Black in the letter he sends to Warren (see note 50):"But it can also be evidenced by conduct which has the evidential effect of a formal document. An extreme example would be joining a foreign army to invade United States." Letter of Black to Warren, In re Dissents in No. 70-44, Box 583, Warren Papers.

71. 356 U.S. 44, 65.

72. 356 U.S. 44.

73. See Leonard B. Boudin, "Involuntary Loss of Citizenship," *Harvard Law Review* 73, no. 8, (June 1960): 1510, 1517.

74. In response to a question from the chief justice during the oral argument of October 28, 1957, the solicitor general gave the Supreme Court an assessment of the number of Americans— seven thousand—who were deprived of their citizenship under section 401(g) of the 1940 Nationality Act. Box A65, folder 4, Tom C. Clark Papers, Tarleton Law Library, University of Texas–Austin.

75. The association between statelessness and the "cruel and unusual punishment" forbidden by the Eighth Amendment had been made earlier in a draft prepared for the dissenting opinion of Justice Wiley Rutledge in *Knauer v. United States*, 328 U.S. (1946). But it was suppressed from the last version of the dissent. Box 127, Wiley Rutledge Papers, Library of Congress, Washington, D.C.

76. Stephen Pollak, interview with the author, Washington, D.C., April 25, 2011. Pollak said in a published interview on his article: "The Smith Act was a criminal statute aimed at persons who were members of the communist party and advocated overthrow of the government by force and violence. . . . The Expatriation Act added a condition of statelessness to the court-imposed punishment of persons convicted of Smith Act crimes," which is what he argued should be considered "cruel and unusual punishment." He noted that in *Trop*, the Court "struck down on Eighth Amendment grounds a companion provision taking nationality away from persons court-martialed for desertion" and cited his article. See "Legends in the Law: A Conversation with Stephen J. Pollak," *Bar Report*, December/January 2000.

77. *Trop*, 239 F.2d 527.

78. The Eighth Amendment includes three parts: the excessive bail clause, the excessive fines clause, and the cruel and unusual punishment clause.

79. The first major "cruel and unusual punishment case" heard by the Supreme Court was *Pervear v. Massachusetts*, 72 U.S. 475 (1866). The Court ruled that a fifty dollar fine and three months' sentence of hard labor imposed on a man who had illegally stored and sold liquor did not violate the Eighth Amendment. There was "nothing excessive, or cruel, or unusual" in the punishment because "the law was to protect the community against the manifold evils of intemperance," which was "the usual mode adopted in many, perhaps, all of the States." 72 U.S. 475, at 480. In *Wilkerson v. Utah*, 99 U.S. 130 (1878), the Court held that the state of Utah was not prohibited by the Eighth Amendment from executing by firing squad a man who had been convicted of first degree murder. Despite ruling against the petitioner, the Supreme Court did note, however, that the Eighth Amendment proscribes torture and other unnecessary cruelty. The Court further refined its conception of cruel and unusual punishment in *In re Kemmler*, 136 U.S. 436 (1890). In that case, the Court held that the Fourteenth Amendment did not incorporate the Eighth Amendment against the states and that the use of the electric chair to execute individuals convicted of murder was not considered cruel and unusual punishment. The Court also provided several examples of specific punishments that it considered to violate the Eight Amendment: "burning at the stake, crucifixion, breaking on the wheel, or the like."

80. In *Weems v. United States*, 217 U.S. 349 (1910), a man living in the Philippines was convicted of falsifying a public document and sentenced to fifteen years imprisonment and a fine of four thousand pesetas. Over the dissent of Chief Justice Edward White (with Justice Holmes concurring in the dissent), Justice McKenna ruled for the Court that the petitioner's punishment violated the Eighth Amendment. Justice McKenna found first that "it is a precept of justice that punishment for crime should be graduated and proportioned to offense." 217 U.S. 367. Next, he held that the phrase "cruel and unusual punishment" extends beyond mere bodily punishment to other acts that are excessive in their severity or length.

81. *Trop*, 356 U.S. 125.

82. Jon Newman, *Trop v. Dulles*, 70, undated draft, box 583, Warren Papers. Cf. 356 U.S. 98 for the final version.

83. Ed Cray, *Chief Justice: A Biography of Earl Warren* (New York: Simon and Schuster, 1997), 359.

84. 356 U.S. 97.

85. *Trop*, Warren dissent, February 26, 1958, box 331, 16, Black Papers.

86. Dissenting draft opinion of Chief Justice Warren in *Trop*, March 1958, Box I-11, Brennan Papers.

87. According to his biographer, it was a condition to keep Whittaker in the majority. See Craig Alan Smith, *Failing Justice: Charles Evans Whittaker in the Supreme Court* (Jefferson, N.C.: McFarland, 2005), 141.

88. On the use of foreign and international law in *Trop*, see Judith Resnik, "Law's Migration: American Exceptionalism, Silent Dialogues, and Federalism's Multiple Ports of Entry," *Yale Law Journal* 115 (May 2006).

89. A verifier of governmental action "is to respect the actions of the two branches of our Government directly responsive to the will of the people and empowered under the Constitution to determine the wisdom of legislation. The awesome power of this court to invalidate such legislation, because in practice it is bounded only by our own prudence in discerning the limits of the court's constitutional function, must be exercised with the utmost restraint." *Trop*, 356 U.S.

90. *Trop*, 356 U.S., 92, 93.

91. There was then a majority of a 7-2 in the Supreme Court to reestablish Nishikawa's U.S. citizenship on the ground that the government did not prove "beyond a reasonable doubt" that he had acted voluntarily in joining the Japanese army.

92. See letter of Brennan to Frankfurter, March 26, 1958, box 30, Frankfurter Papers, Library of Congress.

93. See letter of Frankfurter to Harlan, March 27, 1958, box 605, Harlan Papers.

94. In the *Perez* case, there were in fact two votes: on the constitutionality of Perez's expatriation based on his desertion of military service in time of war (§401[g] of the Nationality Act), Brennan voted no; on the constitutionality of Perez's expatriation based on his voting in foreign elections (§401[e] of the Nationality Act), Brennan voted yes. Box I-8-3, Brennan Papers.

95. "The Supreme Court: The Judges or the Congress?" *Time*, April 14, 1958.

96. Anthony Lewis, "Conflict in the Court: A Discussion of Sharp Disagreement Among the Justices on Their Function," *New York Times*, April 3, 1958, 22.

97. After been informed of the Court decision on his case, Trop, then an employee of Air France in Gander Airport, Newfoundland, Canada, wrote to the ACLU: "Gentlemen, I have just received the official word from Mr. Fraenkel regarding the successful conclusion of three years of legal strife. Needless to say that the decision of the Supreme Court, in spite of the minority opinion, did spare me from 'a fate worse than death.' I do not only consider the results in the light of the personal benefits I may have derived from this decision, for I sincerely believe that the 'victory' if one chooses to call it that, belongs completely to the ACLU and thus to those that sustain and support it. That 7000 men who had been disenfranchised are no longer second class human beings, bears to testimony that the functions and efforts of the ACLU are, without a doubt, not only justified but necessary. One of the greatest contributions to our complex society is to give hope to the hopeless. This you have done." Letter of Albert L. Trop to the ACLU, April 5, 1958, box 1740, ACLU Papers, Mudd Manuscript Library.

Chapter 12. American Citizenship Is Secured

1. *Mendoza-Martinez v. Mackey,* 356 U.S. 258 (1958).

2. Ibid.

3. Bernard Schwartz, *The Unpublished Opinions of the Warren Court* (New York: Oxford University Press, 1985), 109. This was premised on his remaining outside the United States to avoid military service after September 27, 1944, when §401(j) of the Naturalization Act took effect.

4. In 1944 §401(j) had been added; its successor and still present counterpart is §349(a)(10) of the Immigration and Nationality Act of 1952.

5. Draft opinion of Justice Brennan, January 8, 1960, Douglas Papers, Library of Congress, box 1221. At this point the majority was 6–3, with the other five backing the opinion of Stewart. Schwartz, *The Unpublished Opinions of the Warren Court*, 110.

6. See Memorandum of Brennan to the Conference, October 5, 1961 and in reply memorandum of Frankfurter to the conference, October 10, 1961, box 17, folder 157, Potter Stewart Papers.

7. See the text of the February 1952 Stewart draft in Schwartz, *The Unpublished Opinions of the Warren Court*, 113.

8. *Kennedy v. Mendoza-Martinez,* Memorandum of Charles Whittaker, February 2, 1962, 1.

Whittaker concurred in the result because he thought it was constitutional to consider the voluntary conduct of avoiding service in the army in time of war as a voluntary abandonment of U.S. citizenship. Douglas Papers, Library of Congress, box 1286.

9. *Cort v. Herter*, 187 F. Supp. 683 (1960).

10. 372 U.S. 50.

11. See December 7, 1962 Conference notes of Douglas, box 1287, Douglas Papers.

12. Peter Edelman, interview with the author, April 22, 2011. Edelman said, in another interview published in 2008, "His first question in approaching a case always was, 'What is the just result?' Then he would work backward from the answer to that question to see how it would comport with relevant theory or precedent. It took me a while to get used to that approach. The way I had learned the law at Harvard was that you looked up the answer in a book. The law was composed of 'neutral principles' that you could apply to get the proper result, and you never really asked whether it was just or not. Justice Goldberg opened my consciousness to the fact that the overarching purpose is about justice." "Legends in the Law: A Conversation with Peter B. Edelman," interview with Tim Wells, April 2008. http://www.dcbar.org/for_lawyers/resources/publications/washington_lawyer/april_2008/legends.cfm.

13. *Cort*, 372 U.S. 144 (1963).

14. See Charles Gordon, "The Citizen and the State: Power of Congress to Expatriate American Citizens," *Georgetown Law Journal* 53 (1936): 315, 330.

15. 372 U.S. 167.

16. Alexander M. Bickel, *Politics and the Warren Court* (New York: Harper and Row, 1965), 163.

17. 372 U.S. at 188. Privately he said to he was "just dead wrong" on *Perez*, highly unusual for a judge who rarely second-guessed himself, acknowledge his biographers, Seth Stern and Stephen Wermiel, in *Justice Brennan: Liberal Champion* (New York: Houghton Mifflin Harcourt, 2010), 135.

18. "Man with a Country," *Washington Post*, February 21, 1963, A26. Pressure was thus coming also from the media: the Court did not go so far as excluding loss of citizenship in cases where Congress's acts introduced a criminal trial, but the *Post* urged Congress to not leave the provision in limbo.

19. *Schneider v. Rusk* 377 U.S. 163 (1964).

20. Certiorari Memorandum on *Schneider v. Rusk,* No. 251, of David L. Shapiro to Harlan, October 6, 1962, Harlan Papers.

21. See *Schneider v. Rusk,* U.S. District Court for the District of Columbia, 218 F. Supp. 302 (1963).

22. The Court reversed an earlier district court refusal to convey a three-judge court decision in a per curiam decision *Schneider v. Rusk,* 372 U.S. 224 (1963) prepared by Justice Goldberg "after discussion with the Chief Justice and at his request." See memorandum of Arthur Goldberg to the brethren January 30, 1963, Warren Papers, Library of Congress, box 642.

23. John M. Goshko, "Suit Raises Constitutional Issue of Rights of Naturalized Citizens," *Washington Post*, May 27, 1963, B2.

24. Ibid.

25. Ibid.

26. Ibid.

27. 377 U.S. at 168.

28. Ibid. At the request of Potter Stewart, Douglas amended an earlier version of his opinion so as to add that the naturalized citizen was equally protected only if his naturalization was "free of

fraud." See correspondence between Justices Potter and Douglas, April–May 1964, box 1325, Douglas Papers.

29. The total of the expatriations performed after between 1940 and 1964 was 99,100.

30. The lower court decision was thereby confirmed.

31. *Marks v. Esperdy*, 315 F.2d 673 (1963).

32. Bench Memorandum of James K. Hoenig, box 250, Warren Papers.

33. *Marks v. Esperdy*, 315 F.2d 673 (1963).

34. See Justice Douglas's notes of April 3, 1964, conference, no. 253, *Marks v. Esperdy*, box 1304,
Douglas Papers. See also box 130, no. 253, Douglas Papers.

35. On April 4, 1964, Justice Brennan informed his colleagues that the previous night he had
learned that his son, who was employed by the firm Arnold, Fortas and Porter, had discussed the
Schneider case with Milton V. Freeman—from the same firm that argued the case for Schneider.
This fact disqualified him from participating in the decision in the case, and since his vote on *Schneider* "was on the same constitutional ground" as his vote in *Marks v. Esperdy*, he decided not to
participate in both cases. Memorandum to the conference, part I, box 110, folder 63-253, Brennan
Papers.

36. Marks added that "He was eligible for Cuban citizenship but did not apply to it," and that
like Nishikawa in that case, he had to obey an order of Che Guevara and that it would have been
suicide to refuse. Bench Memorandum of James K. Hoenig, box 250, Warren Papers, 6 and 8.

37. Justice Douglas's notes of April 3, 1964 Conference, no. 253, *Marks v. Esperdy*, box 1304,
Douglas Papers.

38. Philip Kurland, "Supreme Court, 1963 Term," *Harvard Law Review* 78 (November 1964):
170, 175.

39. Box 393, Black Papers.

40. In *Mendoza-Martinez* decision, Black together with Douglas, while joining the opinion of
the Court, reaffirmed their adgerence to "the views expressed in the dissent of MR. JUSTICE DOUG-
LAS, in which MR. JUSTICE BLACK joined, in Perez v. Brownell, 356 U.S. 44, 356 U.S. 79, that Congress
has no power to deprive a person of the citizenship granted the native-born by §1, cl. 1, of the Fourteenth Amendment." 372 U.S. 186.

41. 387 U.S. 253 (1967).

42. T. Alexander Aleinikoff, "Theories of Loss of Citizenship," *Michigan Law Review* 84, no.7
(1986): 1471, 1482.

43. See Certiorari 456 *Afroyim v. Rusk*, October 17, 1966, Box 286, Harlan Papers.

44. Ibid. The shift in *Afroyim* occurred because Justice Abe Fortas had replaced Justice Frankfurter and voted with the majority in *Afroyim* and because Justice Brennan changed his view.

45. *Afroyim v. Rusk*, 361 F.2d. 102 (1966).

46. Fortas replaced Goldberg, whom Lyndon Johnson persuaded to accept the position of
permanent representative of the United States at the United Nations.

47. 387 U.S. 257.

48. 372 U.S. 186.

49. Black's historical interpretation was contested in this case in Harlan's dissent. Harlan found
"positive evidence that the Court's construction of the clause is not that intended by its draftsmen.
Between the two brief statements from Senator Howard [the sponsor of the citizenship clause] relied upon by the Court, Howard, in response to a question, said the following: 'I take it for granted
that, after a man becomes a citizen of the United States under the Constitution, he cannot cease to

be citizen *except by* expatriation or *the commission of some crime by which his citizenship shall be forfeited.'*" 387 U.S. 253, 287 (1967).

50. Draft of Hugo Black's concurring opinion in *Nishikawa*, March 3, 1958, box 333, Black Papers.

51. On May 17, 1967, Fortas's clerk penciled the Harlan's dissent opinion on *Afroyim* sent two days earlier by Harlan to Fortas. "H. seems to put most of the history out from under Black. You have joined Black already. H's history doesn't matter much however, since Black also relied explicitly on the Chief's masterful Perez dissent which didn't depend on the 'history' Black dredges up here." Box 42, Abe Fortas Papers,.

52. 387 U.S. at 268.

53. 372 U.S. 253, 187 fn. 5.

54. Letter of Warren to Black, April 13, 1967, box 537, Warren Papers.

Conclusion

1. He had replaced Arthur Goldberg whom Lyndon Johnson persuaded to accept the position of permanent representative of the United States at the United Nations.

2. *Rogers v. Bellei*, 401 U.S. 815 (1971).

3. *Bellei v. Rusk*, 296 F.Supp. 1247 (DC 1969).

4. Memorandum of Daniel B. Edelman, clerk of Justice Blackmun, September 16, 1970, box 120, Blackmun Papers, Manuscript Division, Library of Congress, Washington, D.C.

5. Abe Fortas had resigned on May 14, 1969, and Harry Andrew Blackmun did not replace him as an associate justice until June 9, 1970.

6. Memorandum from Blackmun, November 2, 1970, box 120, Blackmun Papers.

7. Tinsley E. Yarbrough, *John Marshall Harlan, Great Dissenter of the Warren Court* (New York, Oxford University Press, 1992), 150.

8. Memorandum of Justice Harlan in *Gibson v. Thomson, Trustee*, 355 U.S. 18 (1957). In his memo he refers to a precedent case *Rogers v. Missouri Pac. R. Co.,* 352 U.S. 500 (1957) and he said: "much as I disagree, 352 U.S. 559, 562–564, with the reasoning and philosophy of the *Rogers* case, which strips the historic role of the judge in a jury trial of all meaningful significance, I feel presently bound to bow to it."

9. Yarbrough, Ibid, 151.

10. Copy of a letter re: no. 179—*Rogers v. Bellei*, of John M. Harlan to Hugo Black, February 16, 1970, box I 214/2, Brennan Papers.

11. In 1790, in the statute titled "an Act to establish an uniform rule of Naturalization," a clear indication that Congress was legislating under the Constitution's authorization to establish such uniform rules, Congress granted citizenship at birth to persons born abroad to United States citizens and for the naturalization of qualified aliens and the derivative naturalization of their minor children.. "At the earliest period of United States constitutional history, then, citizenship obtained by birth abroad was believed to be citizenship by naturalization." Steven S. Bell, "Expatriation: Constitutional and Non-Constitutional Citizenship," *California Law Review*, 60, no. 6 (November 1972): 1587, 1600.

12. 401 U.S. 828.

13. Gerald Gunther, "The Supreme Court, 1971 Term," *Harvard Law Review* 86, no. 1 (November 1972): 48, 50.

14. 444 U.S. 252 (1980). Lawrence J. Terrazas was born in 1948 as a dual citizen. While executing at the age of twenty-two an application for a certificate of Mexican nationality, he swore allegiance to Mexico and expressly renounced his U.S. citizenship. The question was whether doing so cost him his U.S. citizenship. The State Department said yes. The district court agreed, but the appeals court reversed the decision, asserting that Congress could not legislate a standard of proof (pre-ponderance of evidence) when the Supreme Court had required a different one (clear, convincing, and unequivocal evidence). Going back to *Afroyim*, the Supreme Court noted that the government could not deduce that a person had voluntarily relinquished his nationality by the accomplishment of some of the acts mentioned in the statute: "the record [must] support a finding that the expatri-ating act was accompanied by an intent to terminate United States citizenship." But the Court also decided that contrary to the appeals court's decision, the standard of proof of expatriation could be determined by Congress. The Court had decided in *Nishikawa v. Dulles*, 356 U.S. 129, 78 S.Ct. 612, 2 L. Ed. 2d 659 (1958), that evidence had to be "clear, unequivocal and convincing," comparable to the burden of proof in denaturalization cases. Congress explicitly modified this conclusion in the Act of September 26, 1961, Pub. L. No. 87-301, §19, 75 Stat.650, 656, which specifies that a claim of loss of nationality can be established by a preponderance of the evidence. INA 1961 349(b), 8 U.S.C. 1481(b). The constitutionality of this statutory provision is what the Court upheld in the *Vance v. Terrazas* case. Alona E. Evans, "*Vance v. Terrazas*. 48 U.S.L.W. 4069 (S.Ct., Jan. 15, 1980)," *American Journal of International Law* 74, no. 2 (April 1980): 438–441.

15. *Vance v. Terrazas* had kept some uncertainty alive; before that decision, on January 23, 1969, Attorney General Ramsey Clark had published a statement of interpretation that left some room for the executive to consider certain acts not explicitly declared unconstitutional by the Supreme Court as an intent to abandon U.S. citizenship, for example enlisting voluntarily in the armed forces of a foreign government engaged in hostilities against the United States. A.G. Clark Statement, 34 *Fed. Reg.* 15 (January 23, 1969). There was a terrible precedent whose memory was still alive, the case of Japanese Americans who had voluntarily renounced their citizenship in 1944. In 1959, of 5,766 Japanese Americans who had renounced, 5,409 had applied for restoration of their citizenship, and 4,987 had been successful. John Christgau, "Collins v. the World: The Fight to Restore Citizenship to Japanese American Renunciants of World War II," *Pacific Historical Review* 54, no. 1 (February 1985).

16. Pub. L. 99-653, 100 Stat. 3658 (1986), amending the Immigration and Nationality Act of 1952 (Pub. L. 82-414, 66 Stat. 163, June 27, 1952) or INA § 349 (a), 8 U.S.C. § 1481 (a).

17. State Department cable to diplomatic and consular post (April 1990) reproduced in 67 Interpreter Releases 1092 (October 1, 1990)., at 1093. See Stephen H. Legomsky and Cristina M. Rodriguez, *Immigration and Refugee Law and Policy* (New York: Foundation Press, 2009), 1367–1368. This presumption of nonexpatriation applies in fact (1) INA §349(a)(1), on naturalization in a foreign state; (2) INA §349(a)(2), on taking an oath of allegiance to a foreign state; and (3) INA §349(a)(4), on serving in a low-level position in the government of a foreign state or on serving in the military of a state not engaged in hostilities with the United States intends to retain one's U.S. citizenship. See http://www.state.gov/documents/organization/109065.pdf.

18. Justice Black had pointed out in *Afroyim* that naturalization unlawfully procured could be set aside. *Afroyim*, 387 U.S. 253, fn. 23 (1967).

19. The proposed Patriot Act II (Domestic Security Enhancement Act of 2003) would have made it possible for the American government to strip citizenship away from U.S. citizens if they were found to have connections with a terrorist organization, by expanding the powers of

expatriation given in 8 USC 1481. See http://www.pbs.org/now/politics/patriot2-hi.pdf. The power was never granted. Yet a new method of deprivation of citizenship was used in October 2004, in the case of Yasser Hamdi, an American born of Saudi parents. Arrested in Afghanistan, he was transferred to a Northern Alliance prison there, then to Guantanamo Bay in Cuba, and finally in a naval brig in South Carolina. He was eventually released and sent back to Saudi Arabia, the country of his family, under the condition that he reported to an American consular official within a week of his arrival in the kingdom and renounce his American citizenship. Hamdi complied with the requirement. See Saad Gul, "Return of the Native? An Assessment of the Citizenship Renunciation Clause in Hamdi's Settlement Agreement in Light of Citizenship Jurisprudence," *Northern Illinois University Law Review* 27 (Spring 2007).

20. The new section was created in 2010 in the Criminal Division of the Department of Justice to handle human rights crimes (Human Rights Enforcement Act, Pub. L. 111–122, 123 Stat. 3480, S. 1472, enacted on December 22, 2009). It is a merger between the OSI (which had jurisdiction on US citizens accused of human rights crimes and the Domestic Security Section who had jurisdiction on aliens in the U.S. accused of human rights crimes.

21. Interview of Eli M. Rosenbaum, Director, Human Rights Enforcement Strategy & Policy Criminal Division, Department of Justice, February 13, 2012.

22. 449 U.S. 490 (1981). The 1948 Displaced Persons Act prohibited admission of any person who «assisted the enemy in persecuting civil[ians]," a clause that mandates the literal interpretation, rejected by the district court, that an individual's service as a concentration camp armed guard—whether voluntary or involuntary—made him ineligible for a visa. Since a misrepresentation must be considered material if disclosure of the true facts would have made the applicant ineligible for a visa, and since in 1970, when Fedor Fedorenko filed his petition for and was admitted to citizenship, the Immigration and Nationality Act required lawfully admission to the United States for permanent residence, which required the possession of a valid visa, the Court ruled that "under the law applicable at the time of petitioner's initial entry into the United States, a visa obtained through a material misrepresentation was not valid" and in consequence his citizenship must be revoked because it was "illegally procured." 449 U.S. at 514, 516. In Abbe L. Dienstag's analysis, *Fedorenko* was decided as a totally mechanical exercise not taking into account the duress claimed by the defendant nor the requirement of voluntariness recognized in the cases involving denaturalization or expatriation. But as Dienstag also astutely notes, it might have been a way for the Court to express "an ideal duress standard for Holocaust participation." The interest of the society in expressing the disapproval of mass murder in this fashion outweighed whatever claims the murderer might have for social indulgence (161). Though the standard is not enough to satisfy the rigor of criminal law, it should certainly be sufficient in the nationality law context, where the constitutional powers of Congress are broad and idealist moral values may find greater expression. Viewed then in the abstract of legal analysis, *Fedorenko* may be said to have been decided rightly, though for the wrong reasons (162). See Abbe L. Dienstag, "Fedorenko v. United States: War Crimes, the Defense of Duress, and American Nationality Law," *Columbia Law Review* 82, no. 1 (January 1982): 120–183.

23. 485 U.S. 759 (1988).

24. Ibid. This case is the Supreme Court's most recent interpretation of what INA §340(a) requires for judicial denaturalization. The plaintiff immigrated in 1948 and was naturalized as a citizen in 1954. In 1982 the Department of Justice commenced denaturalization proceedings on three grounds: (1) Kungys had participated in the slaughter of two thousand Jewish Lithuanian civilians in 1941 during World War II, (2) Kungys made false statements concerning his date and

place of birth as well as his employment and residence during World War II (the "concealment and misrepresentation" claim), and (3) even if Kungys's false statements were not in themselves material to his original naturalization proceeding, their falsity indicates that Kungys lacked the requisite "good moral character" for naturalization (the "illegal procurement" claim). In response, the district court found that the evidence as to (1) was unreliable, that Kungys's false statements were not material to his denaturalization, and that, because they were not material, they could not be used to show Kungys's lack of good moral character. The Third Circuit Court of Appeals upheld the district court regarding claim (1), but reversed its decision as to claims (2) and (3). The Supreme Court then agreed to consider the standards required for the "concealment and misrepresentation" (but only as to the date and place of Kungys's birth) and "illegal procurement" claims. It did not reexamine the question of Kungys's participation in World War II atrocities. Writing for the majority, Justice Antonin Scalia ruled with respect to the "concealment and misrepresentation" claim that "the test of whether Kungys' concealments or misrepresentations were material is whether they had a natural tendency to influence the decisions of the Immigration and Naturalization Service," or if their disclosure might have been useful in an investigation possibly leading to the discovery of other facts warranting denial of citizenship. On the separate question of whether the citizenship was "illegal procured," under INA §101(f)(6), because the plaintiff lacked the good moral character required, the Court held that that section of the act does not contain a materiality requirement because the primary purpose is to identify lack of good moral character, not to prevent false pertinent data from being introduced into the naturalization process.

25. Intelligence Reform and Terrorism Prevention Act of 2004 (IRTPA), 118 Stat. 3638 (2004). See Gregory S. Gordon, "OSI's Expanded Jurisdiction Under the Intelligence Reform and Terrorism Prevention Act of 2004," *United States Attorneys' Bulletin* 54, no. 1 (January 2006): 25.

26. http://www.aila.org/content/default.aspx?docid=32184. Jadranko Gostic agreed to admit to the allegations against him, be denaturalized, surrender his lawful permanent resident status, and leave the United States.

27. Gilberto Jordan was naturalized in 1999. *United States of America v. Gilberto Jordan,* U.S. Court of Appeals for the Eleventh Circuit 432 Fed. Appx. 950; 2011.

28. Pub.L. 101-649, 104 Stat. 4978 §407(d)(18). See Legomsky and Rodríguez, *Immigration and Refugee Law and Policy*, 1338.

29. 219 F 3d 1087. See Jon B. Hultman, "Administrative Denaturalization: Is There 'Nothing We Can Do That Can't Be [Un]Done,'" *Loyola of Los Angeles Law Review* 34 (2001). At least 31 denaturalizations have been decided by courts: *U.S. v. Vo* 2001 WL 845657, 1 (D.Md., 2001); *U.S. v. Tarango-Pena* 173 F.Supp.2d 588, 590 (E.D.Tex., 2001); *U.S. v. Santillan-Garcia* 2001 WL 1442396, 1 (N.D.Ill., 2001); *U.S. v. Kiang* 175 F.Supp.2d 942 (E.D.Mich., 2001); *U.S. v. Vlamakis* 2002 WL 230909, 1 (N.D.Ill., 2002); *U.S. v. Inocencio* 215 F.Supp.2d 1095 (D.Hawai'i, 2002); *U.S. v. Ekpin* 214 F.Supp.2d 707, 709 (S.D.Tex., 2002); *U.S. v. Ep* 2003 WL 22118926, 1 (N.D.Ill., 2003); *U.S. v. Reve* 241 F.Supp.2d 470 (D.N.J., 2003); *U.S. v. Raghav* 2003 WL 22080759, 1 (N.D.Cal., 2003); *U.S. v. Nunez-Garcia* 262 F.Supp.2d 1073 (C.D.Cal., 2003); *U.S. v. Samaei* 260 F.Supp.2d 1223 (M.D.Fla., 2003); *U.S. v. Dang* 2004 WL 2731911, 2 (E.D.Cal., 2004); *U.S. v. Biheiri* 341 F.Supp. 2d 593 (E.D.Va., 2004); *U.S. v. Wang* 404 F.Supp.2d 1159 (N.D.Cal., 2005); *U.S. v. Jean-Baptiste* 395 F.3d 1190, 1191 (11th Cir. 2005); *U.S. v. Cabrera-Rojas* 2007 WL 778181, 1 (D.Idaho, 2007); *U.S. v. Mohalla* 545 F.Supp.2d 1035, 1038 (C.D.Cal., 2008); *U.S. v. Benavides* 2008 WL 362682, 1 (S.D.Tex., 2008); *U.S. v. Montelongo* 2008 WL 4693402, 1 (N.D.Tex., 2008); *U.S. v. Rebelo* 646 F.Supp.2d 682, 685 (D.N.J., 2009); *U.S. v. Okeke* 671 F.Supp.2d 744 (D.Md., 2009); *U.S. v. Arango* 2010 WL 1253212, 1 (D.Ariz., 2010); *U.S. v.*

Mwalumba 688 F.Supp.2d 565 (N.D.Tex., 2010); *U.S. v. Jose Cordero,* Civil Action No. H-09-1232 (S.D. Tex., 2011).

30. 457 U.S. 202 (1982).

31. See Peter H. Schuck and Rogers M. Smith, *Citizenship Without Consent* (New Haven, Conn.: Yale University Press, 1985).

32. Peter H. Schuck, "Birthright of a Nation," *New York Times*, August 13, 2010.

33. Schuck uses this supposed lack of precedent to buttress his argument that, while the children of undocumented immigrants may meet the citizenship clause's first requirement of birth in the United States, the status of their parents as undocumented means they are not subject to U.S. jurisdiction and, therefore, not protected by the citizenship clause.

34. *United States v. Wong Kim Ark*, 169 U.S. 649 (1898).

35. Seth Stern and Steven Wermiel, *Justice Brennan: Liberal Champion* (Boston: Houghton Mifflin Harcourt, 2010), 134.

36. 356 U.S. 44 (1958).

37. Ibid., at 46.

38. Ibid., at 66.

39. 356 U.S. at 129, 131.

40. Ibid., at 491.

41. 372 U.S. 144, 148 (1963).

42. It at least clarifies Justice Gray's reasoning which fluctuate between the affirmation that the meaning of the words "in the United States, and subject to the jurisdiction thereof" as the equivalent of the words "within the limits and under the jurisdiction of the United States," in the tradition of English common law and the solely application of this principle to "Chinese persons, born out of the United States, remaining subjects of the Emperor of China, and not having become citizens of the United States," nevertheless entitled to the protection of, and owing allegiance to, the United States *"so long as they are permitted by the United States to reside here."* 169 U.S. 694 (emphasis added). Gerald Neuman had argued that the authors of the Fourteenth Amendment had the conscious purpose of including tens of thousands of children of illegally imported slaves as citizens and that the meaning of the phrase "subject to the jurisdiction" has been well established for a century. It means actual subjection to the lawmaking power of the United States. It echoes the English common law notion of the king's protection and sovereignty: "The common law exceptions included children of foreign diplomats . . . and children born to women accompanying invading armies, who were practically immune from the protection of domestic law." Committee on the Judiciary, testimony of Professor Gerald L. Neuman, Subcommittee on Immigration and Claims and Subcommittee on the Constitution, House, December 13, 1995. See also Gerald L. Neuman, *Strangers to the Constitution: Immigrants, Borders, and Fundamental Law* (Princeton, N.J.: Princeton University Press, 1996), 178.

43. Earl Warren, *The Memoirs of Chief Justice Earl Warren* (New York: Doubleday, 1977), 6.

44. Ibid.

45. Citizenship is not far from a common-pool resource, as Elinor Ostrom argues (*Governing the Commons: The Evolution of Institutions or Collective Action* [Cambridge: Cambridge University Press, 1990]), but it is still quite different: the limit to access to citizenship is not based on the scarcity of the resources of the state (which could be increased by the production of or the taxes provided by the new citizens) like the one that exists in the domains of fisheries, forests, grazing systems, wildlife, water resources, irrigation systems, agriculture, and land tenure studied

by Ostrom. And in fact there is no limit to the multiplication of the number of citizens through parenthood. The limit to access to citizenship concerns foreigners. It is justified by the arguments developed by Bruce Ackerman in an imagined dialogue between the citizens of a liberal democracy and foreigners raised in an authoritarian state: that a too massive influx of newcomers "will generate such anxiety in the native population that it will prove impossible to stop a fascist group from seizing political power" or that "existing institutions will be unable to function in anything but an explicitly authoritarian manner." Bruce Ackerman, *Social Justice in the Liberal State* (Cambridge, Mass.: Harvard University Press, 1980), 93–95. See Patrick Weil "From Conditional to Secured and Sovereign: The New Strategic Link Between the Citizen and the Nation-State in a Globalized World" *International Journal of Constitutional Law* (2011) 9(3–4): 615–635.

46. Article 15, United Nations' Universal Declaration of Human Rights (December 10, 1948).

47. See for example the Convention On the Nationality of Married Women, G.A. Res. 1040 (XI), U.N. Doc. A/RES/1040(XI) (Jan. 29, 1957 and the European Convention on Nationality, Council of Europe - ETS no. 166 November 6, 1997.

48. Peter J. Spiro, "*Afroyim*: Vaunting Citizenship, Presaging Transnationality," in David A. Martin and Peter H. Schuck, eds., *Immigration Stories* (New York: Foundation Press, 2005), at 165. See also T. Alexander Aleinikoff, "Theories of Loss of Citizenship," *Michigan Law Review* 84 (1985–1986). Yet, the most radical criticism of *Afroyim* had been from Alexander Bickel, an influential professor at Yale Law School and former Frankfurter clerk, who, in the aftermath of the decision, asserted that "the Warren language was a regression to the confusions of Bingham and, what is worse, the majority opinion in *Dred Scott v. Sanford,* which held that the terms 'people of the United States' and 'citizens' are synonymous and that they 'both describe the political body who according to our republican institutions form the sovereignty.'" Bickel continued, unflatteringly, "Who said, 'They are what we familiarly call the single 'sovereign people and every citizen is one of this people and a constituent member of this sovereignty'? Roger B. Taney did, and Earl Warren and Hugo L. Black echoed it a century later, unwittingly to be sure." See Alexander M. Bickel, *The Morality of Consent* (New Haven, Conn.: Yale University Press, 1975), 53.

49. Karen Knop, "Relational Nationality: On Gender and Nationality in International Law," in T. Alexander Aleinikoff and Douglas Klusmeyer, eds., *Citizenship Today: Global Perspectives and Practices* (Washington, D.C.: Carnegie Endowment for International Peace, 2001), 89-124. Patrick Weil, "A la Frontière de l'inégalité entre genres et des politiques d'immigration: La situation de la femme mariée à un homme d'une autre nationalité. Une comparaison internationale (19ème–20ème siècles)," in Riva Kastoryano, ed., *Les Codes de la différence, religions, races et origines (France, Etats-Unis, Allemagne)* (Paris: Presses de Sciences-Po, 2005).

50. Patrick Weil, *How to Be French: A Nationality in the Making Since 1789,* trans. Catherine Porter (Durham, N.C.: Duke University Press, 2009), 241.

51. It is the extension of an idea conveyed by Robert Post when he says that "if public discourse is kept free for the autonomous participation of individual citizens, and if government decision-making is subordinated to the public opinion produced by public discourse, there is the possibility that citizens will come to identify with the state as representative of their own collective self-determination." Robert C. Post, *Constitutional Domains, Democracy, Community, Management* (Cambridge, Mass.: Harvard University Press, 1995), 7.

ARCHIVAL SOURCES AND INTERVIEWS

Franklin D. Roosevelt Presidential Library, Hyde Park, N.Y.

Marshall E. Dimock Papers
Charles Fahy Papers
President's Official File
James H. Rowe Jr. Papers

Harvard Law School Library

Felix Frankfurter Papers
Learned Hand Papers

Library of Congress

Hugo Lafayette Black Papers
Harry A. Blackmun Papers
Charles J. Bonaparte Papers
William J. Brennan Papers
Harold H. Burton Papers
Calvin Coolidge Papers
William Orville Douglas Papers
Felix Frankfurter Papers
Robert H. Jackson Papers
Wiley Rutledge Papers
Harlan F. Stone Papers
Earl Warren Papers

National Archives and Records Administration (NARA), Washington, D.C.

Records of the Immigration and Naturalization Service, Record Group 85

National Archives and Records Administration (NARA), College Park, Md.

General Records of the Department of State, Record Group 59
Records of the Department of Justice, Record Group 60

Mudd Manuscript Library, Princeton University

ACLU Papers
John Marshall Harlan Papers
Philip G. Strong Papers

University of California–Berkeley Archives

Emma Goldman Papers

Bentley Historical Library, University of Michigan

Frank Murphy Papers

University of Texas–Austin Archives

Tom. C. Clark Papers

Yale University Archives

Abe Fortas Papers
Potter Stewart Papers
Harry Weinberger Papers

Interviews and Testimonies

Judge Guido Calabresi, clerk of Justice Black (1958–1959)
Norman Dorsen, clerk of Justice Harlan (1957–1958)
Peter Edelman, clerk of Justice Goldberg (1962–1963)
Judge Jon Newman, senior clerk of Justice Warren (1957–1958)
Robert Girard, clerk of Justice Black (1957–1958)
Dallin H. Oaks, clerk of Justice Warren (1957–1958)
Stephen Pollak, author of the *Yale Law Journal* Note (1954)
Eli M. Rosenbaum, Director, Human Rights Enforcement Strategy &
    Policy Criminal Division, Department of Justice (2012)

INDEX

Aboumossa, Joseph George, 89
Abroad, denaturalization for residence, 2, 7, 56, 83-88, 90, 104, 142-44, 169-71, 176, 198, 207, 211, 215, 228, 230, 250
Acheson, Dean, 102, 200, 204, 251, 254
Acheson v. Okimura and Murata, 200, 251, 254
Ackerman, Bruce, 266
Adamson v. California, 157
Afroyim, Beys, 173, 178
Afroyim v. Rusk, 9, 173-76, 178, 181, 183, 201-2, 260, 262, 266-67
Alabama, 16, 18
Aleinikhoff, Alexander, 260, 266
Algeciras, 84, 229
Alien: status of domiciled, 61; constitutional rights, 62, 96; enemies, 96-97
Allegiance, 7, 27, 88, 90, 98, 125-26, 151, 170, 184, 224, 228, 232, 235, 251, 256, 262, 265. *See also* loyalty
Allen, Clay, 67, 224
Allen, William, 253
American Civil Liberties Union, 95, 112, 143, 250, 252, 258, 268
American Committee for the Protection of the Foreign Born, 112
American Federation of Labor, 193
American Jewish Committee, 143
American Jewish Congress, 143
American Legion, 37, 227
American Red Cross, 71, 73
Americanization Campaign, 37-38
Anarchist Bureau of the Chicago Police Department, 61
Anarchist Law of Congress (1907), 58
Anarchists and anarchism, 35, 57 62, 65-66, 74-75, 120, 139-41, 187, 190-91, 206, 220, 222, 223

Anti-Americanism, 74. *See also* Un-American sentiment
Applefeld, Samuel, 74-75
Arendt, Hannah, 158, 183
Asians: exclusions from naturalization, 7, 75-79, 101; in the military, 79-80
Atomic bomb, 136
Attorney General (U.S.), 11, 26-27, 49, 60, 65, 68-69, 85, 87, 92-93, 98, 100, 105, 125, 179, 207, 209-10
Austria, 70, 141, 194
Austrians, Austro-Hungarians, 69-70, 97, 141, 193
Azores, 85-86, 229

Bagai, Vaishno Das, 81, 227
Baginski, Max, 57
Balch, Dewey, 102, 104-5, 111, 124, 136, 237, 242
Baltimore, 57, 220
Bancroft treaties, 4
Barreyre, Nicolas, 206, 217
Batista, Fulgencio, 171
Baumgartner, Carl, 127, 234, 247
Baumgartner v. United States, 128, 130-32, 135, 137-39, 141, 200, 242-44
Beaud, Olivier, 255
Benedict, Charles, 77-78, 226
Benett, Ira, 223
Berge, Wendell, 103-5, 234-37
Berger, Victor, 67
Bergman, Benjamin, 217-18
Berkman, Alexander, 57, 62-63, 74, 222
Bernard, Louis, 143
Bernard, William, 219
Bernsen, Sam, 216
Bevington, Morris Roscoe, 30, 210, 226
Bickel, Alexander, 266

ACKNOWLEDGMENTS

Since the idea for this book emerged in 2004, several friends and institutions helped make it a reality.

This project could not have been realized without the support of the Russell Sage Foundation, which provided me with a Presidential grant. The German Marshall Fund also supported the project in 2004 and 2005.

A historian starts his research in the archives. At the History Office of the Immigration and Naturalization Service, now of the Department of Homeland Security, Marian Smith was always a thoughtful guide. Her successor, Zack Wilkse, with his sure, smart, and precise knowledge of the entire history of naturalization in the United States, was of invaluable assistance. He deserves my special and respectful gratitude. Many thanks go too to the staffs of the Library of Congress, the National Archives (in College Park and in the District of Columbia), the Mudd Library at Princeton University, the Yale University Archives, the Bentley Historical Library at the University of Michigan, the Harvard Law Library, and the Roosevelt Presidential Library; to Gary Lavergne who agreed to spend few days at the University of Texas–Austin Archives, and to Rahsaan Maxwell who was my special envoy to the Emma Goldman Archives at the University of California Berkeley. The team at the Goldman Archives was always very helpful.

If I had not been invited to teach at the Yale Law School for consecutive fall semesters, this work would have not been completed. The intelligence and friendship of my colleagues, research assistants, students and librarians has been an incomparable stimulation. Day after day they taught me everything from the principles of the American law to the details of its history in many fields and dimensions. Without this invaluable environment, this book would not now exist. Special thanks go to Bruce Ackerman, Akhil Amar, Jack Balkin, Rick Brooks, Guido Calabresi, Owen Fiss, Heather Gerken, Linda Greenhouse, Harold Koh, Jerry Machaw, Daniel Markovics, Tracy Meares,

Gabe Mendlow, Nick Parrillo, Robert Post, Michael Reisman, Judith Resnik, Susan Rose-Ackerman, Peter Schuck, Scott Shapiro, Reva Siegel, Jim Whitman, John Witt, to Blair Kaufman, Richard Hasbany, Teresa Miguel and to Monika Piotrowicz.

Gerald Neuman, a smart and uncompromising reader, followed this project from its origins.

Alice Kaplan encouraged me to visit the Weinberger Papers at the Yale University archives, and she was right: I found a treasure trove. Later she introduced me to Peter Edelman, who clerked for Justice Arthur Goldberg, and she was often there when my energy was failing.

Judge Jon Newman, former clerk of Chief Justice Earl Warren, put me on the path of *Perez* and *Trop*. Always respectful of a law clerk's obligation of confidentiality, he became my guide when the archives yielded extraordinary discoveries that could not be easily decoded or interpreted. He introduced me to many of his fellow former clerks, whose help has been invaluable. Robert Girard, Dallin H. Oaks, and his son, Steven Pollak, and—during the last stage of my research, at NYU Law School—Norman Dorsen all provided me with wonderful help and advice.

With their comments, information and suggestions David Abraham, Nicolas Barreyre, Gwénaële Calvès, Daniel Cohen, Pamela Druckerman, William Frucht, Nancy Green, Patrick Gudridge, Masako Hattori, Tamar Jacoby, Linda Kerber, Thomas Klug, Alison Mackeen, Sara McDougall, Robert McLaughlin, Etienne Ollion, Emma Rothschild, Peter Sahlins, Rebecca Scott, Paul Schor, Norman Silber, and David Todd also contributed to this book.

Jesse Schreger was my first smart entrepreneur-assistant on this project in 2004 and 2005. Josh Gibson worked with me in Paris in 2007–2008 and did a fantastic job. From 2008 to 2011, Alyssa King, Noorain Khan, Itamar Mann, Shi Chi Pan of Yale Law School and, in the last stage of my research, Ashley Lewis, of NYU Law School, were all intelligent, rapid, and efficient research assistants. Alexander Zevin, a talented reader, assisted me very cleverly throughout the different stages of the manuscript. Last but not least, Robby Braun, my research assistant at Yale Law School in the fall of 2010, took the project to heart and worked with me until the completion of the manuscript in 2012. This book owes a lot to his exceptional and multiple research and writing skills.

There is no good book without a great publisher. In 2007, Rogers Smith immediately backed this project. He helped me find my first funding by arranging for me to sign a contract with the University of Pennsylvania Press.

Since the project has evolved to become this first volume of a series, Rogers, together with the patient and professional Peter Agree, helped me complete it in the best conditions. Pamela Haag improved the book's framing by her clever suggestions and made it more readable. Julia Rose Roberts, Robert Milks, and Noreen O'Connor-Abel were fantastic copyeditors.